BUSINESS PROGRAMMING LOGIC

FOURTH EDITION

JAY SINGELMANN

JEAN LONGHURST

William Rainey Harper College

PRENTICE HALL

Englewood Cliffs, New Jersey   07632

Library of Congress Cataloging-in-Publication Data

Singelmann, Jay.
    Business programming logic: a structured approach/Jay
Singelmann, Jean Longhurst.—4th ed.
        p. cm.
    ISBN 0-13-092065-7
    1. Business—Data processing.   2. Flow charts.   I. Longhurst,
Jean.   II. Title.
HF5548.2.S462—1990
005.1—dc20   89–27621
                                                              CIP

Editorial/production supervision: Patrice Fraccio
Interior design: Kenny Beck
Manufacturing buyer: Lori Bulwin
Page layout: Kenny Beck and Maria Piper
Cover design: 20/20 Services

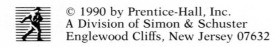

© 1990 by Prentice-Hall, Inc.
A Division of Simon & Schuster
Englewood Cliffs, New Jersey 07632

The author and publisher of this book have used their best efforts in preparing
this book. These efforts include the development, research, and testing of the
theories and programs to determine their effectiveness. The author and
publisher make no warranty of any kind, expressed or implied, with regard to
these programs or the documentation contained in this book. The author and
publisher shall not be liable in any event for incidental or consequential
damages in connection with, or arising out of, the furnishing, performance, or
use of these programs.

Printed in the United States of America
10 9 8 7 6 5 4 3 2 1

ISBN 0-13-092065-7

Prentice-Hall International (UK) Limited, *London*
Prentice-Hall of Australia Pty. Limited, *Sydney*
Prentice-Hall Canada Inc., *Toronto*
Prentice-Hall Hispanoamericana, S.A., *Mexico*
Prentice-Hall of India Private Limited, *New Delhi*
Prentice-Hall of Japan, Inc., *Tokyo*
Simon & Schuster Asia Pte. Ltd., *Singapore*
Editora Prentice-Hall do Brasil, Ltda., *Rio de Janeiro*

CONTENTS

4 DOCUMENTATION 54

5 EXTRACTS 71

6 SINGLE-LEVEL CONTROL BREAKS 108

7 MULTIPLE LEVEL CONTROL BREAKS AND TOTALS 132

8 TABLES 157

14 SYSTEMS FLOWCHARTING

15 ALTERNATIVE CHARTING METHODS

PREFACE

This volume covers the flowcharting of typical types of business application programs. The topics include symbols and their usage, documentation practices, typical applications logic, decision tables, pseudocode, Nassi-Schneiderman charts, hierachical charts, and necessary terminology. A structured approach has been used in flowcharting examples. The material presented is language independent, although examples are shown in COBOL and BASIC for many of the problems.

This volume has several important features. The first is the informal presentation. It is meant for the beginning student in a data processing program at either a community college or a four-year institution. It can be used as the primary book in a business applications logic course or a supplement if logic is taught as part of a programming course.

The depth of the material is sufficient to facilitate the learning of it. Our experience in class testing this text has been that there is sufficient material for a full semester of study. We have also found that students who have studied this material have more success in future programming language courses, because they are then free to concentrate on the syntax of the particular language.

Another feature is the scope of the material. Standard business applications are covered, such as listing programs, input edits, updates, extracts, sorts, table handling, and file matching. Also present is material on pseudocode, documentation, decision tables, and file maintenance. COBOL and BASIC programs are used as figures, showing the ways in which many of the problems can actually be coded. The BASIC programs were run on an IBM PC. There is no attempt to teach either BASIC or COBOL. The programming examples will be most useful to a person who is using this book as a supplement to a programming class.

The whys are emphasized along with the hows so that the student will see the reason for doing something in a particular manner. Throughout the volume there is an abundance of examples, which are explained in detail to aid the student in grasping the topic.

Each chapter starts with a list of behavioral objectives. These emphasize what material the student should master in each chapter. At the end of each chapter are a variety of questions suitable for assignments, class discussions, or quizzes. Projects are included at the end of many chapters as an extension to the exercises.

We would like to extend our appreciation to those who have aided in the preparation of this volume. Credit goes to our students and faculty, whose constructive criticism has been invaluable to us in preparing this material. We are endebted to Patrice Fraccio for her interest and support with regard to this edition of the text.

Jay Singelmann
Jean Longhurst

BUSINESS
PROGRAMMING
LOGIC

DATA PROCESSING

OBJECTIVES

As a result of studying this chapter the student should be able to perform the following activities:

1. Describe the data processing cycle.
2. Define the units of data.
3. Differentiate between hardware and software.
4. Differentiate between device and media, main memory and auxiliary storage, data and instructions.

5. Describe the steps in program development.
6. List the steps required to convert a flowchart to an operational program.
7. List the major types of programs in a system.

INTRODUCTION

A vital competency in computer programming is problem analysis. Only through a clear understanding of what is desired can a reasonable solution to a problem be developed. A business might, for example, require a breakdown of sales by product in order to identify the most and least profitable products, or it might require the breakdown of sales by salesman in order to pay commissions and judge performance. Another business or a different department in the same business might require analysis of freight bills in order to confirm rates charged, analyze the volume shipped from each location, or identify duplicate bills. In each of these cases it hopes to use the information to improve the operation of the business.

DATA PROCESSING CYCLE

When communication begins between the data processing department and a department requiring its services, the discussion is usually in terms of the end result desired. The result of the data processing operation is termed the **output.** If the output is to be in printed form, it is called a **report.**

Next, we need to determine if the necessary data is available to produce the desired output. If not, can it be collected and made available? The data collected and converted to a machine-readable form in order to produce the output is called the **input.**

Knowing what must be produced as output and what input there is to work with, we next ask: How do we go about transforming the input to the output? This is called the **process.**

These three items—input, process, and output—constitute the **data processing cycle.** Its purpose is to change **data** into **information.** Data can be thought of as the raw material and information as the finished product. This book will outline the steps necessary to process the data into information using business computer programs.

UNITS OF DATA

In order to discuss the output that we would like, or the input needed to produce the output, terms are necessary to describe the units of data. Programs are written in order to manipulate data and produce information. There are two types of data, internal data and external data. Internal data is held in primary storage, the storage within the computer itself. The terms bits and bytes are used to describe units of data in memory. Internal data is data which is created by the execution of the program and which ceases to exist once the program finishes executing. External data is data which is stored on some auxiliary (secondary) storage medium such as disk, tape, or paper. External data is organized into units called files. Files may exist before, during and after program execution.

File Structure

A file is a set of related data. A file might contain a business' current orders, last month's payroll data, or names and birthdates of its employees. The units of data which make up a file are listed below.

CHARACTERS

A character is the smallest unit of data which makes up a file. A character is a single symbol. It may be a letter (A through Z), a digit (0 through 9), or a special character (examples: $ # : & = /).

|W

FIELD

A field consists of one or more characters of related data. A field is an individual item of data such as an order number, a payroll period, or a last name. There are two general types of fields, numeric and alphanumeric. Numeric fields consist of digits and in some cases a sign (+ −). In order to perform calculations with a field, it must be numeric. Alphanumeric fields can contain any combination of letters, digits, and special characters.

| |450823 | NUMERIC |

| |1683 LOCUST, APT #3 | ALPHANUMERIC |

RECORD

A record consists of one or more related fields which refer to a particular person, place, or thing. A record could contain the data for one order or for one employee. The record below is made up of four fields: last name, first name, middle initial, and birthdate.

| |WEISS | |DAVID | |Q|450823 |

FILE

A file consists of one or more related records. The file below contains seven employee records. This file may be stored on auxiliary storage such as tape or disk. When a program processes data from this file, the data is read into memory and processed one record at a time.

WEISS	DAVID	Q	450823
OAKEY	BETH	M	360412
HANSEN	CLARICE	H	301218
TINGEY	LEATHA	K	280330
EBNER	MICHAEL	R	321109
GRANGE	LEILA	C	240921
THOMPSON	ELECTA	V	220824

HARDWARE

In order to use the computer to manipulate data, a means of transferring the data into **primary storage** of the computer (storage located within the computer itself) is required. After the data has been manipulated, a means of transferring it back out of storage is needed. Many kinds of **input/output devices** are used for these purposes. Among the common ones are tape drives, disk drives, terminals, optical scanners, and card readers. These devices together with the computer are known as **hardware.** Each input/output device records the data on or reads the data from a **medium,** such as magnetic tape, magnetic disks, optically readable forms, and punched cards. (Notice that there is a difference between a device and a medium. A tape drive is a device, while magnetic tape is a medium.) The term **auxiliary storage** or secondary storage refers to the storage of data outside the computer on some type of media. Among the common auxiliary storage media are disk, tape, and printed reports.

SOFTWARE

Software is a set of instructions written in a computer programming language. It is commonly referred to as a program. There is a large variety of programming languages to choose from. Some of the more commonly used programming languages are COBOL, BASIC, FORTRAN, Pascal, C, RPG, and assembler. Each of these languages has its own rules for instructing the computer to do something. Some of the languages are more suitable for business applications, others are more suitable for scientific applications.

After a program is written it must be converted to machine language before the computer can execute the instructions. This is done through the use of another program which may be called a compiler, interpreter, or assembler depending on the programming language which needs conversion.

DATA VERSUS INSTRUCTIONS

When a program is executed on a computer, two types of items are placed in primary storage, the **instructions** (processing steps) and then the **data** as it is required by the program. It is important to make a distinction between the two items.

An example of a COBOL instruction is ADD A, B GIVING C. This instruction has two parts, an operation code (op code) and operands. The **operation code** tells the computer what we want done (ADD). The operands (A, B, C) give the names of the data items to be used in the addition. These item names (A, B, C) are called variables and represent the storage areas where the actual values of the data can be found. This same instruction in BASIC would appear as 30 LET C = A + B.

This instruction assumes that values of the data items A and B have already been established and stored in memory. The computer will calculate a value for C as this instruction is executed and store it in the storage area referred to as C. To use this instruction, areas for A, B, and C must be provided in primary storage. The method for providing these storage areas depends on the programming language being used.

PROGRAM DEVELOPMENT

The Development Process

When creating a computer program, the development process is the same regardless of which programming language is used. The development process may be divided into four phases:

    I. ANALYSIS
    II. DESIGN
    III. CODING
    IV. TESTING

Depending on the size and complexity of the programming project, a different person (or group of people) might be responsible for each of the phases or one person might complete the entire process alone.

Analysis

The development process begins with a problem to be solved. The analyst meets with the group which has requested a computerized solution to their problem to determine their requirements. He or she then analyzes the current manual and computerized systems that relate to the problem. With this information, the analyst determines the input, output, and processing requirements for the program. In general, the analyst will produce documents which describe these requirements. These documents usually include program specifications, input layouts, output layouts, and system flowcharts.

Design

The designer begins with the information gathered during the analysis phase and develops the logic which will be used to solve the problem. The processing requirements are divided into smaller and smaller pieces until the logic flow is described for the entire program.

There are several design tools available which are useful for describing program logic. These include flowcharts, pseudocode, hierarchy charts, Warnier-Orr diagrams, Nassi-Schneiderman charts, Chapin charts, and IPO diagrams. The tool used for design may be mandated by the institution or organization. Otherwise, the tool used will depend upon the preference of the designer.

Coding

Coding is the process of translating the logic design into programming language code. Each step of the logic must be converted into code which conforms to the rules of the language. In many programming languages each item of data used by the program must be described. If the logic design is complete and comprehensive, coding will consist only of translating the design to fit the syntax of the programming language.

Testing

After a program is coded, it must be tested in order to discover and correct errors which occurred during the analysis, design, and coding phases. Testing involves converting the program into machine language. A computer cannot execute a program unless it is in machine language. Two types of errors may be uncovered during testing; syntax errors and errors causing incorrect output.

Syntax Errors

Syntax errors occur when the program code violates a rule of the programming language. A syntax error might be caused by a typographical error, a misspelling, or a misunderstanding of the language rules. For example, a syntax error would occur if the word MVOE were used instead of the word MOVE. With syntax errors in a program, it may not be possible to run the program.

Errors Causing Incorrect Output

Once syntax errors have been removed from the program, the program is executed to determine if it produces correct output. Test data must be carefully prepared to assure thorough testing of the program. All possible combinations of data, correct and incorrect, should be tested. The output must be carefully examined to locate any errors which might be present. If the output is incorrect, the program needs to be debugged. **Debugging** is the process of locating and removing program errors. Incorrect output may be caused by coding errors or by errors in the logic of the program.

SYSTEM FLOWCHART

A graphic representation of a system is made by drawing a **system flowchart,** which shows the flow of data from the original source such as employment records and time cards through the creation of all the necessary output (printed reports, updated master files, and so on). The system flowchart needs approval from all departments involved before programming is begun. In a system flowchart the individual programs in the system are depicted as rectangles containing a program name; nothing is said about the individual logic steps within the program itself. The system flowchart in Figure 1–1 shows a disk file which contains unedited transactions. Program1 uses this file as input and produces as output a disk file containing only the records without errors (valid records) and a report listing the records which contain errors. Program2 uses the disk file created by Program1 as input and produces as output a listing of the valid records. System flowcharts will be covered in Chapter 14.

LOGIC DESIGN TOOLS

The objective in this text is to take an individual program rectangle shown in the system flowchart and break it down into processing steps. One way to do this is with a **program flowchart.** A program flowchart shows how the data will be manipulated in a step-by-step fashion. Each description is enclosed in a standard symbol, which indicates the type of action to be taken. Other techniques used to break program rectangles down into processing steps are pseudocode, hierarchical diagrams, and Nassi-Schneiderman charts. With pseudocode a somewhat standard set of terminology and indenting is used to express the actions to be taken in the program. Hierarchical diagrams utilize rectangles in a format similar to an organization chart to identify the various routines and their relationships. Nassi-Schneiderman charts place individual routines into rectangles that are broken down by triangles and horizontal lines to show individual steps and decisions. Whichever method is used in logic design, we must later convert the flowchart, pseudocode, hierarchical diagram, or Nassi-Schneiderman charts into a computer program. Figure 1–2 shows a program flowchart for a simple listing.

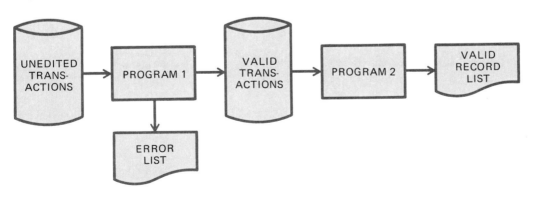

FIGURE 1–1

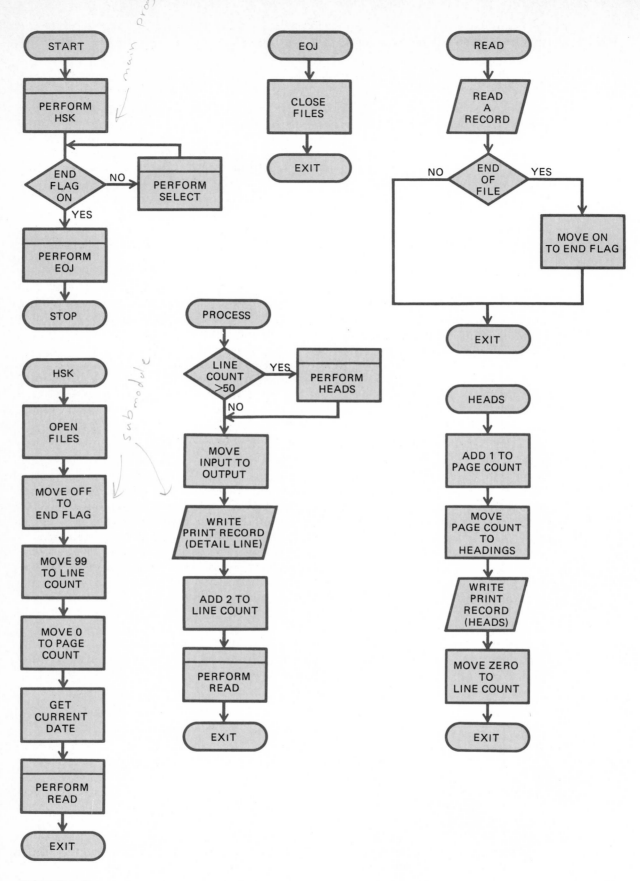

FIGURE 1–2

CONVERSION FROM FLOWCHART TO PROGRAM

Throughout the book, examples of the output will be provided along with the format of the input record or records needed to produce the output. This will allow you to concentrate on the processing required to produce the output.

Flowcharts are used to help quantify and structure the processing step. Once the flowchart is complete, it is tested with all the possible types of input that can reasonably be expected (and some unreasonable types also). This process is called **desk checking.** After we have proved to our satisfaction that the logic will produce the output required, the actual computer program can be coded. Coding is converting the flowchart into a particular programming language. The language used will depend on what is available at the facility. The logic presented in this text can readily be applied in languages such as COBOL and BASIC.

After the program is coded, it should be checked for correctness with respect to both the logic and the rules of the programming language. The coding is then converted to a form which can be accepted by the computer, such as entering the code directly into the computer through a terminal keyboard.

At this point, the instructions are inspected by a program called a compiler, interpreter, or assembler, depending on the programming language being used. Such a program exists for every programming language. This program checks each instruction of our program to see if it complies with all the rules of the programming language being used. It also converts the **source program** written by the programmer into a machine-executable equivalent called an **object program.** If there are errors in any of the program statements, they are identified by diagnostic messages so that they can be corrected. This conversion process concerns itself with the rules of the programming language only; it does not check the logic of the program or, in the case of a report, the spacing of the output.

Once the programming language errors are removed, the program is executed (run) in an attempt to produce output. If input data is required for the program, it is provided at this time. If the logic was developed correctly, the output will be as planned. If the output is incorrect, the reason may be simple errors of spacing or more serious errors of logic. Corrections to logic and spacing are made until the output is acceptable. To go from a flowchart to a properly executing program requires care at each step. Time spent in careful planning during the developmental stages pays dividends in reducing the time required to complete the project.

When the output is acceptable, a **documentation** package is prepared. Documentation is a means of communication between the programming staff, the operations staff, and the personnel in the user department. It is also useful, if the need arises, for a revision of the program.

PROGRAM TYPES

At least six basic types of programs are found in most systems:

1. File creation programs
2. Extract programs
3. Report programs
4. Input edit programs
5. Update programs
6. Utility programs

File creation programs place data on a storage medium such as tape or disk. The data may start as an optically readable form, be entered via a keyboard, or be transferred from another tape or disk.

Extract programs (discussed in Chapter 5) utilize only a portion of the data from a given file to produce a report. The extracted data may be sorted to produce a report in a sequence different from that of the original file.

Report programs (discussed in Chapters 6, 7, and 11) utilize the data from one or more input files to produce a report containing the requested information from the files. The information is produced usually in the same sequence as the files. The majority of the records in the files usually are referenced.

Input edit programs (discussed in Chapter 10) are used to validate the data in a file, making sure that it is as correct as possible in order to avoid errors when the data is used as input to some other program.

Update programs (discussed in Chapter 12) are used to bring a master file up to date, altering it to reflect transactions that have taken place during the period between the last update and the present time.

Utility programs (not discussed elsewhere in the book except for their use in sorting) may be provided by the manufacturer or a software house or written by the user. They perform such standardized functions as sorting data into a particular sequence, merging two or more files into one, copying records from one file to another, and making simple listings of data on reports.

The majority of the chapters in this book are devoted to planning (flowcharting, pseudocoding, and so on) the processing steps necessary to convert the input we have to the output we require. Chapter 4, which discusses the documenting of a program, will present the concept of documentation and the components of a documentation package.

Chapter 2 introduces the flowcharting symbols and structured concepts. It also explains the moving of data from one storage location to another within a computer.

CHAPTER VOCABULARY

Auxiliary storage
Character (numeric, alphabetic, alphanumeric, special)
Code
Data
Data processing
Desk checking
Extract program
Field
File
Hardware
Hierarchical diagrams
Information
Input
Input edit program
Instructions
Medium (media)
Nassi-Schneiderman charts
Object program
Operands
Operation codes
Output
Primary (internal storage)
Process
Pseudocode
Record
Report
Report program
Secondary (external) storage
Software
Source program
System flowchart
Update program
Utility program

REVIEW QUESTIONS

MATCHING

I.

A. Report program
B. Extract program
C. Input edit program
D. Update program

E. Report
F. System Flowchart
G. File
H. Data processing cycle

_____ 1. Utilizes only a portion of the data in a file to produce a report that may be in a different sequence than the original file.

_____ 2. Used to bring a file (usually a master file) up to a point where it reflects the current status of the data in the file.

_____ 3. Used to summarize data from one or more input files into a written form.

_____ 4. Used to validate the data in a file prior to further processing.

_____ 5. Shows the flow of data from the original source through the creation of all necessary output.

_____ 6. Output which is in a printed form.

_____ 7. Consists of input, process, and output.

_____ 8. A collection of records organized for a particular purpose.

II. Indicate whether the following represents a character (C), a field (FD), a record (R), or a file (FL).

_____ 1. The letter X.

_____ 2. A telephone number.

_____ 3. The inventory for a company.

	4.	The data for one student.
————	5.	A $.
————	6.	Orders waiting to be shipped.
————	7.	A zip code.
————	8.	Payroll data for Jane Cohen.

TRUE/FALSE

T   F   1. A system flowchart shows the logic of individual programs.

T   F   2. Utility programs may be provided by the manufacturer, a software house, or the user.

T   F   3. Program flowcharts are used to quantify and structure the process step of the data processing cycle.

T   F   4. In computer programming the words data and instruction have the same meaning.

T   F   5. Once a program is coded, it should be checked for correctness only with respect to the logic.

T   F   6. A file is a collection of related records.

T   F   7. Data is stored on a device.

T   F   8. Storage within the computer is called auxiliary storage.

T   F   9. A character is the smallest unit of data in a file structure.

T   F   10. All programming languages require a compiler to convert their instructions into object code usable by the computer.

EXERCISES

1. Diagram the relationship of the units of data.
2. List any devices of media that you are aware of. Specify whether they are suitable for input or output or both.
3. Describe the steps in the development of a new system.
4. Describe the basic types of programs found in most systems.

DISCUSSION QUESTIONS

1. Why are we likely to use output as our starting point when developing a system?
2. Identify what would constitute a file, record, field, and character in various data processing systems. Examples: student registration, inventory, accounts receivable.
3. Give examples of logic errors versus violations of the rules of a programming language.
4. What business courses would you want a programmer you are going to hire to have taken?

2 INTRODUCTION TO FLOWCHARTING

OBJECTIVES

As a result of studying this chapter the student should be able to perform the following activities:

1. Describe the purpose of program flowcharting.
2. Define desk checking and indicate its importance to the flowcharting process.
3. Identify the various program flowcharting symbols.
4. Describe the difference between the usage of START/STOP and NAME/EXIT in the terminal symbol.
5. Describe destructive readin and its effects on the contents of an input area.
6. Describe the difference between internal and external predefined processes.
7. Identify the various flowcharting structures.
8. Describe and draw the mainline logic for a flowchart.
9. Describe what is involved in moving data from one area to another in storage, including the moving of multiple fields.
10. Describe what is meant by moving data in storage and the effect on both sending and receiving fields.
11. Describe the use of END FLAG in the mainline logic, including when it is turned on and off.

PROGRAM FLOWCHARTS

We are now going to concentrate on program flowcharts. A program flowchart is planned and drawn by a programmer. When it is complete, the programmer tests it by pretending to be a computer. The programmer moves the data through each step of the flowchart, doing with the data what each step in the flowchart specifies. If the flowchart was correctly drawn, then the results (what happened to the data) will be exactly as planned. This process, called **desk checking,** is important, as it helps to discover logic errors in the flowchart or details that have been forgotten. An example of desk checking will be presented at the end of the chapter once the various symbols have been presented.

When satisfied that the flowchart has been drawn correctly, the programmer will code the program in the programming language used at the facility. This involves coding the actions specified in each symbol in a form appropriate for the programming language being used. If the flowchart has been drawn in detail, the result will be one programming statement for each flowcharting symbol. There are many views on how detailed a program flowchart should be; let's simply say that it needs to be only detailed enough to show the logical decisions being made and the general processing to be done. An experienced programmer will recognize situations where one symbol in a flowchart must be expanded into more than one programming statement. It is better for beginners to put too much rather than too little detail into their flowcharts.

The next step is to translate the coded program into a machine-readable form. This is referred to as **compiling** the program (or **assembling** if you are writing in an assembler language). Error diagnostics will be provided by the compiler (assembler) for any rules of the programming language that have been broken. The programmer must correct any errors that the compiler points out. If a language, which uses an interpreter (such as BASIC) is being utilized, then the

10

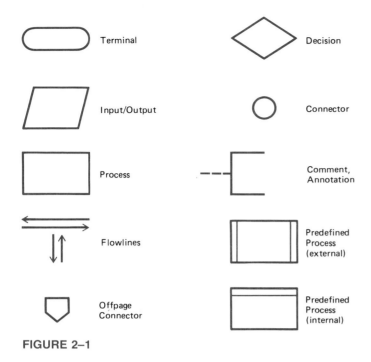

FIGURE 2–1

diagnostics may either be listed at the same time that the statements are entered, or with IBM BASIC as each program statement executes rather than as a separate step. With all the language errors removed, the program will now execute the instructions in the order specified. It is here that any lack of planning in the flowchart will show up. With incorrect planning, the output will be what you asked for—but not what you wanted. Corrections to the logic after it is in the form of a program take an excessive amount of time. An "I'll fix it as it falls apart" attitude leads to sloppy programming and continued headaches.

FLOWCHARTING SYMBOLS

Program flowcharts are the graphic representation of the program logic required to produce the desired output. A number of standard symbols (Figure 2–1) having specific meanings are used in program flowcharting. The ensuing discussion will present these symbols and their meanings. This material* is reproduced with permission from American National Standards x3.5–1970 by the American National Standards Institute, copies of which may be purchased from the American National Standards Institute at 1430 Broadway, New York, New York 10018.

STRUCTURED FLOWCHARTING

Before considering what these symbols mean individually, we need to look at the standard configurations in which they are used. These configurations, called **structures,** are the basic building blocks of structured flowcharting.

Structured flowcharting is only one part of the overall topic of structuring, which includes systems design, programming, and so on. Structured flowcharting is a method of organizing the logic of a program in a standardized manner. This type of organization provides for easier coding of programs, ease of maintenance (changing programs), and uniform coding practices between programming personnel. It has been shown that using structured techniques will dramat-

---

* All flowcharting symbols (except the offpage connector, which is an IBM symbol) and the definitions for the following symbols in Chapter 13: Punched Card Symbols, Online Storage, Magnetic Tape, Punched Tape, Magnetic Drum, Magnetic Disk, Core, Document, Manual Input, Display, Communications Link, Offline Storage, Preparation, Manual Operation, Auxiliary Operation, Merge, Extract, Sort, and Collate.

ically improve the productivity of a programming department. No attempt will be made here to completely cover the topic of structuring. Rather, we will present only the basics of structured program flowcharting.

STRUCTURES—IDENTIFIED

In structured flowcharts the following four structures form the basis for the logical solution to a problem:

1. Sequence structure (Figure 2–2)
2. Decision structure (Figure 2–3)
3. Do while structure (Figure 2–4)
4. Do until structure (Figure 2–5)

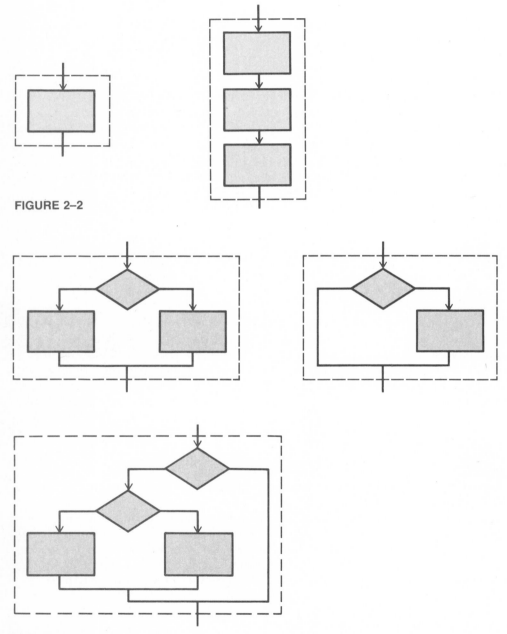

FIGURE 2–2

FIGURE 2–3

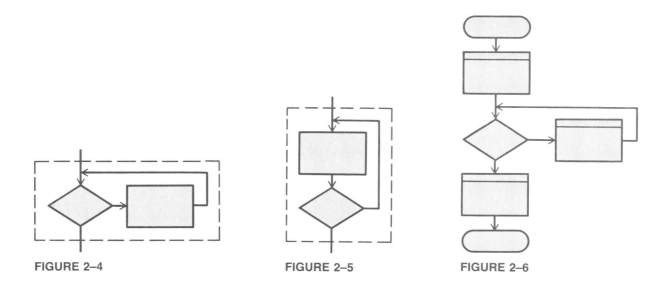

FIGURE 2–4   **FIGURE 2–5**   **FIGURE 2–6**

The structures in Figures 2–2 through 2–5 have been enclosed in dotted lines for reference purposes only. When a flowchart is drawn, the dotted lines will not be present.

Throughout the book we will make use of these structures. We will also use a combination of these structures referred to as the **mainline logic** of a program (Figure 2–6); this will appear in some form in the rest of the flowcharts in the book. The mainline logic is the basic logic of a program which performs the standard routines present in almost any program. What the mainline logic stands for will be explained throughout the rest of the chapter.

SYMBOLS

The individual symbols used in program flowcharting first need to be described so that we can show how they can be combined into the standard structures (as well as the mainline logic).

TERMINAL SYMBOL

The terminal symbol is used to indicate a starting or stopping point in the logic. The use of this symbol in the mainline logic is shown in Figure 2–7.

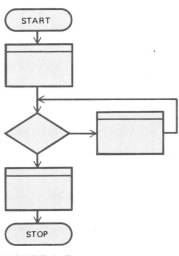

FIGURE 2–7

The terminal symbol at the beginning is identified by the word START, the ending symbol by the word STOP. Another use of the terminal symbol will be indicated later in the chapter, when subroutines are presented.

PROCESS SYMBOL

As a part of doing an overall problem we may be calculating regular pay and adding it to a total. This particular segment of the logic is shown in Figure 2–8. The process symbol is used to depict any single step in the solution to a problem other than reading, writing, or making a decision.

FIGURE 2–8

PREDEFINED-PROCESS SYMBOL

The predefined-process symbol is used to show a series of processing steps which are described elsewhere. Two versions of the predefined-process symbols are shown in Figure 2–9.

Predefined processes are either internal or external. **Internal** processes are found within the same program that are performing the process; **external** processes are not, but they can be referred to and used as needed by being called from a system library. In either case, after the separate set of steps in the process being performed have been executed, control returns to the symbol immediately following the predefined-process symbol that invoked them. Let's return to the mainline logic presented earlier. This time names have been added to the predefined processes, as shown in Figure 2–10.

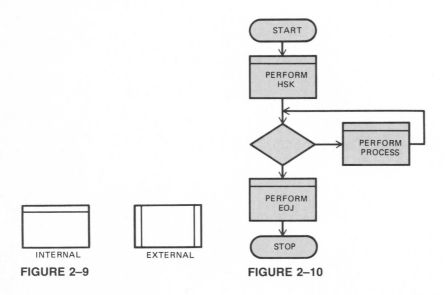

FIGURE 2–9

FIGURE 2–10

HSK, PROCESS, and EOJ are routines that are depicted in predefined-process symbols. Each routine has its own set of processing steps. What these steps are at this point is neither here nor there, but the routines would be drawn as shown in Figure 2–11. The steps in each of these routines will be presented later as the need arises. In Figure 2–11 these steps are indicated by a pair of wavy lines:

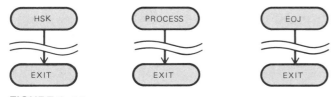

FIGURE 2–11

Several points should be noticed here. Each routine starts and stops with a terminal symbol. START has been replaced by the name of the routine (HSK, PROCESS or EOJ). STOP has been replaced by the term EXIT. Both uses (mainline and routine) of the terminal symbol indicate a starting or stopping point in the logic.

INPUT/OUTPUT SYMBOL

The input/output symbol is used to show the reading or writing of one logical (individual) record. This is a general-purpose input/output symbol. It is general purpose in that it refers to reading or writing a single record from or to any device (tape, disk, printer, drum, optically read document, etc.) More specific symbols which indicate a particular type of input/output device are used in a system flowchart. These special-purpose symbols (which should not be used in program flowcharts) as well as the concept of system flowcharting will be covered in Chapter 14.

DECISION SYMBOL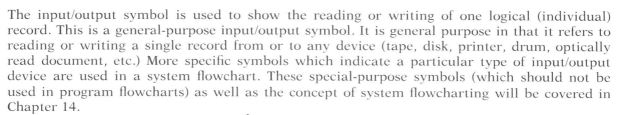

The decision symbol depicts a decision being made and the alternate logic paths to be followed as a result. There is one entrance into a decision symbol and at least two exits from it. The standard form of a decision symbol is a two-way exit. With this type of decision there are only two possible answers, yes or no. The mainline logic is again shown in Figure 2–12, this time with the decision symbol showing what decision is being made and the YES and NO paths.

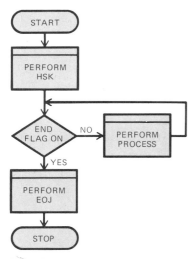

FIGURE 2–12

DECISION SYMBOL—3 OR MORE EXITS

Besides simple two-way tests, there are two other common uses for decision symbols. One is the situation where you are testing to see if one number is greater than, equal to, or less than another number. Two common ways of flowcharting this are shown in Figure 2–13. In this text we will be using the one with two decision symbols rather than showing three separate exits.

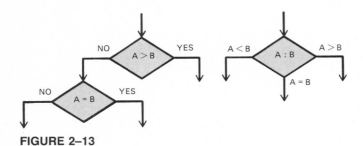

FIGURE 2–13

Another possibility is that one of several exit paths may be taken, depending on the value of some variable. Two common ways of depicting this are shown in Figure 2–14. Again, we will be using the version with multiple decision symbols. Based on the value of the variable (CODE in this case), various paths in the logic may be followed.

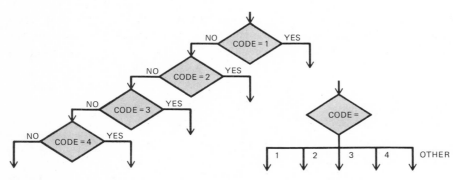

FIGURE 2–14

CONNECTOR SYMBOL

The connector symbol is used to show an exit from or an entrance into the logic of a flowchart. When it shows the logic flow leaving one part of the flowchart and going to some other part, it is called an **exit.** Exits always immediately follow one of the various symbols (other than flowlines) and are usually shown in one of the ways indicated in Figure 2–15.

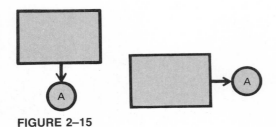

FIGURE 2–15

When a connector symbol is being used as an exit symbol (often called a branch) it is usually identified with a letter that indicates where in the logic a branch is going to for further processing. The point being branched to is indicated by a connector with the same letter in it, and at this point it is called an **entry.** Entries are almost always into flowlines (not into a symbol—unless it is a continuation from a previous page) and are usually drawn as shown in Figure 2–16.

FIGURE 2–16

Exits and entries may also have page references in them indicating (for exits) what page is being branched to and (for entries) what page is being branched from. In most cases connectors are used as replacements for flowlines to avoid having flowlines running all over the place and to present a neater, easier-to-read flowchart. In at least one place connectors are always used in place of flowlines. This is when the branch is to another place in the flowchart on a different page. After all, you can't (or shouldn't) have lines going from one page to another.

Let's take a look at two mainline logic flowcharts. Figure 2–17 utilizes flowlines, while Figure 2–18 utilizes connectors. The individual symbols are numbered to facilitate cross-referencing.

The path to check the END FLAG in Figure 2–17 is done with flowlines, whereas in Figure 2–18 it is done with connectors. The connector leaving block 3B is an exit. The connector going in to test the setting of END FLAG just above block 2B is an entry. Notice that an exit takes place from a symbol and an entry takes place into a flowline. Normally connectors should not be used when the distance is this short but it serves to show how they are used.

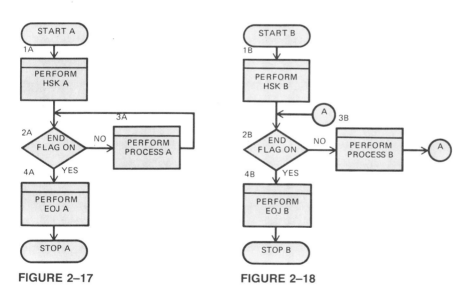

FIGURE 2–17   **FIGURE 2–18**

OFFPAGE CONNECTOR

This is an IBM-only symbol and as such is not an industry standard, although it is commonly used. The offpage connector symbol is used to show a continuation of a logic path from one page to another in a flowchart. Look at the flowchart in Figure 2–19. The small size of the pages is unrealistic, but they serve to illustrate how a page change is made. The pointed end of the symbol should point down.

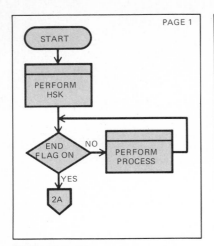
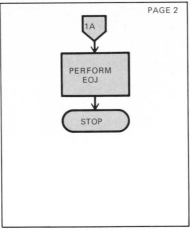

FIGURE 2–19

Notice that the number in the offpage connector symbol is a page reference. The 2A in the symbol on the bottom of page 1 indicates the page being continued to (2) and the path that is being continued (A). The 1A in the symbol on the top of page 2 indicates the page from which the continuation is taking place (1) and the path that is being continued (A). At times the symbolism within the offpage connector symbol becomes more extensive to facilitate the following of a logic path. This is especially true in rather large programs with a great number of subroutines.

ANNOTATION SYMBOL

The annotation symbol is used to add additional comments to a flowcharting symbol. While you normally indicate what action is being taken in any given block, at times additional wording is needed to indicate more detail. For instance, in the reading process above, we said to read a record but did not say from what particular file. If this information is desired, we could provide it as shown in Figure 2–20.

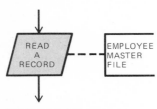

FIGURE 2–20

This note makes it obvious that a record is being read from the employee master file. This same type of notation may be used in many ways on various symbols to provide more detail for purposes of clarification. However, its use should not become so extensive that it clutters up the flowchart and hinders readability.

FLOWLINES

Flowlines are used to connect the various symbols (or structures) in a flowchart and to indicate the direction of flow of the logic. Flowcharts are normally written so that the flow is from top to bottom and from left to right. If the flowlines have no arrowheads, this direction of flow will be assumed. Flow in other directions requires the use of arrowheads to indicate the path of the logic. A flowchart could be drawn as shown in Figure 2–21, but this is not the best way to depict the flow of logic; it is awkward to read and should be avoided. Notice also that if the arrowheads had been left off and just lines used to connect the symbols in Figure 2–21, the flow would be difficult at best to determine. It would not be easy to determine even the starting place in the logic. Every effort should be made to allow the logic to flow from top down and— except for exiting from decision symbols—from the left to right. Decision symbols are listed as an exception because there are always at least two exit paths from a decision symbol and they come out of both sides and potentially the bottom of the decision symbol.

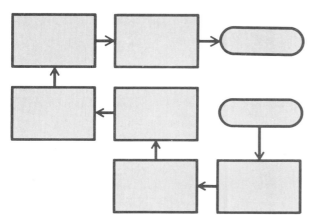

FIGURE 2–21

It is not right or wrong to include or leave out arrowheads when the flow is top down or left to right. You should, however, be consistent in the method that you use. In this text we will use arrowheads at all times to avoid ambiguity.

It is also possible to cross flowlines as shown in Figure 2–22. However, such crossing lends itself to a great deal of ambiguity, and the logic is difficult to follow, so this practice should be avoided.

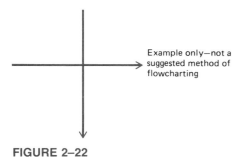

Example only—not a suggested method of flowcharting

FIGURE 2–22

STRUCTURES

Structures are flowcharting symbols or combinations of flowcharting symbols designed for a particular function. These structures are then combined to depict the logic necessary to produce the desired results. The formats for the structures were shown in Figures 2–2 to 2–5. Figure 2–23 shows the mainline logic again, but this time dotted lines have been drawn around the structures. Let us see what these structures are and identify their characteristics.

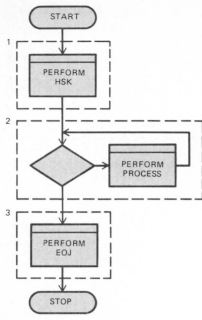

FIGURE 2-23

SEQUENCE STRUCTURE

The dotted areas in Figure 2–23 numbered 1 and 3 are sequence structures. A sequence structure is represented by the process symbol (for such actions ADD or MOVE), the predefined-process symbol, or the input/output symbol.

It is also possible to have multiple process, predefined-process, or input/output symbols within a single sequence structure. There is, however, only one entrance into and one exit from a sequence structure; **this is a very important point which is true for all structures.** Figure 2–24 shows a sequence structure with multiple steps in it.

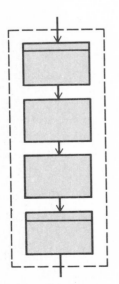

FIGURE 2-24

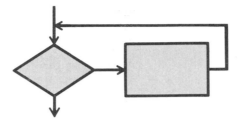

DO WHILE STRUCTURE

Do while structures are used to be able to repeat a series of steps and thus avoid having to code them over and over again in order to accomplish what is desired. The process of reusing a series of steps is referred to as looping. The actual steps involved in looping are presented in Chapter 3. In relation to the mainline logic the PROCESS routine will be done over and over again until some situation (represented by the decision symbol in the mainline logic) becomes true. Notice that with the do while structure the process routine may or may not be performed. Whether the PROCESS routine is performed will depend on the result of the decision. If the result of the decision is not true then the PROCESS routine will be performed. If, however, the result of the decision is true then the process routine will not be performed.

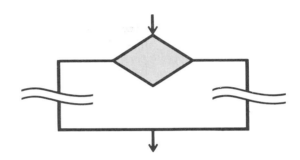

DECISION STRUCTURE

The decision structure is made up of a decision symbol with a sequence structure, do while structure, do until structure, or another decision structure on either or both paths from the decision symbol. Examples of these are shown in Figures 2–25 (with a sequence structure), 2–26 (with a do while structure), 2–27 (with a do until structure), and 2–28 (with another decision structure). This process of combining structures is a basic principle of structured flowcharting.

Figures 2–13 and 2–14 (presented earlier) represent what is called a CASE structure. When there are three or more exits from the decision symbol in a decision structure the structure is called a case structure.

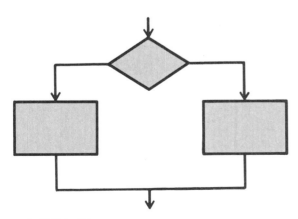

FIGURE 2–25

In using these structures for the first time you may find it difficult to connect the lines and still have structures. Remember the cardinal rule: Structures can have **only one entrance and one exit.** Figure 2–29 indicates both how to and not to connect the lines at the bottom. In

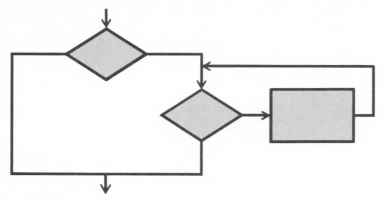

FIGURE 2–26

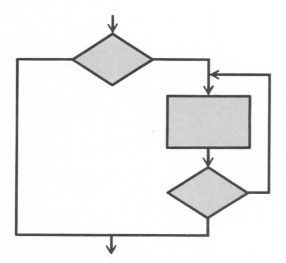

FIGURE 2–27

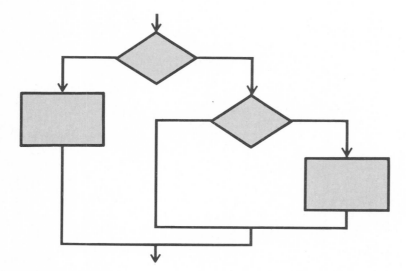

FIGURE 2–28

order to do so it may be necessary to repeat a process in the flowchart. The point here is not whether the flowchart produces the correct output but whether it represents a structured format. The incorrect one is not structured. It violates the one-entrance one-exit rule. You should be able to lift any structure out of the flowchart (although this may alter the results) and connect the entry and exit lines with a single vertical line. This shows us that any structure is sort of "pluggable"; we can fix or change it with new structures by merely taking out the old one and putting in one that produces the new or correct result. An example of this pluggable concept is shown in Figure 2–30. The dotted lines show what has been eliminated.

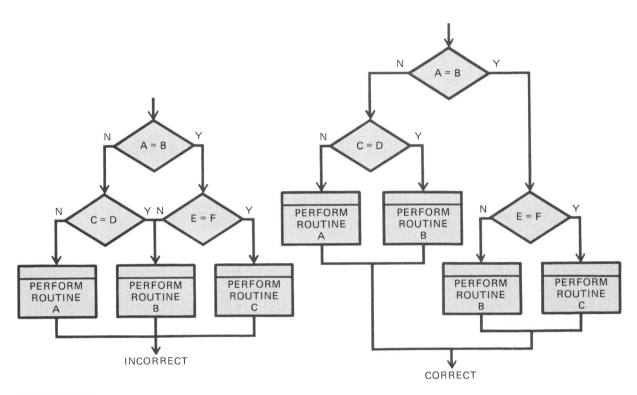

FIGURE 2–29

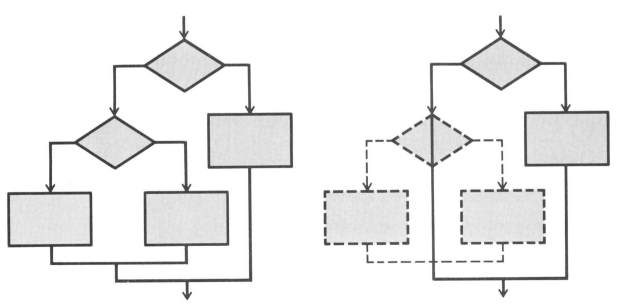

FIGURE 2–30

The one structure that has not yet been described, DO UNTIL, will be covered under looping in Chapter 3.

READING INPUT DATA

There are normally separate areas in primary storage for accepting data that is read into storage and for holding data as it is prepared for output to some device. Figure 2–31 is a diagram of these areas in primary storage.

The area in primary storage shown as INPUT-AREA will be used to hold data that is read into storage from some file. The contents of the records in the file we will use is illustrated in Figure 2–32.

We will assume that INPUT-AREA contains blanks at the beginning of the process. If one 80 character record is read into storage that contains the word APPLES in the first 6 positions and blanks in the remaining 74 positions, the result is as shown in Figure 2–33. The input area has been defined in the program as being 80 positions in size (the same as an input record).

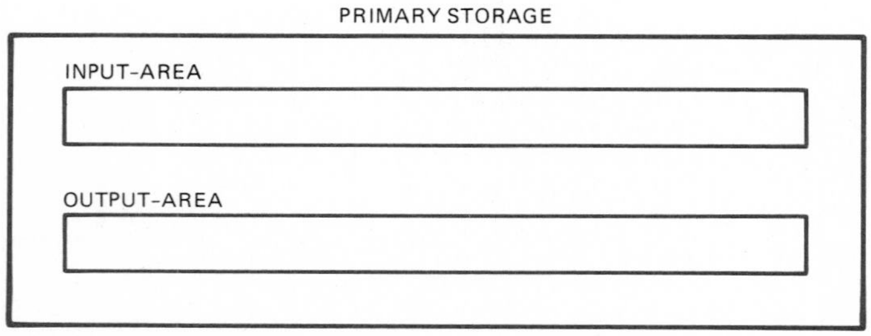

PRIMARY STORAGE

INPUT-AREA

OUTPUT-AREA

FIGURE 2–31

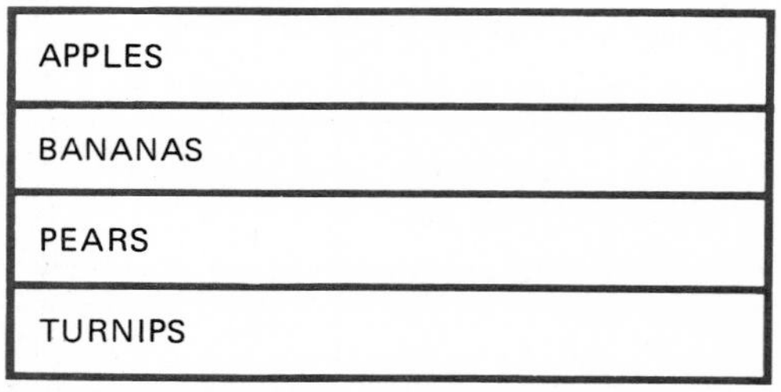

APPLES

BANANAS

PEARS

TURNIPS

FIGURE 2–32

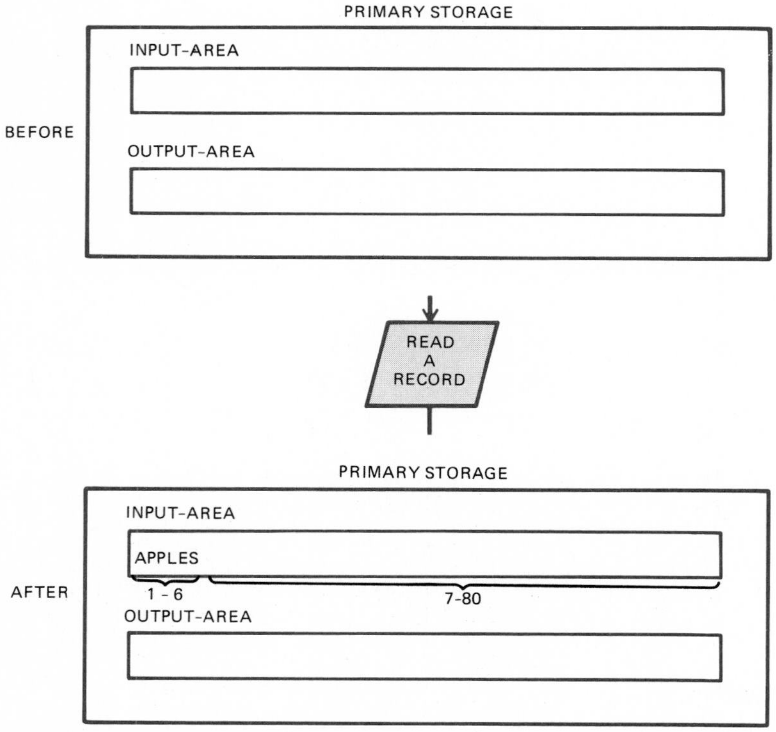

PRIMARY STORAGE

INPUT-AREA

OUTPUT-AREA

BEFORE

READ
A
RECORD

PRIMARY STORAGE

INPUT-AREA

APPLES

1 - 6   7-80

OUTPUT-AREA

AFTER

FIGURE 2–33

Notice that after the reading operation INPUT-AREA contains the data read from the record. In other words, INPUT-AREA contains APPLES and 74 blanks from the record that was read. Notice that the entire record was read into storage, not just one field or area on the record. The blanks from the record are transferred to storage in the same manner as the alphabetic characters. The reading operation had no effect on the contents of OUTPUT-AREA; further processing would be necessary to affect those contents.

DESTRUCTIVE READIN

Now let us assume that all four records in the file are going to be read, one after the other, without doing any other processing. While the odds are not good that any program would just read four records and stop, this example will serve to point out the effect of a repetitive reading process. This process is shown in Figure 2–34.

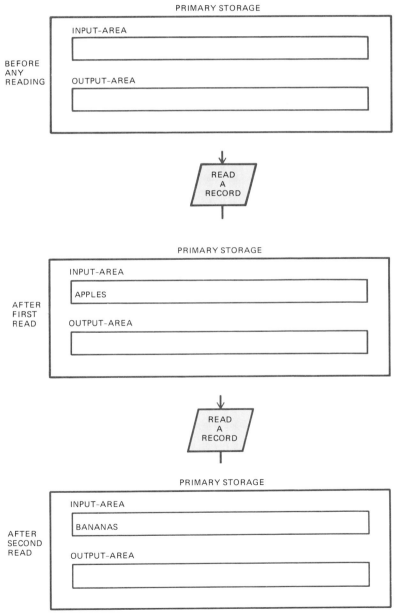

FIGURE 2–34

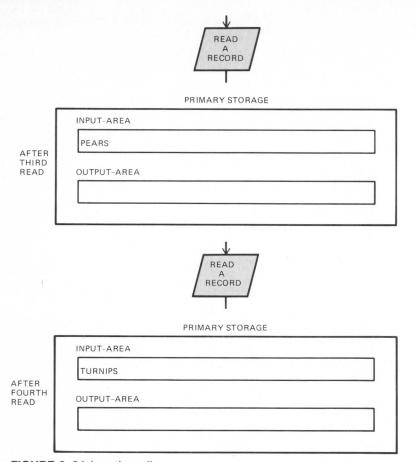

FIGURE 2–34 (continued)

The first read is the same as the previous example. After the first read the contents of INPUT-AREA reflect the contents of the first record. The INPUT-AREA now contains APPLES and the remaining blanks or spaces from the record (74 of them, to be exact).

After the second read the contents of INPUT-AREA have been altered completely; they now reflect the contents of the second record. The word APPLES has been completely replaced with the word BANANAS (and 73 spaces) from the second record.

After the third read the data from the third record (that is PEARS and 75 spaces) has replaced BANANAS (and 73 spaces) in INPUT-AREA. In a similar manner, when the fourth record is read, the data from it (TURNIPS and 73 spaces) will completely replace PEARS (and 75 spaces).

There are two very important concepts in this example. First, only one logical (individual) record at a time is read and not the whole file. Second, since each successive record is read into the same area (INPUT-AREA in this case), the contents of the previous record are lost as each new record is read. The contents can be saved with other types of processing, if desired. The concept of replacing data in the input area as each new record is read is called **destructive readin. (Readin** is a composite term made up of the words **read** and **in.**)

WRITING DATA FROM STORAGE

The other half of the input/output process is that of writing data out of storage to some medium such as tape, disk, or a printed report. In other words, one logical (individual) record is going to be written. Using the original example, where only one record was read that had APPLES and 74 spaces in it, let us assume that the record has already been read and that storage now looks like Figure 2–35.

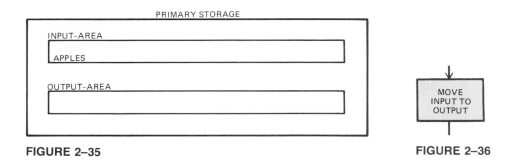

FIGURE 2–35

FIGURE 2–36

In languages such as COBOL or assembler language, transfer of the data from INPUT-AREA is needed before any output that is meaningful can be produced. This transfer requires the use of the MOVE command (Figure 2–36).

Move does not affect the contents of the sending area, which in this case is INPUT-AREA. It merely duplicates the contents of the sending area in some other area of storage, called the receiving area (OUTPUT-AREA in this case). After this action the data will be in storage, as shown in Figure 2–37.

If we now want the contents of OUTPUT-AREA to be written on the printer, we instruct the system to write a line, and the data will be transferred to the output device we indicate (in our example, a printer). The flowcharting form of this instruction is shown in Figure 2–38. The instruction in Figure 2–38 causes the printer output shown in Figure 2–39 to be produced.

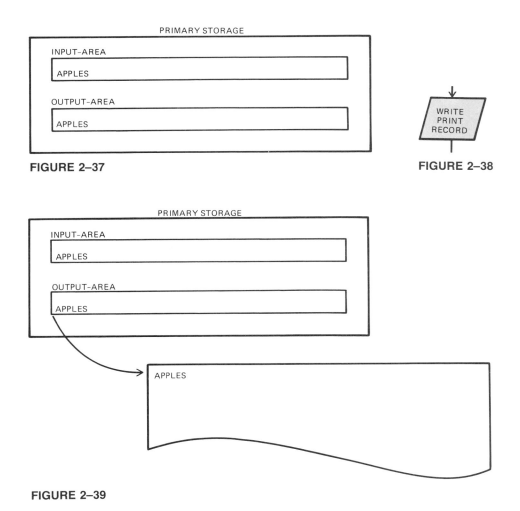

FIGURE 2–37

FIGURE 2–38

FIGURE 2–39

END FLAG AND END-OF-FILE TESTS

One very important decision in the mainline logic of a structured program is determining whether all of the data has been processed (Figure 2–40). If all of the data has not been processed the next step would be to perform the PROCESS routine. If, however, all of the data has been processed the next step is to perform the EOJ routine. The EOJ routine is performed only once and is performed after all of the data items have been processed.

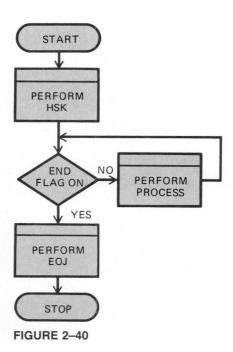

FIGURE 2–40

Upon entering the decision symbol, a check is made to see if END FLAG is on. If the answer is yes, then the logic falls through into the EOJ routine. If the answer is no, the next step is to perform the PROCESS routine and return to test the condition of END FLAG.

END FLAG in this example is called a **switch.** A switch is an area in storage, the contents of which are controlled by the programmer. In this case END FLAG will be set to an on condition (any value can be used by the programmer to indicate an on condition) when the end-of-file record has been read from an input file. Until the end-of-file record has been read, the value of END FLAG will remain set to an **off** condition. END FLAG was initialized to an off condition in the HSK routine (again, this is any value other than that used for **on** and is selected by the programmer). The HSK routine is performed only once at the beginning of the program and is used to get ready for processing. Although switches can be used very effectively in a situation like this, they should not be overused. Cluttering a program with dozens of switches does more to complicate than to simplify the logic.

Let us see how this mainline logic would look in actual programming instructions. In COBOL:

```
MAINLINE-LOGIC.
     PERFORM HSK.
     PERFORM PROCESS UNTIL END-FLAG = 'ON'.
     PERFORM EOJ.
```

In BASIC:

```
100 REM MAINLINE LOGIC
110 GOSUB 1000                          'HSK
120 WHILE END.FLAG$ = "OFF"             'PROCESS
130    GOSUB 2000
140 WEND
150 GOSUB 3000                          'EOJ
160 END
```

This brings up another very important two-way decision: the testing for an end-of-file record when reading an input file. Most computers today provide the ability to test for an out-of-data or end-of-file condition on a sequential reading operation (reading a file from beginning to end, including all the records on the file).

Sequential files are files that have been sorted into some predetermined order such as by social security number or part number. At the end of a sequential file there is usually some sort of record that indicates to the system that all data records have been read and processed. When this record is encountered at the end of a file, it is not to be processed, since it is not data but merely an indicator record. While the format of this record may vary with the specific computer or manufacturer, the principle remains the same. When such a record is not possible (as when data is within the program and is being read via data statements in BASIC), the programmer creates a **sentinel** record after the data records. This sentinel record serves the same function as an end-of-file record; it looks like another data record but has "bogus" values in the fields that can be tested for when the data is processed.

In structured flowcharting the next record on a file is read (via a separate READ routine) at two places: at the end of the HSK and PROCESS routines. Figure 2–41 shows how this is flowcharted.

In both cases if a data record is read the END FLAG will remain unchanged (off). If, however, an end-of-file record is read, the END FLAG will be turned on. After leaving either the HSK or PROCESS routine, the next step is to test the setting of END FLAG. If END FLAG is off, the PROCESS routine will be executed. If END FLAG is on, the EOJ routine will be executed.

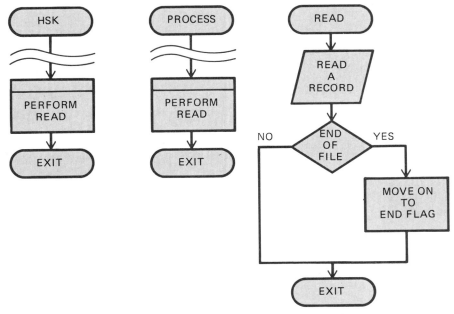

FIGURE 2–41

MOVING SEPARATE FIELDS

We now have enough basics to read and write multiple records and test for end of file. We need one more concept before going further. Most likely any file would have more than one field on each record. To illustrate the fact that in most cases each field must be moved individually, let's read and print each data record from the file shown in Figure 2–42.

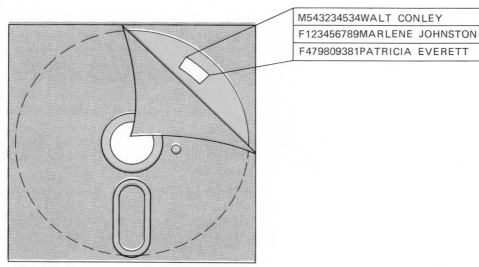

M543234534WALT CONLEY
F123456789MARLENE JOHNSTON
F479809381PATRICIA EVERETT

FIGURE 2–42

On the printed report we want blank space of some size to appear between the fields for readability (see Figure 2–43). We may also desire to alter the sequence of the fields when they are printed.

M   543234534   WALT CONLEY
F   123456789   MARLENE JOHNSTON
F   479809381   PATRICIA EVERETT

FIGURE 2–43

Each record on the disk file contains three fields (sex, social security number, and name). Figure 2–44 shows the flowchart to accomplish the listing of this file. Only the PROCESS and READ routines are shown, so remember that the first record was read in the HSK routine.

The most important idea in Figure 2–44 is that if we are concerned with the individual fields on a record rather than the entire record, then each field from the input record must be moved separately to the output line. In following one record through the process, the actual steps followed should become clearer (see Figure 2–45, steps 1–7).

Step 1. This step performs the HSK routine. The END FLAG is turned off before an attempt is made to read a record. This is to ensure the value of END FLAG prior to any processing. Following this, the first record is read (in the PERFORM READ step) from the input file. Since an end-of-file record is not found, END FLAG is left in its off state.

Step 2. This step tests the setting of END FLAG. Since its value is off, the next step is to execute the PROCESS routine. If it had been on, the next step would have been to execute the EOJ routine.

Step 3. This step moves the contents of the third field (name) to the OUTPUT-AREA.

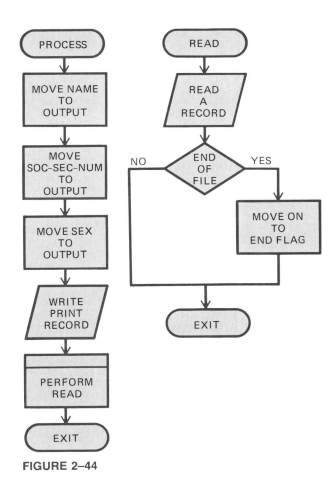

FIGURE 2–44

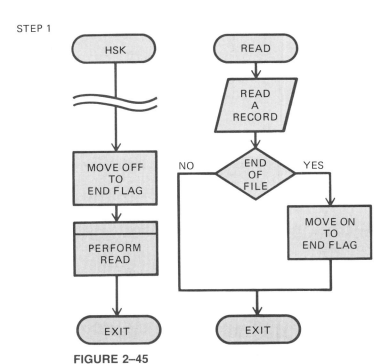

FIGURE 2–45

STEP 2

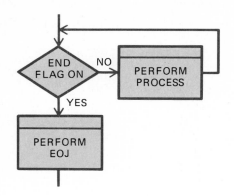

INPUT RECORD

M543234534WALTER CONLEY

PRIMARY STORAGE

INPUT AREA

M543234534WALTER CONLEY

OUTPUT AREA

STEP 3

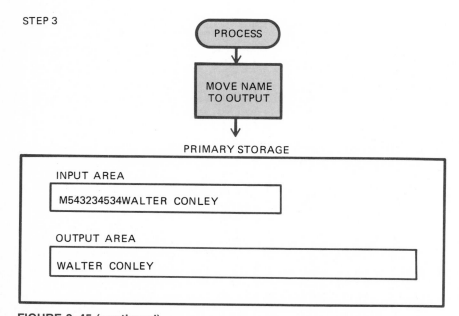

PRIMARY STORAGE

INPUT AREA

M543234534WALTER CONLEY

OUTPUT AREA

WALTER CONLEY

FIGURE 2–45 (continued)

Step 4. This step moves the contents of the second field (soc-sec-num) to OUTPUT-AREA.

Step 5. This step moves the contents of the first field (sex) to OUTPUT-AREA.

Step 6. This step prints the contents of the OUTPUT-AREA on the report. Note that all the fields were moved prior to writing the line and that only one line was written.

Step 7. This step reads (in the PERFORM READ step) the next record on the input file. Since an end-of-file record is not read, the END FLAG is left off. Upon leaving the PROCESS routine the next step is to check the contents of END FLAG (step 2). Once the end-of-file record (the fourth record in this example) has been read, END FLAG will be turned on, which will cause step 2 to proceed to the EOJ routine instead of step 3.

Throughout the rest of the book when you encounter the symbol which says MOVE INPUT TO OUTPUT, remember that this implies moving each field separately before writing a line.

STEP 4

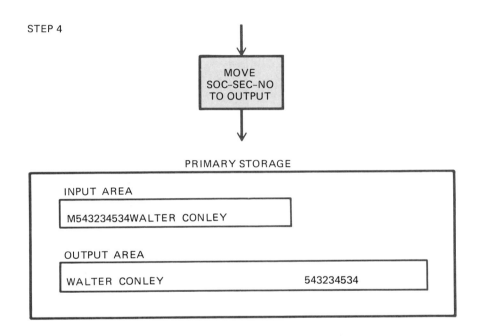

STEP 5

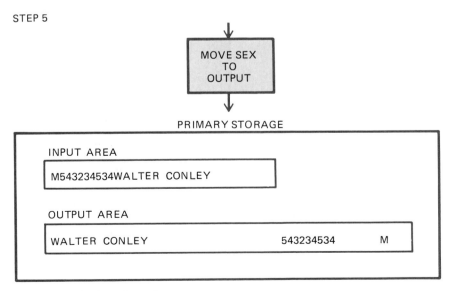

FIGURE 2–45 (continued)

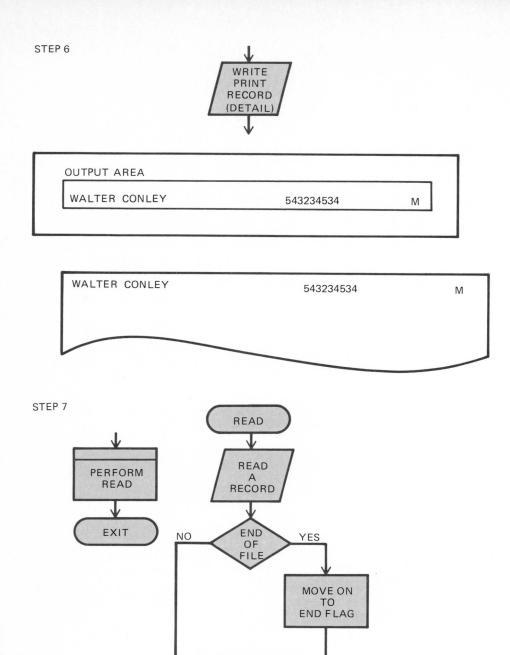

OUTPUT AREA

WALTER CONLEY   543234534   M

WALTER CONLEY   543234534   M

STEP 7

PERFORM
READ

EXIT

READ

READ
A
RECORD

END
OF
FILE

NO   YES

MOVE ON
TO
END FLAG

EXIT

FIGURE 2–45 (continued)

Although such moves are unnecessary when using a programming language such as BASIC they are still quite reasonable in the flowchart.

DESK CHECKING EXAMPLE

It was mentioned previously that once the basics of this chapter were out of the way that we would discuss desk checking in greater detail. We are now at the point. Figure 2–46 is the data that will be used in this exercise and Figure 2–47 is the flowchart that we will be checking. The purpose of the program is to list all of the men who are over 30.

Name	Sex	Age	Phone
Adams, Samuel	M	15	853-8576
Baker, Donna	F	30	853-9687
Conners, Fred	M	41	853-4852
Davis, Abbie	F	24	856-3968
Edwards, Pete	D	36	856-2948

FIGURE 2–46

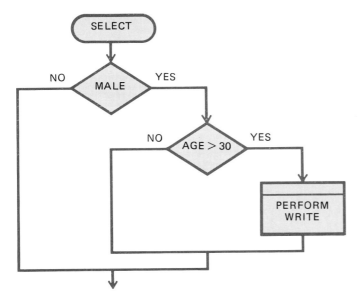

FIGURE 2–47

The first record has been read in the housekeeping routine prior to entering the SELECT routine. Samuel Adams' record is checked to see if it is the record for a male. It is, so his record is checked to see if he is over 30. Since he is not, the next record is read before leaving the SELECT routine.

Returning to the SELECT routine the record for Donna Baker does not have a code for male. The only thing left before leaving the SELECT routine is to read the next record.

The record for Fred Conners is coded as a male and indicates an age greater than 30. He is therefore listed on the report and the next record in the file is read. Having read the next record it is again time to leave the SELECT routine.

The record for Abbie Davis is not coded as a male. Since there are no more checks that are needed the next record is read and it is time to exit the SELECT routine.

When checking the record for Pete Edwards the code is not what is needed for a male. His record is therefore bypassed and he is not shown on the report in any manner. This points out a weakness in the above SELECT routine. By not providing for error conditions records with errors in them may well go undetected. This could be provided for by altering the logic as indicated in Figure 2–48. The following description also incorporates lines on the flowchart to depict the desk checking process as each of the test records is checked.

Prior to entering the SELECT routine the first record has been read in the housekeeping routine. In following it through the flowchart segment (path 1) the first step is to check to see if it is the record for a male. It is, so the next step is to see if it is for a person over 30. It is not, so no further processing is needed for this record and the next record is read. This path through the flowchart is shown by the solid thin line.

In processing the second record (path 2) it is found that it is not the record for a male, it is the record for a female, and therefore no further processing is needed. The next record is read and a branch is taken to exit the SELECT routine. This path through the flowchart is shown by the solid thick line.

Record three (path 3) is a male over 30 so the record is listed on the report. The next

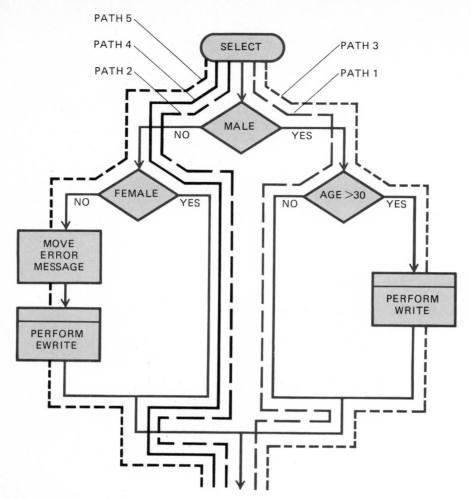

FIGURE 2–48

record is read and the logic path proceeds to the exit for the SELECT routine. This is shown by the thin dotted line through the flowchart.

Record four (path 4) does not represent a male, but does represent a female, so the only thing needed before exiting the SELECT routine is to read the next record. This is shown by the thick dotted line through the flowchart.

When the last record is processed (path 5) it fails the test for being a male (and a female) so an error message is printed and an exit is taken from the select routine after attempting to read the next record. This is shown by the wavey line through the flowchart. Pete Edwards is a male but was incorrectly coded. The alteration to the logic will not allow this to go undetected. Even though Pete is incorrectly coded for a male it would show his record as being in error. In this way it could be corrected for future runs of the program so that he would be properly shown on the report.

CHAPTER VOCABULARY _____

Annotation symbol
Arrowheads
Branching
Connector symbol
Decision structure
Decision symbol
Destructive readin
Do until structure
Do while structure

End flag
Entry
Exit
External process
Flowlines
Input/output symbol
Internal process
Mainline logic
Offpage connector

Predefined process symbol
Process symbol
Program flowchart
Sequence structure
Sequential files
Structured flowcharting
Structures
Switch
Terminal symbol

REVIEW QUESTIONS

MATCHING

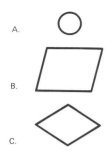

A.

B.

C.

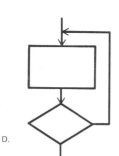

D.

E.

F.

G.

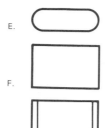

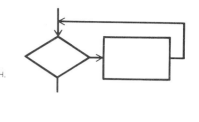

H.

—— **1.** Indicates a do while structure.
—— **2.** Indicates the reading or writing of data.
—— **3.** Indicates a predefined process.
—— **4.** Indicates a decision being made in a flowchart.
—— **5.** Indicates a do until structure.
—— **6.** May be either an exit or an entry point.
—— **7.** Used to represent the statement "MOVE INPUT TO OUTPUT".
—— **8.** Indicates the beginning or ending point in a flowchart.

TRUE/FALSE

T F **1.** Terminal symbols are never used in connection with subroutines.

T F **2.** Two symbols that are interchangeable in program flowcharts are:

T F **3.** Flowcharts are normally read from top to bottom and right to left unless otherwise noted.

T F **4.** An ⬭EXIT symbol on a subroutine indicates that control is to return to that point in the logic immediately following the statement that invoked the subroutine.

T F **5.** Moving data from one storage area to another causes destruction of the contents of the sending area.

T F **6.** Structures always have only 1 entry and 1 exit.

T F **7.** In the following flowchart segment the ③A represents an entry point.

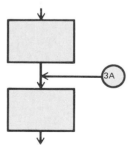

T F **8.** Arrowheads are always required in the construction of a program flowchart.
T F **9.** Decision symbols always have at least two exit paths.
T F **10.** Reading two consecutive records into an input area causes the data from the second record that is read to replace the data from the first record.

EXERCISES

1. Draw a flowchart to read one card, print its contents, and stop.
2. Draw a structured flowchart to read a file and print the contents of each record. When the input has been

exhausted, print a message that indicates the end of processing and stop. Assume that the data will produce less than one page of output. (Techniques for producing multiple pages of output will be covered in Chapter 5.)

3. Repeat Exercise 2, except that only those records with a code of 1, 2, or 7 are to be printed; all other records are merely to be bypassed.
4. Draw a structured flowchart to read a file and print the contents of the records which represent accounts more than 60 days in arrears. Assume that there will be less than one page of output.

DISCUSSION QUESTIONS

1. What is the purpose of preparing a program flowchart?
2. Why use top-down and left-to-right structure in preparing a flowchart?
3. What is destructive readin and what are its implications?
4. Why would or would not connector symbols be more advantageous at times than flowlines?
5. Why do fields need to be moved separately to the output area?

PROJECTS

Project 1

Locate (circle) the structures in the following flowchart segment.

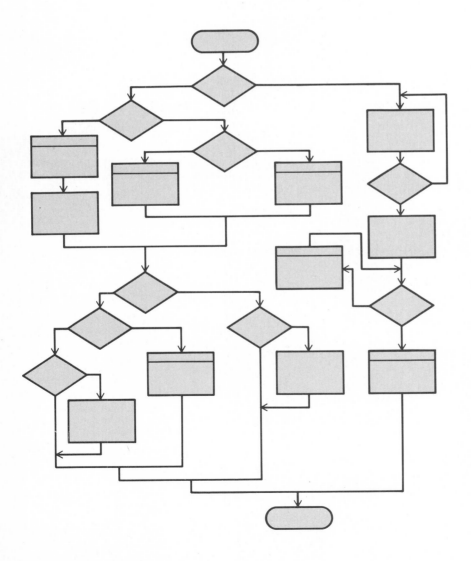

Project 2

Structure the following flowchart segment.

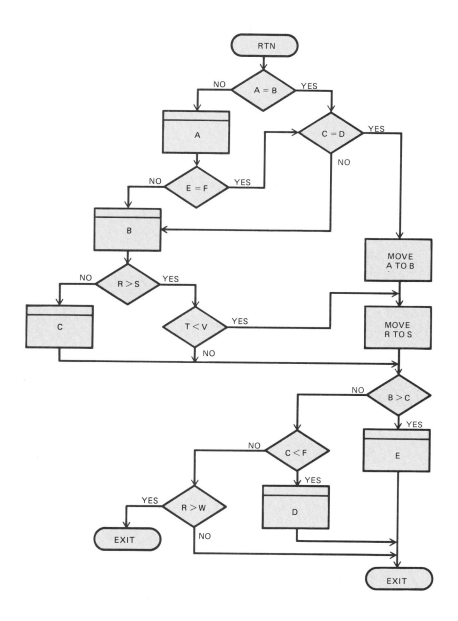

3

BRANCHING

OBJECTIVES

As a result of studying this chapter the student should be able to perform the following activities:

1. Describe the process of branching and explain why it is an important aspect of flowcharting or programming.
2. Differentiate between conditional and unconditional branching.
3. Identify typical places where both conditional and unconditional branching might be found in a flowchart.
4. Describe the process of looping and indicate its importance to flowcharting.

5. Identify and describe the four major steps of the looping process.
6. Describe what is meant by a nested loop.
7. Indicate what pseudocode is and identify the basic rules for using pseudocode.
8. Write the pseudocode for the mainline logic, HSK, PROCESS, and EOJ routines for a simple programming problem.

INTRODUCTION

A computer normally executes the instructions in a program one after the other in the order that they are written. If there were no way of altering this sequential flow, programs would be severly limited. They would have to include the same instructions written over and over and over again for each processing cycle to be done. To overcome this limitation, the designers of computers and programming languages developed a way of altering the sequential processing of instructions. This technique is called branching.

UNCONDITIONAL BRANCHING

Branching causes the sequence in which the instructions are executed to be altered. Instructions are normally executed one after the other in the order that they are written. If some other sequence is desired then it is necessary to perform a branch of some type. Two types of branching are possible; the first type is **unconditional** branching. An unconditional branch is an instruction that alters the flow regardless of what situation is present.

An example of unconditional branching is shown in Figure 3–1. Notice that after printing the line a branch is taken to read the next record. This is an example of an unconditional branch. Due to the constraints of structured programming unconditional branching is an almost non-existent type of operation. Almost any branch that can be shown is in some way controlled by a decision.

40

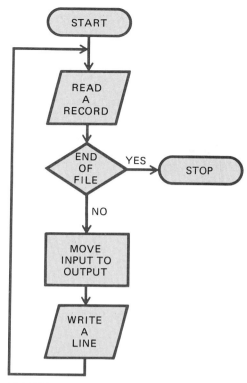

FIGURE 3–1

CONDITIONAL BRANCHING

The second type of branching used in programs is **conditional** branching. A conditional branch is an instruction that causes one of two or more paths in the logic to be followed based on whether some condition is true or not true. A common form of conditional branching is found in the mainline logic shown in Figure 3–2, where a test is issued to see if the END FLAG is on. If the END FLAG is off, the PROCESS routine is executed; otherwise the EOJ routine is executed. The particular path in the logic that is followed at this point depends on whether the contents of END FLAG represent an on or off condition.

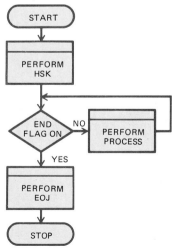

FIGURE 3–2

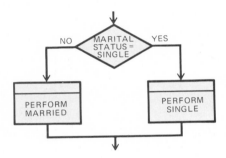

FIGURE 3–3

Conditional branching was also used in Chapter 2 (Figure 2–41), where we checked to see if the end-of-file condition had been found when attempting to read another record.

Now let's look at a problem for computing an employee's federal income tax. Income tax is computed for two basic categories: single and married. Therefore, some place in the program(s) for producing a payroll register and eventually the paychecks, the marital status will need to be checked. The record layout, report format, and segment of the flowchart for doing this are shown in Figure 3–3.

Figure 3–4 shows how this would appear in COBOL and in BASIC.

After testing to see whether a person is single (or married as the default), the appropriate internal subroutine is performed to compute his or her federal tax. Which type of tax calculation is performed is based on a comparison and a conditional branch to the appropriate logic. This

COBOL VERSION

```
IF MARITAL-STATUS = 'S'
      PERFORM SINGLE-INCOME-TAX
ELSE
      PERFORM MARRIED-INCOME-TAX.
```

BASIC VERSION

```
360 IF MARITAL.STATUS$ = "S" THEN GOSUB SINGLE
        ELSE GOSUB MARRIED
```

FIGURE 3–4

same type of process (conditional branching) could be carried to decisions where one of three or more paths in the logic could be followed based on the result of some comparison or series of comparisons.

THREE-WAY BRANCHING

A common type of three-way decision depends on how the contents of two items compare with each other—which item has a value that is high or whether they are equal in value. An example is shown in Figure 3–5. As pointed out in Chapter 2, there is more than one possible method of flowcharting the material shown in Figure 3–5.

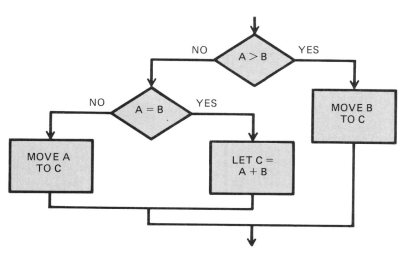

FIGURE 3–5

If the value in A is greater than the value in B, then the value in B will be moved to C. If the values in A and B are equal, then C will be set equal to the sum of the values in A and B. If the value in A is less than the value in B, the value in A will be moved to C. Given the instructions in Figure 3–5, the following values present in A and B would produce the values shown for C.

VALUE IN A	VALUE IN B	RESULTING VALUE IN C
24	19	19
36	82	36
54	54	108

Not only can a separate item such as C be changed as a result of the comparison of A and B, but the logic might require the contents of A or B to be altered after the comparison. What is important is not so much the process used in Figure 3–5 as it is the taking of one of several paths based on the results of a series of decisions and which path is taken when leaving any one of the decisions. Each exit path from the decision will have different activities associated with it.

This same process could be extended to something such as checking a particular code for its value and performing various activities depending on the value of the code, as shown in Figure 3–6. Notice in Figure 3–6 that each decision structure has only one entrance and one exit.

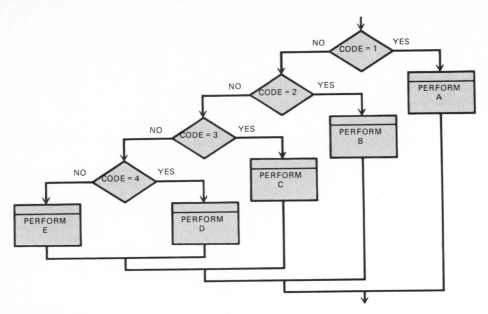

FIGURE 3–6

LOOPING

In flowcharts where a file is being read (most of the time) a branch back to the END FLAG check is taken after reading another record at the end of the PROCESS routine. This process of reusing the same set of logic for each record to be processed is an example of looping. **Looping** is executing any series of instructions repeatedly. Loops, however, do not have to include the whole PROCESS routine; they may cover only a small portion of the routine (PROCESS or otherwise). It is also possible for a flowchart to have multiple loops in it and for one loop to be inside a larger loop. When a loop is inside a larger loop, the one on the inside is said to be nested.

Let's start with a relatively simple looping operation. Assume that we have a file where each record has ten fields in it that contain numeric data. As each record is read each of the amounts in each of the ten fields needs to be added together, and the total needs to be printed. Since we are going to be producing a total of the fields, we are going to need someplace to accumulate the total. For lack of a better name let's accumulate the total in an area of storage that we will call TOTAL. In order to control how many times the next field is added to TOTAL we will also need a counter. The value that is put into this counter will control how many times the steps in the loop are performed. Let's name our counter COUNT. The logic needed to accomplish the process of totaling the values in the ten fields is shown in Figure 3–7.

Let's follow one record through this process to see how it operates. Upon entering the PROCESS routine the first data record has been read (in HSK), thus CALCS will be the first step in the PROCESS routine to be done. It is the CALCS routine that will actually produce the total and contains the loop for adding the ten fields. The first step in CALCS is to zero out the area called COUNT. Count needs to be initialized to some value, since we are going to use the value in COUNT to determine when the values in all ten fields have been added to TOTAL or, in other words, to indicate when the loop has been completed. It will also be used to identify which field is being added to TOTAL. A complete description of how it identifies which field is being processed is given in chapter 8, when tables and subscripts are presented.

The next step is to zero out the total (TOTAL). This is necessary if the total is to be only for the fields in the record currently in storage. If TOTAL were not initially set to zero, the total would be erroneous. Whatever was left over from the last program that used the same area in storage or what is in the storage area from the previous record processed is the value to which the current records fields would be added. Notice that both of these operations (zeroing

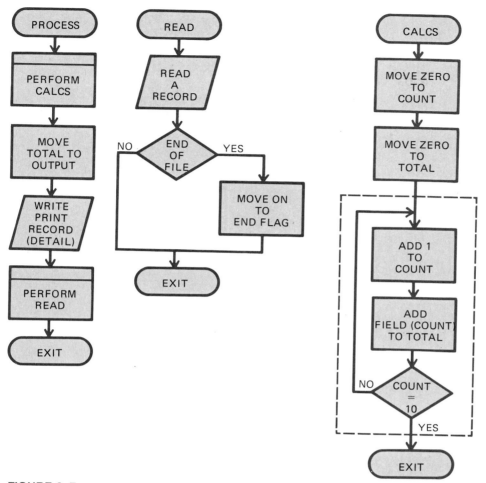

FIGURE 3-7

out COUNT and TOTAL) are done at the beginning of the CALCS routine so that each record processed will start at the same point.

The next step in CALCS is to increment COUNT by 1. A 1 is being added to indicate that 1 more field is being processed. This process will take place as each of the 10 fields is processed (added to TOTAL). The value in COUNT can be used to point to the field to be added to TOTAL by indicating FIELD (COUNT). Again, the concept of using a subscript to refer to a specific item in a list of items via a subscript will be covered in Chapter 8. After COUNT is incremented, the next field's value is added to TOTAL.

At this point the value in COUNT is checked to see if it is equal to 10. If it is, then the contents of all ten fields have been added, and it is time to exit the routine. If the value in COUNT is not yet equal to 10, then a return is taken to the step that increments COUNT.

Once the exit path in CALCS is taken, it is time to return to the next step in the logic of the program. This is immediately after the perform that invoked the CALCS routine. At this point the total is moved and printed and the next record is read.

The symbols containing ADD 1 TO COUNT, ADD FIELD (COUNT) to TOTAL, and COUNT = 10 comprise the loop. These are executed over and over until the value in COUNT has progressed from 1 to 10.

Notice that the steps in the loop are enclosed in a dotted line. These steps comprise a DO UNTIL structure. In a DO UNTIL structure the actions take place at least once before the testing of a condition. In the DO WHILE structure (Chapter 2), on the other hand, the test occurs first and the actions may or may not be performed at all.

LOOPING STEPS

Some standard steps are present in any looping process. These steps, except for the first, may be in just about any order needed to produce the desired effect. The major difference is in where in the loop the modification and testing are done, which will cause the loop to be referred to as either top driven or bottom driven. Depending on the language being used to implement the flowchart, the processes of initialization, modification, and testing may require two or more actual programming instructions to accomplish the necessary actions.

1. **Initialization**—the step in which variable items are given a beginning value. One or more of these items will be used to determine when the loop should be terminated. This step may involve moving a value such as 1 to an area. In the case of the loop used to add the contents of ten fields in a record, this step is when zero is moved to COUNT and TOTAL. The initialization step comes before the loop itself.
2. **Processing**—the step or steps in the loop in which the actual data manipulation present within the loop is performed.
3. **Modification**—the step in the loop in which some sort of alteration is done to the item used to control how often the loop will be performed and which was initialized in Step 1. This might be adding 1 to a counter or reading the next available record.
4. **Testing**—the step in the loop in which the value of an item is tested (such as whether the record is a data record or whether the value in a counter has exceeded a given value) to determine whether the loop should be continued or terminated.

The sample loop added the values in the fields on a record and printed the result. The initialization step in this sample is moving zero to COUNT and TOTAL. The processing step is the addition of the contents of the FIELD (COUNT) to TOTAL. Modification takes place when 1 is added to COUNT. Testing is when the value in COUNT is checked to see if it is equal to 10.

NESTED LOOPS

In order to discuss nested loops let's use the flowchart in Figure 3–8. Both ROUTINE A and ROUTINE B contain loops. In this case ROUTINE B contains a nested loop, in that it is executed for each repetition of the loop within ROUTINE A. Following a single record through this process should help to make this clearer.

After reading of a data record in HSK, the first thing in PROCESS is to perform ROUTINE A. The loop in ROUTINE A will continue to be performed until the value in COUNT1 is greater than 3 (a total of 4 times). The reason for the extra execution is that the steps in the loop are executed for the values of 0, 1, 2, and 3 in COUNT1. Each time the loop in ROUTINE A is performed, ROUTINE B is invoked. The steps in the loop within ROUTINE B will be executed a total of 6 times (for values of 0, 1, 2, 3, 4, and 5 in COUNT2). Since the loop in ROUTINE B is executed 6 times, once for each execution of the loop in ROUTINE A, then the loop in ROUTINE B will be executed a total of 24 times during the processing of each record. PROCESS A and PROCESS B could contain any type of processing and have no affect on how the loops are handled as long as neither does anything to the contents of COUNT1 and COUNT2. This is because COUNT1 and COUNT2 are loop-control counters, whose values determine how many times the loop in ROUTINE A and ROUTINE B, respectively, will be executed. Any alteration of their contents will affect how many times the loop is executed.

In a similar manner ROUTINE A is a nested loop. It is performed or invoked for each record that is read, until an end-of-file condition occurs. This loop, however, is not controlled by a counter. It continues to be executed until an end-of-file condition causes END FLAG to be set on.

PSEUDOCODE

Pseudocode is a listing of English-like statements, each of which identifies a processing step to be done. To explain this concept let's work with the following problem.

We need to produce a report of overdue charges for a local library. All the records in the file we will use are for persons with overdue books. No records are present for persons without overdue books. The format of the records in this file is shown in Figure 3–9.

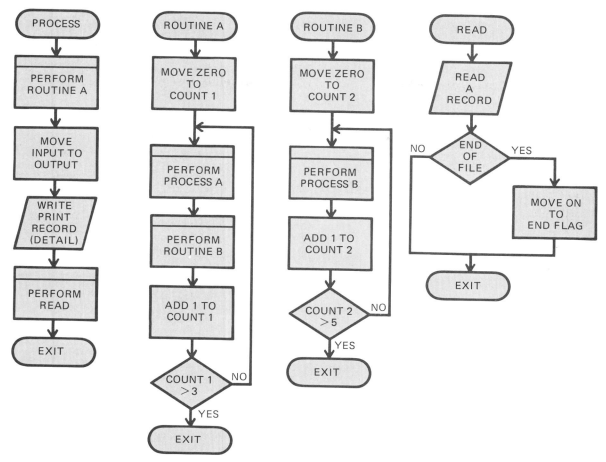

FIGURE 3-8

In producing this report all the fields will be listed as well as the amount of overdue charges for each input record on the file. The computation of the overdue charges should also make provision for a second-notice charge. If the person's record has a 1 in the second-notice field, add $.50 to his or her overdue charges. The regular charge for overdue books is 10 cents per day per book. The input record format and report format are shown in Figure 3-10. The logic is shown in Figure 3-11. The pseudocode for this problem is shown in Figure 3-12.

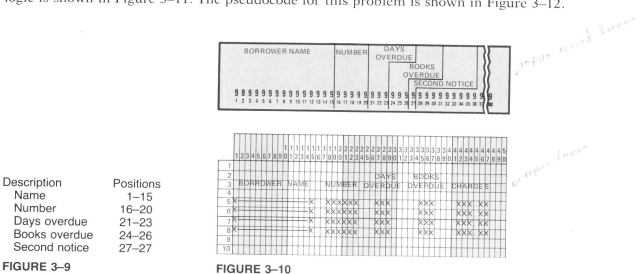

Description	Positions
Name	1–15
Number	16–20
Days overdue	21–23
Books overdue	24–26
Second notice	27–27

FIGURE 3-9

FIGURE 3-10

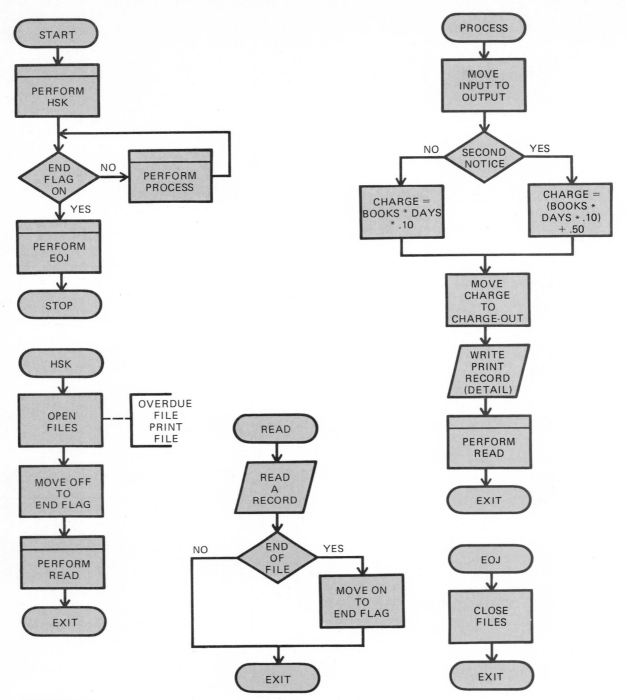

FIGURE 3–11

Many forms of pseudocode exist in data processing, and to date there are only a few relatively constant rules concerning their usage. In this book these are the basics we will follow when using pseudocode:

1. The mainline logic is listed first, followed by each of the subroutines that are present.
2. The first word in each statement (including such items as ENDIF, which is a word made up of two words) is always in capital letters. The rest of the items in the statement are always in lower-case letters.
3. Every IF statement will be ended by an ENDIF.
4. If the ELSE portion of an IF statement (or of multiple IF's, if present) shows no action, then you proceed to the ENDIF.

```
MAINLINE LOGIC
      PERFORM hsk routine
      PERFORM process routine until end flag is on
      PERFORM eoj routine
HSK ROUTINE
      OPEN files
      MOVE off to end flag
      PERFORM read routine
PROCESS ROUTINE
      MOVE input fields to output
      IF second notice
            COMPUTE second notice charges
      ELSE
            COMPUTE normal charges
      ENDIF
      MOVE charges to output
      WRITE print record (detail)
      PERFORM read routine
EOJ ROUTINE
      CLOSE files
READ ROUTINE
      READ a record
            AT END of file
                  MOVE on to end flag
```

FIGURE 3–12

5. Indention is present only to identify actions related to the first word in a statement.
6. Punctuation—if used—has no specific meaning.

The COBOL and BASIC programs for the logic depicted in Figure 3–11 are shown in Figure 3–13 and Figure 3–14 respectively. Both the COBOL and the BASIC program produce the same

COBOL EXAMPLE

```
PROCEDURE DIVISION.
MAINLINE-LOGIC.
      PERFORM HSK-ROUTINE.
      PERFORM PROCESS-ROUTINE UNTIL END-FLAG = 'ON'.
      PERFORM EOJ-ROUTINE.
      STOP RUN.
HSK-ROUTINE.
      OPEN INPUT OVERDUE-FILE
            OUTPUT PRINT-FILE.
      MOVE 'OFF' to END-FLAG.
      PERFORM READ-ROUTINE.
PROCESS-ROUTINE.
      MOVE NAME                TO NAME-OUT.
      MOVE NUMBER              TO NUMBER-OUT.
      MOVE DAYS-OVERDUE        TO DAYS-OVERDUE-OUT.
      MOVE BOOKS-OVERDUE       TO BOOKS-OVERDUE-OUT.
      IF SECOND-NOTICE = '1'
            COMPUTE CHARGE = BOOKS-OVERDUE*DAYS-OVERDUE*.10.+ .50
      ELSE
            COMPUTE CHARGE = BOOKS-OVERDUE* DAYS-OVERDUE*.10.
      MOVE CHARGE TO CHARGE-OUT.
      WRITE PRINT-RECORD FROM DETAIL AFTER ADVANCING 1 LINES.
      PERFORM READ-ROUTINE.
EOJ ROUTINE.
      CLOSE OVERDUE-FILE
            PRINT-FILE.
READ-ROUTINE.
      READ OVERDUE-FILE
            AT END
                  MOVE 'ON' TO END-FLAG.
```

FIGURE 3–13

```
'PROGRAMMERS: J AND J, INC.
'DATE: 10/11/89
'PROGRAM NAME: CASE 3
'****************************************************************
'*                        MAINLINE LOGIC                       *
'****************************************************************
GOSUB HOUSEKEEPING.ROUTINE
WHILE END.FLAG$ = "OFF"
    GOSUB PROCESS.ROUTINE
WEND
GOSUB EOJ.ROUTINE
END
'****************************************************************
'*                     HOUSEKEEPING ROUTINE                    *
'****************************************************************
HOUSEKEEPING.ROUTINE:
OPEN "A:C3B1DATA" FOR INPUT AS #1
D$ = "SCRN:":CLS
INPUT "OUTPUT TO THE PRINTER - ANSWER Y OR N";ANSWER$
IF ANSWER$ ="y" OR ANSWER$ = "Y" THEN
    D$ = "LPT1:":WIDTH "LPT1:",80:LPRINT CHR$(15)
END IF
OPEN D$ FOR OUTPUT AS #2
LET END.FLAG$ = "OFF"
GOSUB READ.ROUTINE
RETURN
'****************************************************************
'*                       PROCESS ROUTINE                       *
'****************************************************************
PROCESS.ROUTINE:
IF SECOND.NOTICE = 1 THEN
    CHARGE = BOOKS.OVERDUE * DAYS.OVERDUE * .1  +  .5
ELSE
    CHARGE = BOOKS.OVERDUE * DAYS.OVERDUE * .1
END IF
LET F$ = "\                \"  +  SPACE$(2)  +  "######"  +  SPACE$(3)  +  "###"  +
    SPACE$(5)  +  "###"  +  SPACE$(4)  +  "###.##"
PRINT #2,USING F$; NAM$, NUMBER, DAYS.OVERDUE, BOOKS.OVERDUE, CHARGE
GOSUB READ.ROUTINE
RETURN
'****************************************************************
'*                         EOJ ROUTINE                         *
'****************************************************************
EOJ.ROUTINE:
CLOSE #1,#2
RETURN
'****************************************************************
'*                        READ ROUTINE                         *
'****************************************************************
READ.ROUTINE:
IF EOF(1) THEN
    END.FLAG$ = "ON"
ELSE
    INPUT #1, NAM$, NUMBER, DAYS.OVERDUE, BOOKS.OVERDUE, SECOND.NOTICE
END IF
RETURN
```

FIGURE 3–14

output. There are, however, differences between the two languages. For instance, there are no moves in the BASIC program. BASIC does not require data to be moved to the output area when writing sequential files. Data can be printed directly (or written to any medium) from input areas or areas that have been computed such as overdue charges. In spite of this and other differences both programs have the same structured design and were coded from the same flowchart. Neither program provides for headings or reaching the end of a printed page. These topics are introduced in Chapter 5.

Given these basics, if you look back at both the flowchart and the pseudocode in the previous example they represent the same things being done. Which comes first or whether both need to be present will depend on an organization's standards for program planning and documentation.

CHAPTER VOCABULARY

Conditional branching
Counter (loop control)
Initialize
Looping

Modify
Nested loops
Process

Pseudocode
Test
Unconditional branching

REVIEW QUESTIONS

MATCHING

A. Unconditional branch
B. Loop
C. Connectors or flowlines
D. Modification
E. Initialization

F. Conditional branch
G. Nested loop
H. Normal instruction sequence
I. Testing
J. Pseudocode

___A___ 1. An alteration in the flow of the logic that takes place regardless of whether anything is or is not true.

___B___ 2. The reuse of a series of instructions or symbols in a flowchart over and over again.

___E___ 3. The step in the looping process that must always be first.

___G___ 4. A loop which is performed inside another loop.

___F___ 5. An alteration in the flow of the logic based on whether some situation is true or not true.

___H___ 6. The order in which they are written.

___D___ 7. The step in the looping process responsible for the alteration of some variable which will be used to determine whether or not the loop should be continued.

___C___ 8. A way of showing where either type of branch will proceed to next.

___J___ 9. A listing of English-like statements that specify the actions to be taken in the solution of a problem.

___I___ 10. The step in the looping process which determines whether the loop should be terminated or continued.

TRUE/FALSE

T **F** 1. Loops may not be performed more than 500 times in a program or flowchart.

T **F** 2. Altering the sequence in which the instructions will be executed is called sequencing.

T **F** 3. The step(s) in which the processing in a loop takes place is referred to as modification.

T **F** 4. Conditional branching requires that there be at least three exit paths out of any decision symbol on a flowchart.

T F 5. You can avoid using a loop by merely rewriting the desired instructions as many times as you want them performed.

T F 6. DO UNTIL structures perform the process before testing the condition.

T **F** 7. Connectors are used commonly and plentifully in structuring.

T **F** 8. Pseudocode is always preferable to flowcharts and eventually will replace them completely.

EXERCISES

1. Draw a flowchart segment to depict conditional branching to a routine called TALLY GRADES if the record is for sophomore students. Perform the NO TALLY routine for students' records of students who are not sophomores.

2. Draw a flowchart segment that shows the logic in a program performing RTN-A, RTN-B, RTN-C, RTN-D,

and RTN-E depending on whether the contents of a field called CODE is 1, 2, 3, 4, or 5 respectively. If the value in code is none of these, the program should perform ERR-RTN.

3. Draw a flowchart to show the reading of 20 records and stop. The contents of the records should be printed as they are read. Use a loop to control the reading/listing process.

4. Repeat exercise three with the following additions. Each record now contains five fields with numeric data in them. As each record is read, these fields are to be summed and the sum is to be printed along with the contents of the record. Use a nested loop to solve the problem.

DISCUSSION QUESTIONS

1. Differentiate between conditional and unconditional branching and give an example of where each of them might be used.
2. Describe what branching is and why it is necessary in the construction of flowcharts.
3. Describe what pseudocode is and how it is used.
4. Describe looping and why it is an important part of the flowcharting process.
5. Identify the steps in the looping process and what their function is within this process.
6. Describe the effects of having the initialization step as something other than the first step in a loop.
7. Describe nested looping and how it works.
8. Using structured concepts, depict and describe the general mainline logic of a program both as a flowchart and using pseudocode.

PROJECTS
Project 1

Given the following flowchart segment and values for A, B, and C, show the resulting values in A, B, and C after each set of values is processed by the flowchart segment.

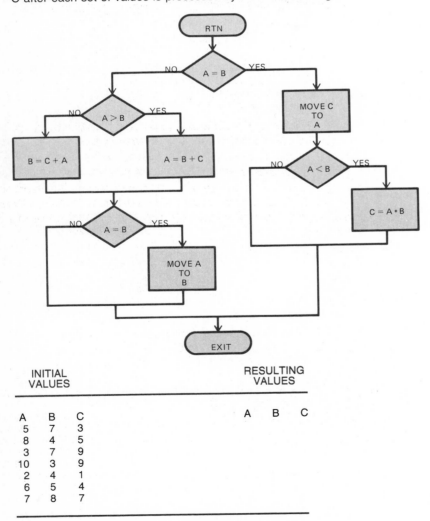

INITIAL VALUES				RESULTING VALUES		
A	B	C		A	B	C
5	7	3				
8	4	5				
3	7	9				
10	3	9				
2	4	1				
6	5	4				
7	8	7				

Draw the flowchart segment for the following TEST ROUTINE pseudocode.

TEST ROUTINE

```
PERFORM alpha routine
IF A = B
     IF C > D
          IF E < F
                    PERFORM beta routine
                    PERFORM delta routine
          ELSE
                    PERFORM delta routine
          ENDIF
     ELSE
          PERFORM gamma routine
     ENDIF
ELSE
     PERFORM beta routine
     IF D = S
          IF A = C
                    PERFORM theta routine
          ELSE
                    PERFORM chi routine
          ENDIF
     ELSE
     ENDIF
ENDIF
PERFORM omega routine
```

4

DOCUMENTATION

OBJECTIVES

As a result of studying this chapter the student should be able to perform the following activities:

1. Describe the need for documentation.
2. Describe the need for and create a program specification.
3. Describe the need for and create a record layout.
4. Describe the need for and create a record description.
5. Describe the need for and design a print chart.
6. Describe the need for and create a simple flowchart.
7. Describe the need for and create a pseudocode listing.
8. Describe the need for and create a hierarchy chart.
9. Describe the need for and prepare a run sheet.
10. Assemble a documentation package upon completion of a programming project.

INTRODUCTION

Flowcharting, while essential to the planning of a program, is only one part of the documentation usually required by a company. Each company has its own standards for documentation, and the forms used vary from company to company. No matter what the format, the underlying concept is the desire to communicate information about a program or an entire system as completely and efficiently as possible.

Documentation for every program and system is usually kept in a centralized location within the data processing department. This makes it easily accessible to all members of the department. A set of standards for documentation is usually supplied to each programmer so that documentation packages can be prepared in accordance with the company's standards.

Programmers and systems analysts come and go within an organization, but the projects they work on remain as a part of the company's data processing system. As the needs of the company change, systems and programs require revision. If the program or system has not been documented, then changes will require an excessive amount of time. This extra time is required to track down all the details of the project.

SYSTEM FLOWCHART

The examples of documentation in this chapter will draw from a payroll system. We will use a portion of a system flowchart to show the section of a payroll system we are going to document.

A system flowchart depicts the flow of data through a system. Symbols are used to represent the various files in the system. The shape of the symbol represents the media on which the data files are recorded. Rectangles are use to indicate programs which process the data in the files. The system flowcharting symbols are described in Chapter 14.

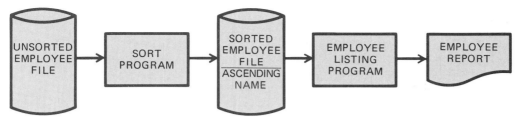

FIGURE 4–1

This portion of a system flowchart indicates that a disk file containing information about each employee will be input to a sort program. The sort program creates as output a disk file whose records are sorted in ascending order by employee last name. This sorted file is then used as input to a listing program which produces a printed version of the records from the file. See Figure 4–1.

The purpose of printing the listing is to provide a visual check of the contents of the records loaded on the disk file. Such a listing would become a reference document for the payroll department.

The planning and design for a system flowchart are done by a systems analyst/designer. This flowchart is the graphic way of showing the flow of data through a portion of the system.

PROGRAM DOCUMENTATION COMPONENTS

Each program in the system flowchart must be planned and developed. In the planning process for the program some of the planning tools become documentation for the system. This chapter will provide examples of commonly used types of program documentation. It will point out when each piece of documentation is created and by whom. We will identify the users of the documentation and reasons for their need of each item. Seven of the more common documentation items are listed below. Some or all of these items are prepared before the program is coded:

1. Program specification
2. Record layout
3. Record description
4. Print chart
5. Flowchart
6. Pseudocode
7. Hierarchy chart

When a program has been completed (written and tested), a final documentation package is prepared. Final versions of the above items are prepared, and the following items are added:

1. A listing of the source program (a machine-produced listing of the program as coded by the programmer). This is the final version of the source program after all errors have been corrected and the program has produced correct output.
2. Samples of any printed reports produced by the program and, in particular, any special preprinted forms that may be used when producing output.
3. A run sheet that provides instructions to the operations staff.
4. A table of contents for the documentation package.

PROGRAM SPECIFICATION

Program specifications are prepared by the designer of the system. The program specification outlines what that particular program of the system should accomplish. It should provide the program function and a general description of the files involved, as well as processing and output requirements. The output requirements should include the formatting requirement of any reports that are to be prepared. The programmer will use the specification along with detailed descriptions of the records and a logic planning tool (flowchart, pseudocode, etc.) as his or her guide to coding the program.

PROGRAM SPECIFICATION

PROGRAM NAME: Employee Listing
PROGRAM FUNCTION:
    The program will produce a printed listing of all employees from the sorted payroll file.
INPUT FILES:
    I. SORTED PAYROLL FILE
        INPUT DEVICE: Disk
        FILE ORGANIZATION: Sequential
        RECORD LENGTH: 91 bytes
        FILE SEQUENCE: Ascending on Employee Last Name
OUTPUT FILES:
    II. PRINT FILE
        OUTPUT DEVICE: Printer
        RECORD LENGTH: 133 Bytes
OUTPUT REQUIREMENTS:
    Each record read from the sorted payroll file should be printed on one line of the output report. All fields from the input record are to be included on the output.
    The following are formatting requirements for the report:
    1. The first page of the report should contain:
        (a) a main heading which includes the report name.
        (b) column headings which describe the items printed underneath them.
    2. The detail lines should include all fields from the input.
    3. The detail lines should be double spaced.

FIGURE 4–2

Figure 4–2 is the program specification for a simple listing program. It has one input and one output file. There are no processing requirements since the data is simply transferred from the input file to the output file. Details of the report format are included under output requirements.

THE RECORD LAYOUT

Record layouts are developed as a part of the design for a system. Whenever disk or tape is to be used as the input or output medium for a program, a layout is drawn of the record. Programmers using the records can then have a visual reference of the record's contents. Consistency between programmers working on a system is essential, and a record layout provides a portion of the information and standards for this purpose.

The design of the record entails both data entry and programming considerations not covered in this book. Such information is found in many systems analysis and design books. The conventions for drawing a record layout, given the size and relative positions of the fields, will be sufficient for our purposes. The process usually begins with a list similar to the one in Figure 4–3.

Under DATA ITEM we find the name to be used when referring to this item of data. POSITIONS gives us the size of each field and its relative position in the record. The notation in parentheses after EMPLOYEE PAY RATE indicates the placement of a decimal in the field. In the case of EMPLOYEE PAY RATE, the field is six positions wide. Two of the six positions are to the right of the decimal point. For COBOL data no decimal point is actually entered into the record. We identify its position when coding the program so that proper alignment of the digits can be made when making calculations or printing the number. Each field on the list is then transferred to a record layout as shown in Figure 4–4.

Accuracy in transferring the information from the list to the record layout is important. This record layout will be used by the programmer to describe to the computer where the data can be found in the record. The programmer will also use it to specify under what name the areas of the record will be stored in the computer. An example of how this information might be conveyed to the computer in the COBOL programming language is shown in Figure 4–5. Each 9 represents a position to be occupied by numeric data. Each X represents a position to be occupied by alphanumeric (either alphabetic, numeric, or special characters) data. A V represents the position for an *assumed* decimal. The V does not occupy a position, and no decimal point is entered in the record.

DATA ITEM	POSITIONS
EMPLOYEE NUMBER	
EMPLOYEE NUMBER 1	1– 3
EMPLOYEE NUMBER 2	4– 5
EMPLOYEE NUMBER 3	6– 9
EMPLOYEE NAME	
EMPLOYEE LAST NAME	10–22
EMPLOYEE FIRST NAME	23–32
EMPLOYEE MIDDLE INITIAL	33–33
EMPLOYEE STREET ADDRESS	34–55
EMPLOYEE CITY	56–67
EMPLOYEE STATE	68–69
EMPLOYEE ZIP	
EMPLOYEE ZIP 1	70–74
EMPLOYEE ZIP 2	75–78
EMPLOYEE HIRE DATE	
EMPLOYEE MONTH	79–80
EMPLOYEE DAY	81–82
EMPLOYEE YEAR	83–84
EMPLOYEE PAY RATE	85–90 (6.2)
EMPLOYEE SEX CODE	91–91

FIGURE 4–4

```
01   EMPLOYEE-RECORD.
     05   EMPLOYEE-NUMBER.
          10   EMPLOYEE-NUMBER-1        PIC 9(3).
          10   EMPLOYEE-NUMBER-2        PIC 9(2).
          10   EMPLOYEE-NUMBER-3        PIC 9(4).
     05   EMPLOYEE-NAME.
          10   EMPLOYEE-LAST-NAME       PIC X(13).
          10   EMPLOYEE-FIRST-NAME      PIC X(10).
          10   EMPLOYEE-MIDDLE-INITIAL  PIC X(1).
     05   EMPLOYEE-STREET-ADDRESS       PIC X(22).
     05   EMPLOYEE-CITY                 PIC X(12).
     05   EMPLOYEE-ZIP.
          10   EMPLOYEE-ZIP-1           PIC X(5).
          10   EMPLOYEE-ZIP-2           PIC X(4).
     05   EMPLOYEE-HIRE-DATE.
          10   EMPLOYEE-MONTH           PIC 9(2).
          10   EMPLOYEE-DAY             PIC 9(2).
          10   EMPLOYEE-YEAR            PIC 9(2).
     05   EMPLOYEE-PAY-RATE             PIC 9(4)V9(2).
     05   EMPLOYEE—SEX-CODE             PIC X(1).
```

FIGURE 4–5

If the record layout is made incorrectly or the storage description made from it is inaccurate, the consequences are incorrect information on the output or a program interrupt. A *program interrupt* occurs when the computer stops processing the program and prints a message indicating a problem of some type. One reason for this occurrence is that the computer does not find the appropriate numeric values in storage areas where it attempts to perform arithmetic operations.

Any unused areas in the record should be identified and space allocated so that they may be described to the computer as physically occupying space in the record. Otherwise, the alignment of each succeeding field will be off. The same thing will happen if we describe the length of the field incorrectly. On the record layout itself, if the area is not used it should be marked as unused to make it clear that this area has not been overlooked.

When a decimal point is not entered its assumed position is shown on the record layout and conveyed to the computer when storage of the record is described to the computer as in the COBOL example (Figure 4–5), where the V indicates the assumed position of the decimal point. In the record layout (Figure 4–4) the broken lines extending part of the way up the field indicate the assumed decimal position.

The record layout is a preliminary piece of documentation. This means that it is created prior to the coding of the program. The size of the company has a great deal to do with who creates the record layout. Large companies often have documentation analysts whose primary job is to create documentation for systems. If such a position does not exist, the record layout may be done by the systems designer. In an even smaller shop, the programmer may double as system designer and create the documentation. Data entry operators usually keep their own record layout for every record format they have occasion to enter.

RECORD DESCRIPTION

Often a listing of the fields in a record is created with more extensive explanation of each field than the space on a card or record layout form will allow. Such a record description, created from the record layout in this chapter, would be prepared as shown in Figure 4–6.

Some of the columns in Figure 4–6 need explanation. *Position* numbers refer to the position of the field within the record relative to the beginning of the record. The *data name* portion should be the same name that will be used when the program is actually written in a programming language. The computer program is not concerned with what a data name means in the English language. It requires only that when you use a data name to refer to a particular field on a record, it follows the rules for names in the language being used and is spelled exactly the same way every time it is used. The rules for constructing data names vary with each programming

RECORD DESCRIPTION
EMPLOYEE RECORD

POSITION	DATA NAME	CLASS	SIZE	EXPLANATION
	EMPLOYEE-NUMBER			Social security nbr
1–3	EMPLOYEE-NUMBER-1	9	3	
4–5	EMPLOYEE-NUMBER-2	9	2	
6–9	EMPLOYEE-NUMBER-3	9	4	
	EMPLOYEE-NAME			
10–22	EMPLOYEE-LAST-NAME	X	13	
23–32	EMPLOYEE-FIRST-NAME	X	12	
33–33	EMPLOYEE-MIDDLE-INITIAL	X	1	
34–55	EMPLOYEE-STREET-ADDRESS	X	22	
56–67	EMPLOYEE-CITY	X	12	
68–69	EMPLOYEE-STATE	X	2	
	EMPLOYEE-ZIP			
70–74	EMPLOYEE-ZIP-1	9	5	
75–78	EMPLOYEE-ZIP-2	9	4	
	EMPLOYEE-HIRE-DATE			
79–80	EMPLOYEE-MONTH	9	2	
81–82	EMPLOYEE-DAY	9	2	
83–84	EMPLOYEE-YEAR	9	2	
85–90	EMPLOYEE-PAY-RATE	9	6.2	
91–91	EMPLOYEE-SEX-CODE	X	1	F = female M = male

FIGURE 4–6

language. The names we have chosen for our example are suitable for the COBOL programming language.

The *class* portion of the record description has three possibilities in the COBOL language. The three classes used in COBOL are shown in the table below. In the BASIC language two classes are used, numeric (integer, single-precision, or double-precision) and alphanumeric (string).

SYMBOL	CLASS OF DATA	ALLOWABLE CHARACTERS
N	Numeric	Includes 0–9 and sign
X	Alphanumeric	Includes 0–9 and sign, A-Z and special characters
A	Alphabetic	Includes A-Z and blanks

When writing a computer program, we usually need to declare a class for each field. The ways in which we can use the field within the program depend partially on its class. For example, arithmetic can be done only with fields that have been declared numeric.

The *size* of a numeric field is of the form *w.d.* where *w* is equal to the total size of the field and *d* equals the positions to the right of the decimal.

The *explanation* column is used to explain the codes used and provide other useful information. A record description is useful to departments of a company that prepare source (original) documents or forms for eventual input to the computer. It provides guidance for these people in assigning codes to various items. In our example, F represents female and M represents male. The use of such codes saves considerable storage space on a record and at the same time reduces the cost of preparing the input record. Upon receiving the source documents, the data input operators use the record description as a reference to insure that the data they are entering is coded properly and appropriate for each field.

Programmers will use the record description as reference when they describe the record for storage in the computer. Some of their programming techniques will depend upon the class of the data, as well as its possible values. The record description is a part of the preliminary documentation and is created in conjunction with the record layouts.

PRINT CHART

When a printed copy of information from a file is needed, someone must design the format of the printed copy. This must be done before the program can be written, as the design will be used as an aid in coding the program. A special form called a *print chart* or *printer layout* is used for this purpose. This form is marked off in boxes corresponding to a print position. The standard print chart has 150 vertical columns and 50 horizontal rows to accommodate almost any needed design. Preprinted forms and blank paper stock for a computer printer come in a variety of sizes. If smaller paper or forms are used, the print chart can be lined off to indicate the form size and shape.

We generally print 10 columns (vertical) to an inch and 6 rows (horizontal) to an inch. Many printers can be adjusted to 12, 15, or 17 columns per inch and 6 or 8 lines per inch. When preprinted forms are designed care should be taken to consider the type size that will be used. In designing forms it is also important to provide adequate space for all field lengths.

If 91 columns of input data, as described by the record description in Figure 4–6, were transferred directly to output with no space inserted between fields, the result would look like Figure 4–7. Figure 4–7 contains all the necessary data, but its readability leaves something to be desired. In order to create a readable report, spaces need to be inserted between each field, thus forming the data into columns. While some of the columns appear to have space between them it is only because the data provided does not fill the entire field.

Normally when a printed output is described to the computer, space is allotted to each variable to be printed on a line, and space is also allotted between each variable for readability. Each variable is transferred to the output line individually, then the write command is executed to print the entire line. Every variable on the line should have a current value in the output

```
     1         1         2         2         3         3         4         4         5         5         6         6         7         7         8         8         9
...5....0....5....0....5....0....5....0....5....0....5....0....5....0....5....0....5....0.

519325678ADOLPHSON    OLGA        FIRTH        150 RIVER DRIVE         ID834011234010155240000F
519384646BABCOCK      MARGARET    BASALT       12 LOST BUTTE ROAD      ID834011345030272160000F
519237657BUTLER       ORVAL       SHELLEY      3100 QUAKING ASP DRIVE  ID834011456050374180000M
519188787EBNER        MICHAEL     WOODVILLE    84 SITE AVENUE          ID834011567070481170000M
519433434EVERETT      WAYNE       NEW SWEDEN   32 N. YELLOWSTONE DR    ID834011678090588140000M
519181618FERGUSON     BETH        CHUBBUCK     486 TETON AVENUE        ID834011789110680190000F
519148189GRANGE       LEILA       TYHEE        55 RESERVATION ROAD     ID834011890020768170000F
519454243HANSEN       CLARICE     POCATELLO    46 N. POLE LINE ROAD    ID834011902040887160000F
519387645HUMPREYS     KENNETH     BLACKFOOT    449 FAIRMONT AVENUE     ID834011023060960340000M
519835795MCGARY       DWAIN       ROSE         98 LAVA HOT SPRINGS RD  ID834011234081061280000M
519425798NEAL         WILBUR      AMMON        269 EAST CENTER         ID834011345101160260000M
519243253OAKEY        ELIZABETH   ARCO         169 SOUTH MILTON        ID834011456121284150000F
519904523TINGEY       LEATHA      LOST RIVER   680 GRAYS LANE          ID834011567011353340000F
519138367THOMPSON     ELECTA      JAMESTON     54 OLD SCHOOL ROAD      ID834011678071454360000F
```

FIGURE 4-7

PRINTER LAYOUT

(Printer spacing chart with row numbers 1–12 and column positions 1–130)

```
Row 7:  XXX-XX-XXXX  XXXXXXXXXX  XXXXXXXXX  X  XXXXXXXXXXXXXXX  XXXXXXXXX  XX  XXXXX-XXXX  XX-XX-XX  XXXX.XX  XXXXXXX
```

FIGURE 4-8

PRINTER LAYOUT

(Printer spacing chart with row numbers 1–12 and column positions 1–130)

```
Row 1:  XX-XX-XX                                                                                          PAGE XXX

Row 4:  EMPLOYEE     EMPLOYEE     EMPLOYEE     EMP   EMPLOYEE          EMPLOYEE       EMP    EMPLOYEE    EMPLOYEE    EMP       EMP
Row 5:  NUMBER       LAST NAME    FIRST NAME   M I   STREET ADDRESS    CITY           STATE  ZIP CODE    HIRE DATE   PAY RATE  SEX

        EMPLOYEE LISTING

Row 7:  XXX-XX-XXXX  XXXXXXXXXX   XXXXXXXXX    X     XXXXXXXXXXXXXXX    XXXXXXXXX      XX     XXXXX-XXXX  XX-XX-XX    XXXX.XX   XXXXXXX
```

FIGURE 4-9

record before a write command is issued for that line. For the sake of brevity, our flowchart will say **MOVE INPUT TO OUTPUT** and then **WRITE PRINT RECORD.**

Based on the 14 × 11 inch paper used, our report will use 132 possible horizontal print positions on the paper and 66 vertical print lines. At least twelve of the 66 print lines on 11 inch paper are usually reserved for the top and bottom margins. This leaves 54 lines for our printout. We divide the available lines between heading and detail lines. One combination would be six lines for headings and 48 lines for detail. Our job is to make the form look as attractive and readable as possible within our space constraints.

Although in a number of places judgment and not simple mathematics is useful in laying out a form, let's approach this first layout on a mathematical basis. It is usually easier to create the detail line first and then work upward, filling the headings in later. In order to create the detail line first, we need to know the number of heading lines there will be and the blank lines we wish between them. For this form there will be one line of report headings and two lines of column headings, with three blank lines. Since we are devoting six lines to headings, we will start the detail line on line seven of the print chart.

Ninety-one columns of data on the record (shown in Figure 4–3) must be printed out. Hyphens would improve the readability of the EMPLOYEE-NUMBER, EMPLOYEE-ZIP-CODE, and the EMPLOYEE-HIRE-DATE. This will require 5 additional spaces for the three fields raising the used positions on the print chart to 96. One of the fields represents money and would be more understandable if a decimal point were inserted in the proper space. The addition of the decimal point will increase the needed print positions from 96 to 97. The F or M used for EMPLOYEE-SEX-CODE needs to be expanded to the words female or male. This will take as many as 5 additional positions bringing the total to 102.

$$
\begin{array}{rl}
132 & \text{positions possible} \\
-102 & \text{positions used} \\
\hline
30 & \text{positions available for spacing}
\end{array}
$$

With 11 columns to be printed there are

$$
\begin{array}{rl}
10 & \text{gaps between columns} \\
+\ 2 & \text{margins needed} \\
\hline
12 & \text{areas which require spacing}
\end{array}
$$

The object is to divide the 30 spaces available among the 12 blank areas. Twelve will not go into 30 evenly, it will go two times with six left over. The extra six can be distributed a number of ways. It is usually added to the margins or around narrow columns of data to make room for headings. We will add one space on either side of state and two extra spaces for each margin. One solution for printing out the contents of the file is shown in Figure 4–8.

Notice the characters that are used to express the fields on the detail line. We have used X's to indicate both variable numeric and alphanumeric data fields. It is also possible to use 9s for the numeric fields and Xs for the alphanumeric fields. If other editing characters or constant information are to be a part of the output ($, -, *, page, and so on), they can be shown on the print chart as they would actually appear on the printed listing.

After we have placed the detail line on the print chart, we can center the column headings above each column. Working from the detail line up make the centering of the column headings easier. Most of the placement can be done by sight at this point. The report name, date, and page numbering can be added at the end of the process to finish off the report (see Figure 4–9).

PROGRAM FLOWCHART

A program flowchart is first drawn by the programmer when the portion of the system that includes the program is assigned. Planning items listed previously are used in the preparation of the program flowchart. The first program flowchart is generally a rough planning tool. Then, depending upon the company's size and procedures, the programmer will either code from this rough flowchart or produce a more finished copy and have it reviewed by the project leader. The programmer will then code the program. When the coding is complete and the program has been tested, a finished flowchart should be drawn, reflecting any changes that may have occurred between the planning stage and the operational program. Figure 4–10 is a flowchart designed to produce a simple listing of the sorted payroll file.

PROGRAM FLOWCHART

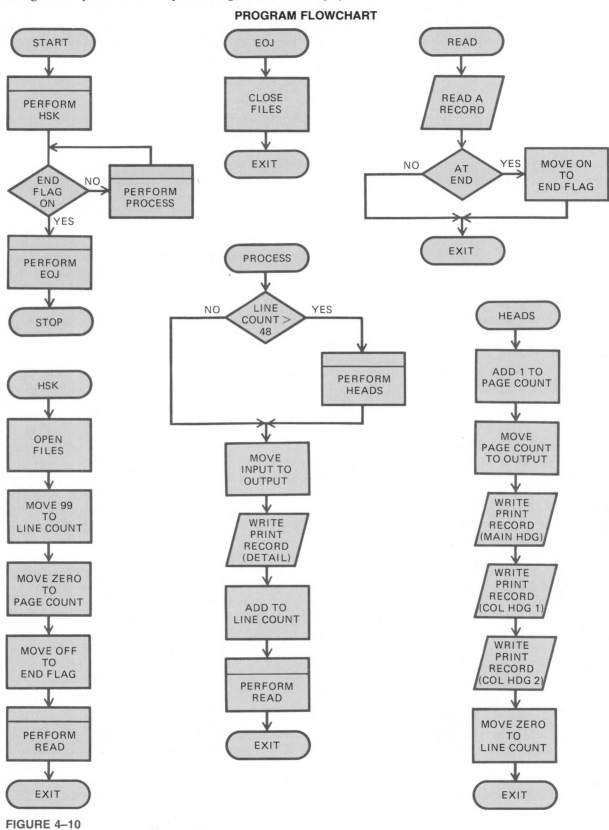

FIGURE 4–10

PSEUDOCODE

Another choice of logic planning tools is pseudocode. It reflects the logic steps but is not restricted to the syntax of a programming language. Pseudocode is an easier type of documentation to maintain than a flowchart because of easy access to word processing. The pseudocode for the simple listing is shown in Figure 4–11.

```
MAINLINE
PERFORM hsk routine
DO WHILE end flag = off
        PERFORM process routine
ENDDO
PERFORM eoj routine
END

HSK ROUTINE
OPEN files
MOVE 99 to line count
MOVE 0 to page count
MOVE off to end flag
PERFORM read routine

PROCESS ROUTINE
IF line count > 48
        PERFORM heads routine
ENDIF
MOVE input to output
WRITE print record (detail)
ADD 2 to line count
PERFORM read routine

EOJ ROUTINE
CLOSE files

READ ROUTINE
READ a record
        AT END of file
                MOVE on to end flag

HEADS ROUTINE
ADD 1 to page count
MOVE page count to output
WRITE print record (main heading)
WRITE print record (column heading 1)
WRITE print record (column heading 2)
MOVE zero to line count
```

FIGURE 4–11

HIERARCHY CHART

A hierarchy chart identifies the routines in a program and their relationship to each other. Each level of routines is performed from the one above it, with the top box representing the mainline or controlling portion of the program. If a routine is performed from more than one location, a corner of the box is shaded to reflect this. A hierarchy chart shows only routines, it does not provide details of the logic steps in each routine. See Figure 4–12.

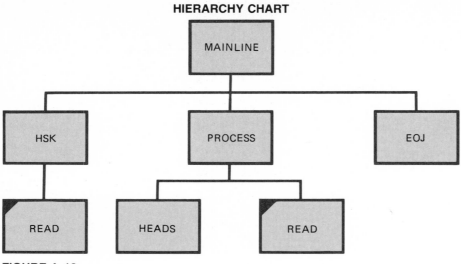

HIERARCHY CHART

FIGURE 4–12

FINAL DOCUMENTATION

Using the program specification, record layouts and descriptions, a print chart, and the programmer's choice of logic planning tools the program is written and tested. When the output produced is satisfactory the documentation package is completed. This package should include a listing of the program (Figure 4–13), a sample of the output (Figure 4–14), a run sheet (Figure 4–15), and job control (Figure 4–16). All of the documentation components are then tied together with a table of contents.

RUN SHEET

Once the programming and testing of a system have been completed, the system is turned over to the operations department. An important part of the documentation sent to the operations department is the run sheets for the program. See Figure 4–15. A copy of these sheets is incorporated into a run book. Depending on the complexity of the installation, there may be a run book for each system or just one run book for the entire shop.

A run sheet provides operations with a detailed list of all inputs and outputs for each program as well as their source and disposition. The amount of information on the run sheet varies with the size of the organization. In a large organization the source and disposition of files may only be the input/output room, where a more detailed set of instructions has been developed for the handling of these items. Assuming the existence of an input/output room shifts much of the detail away from operations with respect to the handling, storage, and distribution of files. Existence of a mailroom may further isolate some of the functions that could be found on a run sheet in a small company.

The printer portion of the form tells the operator the appropriate size paper or special form to be loaded into the printer and how to align the form in the printer so that the output will be placed properly on the form. At the end of the form (bottom of Figure 4–15) is the information about the treatment of the report after it has been produced. *Burst* means to separate continuous forms into single units or pages, as one would do with paychecks. *Decollate* means to separate multiple-ply forms and remove any carbon paper they may contain.

The mass storage portion of the form identifies any disk, tape, drum, or other files used by the program. It shows their name, ID number, where they are coming from, type of file (tape, disk, or whatever), and where they will be used or should go to after processing is completed.

Recovery procedures represent special situations which the programmer anticipates may occur and the actions the operations department is expected to take if they do. The operations department usually runs two or three shifts a day. It is to the advantage of the programmer,

```
10 REM JULIE REED
20 REM 4/15/89
30 REM PROGRAM NAME C4B1
100 REM ********************************************************************
110 REM *                         MAINLINE LOGIC                          *
120 REM ********************************************************************
130 REM
140 GOSUB 1000                                       'HSK ROUTINE
150 WHILE END.FLAG$ = "OFF"
160    GOSUB 2000                                    'PROCESS ROUTINE
170 WEND
180 GOSUB 3000                                       'EOJ ROUTINE
190 END
1000 REM *******************************************************************
1010 REM *                         HSK ROUTINE                            *
1020 REM *******************************************************************
1030 'OPEN "I",#2,"B:C4B1DATA"
1040 INPUT "DO YOU WANT THE OUTPUT TO BE PRINTED - ENTER Y OR N", ANSWER$
1050 IF ANSWER$ = "Y" OR ANSWER$ = "y" THEN DEVICE$ = "LPT1:"
                                       ELSE DEVICE$ = "SCRN:"
1060 OPEN "O", #1, DEVICE$
1070 LET LINE.COUNT = 99
1080 LET PAGE.COUNT = 0
1090 LET END.FLAG$ = "OFF"
1100 DETAIL$ = SPACE$(4)+"&-&-&"+SPACE$(2)+"\          \"+SPACE$(2)+"\       \
"+SPACE$(2)+"!"+SPACE$(2)+"\            \"+SPACE$(2)+"\          \"+SPAC
E$(3)+"\\"+SPACE$(3)+"&-&"+SPACE$(2)+"&-&-&"+SPACE$(2) + "####.##" + SPACE$(2) +
"\  \"
2000 REM *******************************************************************
2010 REM *                         PROCESS ROUTINE                        *
2020 REM *******************************************************************
2030 IF LINE.COUNT > 48 THEN GOSUB 5000         'HEADS ROUTINE
2040 PRINT #1, USING DETAIL$; MID$(NBR$,1,3),MID$(NBR$,4,2),MID$(NBR$,6,4),LNAME
$, CNAME$, MI$, STR.ADDR$, CITY$, STATE$, MID$(ZIP,1,5), MID$(ZIP,6,4), MID$(HI
RE.DATE$,1,2), MID$(HIRE.DATE$,3,2),MID$(HIRE.DATE$,5,2), PAY.RATE, SEX$
2050 LET LINE.COUNT = LINE.COUNT + 2
2060 GOSUB 4000                                      'READ ROUTINE
2070 RETURN
3000 REM *******************************************************************
3010 REM *                         EOJ ROUTINE                            *
3020 REM *******************************************************************
3030 CLOSE
3040 RETURN
4000 REM *******************************************************************
4010 REM *                         READ ROUTINE                           *
4020 REM *******************************************************************
4030 IF NOT EOF(2) THEN
        INPUT #2, NBR$, LNAME$, FNAME$, MI$, STR.ADDR$, CITY$, STATE$, ZIP$, HI
RE.DATE$, PAY.RATE, SEX.CODE$ ELSE LET END.FLAG$ = "ON"
4040 RETURN
5000 REM *******************************************************************
5010 REM *                         HEADS ROUTINE                          *
5020 REM *******************************************************************
5030 LET PAGE.COUNT = PAGE.COUNT + 1
5040 PRINT #1, USING "     &                                              EMP
LOYEE LISTING                                        PAGE ###"; DATE$, PAG
E.COUNT
5050 PRINT #1, "       EMPLOYEE      EMPLOYEE       EMPLOYEE   EMP        EMPLOYEE
        EMPLOYEE     EMP    EMPLOYEE   EMPLOYEE    EMP       EMP"
5060 PRINT #1, "        NUMBER      LAST NAME     FIRST NAME M I      STREET ADDRES
S        CITY     STATE    ZIP CODE   HIRE DATE PAY RATE    SEX"
5070 LET LINE.COUNT = 0
5080 RETURN
```

FIGURE 4–13

who normally works a day shift, not only to make his or her instructions as clear as possible but to cover all potential trouble spots with error-handling instructions. The alternative is loss of sleep when a call comes from the operations department in the middle of the night.

SAMPLE OUTPUT

EMPLOYEE NUMBER	EMPLOYEE LAST NAME	EMPLOYEE FIRST NAME	EMPLOYEE STREET ADDRESS	EMPLOYEE CITY	EMP STATE	EMPLOYEE ZIP CODE	EMPLOYEE HIRE DATE	EMP PAY RATE	EMP SEX
519-32-5678	ADOLPHSON	OLGA	150 RIVER DRIVE	FIRTH	ID	83401-1234	01-01-52	2400.00	F
519-38-4646	BABCOCK	MARGARET	12 LOST BUTTE ROAD	BASALT	ID	83401-1345	03-02-72	1600.00	F
519-23-7657	BUTLER	ORVAL	3100 QUAKING ASP DRIVE	SHELLEY	ID	83401-1456	05-03-74	1800.00	M
519-18-8787	EBNER	MICHAEL	84 SITE AVENUE	WOODVILLE	ID	83401-1567	07-04-81	1700.00	M
519-43-3434	EVERETT	WAYNE	32 N. YELLOWSTONE DRIVE	NEW SWEDEN	ID	83401-1678	09-05-88	1400.00	M
519-18-1618	FERGUSON	BETH	486 TETON AVENUE	CHUBBUCK	ID	83401-1789	11-06-80	1900.00	F
519-14-8189	GRANGE	LEILA	55 RESERVATION ROAD	TYHEE	ID	83401-1890	02-07-68	1700.00	F
519-45-4243	HANSEN	CLARICE	46. N. POLE LINE ROAD	POCATELLO	ID	83401-1902	04-08-87	1600.00	F
519-38-7645	HUMPHREYS	KENNETH	449 FAIRMONT AVENUE	BLACKFOOT	ID	83401-1023	06-09-60	3400.00	M
519-83-5795	MCGARY	DWAIN	98 LAVA HOT SPRINGS RD	ROSE	ID	83401-1234	08-10-61	2800.00	M
519-42-5798	NEAL	WILBUR	269 EAST CENTER	AMMON	ID	83401-1345	10-11-60	2600.00	M
519-24-3253	OAKEY	ELIZABETH	169 SOUTH MILTON	ARCO	ID	83401-1456	12-12-84	1500.00	F
519-90-4523	TINGEY	LEATHA	680 GRAYS LANE	LOST RIVER	ID	83401-1567	01-13-53	3400.00	F
519-13-8367	THOMPSON	ELECTA	54 OLD SCHOOL ROAD	JAMESTON	ID	83401-1678	07-14-54	3600.00	F

FIGURE 4-14

RUN SHEET

JOB NUMBER ___PAY190___   JOB NAME ___EMPLOYEE LIST___

PARTITION/CLASS ___F1___   EST. RUN TIME ___5___   DATE ___11/09/90___

(X) SEE SPECIAL INSTRUCTIONS ON REVERSE

PRINTER

LOGICAL UNIT	FORM NUMBER	CARRIAGE TAPE #	ALIGNMENT		
SYS020	STD 1	STD	CHANNEL 1 = LINE 7		

CARD

LOGICAL UNIT	I/O	POCKET	CARD IDENTIFICATION VOLUME	SOURCE/ DISPOSITION

MAGNETIC STORAGE DEVICES

LOGICAL UNIT	I/O	T/D	FILE IDENTIFICATION	VOLUME ID	SOURCE/ DISPOSITION
SYS005	I	D	EMPLOYEE MASTER	072540	
SYS001	S	D	SORTWORK	022335	TEMP
SYS006	0	D	SORTED MASTER	060161	

FIGURE 4-15

PHASE NAME	STEP DESCRIPTION	EST TIME	STEP NUMBER
S1	SORT BY NAME ASCENDING	3	1
R1	LISTING OF SORTED FILE	2	2

PROCEDURE

SPECIAL INSTRUCTIONS

BURST   NO

DECOLLATE NO

FIGURE 4–15 (continued)

JOB CONTROL

A listing of the job control language is also provided (see Figure 4–16). Job control language is a set of instructions to the computer concerning the actions it is to perform. Each type of computer system has a different operating system and uses different job control language. The example in Figure 4–16 is from a disk operating system on an IBM mainframe; it is presented here only as a general example. This example is explained briefly below to make you aware of some of the functions job control languages serve.

The // JOB statement identifies a new job to the computer.
The // OPTION statement allows us to request special options, otherwise, we take the standard options available.
The // ASSGN statements specify the input/output devices we will use.

```
// JOB PAY20J
// OPTION DUMP
// ASSGN SYS005, X'193'
// ASSGN SYS020, X'00E'
// DLBL MASTER, 'SORTED PAYROLL FILE',,SD
// EXTENT SYS005,072540,1,1,100,40
// EXEC EMPLIST
   (the program
/*
   (data)
/*
/&
```

FIGURE 4–16

The // DLBL and // EXTENT statements identify our disk pack and the storage area on it we will use.

The // EXEC statement begins the execution of the program. The data is read as required by the instructions in the program.

The /* statement identifies the end of the program or data.

The /& statement identifies the end of the job.

A more complete explanation of job control suitable for your assignments will be covered in programming courses as the need arises.

CHAPTER VOCABULARY

Documentation
Flowchart
Hierarchy chart
Job control
Print chart

Printer layout
Program interrupt
Program narrative
Pseudocode

Record description
Record layout
Run sheet
System flowchart

REVIEW QUESTIONS

MATCHING

A. Pseudocode
B. Record layout
C. Record description
D. Print chart
E. Program specification
F. Run sheet

G. Documentation
H. Vertical spacing
I. Decimal alignment
J. Job control
K. Class
L. Hierarchy chart

_____ **1.** A logic planning tool which outlines routines but does not provide individual logic steps.

_____ **2.** Spacing between lines on a printed report.

_____ **3.** Graphic representation of the fields in a record.

_____ **4.** Written description of a group of fields.

_____ **5.** Written instructions to the operations staff concerning all details of running a program.

_____ **6.** The sum total of information conveyed in written form concerning an entire system or an individual program.

_____ **7.** A written description of the logic steps in a program.

_____ **8.** Positioning of a numeric field in storage.

_____ **9.** Graphic description of a tape or disk file.

_____ **10.** Indication of whether a field is alphabetic, numeric, or alphanumeric.

_____ **11.** An overview of the purpose and mechanics of a program.

_____ **12.** A design for printed output.

TRUE/FALSE

T   F   **1.** Vertical spacing on a print chart means the space left between columns.

T   F   **2.** When no actual decimal point is entered in a record, its location is ignored on a record layout.

T   F   **3.** Class, on a record description, describes the contents of a field such as alphabetic, numeric, or alphanumeric.

T   F   **4.** The print chart is usually drawn after the program is written.

T   F   **5.** Blank fields or areas on a record layout should be identified.

T   F   **6.** Record descriptions are superfluous if a layout of the record has been made.

T   F   **7.** A documentation package consists only of a flowchart and a copy of the program.

T   F   **8.** A run sheet is used by the data entry operator for entering data.

T   F   **9.** If the operator maintains job control in some other form, a listing of it is unnecessary.

EXERCISES

1. Create a record layout, record description, and print chart for the following case. Add any editing characters you think appropriate to the output.

Problem Description

A listing will be produced from the card input showing the personal information for each employee. The input is already in sequence. Output formats will be designed by the student and will include the items indicated below. Page and column heads should appear at the top of each page. The current date, page number, company name, and report title should be included in the page headings.

INPUT

DATA NAME	POSITIONS
EMPLOYEE NAME	1–15
EMPLOYEE NUMBER	16–20
SOCIAL SECURITY NUMBER	21–29
SEX CODE	30–30
MARITAL STATUS CODE	31–31
START DATE (MMDDYY)	32–37
SALARY CODE	38–39
POSITION	40–54
RATE	55–61 (7.2)
DATE OF BIRTH (MMDDYY)	69–74
NUMBER OF DEPENDENTS	75–76
DATE OF LAST RAISE (MMYY)	77–80

OUTPUT

All fields on the input should be included on the output.

2. Prepare a record layout and printer layout for the following case.

INPUT

DATA NAME	POSITIONS
NAME	1–15
ADDRESS	16–35
CITY/STATE	36–50
ZIP	51–55
DATE	56–61
DESCRIPTION	62–74
AMOUNT	75–80 (6.2)

PROCESSING

You have been presented with a large supply of a poorly designed mailer. Print a politely worded threat on the left and a list of the items that will be repossessed by a collection agency on the right. The shaded areas can be used only for addresses because of the placement of the carbon. There may be as many as 12 records per customer (items to be repossessed). Put all items for each customer on a single sheet.

OUTPUT (ACTUAL SIZE)

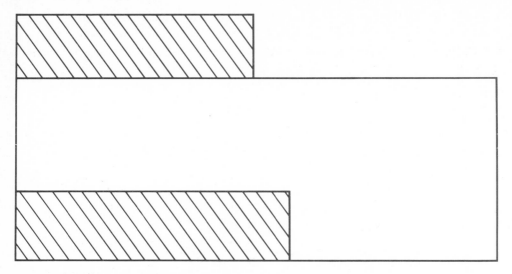

DISCUSSION QUESTIONS

1. Which pieces of documentation must be prepared before the program can be written? Why?
2. Which pieces of documentation are likely to be prepared after the program is written? Why?
3. List the pieces of documentation in the order they would be created (include the flowchart). Give your reasons for the order you selected.
4. Is a documentation package really worth all the time it takes to prepare it?
5. How large should a company be before it documents formally?
6. Once a program or system is put into operation, will the documentation ever require modification?

PROJECTS

Given the following input record description with a list of the actual data, transfer the actual data to a print chart. Design the printer layout to include appropriate column headings. For this project only, do *not* use Xs or 9s—use the actual data provided.

RECORD DESCRIPTION

1–2	INVENTORY RECORD CODE	
	INVENTORY STOCK NUMBER	
3–3	INVENTORY TYPE	has a range of 1–5
4–5	INVENTORY CLASS	has a range of 1–10
6–9	INVENTORY PART	
10–29	INVENTORY DESCRIPTION	
30–30	INVENTORY LOCATION CODE	
31–34	INVENTORY QUANTITY ON HAND	
35–38	INVENTORY QUANTITY ON ORDER	
39–42	INVENTORY REORDER LEVEL	
43–43	INVENTORY UNIT SIZE CODE	
44–48	INVENTORY UNIT PRICE	(5.2)
49–49	INVENTORY DISCOUNT CODE	
50–55	INVENTORY ANNUAL USAGE (Units)	
56–58	INVENTORY VENDOR CODE	
	INVENTORY TRANSPORTATION CODE	
59–59	INVENTORY CATEGORY	
60–60	INVENTORY DISTANCE	
61–80	Filler	

DATA

```
10102222PERSONAL COMPUTERS     50004000500108000109444444433366
102023333FLOPPY DISKS          50005000900028900009666666644467
102034444DISK DRIVES           60007000800039007779555555588876
```

EXTRACTS

OBJECTIVES

As a result of studying this chapter the student should be able to perform the following activities:

1. Identify the three standard subroutines that will be used in all programs.
2. List the logic steps found in a HOUSEKEEPING routine.
3. Describe why the reading of a record is placed at the end of the PROCESS routine.
4. List the logic steps found in an END OF JOB routine.
5. Describe when headings are produced.
6. Define a listing program.

7. Define an extract program.
8. Describe a collating sequence.
9. Formulate the necessary decision steps to meet particular criteria.
10. Flowchart AND/OR logic.
11. Arrange the decision steps in an efficient manner.
12. Describe how selected records as well as total records processed are counted.

INTRODUCTION

This chapter will introduce the more commonly used subroutines and combine them to create two types of reports. The first type of report is a simple listing in which each record from a file is read and then printed as one detail line on the report. The second type of report is an extract. In this type of report each record is read and tested for a set of criteria. If the fields in the record meet all of the criteria, the record is listed as a detail line on the report; otherwise, no printing takes place and the next record is read and tested.

SIMPLE LISTING

A simple listing is made when each record from a file is read and then printed as a line on a report. Each of these lines is called a detail line. Headings are used to identify the contents of the listing. Report or page headings appear at the top of each page to provide such information as the name of the report, page numbers, and dates. Column headings are placed above each column of the detail lines to identify the data printed underneath them. Care should be taken to ensure that all items are identified and spaced attractively. The discussion of a simple listing will include the source of the program data, switches, and the commonly used subroutines for a simple listing. See Figure 5–1 for a simple listing.

NAME	SOCIAL SECURITY NUMBER	SEX
KENNEDY, KENNETH	123456789	M
EBNER, MICHAEL	163234534	M
SIMPSON, JANET	203469729	F
CARUSO, LUCY	239659387	F
GONZALES, JUANITA	316249532	F
EDISON, KEITH	326498765	M
HILL, ANNA	261269016	F
SMITH, ALICE	385312117	F
JOHNSON, EDWARD	396942219	M
TERRY, EUGENE	419623491	M
EVERETT, GRACE	479809381	F
SWANSON, SHARON	491236125	F
JONES, JAMES	543234534	M
LONG, MARILYN	591632701	F
STANDFORD, ALLEN	619211613	M
METTLESON, GREGORY	632912365	M

FIGURE 5–1

PROGRAM DATA

When a piece of data is needed by a program, the data can be made available in two ways: constants or variables. To create a constant the actual characters are coded as a part of the program without assigning a variable name to them. A COBOL example would be MULTIPLY 12 BY FEET GIVING INCHES. A BASIC example would be LET INCHES = FEET * 12. The 12 is called a literal or constant in the program. Data of this type cannot be changed unless the program is revised and recompiled or reinterpreted. FEET and INCHES are variables, their value can change as the program is executed.

When a program has been written and debugged, it is normally stored in a disk library (catalogued) in a form ready to be executed. Any change to data coded in the program will require that the program be recompiled and recatalogued. If we expect a piece of data to change often, it is better to enter the data at execution time rather than coding it in the program and having to recompile and recatalogue the program constantly.

Variables can be assigned an initial value using a constant at the time the program is written by coding the characters required and assigning them a variable name. This is done when we want to start an area of memory out with an original value but plan to change the value during the execution of the program. The value can be changed during the execution of the program by moving new data to the area or performing a calculation whose results will replace the original data in the area.

The second way of using variables in a program is to establish variable names in an input area and read records containing the data into the input area from a tape or disk at the time the program is executing. This is the way the majority of data enters a program—through the reading of a file as a part of the program logic. The order of the variable names in the program establishes a position for each data element in the data set to be read. These variable names are used to establish an input area in memory so that, when data is read from the data set into memory, the data will be matched to the appropriate variable name.

SWITCHES

Although switches have been used in previous chapters, we have not provided a full explanation of their nature. A switch is simply an area of storage set aside by the programmer who gives it a variable name. The contents, size, and type of the area are up to the programmer. The contents of the storage area are usually given an initial value and changed as necessary to control the logic flow of the program. The size of the switch can range from a single bit (BInary digiT) to several characters. The type can be numeric or alphanumeric.

Switches are used to signal a change of status in a program. END FLAG is an example of a switch. As long as there are records to be read, the END FLAG remains OFF. When a record is read and it is not a regular data record, but rather an end-of-file indicator, END FLAG is changed to ON. This switch is tested as a part of processing each record to see whether regular processing should continue.

We initialize a switch by naming it, specifying its initial contents, and in some programming languages specifying its size and type. What name it is given depends only on the rules of the particular programming language for forming variable names and the concept of using meaningful names. Examples in the COBOL and BASIC programming languages would be:

```
(COBOL) 05    END-FLAG          PIC 9      VALUE ZERO.
(BASIC)  10   LET ENDFLAG = 0
```

or

```
(COBOL) 05    END-FLAG          PIC XXX    VALUE 'OFF'.
(BASIC)  10   LET ENDFLAG$ = "OFF"
```

END FLAG is the name of the switch. In the first example it requires only one character, should contain a numeric value, and is initialized at zero. What the initial value of zero means to the program is up to the programmer, however, it should be documented for future users of the program. In the second example is a three-position alphanumeric field whose initial value is OFF. What the initial value is and what it is changed to is not of prime importance. The important thing is that the storage area can be changed from one value to another and tested for the change in the logic steps.

Contents of a switch are usually changed with a programming statement that causes the value of the storage location to be changed through a transfer of data to that location. Examples are the MOVE statement in COBOL and the LET statement in BASIC.

```
(COBOL)    MOVE 'ON' TO END-FLAG.
(BASIC)    LET ENDFLAG$ = "ON"
```

For ease of understanding in the maintenance of programs it is recommended that the use of switches be restricted. Because of the limitations of some programming languages, structured programming requires the use of a few switches. However, the number of switches used is limited, and most switches that are used have a constant meaning from one program to the next.

SUBROUTINES

General

A **subroutine** is a group of instructions that performs one identifiable part of the overall problem. Typical examples of subroutines are:

1. Housekeeping routines
2. Process routines
3. End of job routines
4. Heading routines
5. Read routines
6. Extract routines

Subroutines may be either internal or external. **Internal subroutines** are coded as a part of the program and are used by it in processing. **External subroutines** are used by the program but are not coded as a part of it. They must be accessed from a library (stored on disk) to be used. In this text we will code all routines as internal subroutines. Flowcharting distinguishes between the two by the use of horizontal or vertical lines in a process symbol. The symbols used in a flowchart to represent these two types of subroutines are shown in Figure 5–2.

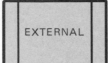

FIGURE 5–2

Internal subroutines are outside the mainline logic of the program (but still part of the program) and must be branched to in order to be executed. Subroutines are normally used for the three major parts in the mainline logic and any time a routine is to be executed at several points in the program. Without subroutines the logic steps done by the subroutine would need to be redone or recoded everywhere in the program the routine is needed.

PERFORM (GOSUB in BASIC) indicates that at this point in the logic a subroutine is to be executed. Control is transferred to the routine being performed and its logic steps are completed. After the routine has been completed, control is returned to the next symbol or instruction following the PERFORM that invoked the routine. This is shown in Figure 5–3 by the solid and dotted line. The solid lines show one execution of the CALC routine. The dotted lines show another execution of the same routine at another point in the program.

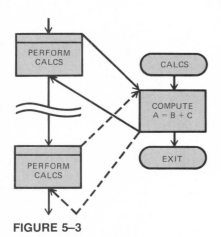

FIGURE 5–3

It is also worth noting how the subroutine itself is depicted. The first symbol is always a terminal symbol with the name of the subroutine. The last symbol is always a terminal symbol with EXIT (or RETURN) in it. EXIT (or RETURN) indicates a return to the logic immediately following where the subroutine was invoked.

HOUSEKEEPING ROUTINES

A housekeeping or initialization routine is one that is executed only one time at the beginning of a program. It contains those logic steps which need to be executed only once and which need to be done prior to the loop which processes each record from a file. Logic steps which fit into this category are:

1. opening files.
2. initializing variables.
3. accessing the system date.
4. reading the first record from the main file.
5. reading special records (date, parameter).
6. loading tables of data to be used in processing the main file(s).

Opening Files

Files reside on auxiliary storage media such as tape or disk where the data is organized into records. The data is normally read into storage and processed one record at a time. To prepare a file for processing it must be opened. Tapes and disks normally have magnetically encoded labels which include information about the file or files included on the media. These labels can be read by the computer system, not by the human eye. On tapes these are called header labels as they appear before the data. On disk an area of the disk is set aside as a directory. This directory contains labels for each file on the disk. It is the function of the open statement to check these labels and ensure that the correct file is available.

Files may be opened as input, output or random. An input file is one that has been created previously. It already resides on tape or disk. A file is opened as input when we wish to have the contents transferred from that tape or disk into memory for processing. The open statement checks for the presence of a label and sets a pointer to the beginning of the file. If no label for that file is found an error message is generated. An output file is a file we expect the program to produce. Therefore, it does not yet exist on the tape or disk. The open statement will create a label for the file. Random is used here as a general term for a file that can be open as input and output at the same time. The computer will check or create labels as necessary for such a file when the open statement is executed. In a flowchart we can specify the opening of files in general terms. See Figure 5–4.

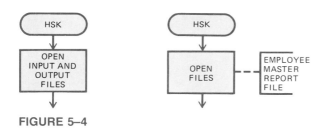

FIGURE 5–4

Initializing Variables

It is a common practice to give some variables an initial value at the beginning of a program. This is most often done with variables which are used to store totals, count lines, count pages, and test relationships. Although there are exceptions where all variables are initialized by the system to the same value, we normally cannot depend on an area of memory where a variable is stored to have any particular initial value. To ensure proper execution of the program totals, line counts, and page counts are set to zero or a special value at the beginning of the program.

Two types of fields, switches and holds are used for testing relationships. A switch is set to an initial value (0, OFF) with the intent of changing it to another specific value (1, ON) when a particular event occurs. This is the case with END FLAG which is initialized as OFF with the intent to change it to ON when an end-of-file indicator is read. See Figure 5–5. A hold is also set to an initial value. Its value will be changed when an event occurs. Its new value will not be a predetermined constant, rather, it will be the data from a variable whose contents

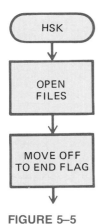

FIGURE 5–5

are moved to the hold. This technique is used to compare a field in a record to the contents of the same field in the previous record.

Accessing the System Date

Most computer systems have the current date stored in them. The programming to access this date varies with the programming language and the computer being used. The date is normally accessed in the housekeeping routine and stored in an area set aside by the program for headings. It can then be printed each time the headings are printed. This avoids the need to retrieve the date from the system more than once. See Figure 5–6.

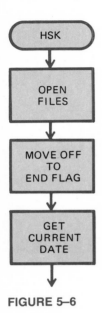

FIGURE 5–6

Reading the First Record from the Main File

A routine to read the first record from the main file(s) is included in housekeeping. All subsequent records will be read by the READ routine performed at the end of PROCESS. In each case a test for end-of-file is made. If the end-of-file indicator is read, ON is moved to END FLAG. This approach allows a test of the END FLAG prior to every execution of PROCESS including the first. Therefore, if no file is present, the program will terminate without ever performing PROCESS. See Figure 5–7.

Reading Special Records

Some programs require a few items of data that are not included in the main file(s). The data items might be a special date for a report that differs from the current date or a set of criteria against which the records in the file(s) will be tested. Since data of this type needs to be read only once and then stored for future printing or testing, housekeeping is the appropriate routine in which to place the logic steps that read the data.

Loading Tables

Some programs require extensive amounts of data that are not included in the main file(s). The volume of the data often makes a table in memory the better choice for storage of the items. The data may be needed to provide current rates for calculations, lists of valid codes for editing purposes, or descriptions used to interpret codes in the file(s). The data needs to be loaded into memory prior to processing the data from the main file(s) making housekeeping the appropriate place to load the table.

FIGURE 5-7

PROCESS

Since the first record is read in HSK, PROCESS is started by moving the data from the input area where it was placed by the read to an area which describes how it will look when it is output (detail line). If spaces between the columns of data are required (as is usually the case), some programming languages require that the data items from the input record be moved to the detail line one at a time. Each of these moves could have been shown in a separate symbol, but we have elected to consolidate them in the flowchart as MOVE INPUT TO OUTPUT.

After the data from the input record has been moved to the detail line, the detail line will contain all of the data needed for printing one line. Next the line is written, this transfers the data from computer memory, through a printer, to paper.

Now the READ routine is performed. This perform will cause the next record to be read. As with all reads from a sequential file, a test will be made to see if an end-of-file indicator is encountered. If it is, END FLAG will be changed to ON and the EOJ routine will be performed rather than repeating PROCESS.

Notice the general order of the PROCESS routine in Figure 5-8; it is probably not what you expected.

    MOVE
    WRITE
    READ

The PROCESS routine starts with MOVE because the first record was read in HSK, therefore, as PROCESS is entered there is a record available to be moved and written. The perform for the READ routine is at the end of the PROCESS routine so that immediately after reading, the test to see if END FLAG has been changed to ON can be made. If END FLAG is ON the EOJ routine will be performed.

FIGURE 5–8

What if the arrangement were as follows with no read in HSK?

```
READ
MOVE
WRITE
```

With this arrangement a logic error occurs when the read finds the end-of-file indicator. END FLAG is changed to ON, but the switch cannot be tested yet. The next step is to MOVE and WRITE. Unfortunately, there is no data to MOVE or WRITE.

END OF JOB

The end of job routine should include the logic steps that need to be performed only once after all records have been processed. Logic steps which fit into this category are:

1. Closing files.
2. Printing record counts or totals.

The close process is the reverse of the open process. The close statement makes the files unavailable for processing. Record counts or totals which have been accumulated as records were processed are normally printed at this time. See Figure 5–9.

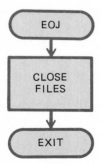

FIGURE 5–9

HEADINGS

Headings are descriptive information at the top of a page that indicate what the report is and what information is contained on the page. Headings may be quite simple or very complex;

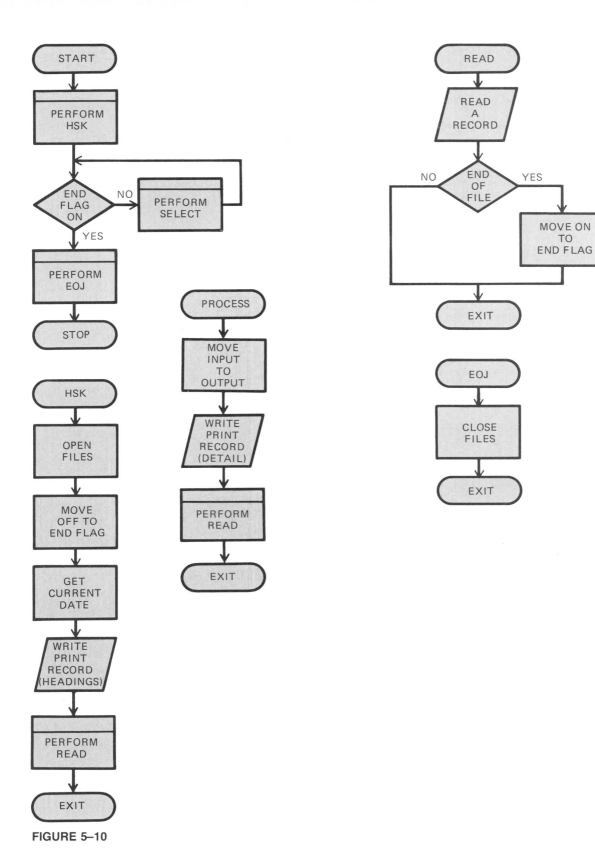

FIGURE 5–10

we will start with the simplest of headings. A small number of records will be printed under appropriate headings before stopping. This flowchart is shown in Figure 5–10. The pseudocode for this flowchart is shown in Figure 5–11.

MAINLINE LOGIC

PERFORM hsk routine
PERFORM process routine until end flag = on
PERFORM eoj routine

HSK ROUTINE

OPEN files
MOVE off to end flag
GET current date
WRITE print record (headings)
PERFORM read routine

PROCESS ROUTINE

MOVE input to output
WRITE print record (detail)
PERFORM read routine

EOJ ROUTINE

CLOSE files

READ ROUTINE

READ a record
    AT END of file
        MOVE on to end flag

FIGURE 5–11

It is realistic to assume that the input file contains many records and there is a possibility of forms overflow (that is, more than one page will be needed for the output). Forms overflow means that the end of page has been reached and that before any more detail lines are printed the paper should be moved to a new page and the headings should be printed on the new page. We have elected to print fifty detail lines on a page before going to the next page. The logic for this can be seen in Figure 5–12. The pseudocode is shown in Figure 5–13 and the print chart is in Figure 5–14.

Checking for forms overflow is typically done with a line counter. Once the value in the line counter reaches some predetermined limit, the heading routine is performed. In this routine headings are printed and the line counter is reset to an initial value. There are many approaches to counting lines. One of the most common is to count only the detail lines that are printed, with overflow occurring when the maximum number of detail lines that will fit on one page of the report have been printed. Remember, headings use space on the paper also. Take this into account when you decide how many detail lines to allow.

The way in which the paper is moved to the top of a new page varies with the programming language being used to implement the flowchart. When the heading routine is coded in a programming language it will include instructions to skip to the top of a new page before printing any headings. Therefore when the routine or symbol says WRITE PRINT RECORD (HEADS), it implies that this is to be done at the top of a new page.

Notice that the line counter in Figure 5–12 was initially set to 99. This is to make sure that heads will appear at the top of the first page, since we are producing headings if LINE COUNT is greater than 50. There are many approaches to printing the first set of headings, but this is one of the easiest. Since the test is made in the PROCESS routine it will not produce a set of useless headings if the file is not present.

In following through the flowchart, after each record is read and found to be a data record (that is, no end-of-file indicator has been found, so the END FLAG is still off), LINE COUNT is

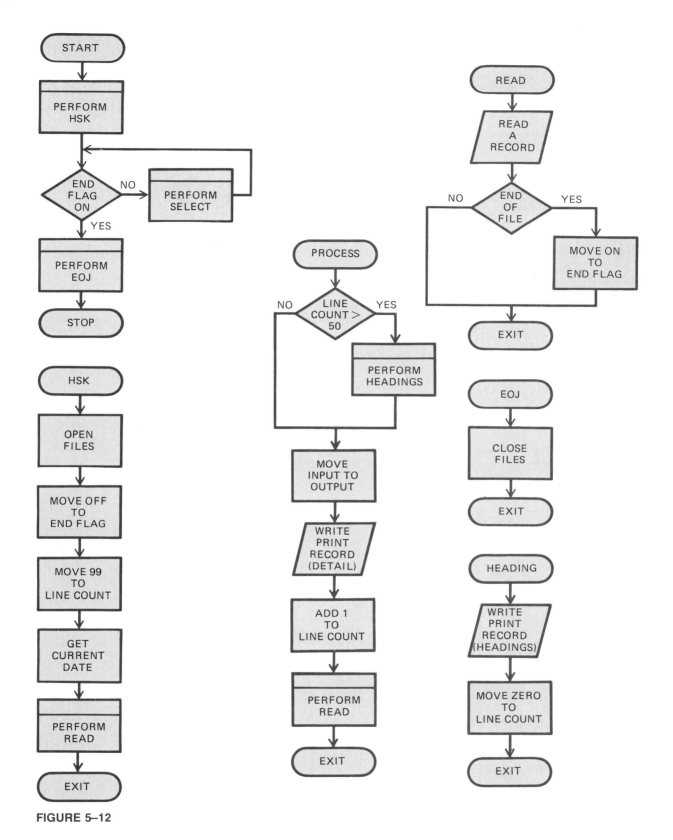

FIGURE 5–12

tested for > 50. If it is not, the input items are moved to the output areas and the detail line is written. After each detail line is written, LINE COUNT is incremented by 1; this counter reflects the number of lines used by detail lines on the page. If, for example, the output is double-spaced two would be added to line count for each detail line written. If, on any pass through

MAINLINE LOGIC

PERFORM hsk routine
PERFORM process routine until end flag = on
PERFORM eoj routine

HSK ROUTINE

OPEN files
MOVE off to end flag
MOVE 99 to line count
GET current date
PERFORM read outline

PROCESS

IF line count > 50
        PERFORM heading routine
ENDIF
MOVE input fields to output
WRITE print record (detail)
ADD 1 to line count
PERFORM read routine

EOJ ROUTINE

CLOSE files

READ ROUTINE

READ a record
        AT END of file
                MOVE on to end flag

HEADING ROUTINE

WRITE print record (headings)
MOVE zero to line count

FIGURE 5–13

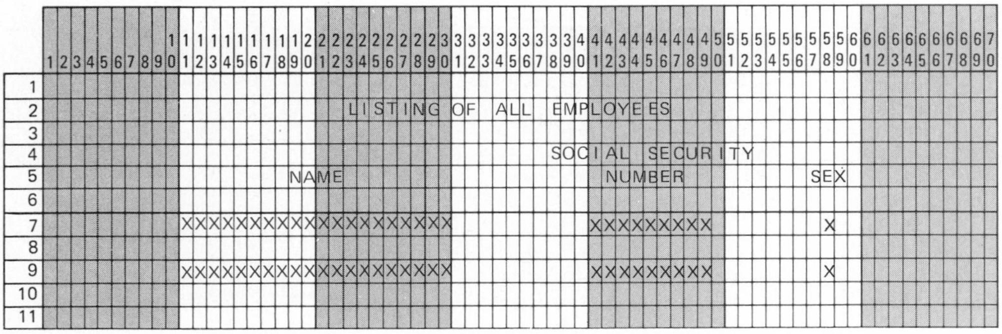

FIGURE 5–14

the logic, LINE COUNT is greater than 50, the page is full. According to the specifications when the page is full another set of headings is printed and LINE COUNT is reset.

It is also important to note that the test for LINE COUNT greater than 50 comes before the building or printing of the output line. This is usually preferable to prevent an extra set of headings from being produced. For instance, suppose we have just printed the 51st line on a page and incremented the line counter after doing so. If we check the value of LINE COUNT at this point (after writing the line and adding to the line counter rather than before), we find it to be greater than 50. According to the plan another set of headings is printed. Next, another record is read. If the end-of-file indicator is read, the flowchart indicates END FLAG is turned on, the files are closed, and execution stops. Thus, a set of headings have been created which will have no detail line under them.

Read Routine

The read routine reads one record from the file, and if no record is present, the end-of-file indicator is recognized and ON is moved to END FLAG. This change in value for END FLAG will be recognized when the test is made in the mainline.

EXTRACTS

An **extract program** is used to select certain records, or fields in a record, from a data file. These records are used to create a new file. The new file may be a printed listing or may be created on a medium suitable for input to another program within the system.

The first type of extract program creates a file in printed form containing only those items which meet a particular set of criteria. Then the user of the data processing output no longer has to scan through a long list of items looking for those of interest. The user will have specified in advance the items that are to be on the report. The input file to this process may be read sequentially in its normal order, or it may be sorted first into some other order.

The second type of extract program selects records based on the contents of one or more fields in a record, creates a new file of the selected records (usually on tape or disk), and then sorts the new file into the desired order if necessary. The extract file is smaller than the original. This saves storage space and saves reading time when the extract file is used as input to other programs in the system.

PRINTED REPORTS

For the discussion of the first type of extract process, we will start with a printed listing as the output to be created. Assume a file containing records of both male and female employees. See Figure 5–15 for a description of the input. Figure 5–16 is the printer spacing chart. A listing of all the records is shown in Figure 5–17.

FIGURE 5–15

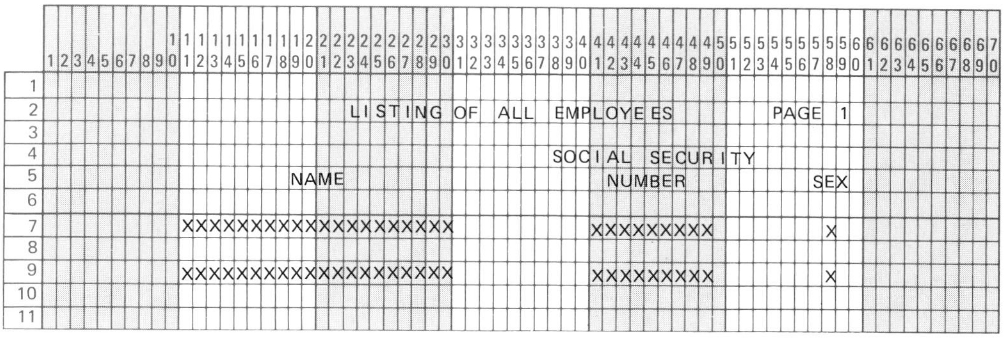

FIGURE 5–16

NAME	SOCIAL SECURITY NUMBER	SEX
KENNEDY, KENNETH	123456789	M
EBNER, MICHAEL	163234534	M
SIMPSON, JANET	203469729	F
CARUSO, LUCY	239659387	F
GONZALES, JUANITA	316249532	F
EDISON, KEITH	326498765	M
HILL, ANNA	261269016	F
SMITH, ALICE	385312117	F
JOHNSON, EDWARD	396942219	M
TERRY, EUGENE	419623491	M
EVERETT, GRACE	479809381	F
SWANSON, SHARON	491236125	F
JONES, JAMES	543234534	M
LONG, MARILYN	591632701	F
STANDFORD, ALLEN	619211613	M
METTLESON, GREGORY	632912365	M

FIGURE 5–17

Instead of this list of all employees, we wish to produce a listing of only the male employees. The input record description will not require change when we restrict the number or type of employees whose data is on the printout. Only the main heading needs to be changed on the printer spacing chart to indicate that the listing is for male employees. The logic for the program must be changed to extract certain records from the file. Figure 5–18 shows the listing of the male employees only. Figure 5–19 illustrates the process steps necessary to extract the records of the male employees from the file. Notice that once a record is read and it can be determined that it is not the record of a male employee, the logic moves downward to read another record. No further processing takes place for the "nonmale" record. Figure 5–20 shows the pseudocode.

In Figure 5–19 only two possibilities for the question, SEX = M (yes or no) were considered. We have assumed that the contents of the records have been verified prior to this program. Such a verification assures us that the field representing sex contains either an M or an F for all the records in the file.

NAME	SOCIAL SECURITY NUMBER	SEX
KENNEDY, KENNETH	123456789	M
EBNER, MICHAEL	163234534	M
EDISON, KEITH	326498765	M
JOHNSON, EDWARD	396942219	M
TERRY, EUGENE	419623491	M
JONES, JAMES	543234534	M
STANDFORD, ALLEN	619211613	M
METTLESON, GREGORY	632912365	M

FIGURE 5–18

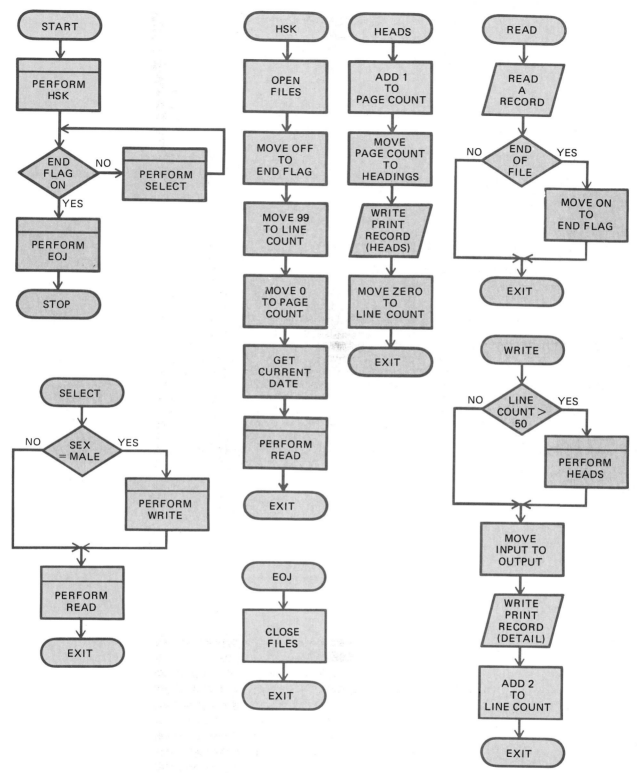

FIGURE 5–19

MAINLINE LOGIC

PERFORM hsk routine
PERFORM select routine until end flag = on
PERFORM eoj routine
STOP

HSK ROUTINE

OPEN files
MOVE off to end flag
MOVE 99 to line count
MOVE zero to page count
PERFORM read routine

SELECT ROUTINE

IF sex = male
       PERFORM write routine
ENDIF
PERFORM read routine

EOJ ROUTINE

CLOSE files

READ ROUTINE

READ a record
       AT END of file
              MOVE on to end flag

WRITE ROUTINE

IF line count > 50
       PERFORM heads routine
ENDIF
MOVE input to output
WRITE print record (detail)
ADD 2 to line count

HEADS ROUTINE

ADD 1 to page count
MOVE page count to headings
WRITE print record (heads)
MOVE zero to line count
FIGURE 5–20

If some prior verification of the contents of the file were not made, we would run the risk of rejecting records of male employees. A data entry error could result in the presence of some character other than an M or an F in the field used for the sex code. Since the character would not be an M, the logic would follow the NO path and bypass writing the record.

If there has been no prior verification of the input data, the records with an incorrect sex code could be identified by testing separately for the M or the F. The select routine of the flowchart for this is shown in Figure 5–21 and the pseudocode in Figure 5–22. Then, when the

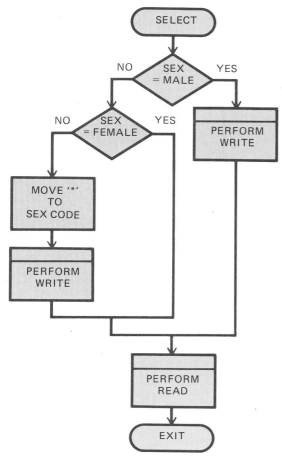

FIGURE 5–21

```
IF sex = male
        PERFORM write routine
ELSE
        IF sex = female
        ELSE
                MOVE '*' to sex-code
                PERFORM write routine
        ENDIF
ENDIF
PERFORM read routine
```
FIGURE 5–22

sex code is neither an M or an F, the record is written anyway. This is done so that the error will be called to the attention of the person using the report. The input description and printer spacing chart remain the same. The format of the input or the output is not changed. The method of selecting which records will be output is changed. A sample of the output is shown in Figure 5–23.

LISTING OF MALE EMPLOYEES   PAGE 1

NAME	SOCIAL SECURITY NUMBER	SEX
KENNEDY, KENNETH	123456789	M
EBNER, MICHAEL	163234534	M
EDISON, KEITH	326498765	M
OSUCHOWSKI, LYNN	372441248	*
JOHNSON, EDWARD	396942219	M
TERRY, EUGENE	419623491	M
JONES, JAMES	543234534	M
STANDFORD, ALLEN	619211613	M
METTLESON, GREGORY	632912365	M

FIGURE 5–23

COLLATING SEQUENCES

We have introduced the idea of comparing or testing relationships in order to select records from a file. Before we go further with material on how to form comparisons, we need a little background on what will be happening within the computer when comparisons are made.

Each computer sytem has a coding scheme which it uses to represent data and instructions. Two of the more popular coding schemes are called EBCDIC (Extended Binary Coded Decimal Interchange Code) and ASCII (American Standard Code for Information Interchange).

Regardless of the coding scheme used, each letter, number, special character, and instruction has been assigned a combination of binary digits called **bits.** This combination is generally referred to as a **byte.** The order in which the letters, numbers, and special characters appear (low to high) is based on the numerical order of the binary code they were assigned. This order is called a **collating sequence.** Portions of the collating sequence for EBCDIC and ASCII are shown in Figure 5–24. Only the capital letters, the numbers, and some special characters are shown so that you can see the relationship of items you are likely to compare. The missing numbers in the chart represent instructions, lower-case letters, and other special characters.

AND/OR

When testing a single field for more than one possible value, we need to look at the arrangement of the decision symbols. The arrangement depends on whether AND or OR logic is appropriate. AND and OR are known as logical operators. Their use in programming is more exacting than we often apply to the words in everyday conversation. Let us assume a single-character field whose value is to be tested for extract purposes. In ordinary conversation we might say, "I want a list of the employees in divisions 1 and 4." Before we can determine the correctness of this statement, we need to look at how AND and OR structures are drawn in flowcharting and

PARTIAL LIST OF ASCII AND EBCDIC

DEC	HEX	BINARY	ASCII	EBCDIC	DEC	HEX	BINARY	ASCII	EBCDIC
32	20	0010 0000	SP		91	5B	0101 1011		$
33	21	0010 0001	!		92	5C	0101 1100		*
34	22	0010 0010	"		93	5D	0101 1101		)
35	23	0010 0011	#		94	5E	0101 1110		;
36	24	0010 0100	$		95	5F	0101 1111		
37	25	0010 0101	%		96	60	0110 0000		—
38	26	0010 0110	&		97	61	0110 0001		/
39	27	0010 0111	'						
40	28	0010 1000	(		108	6C	0110 1100		%
41	29	0010 1001	)		109	6D	0110 1101		—
42	2A	0010 1010	*		110	6E	0110 1110		>
43	2B	0010 1011	+		111	6F	0110 1111		?
44	2C	0010 1100	'						
45	2D	0010 1101	—		122	7A	0111 1010		:
46	2E	0010 1110	.		123	7B	0111 1011		#
47	2F	0010 1111	/		124	7C	0111 1100		@
48	30	0011 0000	0		125	7D	0111 1101		'
49	31	0011 0001	1		126	7E	0111 1110		=
50	32	0011 0010	2		127	7F	0111 1111		"
51	33	0011 0011	3						
52	34	0011 0100	4		193	C1	1100 0001		A
53	35	0011 0101	5		194	C2	1100 0010		B
54	36	0011 0110	6		195	C3	1100 0011		C
55	37	0011 0111	7		196	C4	1100 0100		D
56	38	0011 1000	8		197	C5	1100 0101		E
57	39	0011 1001	9		198	C6	1100 0110		F
58	3A	0011 1010	:		199	C7	1100 0111		G
59	3B	0011 1011	;		200	C8	1100 1000		H
60	3C	0011 1100	<		201	C9	1100 1001		I
61	3D	0011 1101	=						
62	3E	0011 1110	>		209	D1	1101 0001		J
63	3F	0011 1111	?		210	D2	1101 0010		K
64	40	0100 0000	@	SP	211	D3	1101 0011		L
65	41	0100 0001	A		212	D4	1101 0100		M
66	42	0100 0010	B		213	D5	1101 0101		N
67	43	0100 0011	C		214	D6	1101 0110		O
68	44	0100 0100	D		215	D7	1101 0111		P
69	45	0100 0101	E		216	D8	1101 1000		Q
70	46	0100 0110	F		217	D9	1101 1001		R
71	47	0100 0111	G						
72	48	0100 1000	H		226	E2	1110 0010		S
73	49	0100 1001	I		227	E3	1110 0011		T
74	4A	0100 1010	J		228	E4	1110 0100		U
75	4B	0100 1011	K	.	229	E5	1110 0101		V
76	4C	0100 1100	L	<	230	E6	1110 0110		W
77	4D	0100 1101	M	(	231	E7	1110 0111		X
78	4E	0100 1110	N	+	232	E8	1110 1000		Y
79	4F	0100 1111	O		233	E9	1110 1001		Z
80	50	0101 0000	P	&					
81	51	0101 0001	Q		240	F0	1111 0000		0
82	52	0101 0010	R		241	F1	1111 0001		1
83	53	0101 0011	S		242	F2	1111 0010		2
84	54	0101 0100	T		243	F3	1111 0011		3
85	55	0101 0101	U		244	F4	1111 0100		4
86	56	0101 0110	V		245	F5	1111 0101		5
87	57	0101 0111	W		246	F6	1111 0110		6
88	58	0101 1000	X		247	F7	1111 0111		7
89	59	0101 1001	Y		248	F8	1111 1000		8
90	5A	0101 1010	Z		249	F9	1111 1001		9

FIGURE 5–24

then applied in computer programming. Figure 5–25 is an example of an AND logic structure. We are saying, "Does the field contain a 1, AND if it does, does it also contain a 4?" Figure 5–26 is an example of an OR logic structure. We are saying, "Does the field contain a 1, OR if not, does it contain a 4?"

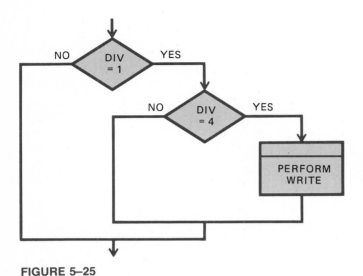

FIGURE 5–25

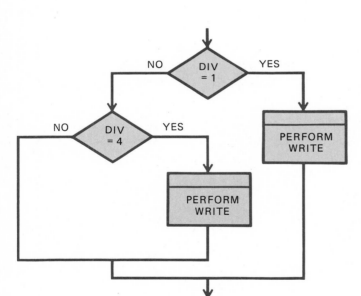

FIGURE 5–26

If we want to write a program which will produce a listing containing all records of either division 1 or division 4, Figure 5–26 (the OR logic) will produce the listing required. Figure 5–25 (the AND logic) will not produce any listing at all. It is not possible for a one-character field in a single record to contain both a 1 and a 4 at the same time. Try two records, one with a division 1 and one with a division 4 on the flowchart segment in Figure 5–25. Did either of the division numbers make it through both tests? Remember, a single field is being tested for an equal condition here. Later we will find that AND logic can be used on a single field if the test is for a value within a range (for example, greater than 0 AND less than 6). A generalized version of pseudocode for AND and OR logic is shown in Figure 5–27.

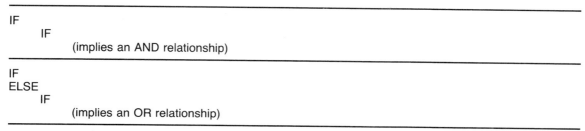

```
IF
    IF
        (implies an AND relationship)

IF
ELSE
    IF
        (implies an OR relationship)
```

FIGURE 5–27

For each criterion that must be met, one or more decision symbols or steps are needed. Although most programming languages allow you to make logical (and, or) decisions which combine a number of tests into one decision statement, most of our examples will make only one test per symbol. If tests are combined into one IF, then we must be satisfied with the same set of YES or NO actions for all the tests combined into one symbol. An example of combining tests in one symbol is given in Figure 5–28. Figures 5–25 and 5–26 would have allowed insertion of commands on either the NO side of DIV = 1 or the NO side of DIV = 4. Figure 5–28 has only one NO side, and any logic steps put there must be for both conditions tested.

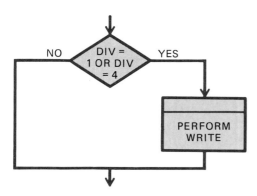

FIGURE 5–28

DECISION SEQUENCE

Most to Least

Often one field has more than two possible values which are reasonable. In such a case the order in which we test for the possibilities will make a difference in the actual number of comparisons the computer makes.

In the company for which we are preparing a payroll, there are five divisions. This means that there are five correct possibilities for the field DIVISION (1–5). There is also the possibility that an incorrect character will appear in this field. We wish to make a listing in which some of the payroll data from division 1 as well as from division 4 is printed. The description of the input we will use is shown in Figure 5–29, the print chart in Figure 5–30, and the flowchart depicting the extract logic in Figure 5–31. Notice that this is OR logic. Figure 5–32 is the pseudocode.

If the possibilities are tested individually, the field must be checked for each additional acceptable possibility after it has been rejected for one. The arrangement which will produce the least number of comparisons is to compare from the *most* likely possibility to the *least* likely.

For our example, the company has 1000 employees with 300 people in division 1 and 100 people in division 4. The number of comparisons made by using the flowchart in Figure 5–31 is 1000 at the first extract decision symbol (DIV = 1), since all records must pass through the first test. At the second decision symbol (DIV = 4) 700 records are tested. The 700 tested at the second decision represent the records rejected at the first test (DIV = 1). The numbers in parentheses represent the numerical results of tests on the actual data. The 300 and 100 represent the number of records in divisions 1 and 4, respectively. A total of 400 records are represented on the report.

If the order of the symbols were reversed, there would be 1000 decisions at the first symbol and 900 at the second. This would mean 200 (or about 12 percent) more decision instructions to be performed by the computer, thus increasing the time necessary to do the job. When OR logic is applied on a single field, the tests should be done from the *most* to the *least* likely to occur. Putting this another way, the fewer we reject, the fewer we have to test again for other possible values.

INPUT RECORD LAYOUT

FIGURE 5–29

PRINT CHART

FIGURE 5–30

FLOWCHART

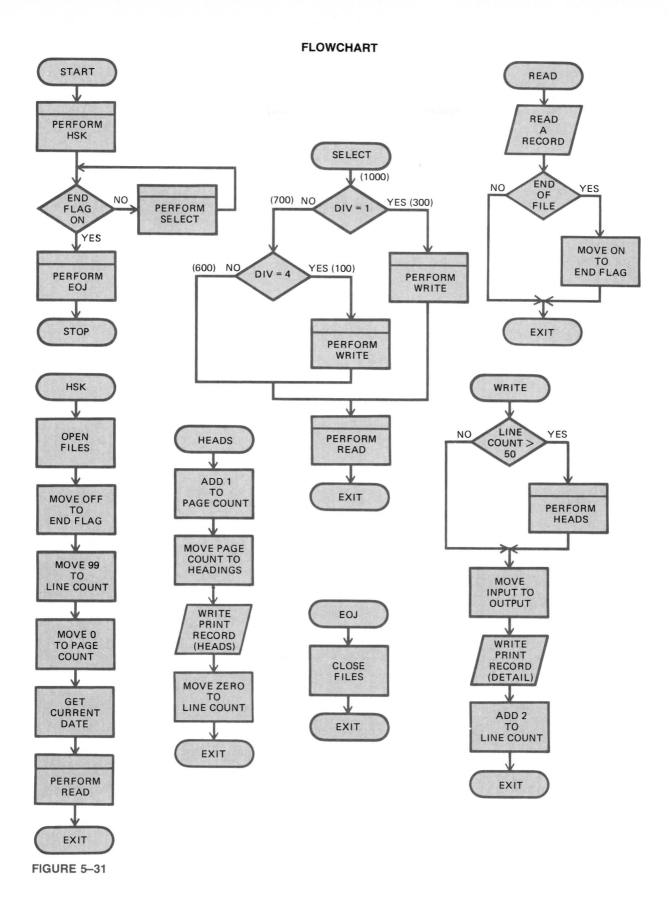

FIGURE 5–31

MAINLINE

PERFORM hsk routine
PERFORM select routine until end flag = on
PERFORM eoj routine
STOP

HSK ROUTINE

OPEN files
MOVE off to end flag
MOVE 99 to line count
MOVE zero to page count
GET current date
PERFORM read routine

SELECT ROUTINE

IF division = 1
        PERFORM write routine
ELSE
        IF division = 4
                PERFORM write routine
        ENDIF
ENDIF
PERFORM read routine

EOJ ROUTINE

CLOSE files

READ ROUTINE

READ a record
        AT END of file
                MOVE on to end flag

WRITE ROUTINE

IF line count > 50
        PERFORM heads routine
ENDIF
MOVE input to output
WRITE print record (detail)
ADD 2 to line count

HEADS ROUTINE

ADD 1 to page count
MOVE page count to headings
WRITE print record (heads)
MOVE zero to line count

FIGURE 5–32

We can test for more than two possibilities in a field if a greater-than or less-than type of decision is used. To print all employees in division 1 or 2, the SELECT routine portion of the flowchart shown in Figure 5–33 could be used. Figure 5–34 is the pseudocode for this logic. Presuming an edited file, this type of testing is possible. However, on an unedited file, this type of test leaves room for error if the division number has been incorrectly entered. With some collating sequences the test "LESS than 3" would produce a yes answer for all the letters of the alphabet, all special characters, and zero as well as the 1 and 2 we are interested in. For this reason a more specific test is safer.

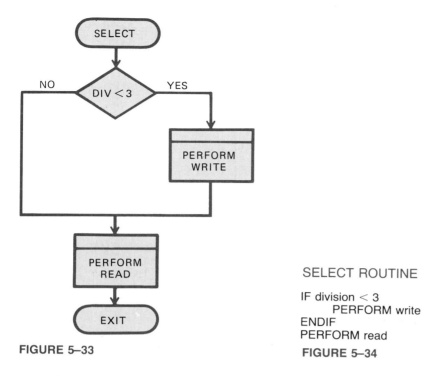

FIGURE 5–33

SELECT ROUTINE

IF division < 3
       PERFORM write
ENDIF
PERFORM read

FIGURE 5–34

Figure 5–35 shows the logic for a more specific test. Only the SELECT routine is shown; all other routines remain the same. Figure 5–36 is the pseudocode.

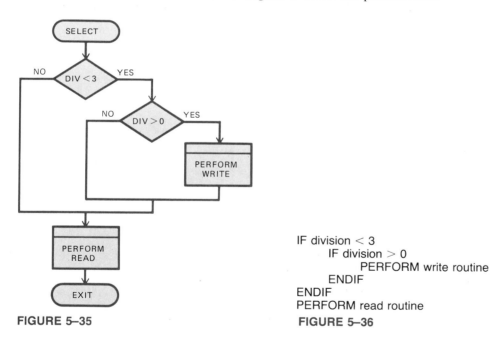

FIGURE 5–35

IF division < 3
     IF division > 0
          PERFORM write routine
     ENDIF
ENDIF
PERFORM read routine

FIGURE 5–36

In Figure 5–35, when any record has a division number less than 3, it is subjected to a second test to make sure that the division is also greater than 0. An assumption is made here that the field containing division number is only one position in length and contains a whole number. Therefore, it must be either a 1 or a 2.

Least to Most

In AND logic we are testing multiple fields in a record and we expect each field to meet some criteria. While it is possible that only one value would be acceptable in some fields and more than one value would be acceptable in others, we will begin with the simple AND logic where only one value in each field is acceptable. The priority of testing for simple AND logic is **least** to **most** likely.

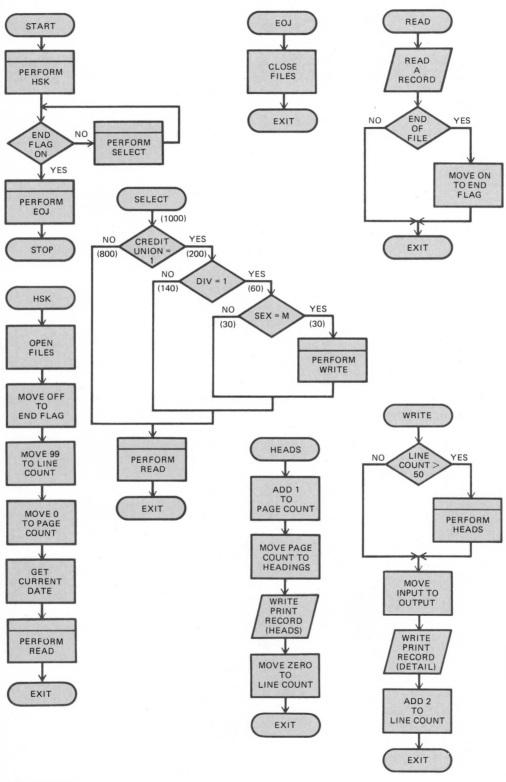

FIGURE 5–37

To illustrate the point, let us produce a list of all males who are in division 1 and who also belong to the credit union. In this case there are three separate criteria, all of which must be met before the record is listed. This means tests must be made on three fields before we can be sure we will accept and list the record. To illustrate the idea of testing for the least likely first, assume a test where we expect only 20 percent of the records to pass. This means 80 percent of the records will not have to be tested on the other two fields, if they fail the first test. An example of such an extract is shown in Figure 5–37. The pseudocode is shown in Figure 5–38.

MAINLINE ROUTINE

```
PERFORM hsk routine
PERFORM select routine until end flag = on
PERFORM eoj routine
STOP
```

HSK ROUTINE

```
OPEN files
MOVE off to end flag
MOVE 99 to line count
MOVE zero to page count
GET current date
PERFORM read routine
```

SELECT ROUTINE

```
IF credit union = 1
    IF division = 1
        IF sex = male
            PERFORM write routine
        ENDIF
    ENDIF
ENDIF
PERFORM read routine
```

EOJ ROUTINE

```
CLOSE file
```

READ ROUTINE

```
READ a record
    AT END of file
        MOVE on to end flag
```

WRITE ROUTINE

```
IF line count > 50
    PERFORM heads routine
ENDIF
MOVE input to output
WRITE print record (detail)
ADD 2 to line count
```

HEADS ROUTINE

```
Add 1 to page count
MOVE page count to headings
WRITE print record (heads)
MOVE zero to line count
```

FIGURE 5–38

The particular order for the decisions was chosen because the members of the credit union represent the smallest percentage of the file 200 members or 20 percent. Division 1 contains 300 employees or 30 percent of the file. Half of the employees are male, making this the decision most likely to produce a yes.

All the records (1000) are tested at the first extract decision. Since 800, or 80 percent, are rejected, we have only 200 records, 70 percent or 140 are rejected, leaving 60 records to be tested at the third decision. Of the 60 tested at the third decision, 30 are accepted and 30 are rejected. A total of 1260 comparisons were made to select the 30 extracted records. Realize that the illustration assumes that the credit union and division 1 are equally divided between male and female members. It also assumes that credit union membership is evenly divided among the divisions of the company. In other words, the company wide percentages are applied at each successive decision.

If we reverse the order of the tests, additional comparisons are necessary when we do not follow the least-to-most-likely sequence. At the first extract decision symbol 1000 records are tested. One-half of these are rejected, leaving 500 records to test at the second decision symbol. Since the middle test is still 30 percent in division 1, 350 of the records are rejected, and 150 of them go on the third test. The third test is for the credit union. Eighty percent or 120 of the records are rejected and 20 percent or 30 records are listed. In this example 1650 comparisons were made instead of 1260; however, the final results were the same.

The process of extracting records using the minimum number of tests is more complex when some fields to be tested have only a yes or no alternative and other fields offer multiple possibilities, such as the division field. The actual arrangement of the decisions will depend upon the probability of a yes or no answer in each case.

The information necessary to determine least or most likely is not always readily available. Any informed judgment made along this line will, however, usually increase the efficiency of the program when it is put into production. If the information is not readily available, it is not practical to spend a lot of time figuring out the frequency factors, chiefly because today's computers are so fast and programming time is so costly.

RECORD COUNTS

The extraction process as explained thus far has not counted records in any way. It has simply listed out the records meeting all the selection criteria. Totals of both the number of records processed and the number of records selected can be useful information. Sometimes in such a count the answer is already known; in the case of the number of records processed it is the number of employees in the company. Even so, producing this count of records provides an important control figure to ensure that the file does actually contain the number of employees assumed to be working for the company. The number of records selected is less likely to be known in advance. Such a count is often a useful summary figure to the user of the extract report. The flowchart depicting the extract and counting the total number of records processed is shown in Figure 5–39. The pseudocode is shown in Figure 5–40.

In Figure 5–39 the portion of the flowchart which does the actual selection (SELECT) is indicated as a subroutine. We now have a basic extract program which counts the records processed, and only the routine called SELECT need be changed to suit the requirements of a particular extract.

Notice, in particular, that the addition of each record to the total records count takes place after the test for end flag = ON in MAINLINE when the logic is in the SELECT routine. Remember, the first record was read in the HSK routine. The ADD 1 to record count could be at the beginning of the SELECT routine or where it is. The important point is that SELECT was chosen instead of EOJ after the read. In many programming languages the end-of-file test is an integral part of the read statement, and no capability exists to insert commands between the read and the end-of-file test. This makes the READ routine a bad choice for counting records.

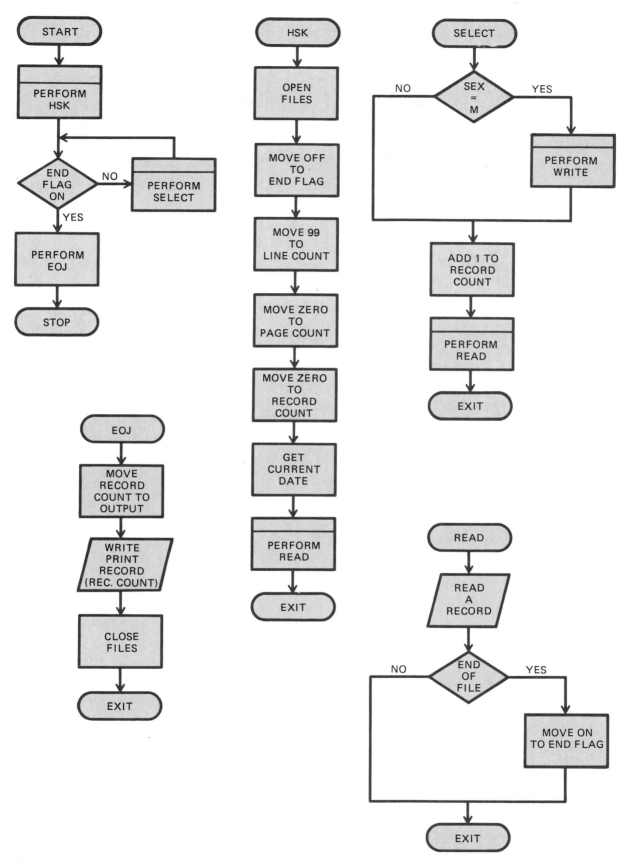

FIGURE 5–39

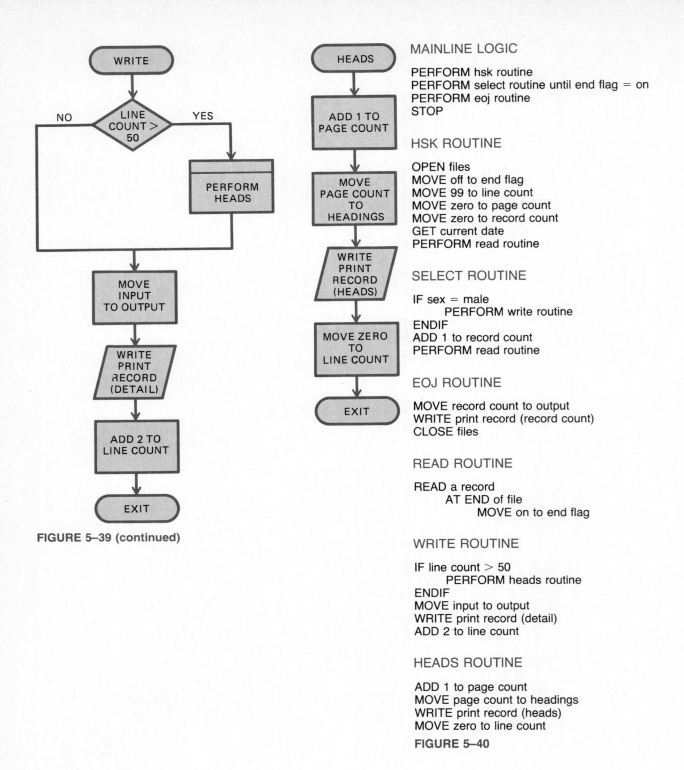

FIGURE 5–39 (continued)

MAINLINE LOGIC

PERFORM hsk routine
PERFORM select routine until end flag = on
PERFORM eoj routine
STOP

HSK ROUTINE

OPEN files
MOVE off to end flag
MOVE 99 to line count
MOVE zero to page count
MOVE zero to record count
GET current date
PERFORM read routine

SELECT ROUTINE

IF sex = male
        PERFORM write routine
ENDIF
ADD 1 to record count
PERFORM read routine

EOJ ROUTINE

MOVE record count to output
WRITE print record (record count)
CLOSE files

READ ROUTINE

READ a record
        AT END of file
                MOVE on to end flag

WRITE ROUTINE

IF line count > 50
        PERFORM heads routine
ENDIF
MOVE input to output
WRITE print record (detail)
ADD 2 to line count

HEADS ROUTINE

ADD 1 to page count
MOVE page count to headings
WRITE print record (heads)
MOVE zero to line count

FIGURE 5–40

SELECTED RECORD COUNTS

In order to count selected records the counting process must come when all selection criteria have been met and before the next record is read. The count is incremented in the WRITE routine which is done only when the selection criteria are met. Figure 5–41 has the flowchart and Figure 5–42 the pseudocode. The COBOL logic is in Figure 5–43 and the BASIC program is shown in Figure 5–44.

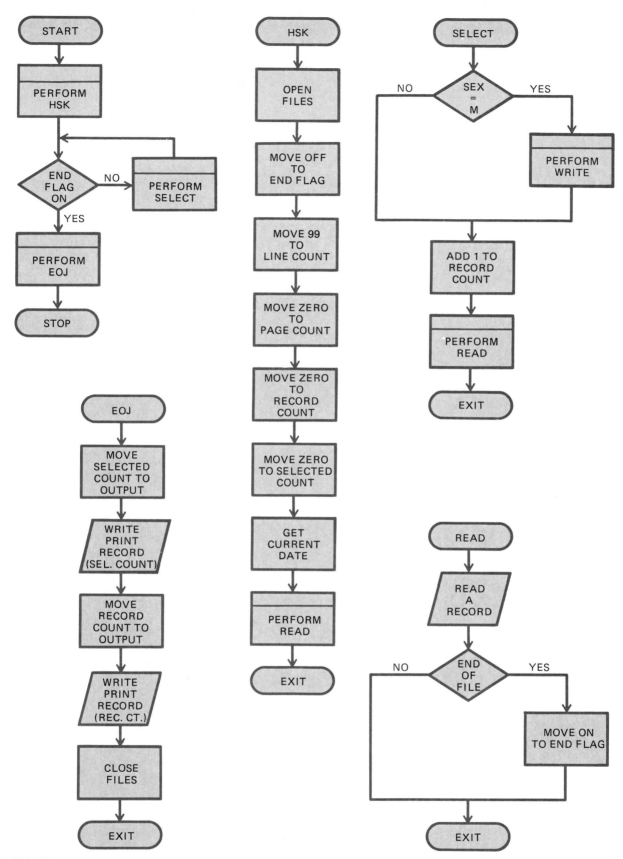

FIGURE 5–41

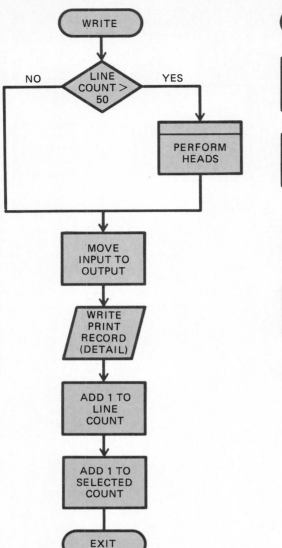

MAINLINE LOGIC

PERFORM hsk routine
PERFORM select routine until end flag = on
PERFORM eoj routine
STOP

HSK ROUTINE

OPEN files
MOVE off to end flag
MOVE 99 to line count
MOVE zero to page count
MOVE zero to record count
MOVE zero to selected count
GET current date
PERFORM read routine

SELECT ROUTINE

IF sex = male
        PERFORM write routine
ENDIF
ADD 1 to record count
PERFORM read routine

EOJ ROUTINE

MOVE selected count to output
WRITE print record (selected count)
MOVE record count to output
WRITE print record (record count)
CLOSE files

READ ROUTINE

READ a record
        AT END of file
                MOVE on to end flag

WRITE ROUTINE

IF line count > 50
        PERFORM heads routine
ENDIF
MOVE input to output
WRITE print record (detail)
ADD 1 to line count
ADD 1 to selected count

HEADS ROUTINE

ADD 1 to page count
MOVE page count to headings
WRITE print record (heads)
MOVE zero to line count

FIGURE 5–42

FIGURE 5–41 (continued)

COBOL VERSION

PROCEDURE DIVISION.

MAINLINE-LOGIC.
        PERFORM HSK-ROUTINE.
        PERFORM SELECT-ROUTINE UNTIL END-FLAG = 'ON'.
        PERFORM EOJ-ROUTINE.
        STOP RUN.

HSK-ROUTINE.
        OPEN INPUT C5B1DATA.
        OPEN OUTPUT PRINT-FILE.
        MOVE 'OFF' TO END-FLAG.
        MOVE 99 TO LINE-COUNT.
        MOVE ZERO TO PAGE-COUNT.
        MOVE ZERO TO RECORD-COUNT.
        MOVE ZERO TO SELECTED-COUNT.
        MOVE CURRENT-DATE TO HDG-DATE.
        PERFORM READ-ROUTINE.

SELECT ROUTINE.
        IF SEX-CODE = 'MALE'
            PERFORM WRITE-ROUTINE.
        ADD 1 to RECORD-COUNT.
        PERFORM READ-ROUTINE.

EOJ-ROUTINE.
        MOVE SELECTED-COUNT TO SELECTED-OUT.
        WRITE PRINT-RECORD FROM SELECTED-LINE AFTER ADVANCING PAGE
        MOVE RECORD-COUNT TO RECORDS-OUT.
        WRITE PRINT-RECORD FROM RECORDS-LINE AFTER ADVANCING 2 LINES.
        CLOSE C5B1DATA PRINT-FILE.

READ-ROUTINE.
        READ C5B1DATA
            AT END
                MOVE 'ON' TO END-FLAG.

WRITE-ROUTINE.
        IF LINE-COUNT > 50
            PERFORM HEADS-ROUTINE.
        MOVE DIV-NBR   TO DIV-OUT.
        MOVE DEPT-NBR   TO DEPT-OUT.
        MOVE NAME   TO NAME-OUT.
        MOVE EMP-NBR   TO EMP-NBR-OUT.
        MOVE SEX-CODE   TO SEX-CODE-OUT.
        WRITE PRINT-RECORD FROM DETAIL-LINE AFTER ADVANCING 1 LINES.
        ADD 1 TO LINE-COUNT.
        ADD 1 TO SELECTED-COUNT.

HEADS-ROUTINE.
        ADD 1 TO PAGE-COUNT.
        MOVE PAGE-COUNT TO PAGE-OUT.
        WRITE PRINT-RECORD FROM HEADING-LINE.
        MOVE ZERO TO LINE-COUNT.

FIGURE 5–43

BASIC VERSION

```
'PROGRAMMERS:    J AND J, INC.
'DATE:           5/11/90
'PROGRAM NAME:   CASE5
'*************************************************************************
'*                          MAINLINE LOGIC                              *
'*************************************************************************
GOSUB HOUSEKEEPING.ROUTINE
WHILE END.FLAG$ = "OFF"
    GOSUB SELECT.ROUTINE
WEND
GOSUB EOJ.ROUTINE
END
'*************************************************************************
'*                       HOUSEKEEPING ROUTINE                           *
'*************************************************************************
HOUSEKEEPING.ROUTINE:
OPEN "B:C5B1DATA" FOR INPUT AS #1
D$ = "SCRN:":CLS
INPUT "OUTPUT TO THE PRINTER - ANSWER Y OR N"; ANSWER$
IF ANSWER$ = "y" OR ANSWER$ = "Y" THEN
    D$ = "LPT1:":WIDTH "LPT1:",80:LPRINT CHR$(15)
END IF
OPEN D$ FOR OUTPUT AS #2
LET DETAIL$ =    "##" + SPACE$(5) + "##" + SPACE$(5) + "\          \" +
    SPACE$(5) + "#####" + SPACE$(5) + "&"
LET SEL.LINE$ = "SELECTED RECORDS" + SPACE$(2) + "###"
LET REC.LINE$ = "TOTAL RECORDS" + SPACE$(5) + "###"
LET END.FLAG$ = "OFF"
LET LINE.COUNT = 99
GOSUB READ.ROUTINE
RETURN
'*************************************************************************
'                           SELECT ROUTINE                              *
'*************************************************************************
SELECT.ROUTINE:
IF SEX.CODE$ = "M" THEN
    GOSUB WRITE.ROUTINE
END IF
LET RECORD.COUNT = RECORD.COUNT + 1
GOSUB READ.ROUTINE
RETURN
'*************************************************************************
'                            EOJ ROUTINE                                *
'*************************************************************************
EOJ.ROUTINE:
PRINT #2,
PRINT #2, USING SEL.LINE$; SELECTED.COUNT
PRINT #2, USING REC.LINE$; RECORD.COUNT
CLOSE
RETURN
'*************************************************************************
'                           READ ROUTINE                                *
'*************************************************************************
READ.ROUTINE:
IF NOT EOF(1) THEN
    INPUT #1, DIV.NBR, DEPT.NBR, ENAME$, ENBR, SEX.CODE$
ELSE
    LET END.FLAG$ = "ON"
```

FIGURE 5–44

```
END IF
RETURN
'******************************************************************
'                        WRITE ROUTINE                            *
'******************************************************************
WRITE.ROUTINE:
IF LINE.COUNT > 50 THEN
    GOSUB HEADS.ROUTINE
ELSE
END IF
PRINT #2, USING DETAIL$; DIV.NBR, DEPT.NBR, ENAME$, ENBR, SEX.CODE$
LET LINE.COUNT = LINE.COUNT + 1
LET SELECTED.COUNT = SELECTED.COUNT + 1
RETURN
'******************************************************************
'                        HEADS ROUTINE                            *
'******************************************************************
HEADS.ROUTINE:
LET PAGE.COUNT = PAGE.COUNT + 1
PRINT #2, "DIV    DEPT           NAME           EMP.NBR    SEX"
PRINT #2,
LET LINE.COUNT = 0
RETURN
```

FIGURE 5–44 (continued)

CHAPTER VOCABULARY

AND logic
Collating sequence
Constant
Decision structure
External subroutine
Extract program
Extract routine
Final totals
Forms overflow

Hold areas
Internal subroutines
Least to most
Line count
Listing program
Logical operators
Most to least
OR logic
Record counts

Selected record counts
Selected records
Special records
Subroutines
Switches
System date
Variables

REVIEW QUESTIONS

MATCHING

A. Extract programs
B. Criteria
C. Least to most
D. Most to least

E. AND logic
F. Total record count
G. Selected record count

_____ **1.** Requires more than one condition to be true.
_____ **2.** Used to make efficient comparisons when only one value is acceptable from each field.
_____ **3.** The sum of all records processed.
_____ **4.** Written to selectively choose records from a file.
_____ **5.** The sum of all records which meet the selection criteria.
_____ **6.** Standards on which decisions may be based.
_____ **7.** Used to make efficient comparisons when multiple possibilities are acceptable from one field.

TRUE/FALSE

T F **1.** Extract programs are used only to create printed files.

T F **2.** One is added to the selected record count after each selection criteria test is passed.

T F **3.** Least to most is efficient for OR logic.

T F **4.** The order in which selection criteria are tested has an effect on the efficiency of the program.

T F **5.** The total record count is accumulated at end-of-file.

T F **6.** When more than one value in a field is acceptable for extract, the most likely value in that field should be tested for first.

T F **7.** Most to least is suitable for simple AND logic.

T F **8.** Selected record counts have little value, since the user can see the length of the listing.

EXERCISES

1. Draw a flowchart to select all males over 25 enrolled in a course. The program should print a report with name and address. Provide appropriate headings for the first page and overflow. Sixty percent of the employees are male and 30 percent of the employees are over 25.

2. Repeat Exercise 1, but also count selected, rejected, and total records. Print these totals at the end of the report.

3. Draw a flowchart to create two nonprint files concurrently. One should contain all males and the other all females. Count selected records for each file as well as total records. Print the results of the counts as a part of a successful end-of-job message. The input data has been previously edited.

4. Draw a flowchart for a personnel search. We are looking for any employees with a business undergraduate degree, an MBA, and two or more years teaching experience whose current salary is under $15,000 per year. Design an input record to help you make the search. Keep the design flexible; next week you may be looking for a dentist.

DISCUSSION QUESTIONS

1. Identify business situations in which a user would request an extract type report.

2. Is there any advantage to putting all selection criteria testing into a subroutine?

3. Why bother to count the number of total records processed if you have a previous count?

4. Since computers are so fast, does it really make any difference whether you arrange decisions for selected criteria in an order that minimizes the number of tests made?

5. Once a non-print extract file has been created, can it be used within the same program?

6. How can you know what order to make tests of selection criteria in?

PROJECTS

Project 1

INPUT

1–2	Inventory Record Code	
	Inventory Stock Number	
3–3	Inventory Type	Has a range of 1–5
4–5	Inventory Class	Has a range of 1–10
6–9	Inventory Part	
10–29	Inventory Description	
30–30	Inventory Location Code	
31–34	Inventory Quality on Hand	
35–38	Inventory Quality on Order	
39–42	Inventory Reorder Level	
43–43	Inventory Unit Size Code	
44–48	Inventory Unit Price	(5.2)
49–49	Inventory Discount Code	
50–55	Inventory Annual Usage (Units)	
56–58	Inventory Vendor Code	
	Inventory Transportation Code	
59–59	Inventory Category	
60–60	Inventory Distance	
61–80	Filler	

PROCESSING

Extract the record of items in types 1 or 4 whose class is less than 7.

OUTPUT

1. Use 132 print positions.
2. Double space the output.
3. Provide report headings including page numbers and current date.
4. Provide appropriate column headings.
5. Print all input fields (except inventory record code) and order quantity, gross order amount, net order amount.
6. Use a line count of greater than 50 for overflow.

Project 2

INPUT

MASTER PERSONNEL FILE

01–02	Personnel Record Code	
03–03	Personnel Division	Has a range of 1–5
04–05	Personnel Department	Has a range of 1–5
	Personnel Employee ID	
06–08	Personnel ID-1	
09–10	Personnel ID-2	
11–14	Personnel ID-3	
15–34	Personnel Name	
35–50	Personnel Street Address	
51–52	Personnel State	
53–57	Personnel Zip	
	Personnel Date of Employment	
58–59	Personnel Month	
60–61	Personnel Day	
62–63	Personnel Year	
64–64	Personnel Experience Code	
65–65	Personnel Responsibility Code	
66–67	Personnel Skill Code	
68–71	Personnel Vacation Days	(4.1)
72–75	Personnel Sick Days	(4.1)
76–80	Personnel Daily Rate	(5.2)

PROCESSING

Extract the records of employees in divisions 1 and 4, whose department is less than 5, and who have less than 5 years of service with the company as of December 31, 1987.

OUTPUT

1. Use 132 print positions.
2. Double space the output.
3. Provide report heading including page numbers and the current date.
4. Provide appropriate column headings.
5. Output the input fields (except record-code).
6. Use a line count of greater than 50 for overview.

6 SINGLE-LEVEL CONTROL BREAKS

OBJECTIVES

As a result of studying this chapter the student should be able to perform the following activities:

1. Describe what a control break is and indicate why it is useful in programming.
2. Identify the function of a control-break hold area.
3. Describe when control-break hold areas are initialized, when they are altered, and why these steps are necessary.
4. Describe when headings are produced in relation to control breaks and how this fits in with forms overflow.
5. Describe what is meant by progressive/end-of-job totals.
6. Describe what control-break totals are and when they are produced.
7. Indicate why control-break totals need to be reset to zero.
8. Describe the use of a first-record switch and indicate other methods of accomplishing the same result.

INTRODUCTION

When reports are being produced within a company it is very likely that a report will be broken up and distributed to various sub-groups within the company. When changing from one group to another the data for the group that just ended needs to be completed and the data for the new group should start on the top of a new page. This chapter will deal with the following topics:

What is a control break?
How is it determined when a control break has occurred?
When and how are headings produced on a control break?
What are progressive and end-of-job totals and how are they processed?
How are control-break totals processed?
How do headings on control breaks and forms overflow interrelate?

CONTROL BREAKS

Control breaks are a method of breaking reports down into smaller units to make the data more meaningful. A control break exists when there is a change in the contents of a given field or fields usually referred to as control field(s). Typically, the records in the file are sequenced on this field(s). For example, suppose a file is in sequence by the divisions within a company; when the contents of the division number field change from division 1 to division 2, a control break has occurred.

HOLD AREAS

In an example in a previous chapter the employee data within a file was listed for verification by personnel at the various divisions. It would be better if the listing were broken down so that each division's information started on a new page. This way the report could easily be separated and sent to the various divisions. In looking at this as a manual process, it sounds rather easy—the paper should merely be moved to the top of a new page as each new division is encountered.

In essence this is what happens in a computerized version of the problem. To know if a new division has been encountered in computer processing it is necessary to have some way of comparing the contents of the control field in the current record being processed with the contents of that field in the previous record processed. This comparison process requires that the number

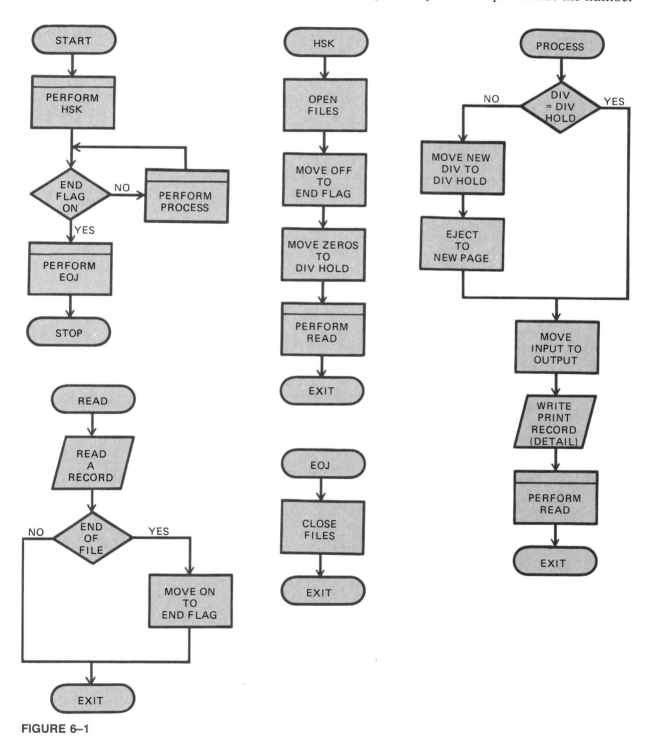

FIGURE 6–1

from the previous record be maintained or stored somewhere. To accomplish this, an area needs to be established in memory in which the division number (control field) from a record can be saved. This area is typically referred to as a **hold area.** The number that has been saved from the previous record can then be compared with the number on the current record. If a difference is found during the comparing process, then a new division has been encountered. When a new division is encountered, the new division number is stored in the hold area. Figure 6–1 shows this process, including modification of the contents of the hold area in storage. This hold area is designed by the programmer to be the same size as the field being compared. The pseudocode for this process is shown in Figure 6–2.

Notice that at the beginning of the flowchart (in HSK) the hold area is set to zero. This is done to force a new-division condition on the first record read. The assumption is that there are no divisions numbered zero. Without initializing this area to zero (or less than the lowest division number) there would be no way of knowing its contents and we would be playing control-break roulette on the first record.

It is very important when a new division (or whatever the control-break field happens to be) is encountered that the new division number (or other contents of the control-break field) is moved to the hold area. Otherwise every record would be considered to be a new division (or control break). The reason is that we would be comparing each record's division number with the original contents of the hold area. Since the hold area was initialized to zero, every record would cause a control break. Failure to update the hold area would produce a report with only one detail line per page.

The process of saving the number as each new division is encountered can be shown with the data in Figure 6–3. The process is called updating the hold area. Figure 6–3 also shows the format of the data on the records and a printer layout of what the report is to look like. These records will be read and processed one at a time.

Let's follow the first few of these records through the flowchart in Figure 6–1; the comparing/updating process should become clear. The division hold area is initially set to zero. After the first record is read and it is determined that the END-FLAG is off, the contents of the division

MAINLINE LOGIC

PERFORM hsk routine
PERFORM process routine until end flag = on
PERFORM eoj routine

HSK ROUTINE

OPEN files
MOVE off to end flag
MOVE zero to division hold
PERFORM read routine

PROCESS ROUTINE

IF division not = division hold
        MOVE division to division hold
        EJECT to new page
ENDIF
MOVE input fields to output
WRITE a record (detail)
PERFORM read routine

EOJ ROUTINE

CLOSE files

READ ROUTINE

READ a record
        AT END of file
                MOVE on to end flag

FIGURE 6–2

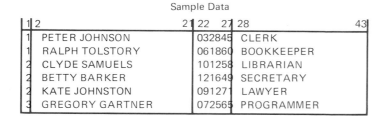

Sample Data

1|2		21|22 27|28	43|
1	PETER JOHNSON	032845	CLERK
1	RALPH TOLSTORY	061860	BOOKKEEPER
2	CLYDE SAMUELS	101258	LIBRARIAN
2	BETTY BARKER	121649	SECRETARY
2	KATE JOHNSTON	091271	LAWYER
3	GREGORY GARTNER	072565	PROGRAMMER

FIGURE 6–3

field in the record (division 1) is compared to the hold area. Since 1 is not equal to zero, a new division (control break) is indicated. Thus, the new division number is stored (moved) in the hold area and it is necessary to eject to a new page. The hold area now contains a 1. Next, the data from the record is moved to the print area and a line is written. Figure 6–4 shows the current contents of the hold area and the line of the report. After this the next record is read.

1	Hold area

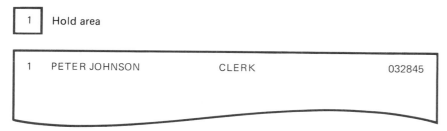

FIGURE 6–4

After reading the second record and finding END-FLAG still off, the contents of the division field in the record (also division 1) are compared to the hold area. Since 1 is equal to 1, the line is built and written and the next record is read. Figure 6–5 shows the current status of the hold area and the report.

1	Hold area

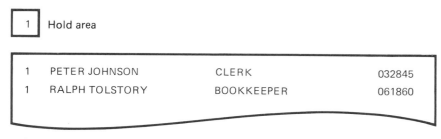

FIGURE 6–5

When the third record is read and found to be a data record, the contents of the division field in the record (division 2) are compared with the hold area. Since 2 is not equal to 1 (from the hold area), a new division has been encountered. This forces the new division number (2) to be stored in the hold area and the paper to be ejected to a new page. The data is then moved and printed, and the next record is read. The result is shown in Figure 6–6. The dashed line is used to indicate the top of a new page.

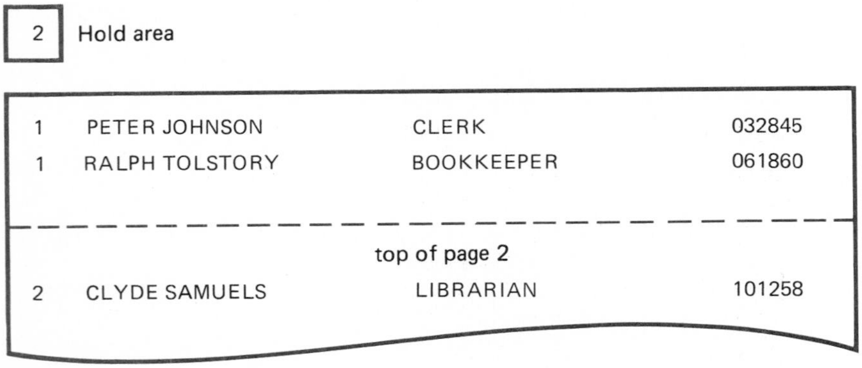

| 2 | Hold area |

1	PETER JOHNSON	CLERK	032845
1	RALPH TOLSTORY	BOOKKEEPER	061860
	top of page 2		
2	CLYDE SAMUELS	LIBRARIAN	101258

FIGURE 6–6

The process of comparing the contents of the control field in the current record with the hold area and moving the new division number to the hold area when one is encountered is a standard method of handling control breaks. It continues until the end-of-file is reached. At the end of the input file the END-FLAG is turned on. When the END-FLAG is again tested, it is found to be on, so we close the files and stop. The completed output for our example is shown in Figure 6–7. Notice that the contents of the hold area after the file has been closed is equal to the value in the control field from the last data record. In Chapter 7 this process will be expanded to cover multiple-level breaks, but the basics will not change.

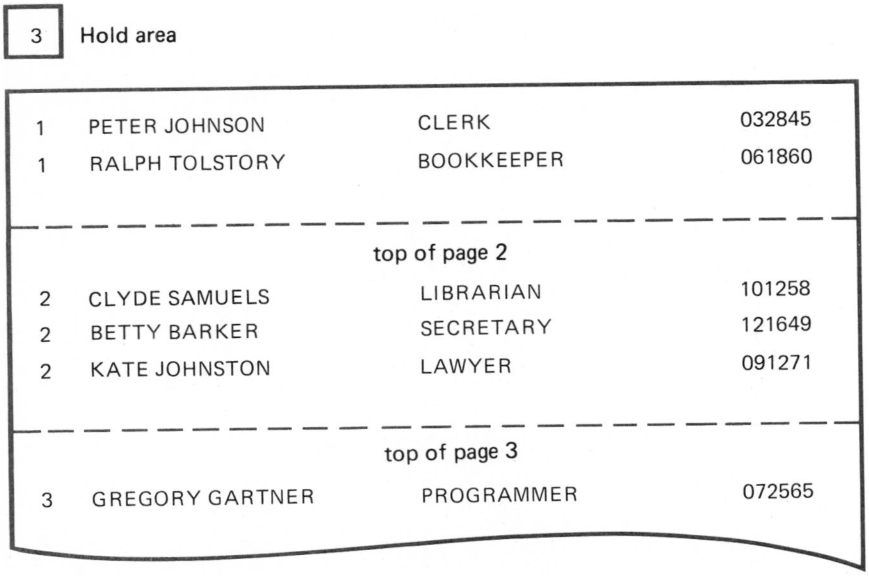

| 3 | Hold area |

1	PETER JOHNSON	CLERK	032845
1	RALPH TOLSTORY	BOOKKEEPER	061860
	top of page 2		
2	CLYDE SAMUELS	LIBRARIAN	101258
2	BETTY BARKER	SECRETARY	121649
2	KATE JOHNSTON	LAWYER	091271
	top of page 3		
3	GREGORY GARTNER	PROGRAMMER	072565

FIGURE 6–7

CONTROL-BREAK HEADINGS

Another item to be introduced into our problem is that of control-break headings. If a control break occurs (that is, a new division is encountered) a new set of headings usually needs to be printed to identify the new division. This may require that certain data in the headings be updated or changed to properly reflect the new division. Producing headings on a control break is in addition to the headings needed for forms overflow, which was discussed in Chapter 5.

For the purpose of discussion a flowchart will be developed to produce a divisional listing (that is, each new division will be started on a new page) of the data in an employee master file. The format for this report along with the input record layout and data in the file is shown in Figure 6–8.

```
1SANDRA ABBOTT       213746000081369SECRETARY      072135
1CINDY BABCOCK       420715250010147PROGRAMMER      111840
1THOMAS CONWICKE     394627250004277SALESMAN        021550
1JAMES DAVIDS        785258250009117SALESMAN        062542
1GRACE EVERETT       102747500011227SALESMAN        090451
1ED FRANKLIN         824438000003197SALESMAN        112748
1FRAN GAREIS         572244900006107MANAGER         021357
1WILSON PICKETT      683929800012286CLERK           102234
1SALLY SMITH         908745700006017CLERK           102356
2MARGE ISAACSON      423676500011226SECRETARY       052440
2SEAN JOHNSTON       387646540011046PROGRAMMER      032644
2CLAUDIA KENT        73215800005177SECRETARY        091966
2BILL LAWSON         275367400009077SALESMAN        111252
2DAN MEYER           589478100003187SALESMAN        120255
2HAWKEY MEYER        445659900012217MANAGER         102669
2ROBERTA NELSON      932717500010026SALESMAN        052554
2SUE OBRYCKI         607259000004157SALESMAN        080751
2TERRY PETERS        303418300006256SALESMAN        020642
2NAN RILEY           218967700012306ANALYST         102538
2CHARLES SMITH       621846800010137SALESMAN        083045
2SALLY THOMAS        154234800007107CLERK           111455
2JOE ULRICH          357924959504057CLERK           040754
2SANDOR VASQUEZ      575628900007137SALESMAN        051242
2DAVID WEISS         738368800011176MANAGER         072244
2THOMAS YOUNG        362439900009217SALESMAN        121539
```

DIVISION		EMPL NUMB	PAY RATE	START DATE			POSITION	BIRTH DATE			UNUSED
	EMPLOYEE NAME			MM	DD	YY		MM	DD	YY	

```
9 99999999999999 99999 99999 999 9999 9999999999999 99999999 9
1 2 3 4 5 6 7 8 9 10 11 12 13 14 15 16 17 18 19 20 21 22 23 24 25 26 27 28 29 30 31 32 33 34 35 36 37 38 39 40 41 42 43 44 45 46 47 48 49 50 51 52 53 80
```

PRINTER LAYOUT

```
            1111111111222222222233333333334444444444555555555566666666667
  1234567890123456789012345678901234567890123456789012345678901234567890
1
2                    EMPLOYEE LISTING
3
4                    DIVISION X
5
6              EMPL    PAY      START                        BIRTH
7 EMPLOYEE NAME NUMB   RATE     DATE          POSITION        DATE
8
9 X----------X XXXXX  XXX.XX  XX/XX/XX  X----------X  XX/XX/XX
10 X----------X XXXXX  XXX.XX  XX/XX/XX  X----------X  XX/XX/XX
11
12
```

FIGURE 6–8

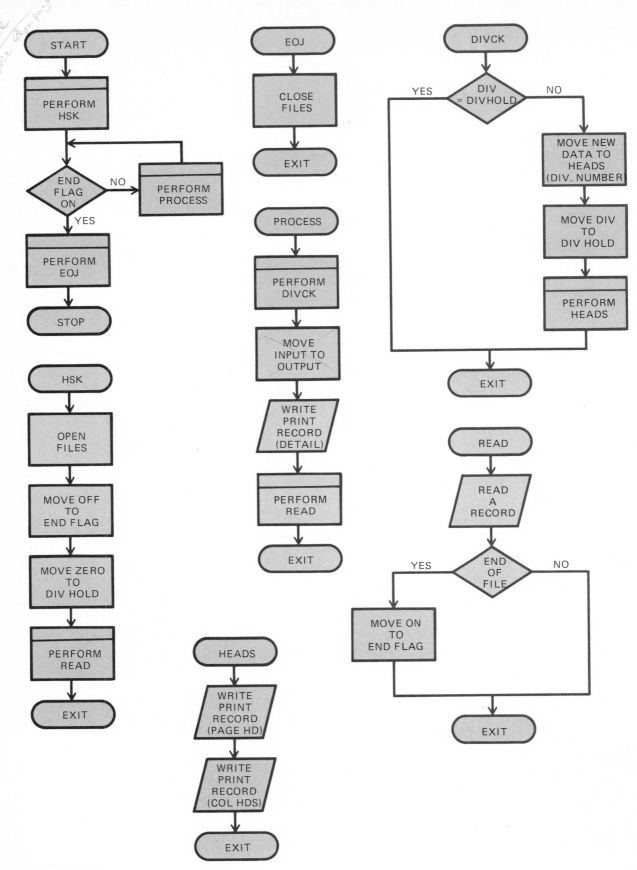

FIGURE 6–9

114   SINGLE-LEVEL CONTROL BREAKS

The actual flowchart for this expanded problem is shown in Figure 6–9. It incorporates new headings as each new division is encountered. Headings for an overflow condition are not included in this problem. The pseudocode is shown in Figure 6–10, and a segment of the output is shown in Figure 6–11.

MAINLINE LOGIC

PERFORM hsk routine
PERFORM process routine until end flag = on
PERFORM eoj routine

HSK ROUTINE

OPEN files
MOVE off to end flag
MOVE zero to division hold
PERFORM read routine

PROCESS ROUTINE

PERFORM divck routine
MOVE input fields to output
WRITE print record (detail)
PERFORM read routine

EOJ ROUTINE

CLOSE files

DIVCK ROUTINE

IF division not = division hold
        MOVE new data to headings (division number)
        MOVE division to division hold
        PERFORM heads routine
ENDIF

HEADS ROUTINE

WRITE print record (page heads)
WRITE print record (column heads)

READ ROUTINE

READ a record
        AT END of file
                MOVE on to end flag
FIGURE 6–10

EMPLOYEE LISTING
DIVISION 1

EMPLOYEE NAME	EMPL NUMB	PAY RATE	START DATE	POSITION	BIRTH DATE
SANDRA ABBOTT	21374	600.00	08-13-69	SECRETARY	07-21-35
CINDY BABCOCK	42071	525.00	10-14-70	PROGRAMMER	11-18-40
THOMAS CONWICKE	39462	725.00	04-27-73	SALESMAN	02-15-50
JAMES DAVIDS	78525	825.00	09-11-71	SALESMAN	06-25-42
GRACE EVERETT	10274	750.00	11-22-75	SALESMAN	09-04-51
ED FRANKLIN	82443	800.00	03-19-72	SALESMAN	11-27-48
FRAN GAREIS	57224	490.00	06-10-76	MANAGER	02-13-57
WILSON PICKETT	68392	980.00	12-28-64	CLERK	10-22-34
SALLY SMITH	90874	570.00	06-01-71	CLERK	10-23-56

EMPLOYEE LISTING
DIVISION 2

EMPLOYEE NAME	EMPL NUMB	PAY RATE	START DATE	POSITION	BIRTH DATE
MARGE ISAACSON	42367	650.00	11-22-63	SECRETARY	05-24-70
SEAN JOHNSTON	38764	654.00	11-04-67	PROGRAMMER	03-26-44
CLAUDIA KENT	73214	580.00	05-17-74	SECRETARY	09-19-66
BILL LAWSON	27536	740.00	09-07-73	SALESMAN	11-12-52
DAN MEYER	58947	810.00	03-18-77	SALESMAN	12-02-55
HAWKEY MEYER	44565	990.00	12-21-43	MANAGER	10-26-69
ROBERTA NELSON	93271	750.00	10-02-69	SALESMAN	05-25-54
SUE OBRYCKI	60725	900.00	04-15-74	SALESMAN	08-07-51
TERRY PETERS	30341	830.00	06-25-66	SALESMAN	02-06-42
NAN RILEY	21896	770.00	12-30-62	ANALYST	10-25-38
CHARLES SMITH	62184	680.00	10-13-71	SALESMAN	08-30-45
SALLY THOMAS	15423	480.00	07-10-75	CLERK	11-14-55
JOE UHLRICH	35792	495.95	04-05-74	CLERK	04-07-54
SANDOR VASQUEZ	57562	890.00	07-13-70	SALESMAN	05-12-42
DAVID WEISS	73836	880.00	11-17-68	MANAGER	07-22-44
THOMAS YOUNG	36243	990.00	09-21-71	SALESMAN	12-15-39

FIGURE 6–11

Like previous flowcharts, the flowchart in Figure 6–9 has the logic in separate subroutines, one of which is called PROCESS. PROCESS is in fact a subroutine, which is performed as long as END-FLAG remains off. END-FLAG will continue to be off until an end-of-file condition is encountered. The HEADS routine also is a subroutine, which is performed as needed as a part of the DIVCK subroutine. When a subroutine is performed within a subroutine that is itself being performed, it is said to be nested.

The hold area for division was set to zero in the HOUSEKEEPING routine. This was done to set it up for control-break testing. As each new division is encountered, this hold area is updated to reflect the new division number (MOVE DIV TO DIV HOLD). When a new division is encountered, the heading information is also updated (MOVE NEW DATA TO HEADS) to reflect the new divisional information. Notice in Figure 6–11 that as a control break (page 1 to page 2) occurred, headings were printed at the top of the new page. The headings were also altered to reflect the new division.

For comparison purposes the COBOL and BASIC versions are shown in Figures 6–12 and 6–13, respectively.

COBOL VERSION:

PROCEDURE DIVISION.

MAINLINE-LOGIC.

PERFORM HSK-ROUTINE.
PERFORM PROCESS-ROUTINE UNTIL END-FLAG = 'ON'.
PERFORM EOJ-ROUTINE.
STOP RUN.

HSK-ROUTINE.

OPEN INPUT EMP-MASTER
    OUTPUT EMP-LISTING.
MOVE 'OFF'   TO END-FLAG.
MOVE ZERO   TO DIV-HOLD.
MOVE ZERO   TO LINE-COUNT.
PERFORM READ-ROUTINE.

PROCESS-ROUTINE.

PERFORM DIVCK-ROUTINE.
MOVE NAME-IN   TO NAME-PRINT.
MOVE EMP-NUMB-IN   TO EMP-NUMB-PRINT.
MOVE PAY-RATE-IN   TO PAY-RATE-PRINT.
MOVE S-DATE-IN   TO S-DATE-PRINT.
MOVE POSITION-IN   TO POSITION-PRINT.
MOVE BIRTH-DATE-IN   TO BIRTH-DATE-PRINT.
WRITE PRINT-RECORD FROM DETAIL-LINE
    AFTER ADVANCING 1 LINES.
PERFORM READ-ROUTINE.

EOJ-ROUTINE.

CLOSE EMP-MASTER
    EMP-LISTING.

DIVCK-ROUTINE.

IF DIVISION-IN IS NOT = DIV-HOLD
    MOVE DIVISION-IN   TO DIV-HEAD2
    MOVE DIVISION-IN   TO DIV-HOLD
    PERFORM HEADS-ROUTINE.

HEADS-ROUTINE.

WRITE PRINT-RECORD FROM HEAD-1 AFTER ADVANCING
    PAGE.
WRITE PRINT-RECORD FROM HEAD-2 AFTER ADVANCING
    2 LINES.
WRITE PRINT-RECORD FROM COL-HD-1 AFTER ADVANCING
    2 LINES.
WRITE PRINT-RECORD FROM COL-HD-2 AFTER ADVANCING
    1 LINES.
WRITE PRINT-RECORD FROM BLANK-LINE AFTER ADVANCING
    1 LINES.

READ-ROUTINE.

READ EMP-MASTER
    AT END MOVE 'ON' TO END-FLAG.

FIGURE 6–12

BASIC VERSION:

```
'PROGRAMMERS: J AND J, INC.
'DATE: 10/11/89
'PROGRAM NAME: CASE 6
'********************************************************************************
'*                          MAINLINE LOGIC                                     *
'********************************************************************************
MAINLINE.LOGIC:
GOSUB HOUSEKEEPING.ROUTINE
WHILE END.FLAG$ = "OFF"
   GOSUB PROCESS.ROUTINE
WEND
GOSUB EOJ.ROUTINE
END
'********************************************************************************
'*                          HOUSEKEEPING ROUTINE                               *
'********************************************************************************
HOUSEKEEPING.ROUTINE:
OPEN "A:C6B1DATA" FOR INPUT AS #1
LET END.FLAG$ = "OFF"
LET DIVISION.HOLD = 0
LET LINE.COUNT = 0
D$ = "SCRN:":CLS
INPUT "OUTPUT TO THE PRINTER - ANSWER Y OR N";ANSWER$
IF ANSWER$ = "Y" OR ANSWER$ = "y" THEN
   D$ = "LPT1:"
END IF
OPEN D$ FOR OUTPUT AS #2
GOSUB READ.ROUTINE
RETURN
'********************************************************************************
'*                          PROCESS ROUTINE                                    *
'********************************************************************************
PROCESS.ROUTINE:
GOSUB DIVISION.CHECK.ROUTINE
LET F$ = "\             \" + SPACE$(2) + "#####" + SPACE$(2) + "###.##"
   + SPACE$(2) + "&-&-&" + SPACE$(1) + "\          \" + SPACE$(1) + "&-&-&"
PRINT #2,USING   F$;  NAMES$,   NUMBER,   PAY.RATE,   MID$(START.DATE$,1,2),
   MID$(START.DATE$,3,2)    ,          MID$(START.DATE$,5,2)    ,          POSITION$,
   MID$(BIRTH.DATE$,1,2) , MID$(BIRTH.DATE$,3,2) , MID$(BIRTH.DATE$,5,2)
LET LINE.COUNT = LINE.COUNT + 1
GOSUB READ.ROUTINE
RETURN
'********************************************************************************
'*                          EOJ ROUTINE                                        *
'********************************************************************************
EOJ.ROUTINE:
CLOSE #1,#2
RETURN
'********************************************************************************
'*                          DIVISION CHECK ROUTINE                             *
'********************************************************************************
DIVISION.CHECK.ROUTINE:
IF DIVISION <> DIVISION.HOLD THEN
   LET DIVISION.HOLD = DIVISION:
   GOSUB HEADS.ROUTINE
ELSE
   GOSUB LINECHECK.ROUTINE
```

FIGURE 6–13

```
END IF
RETURN
'*******************************************************************************
'*                          LINECHECK ROUTINE                                 *
'*******************************************************************************
LINECHECK.ROUTINE:
IF LINE.COUNT > 11  THEN
    GOSUB HEADS.ROUTINE
END IF
RETURN
'*******************************************************************************
'*                          HEADS ROUTINE                                     *
'*******************************************************************************
HEADS.ROUTINE:
PRINT #2,CHR$(12)
PRINT #2,SPC(24);"EMPLOYEE LISTING ": PRINT #2,
PRINT #2,SPC(27); "DIVISION "; DIVISION: PRINT #2,
PRINT #2,SPC(17); "EMPL     PAY      START";SPC(19);"BIRTH"
PRINT #2,"EMPLOYEE NAME    NUMB   RATE    DATE      POSITION      DATE"
PRINT #2,
LET LINE.COUNT = 0
RETURN
'*******************************************************************************
'*                          READ ROUTINE                                      *
'*******************************************************************************
READ.ROUTINE:
IF EOF(1) THEN
    END.FLAG$ = "ON"
ELSE
    INPUT #1,  DIVISION,  NAMES$,  NUMBER,  PAY.RATE,  START.DATE$,  POSITION$,
        BIRTH.DATE$
END IF
RETURN
```

FIGURE 6–13 (continued)

PROGRESSIVE AND END-OF-JOB TOTALS

Progressive totals are totals which are incremented but never reset to zero. This type of total may be printed at various places throughout the report or only at the end of the report. One very standard type of progressive total is a record count. It can be used to indicate the number of records processed. A record count can be produced either as a new file is being created or as an existing file is being read. It can also be recorded at the end of the file in a special record-count record if it is for a file that is being created. The record count may also be printed out at the end of the report as a form of control total. The process of producing a record count and creating a record-count record is flowcharted in Figure 6–14. The pseudocode is shown in Figure 6–15. The record count could just as easily have been printed at the end of the report, with or without the record-count record being created. Notice that the record counter was set to zero at the beginning of the program in the HSK routine. This is a type of progressive total that is only printed (or written to the output file being created) at the end of job.

Another very common type of progressive total is a page counter. Most reports have their pages numbered from 1 to n with n being the number of the last page. The page counter is typically set to zero in the housekeeping routine and incremented in the heading routine. From previous material you will remember an operation that moved data to the headings. One of the actions needed to update the headings is to increment the page counter. The logic for this

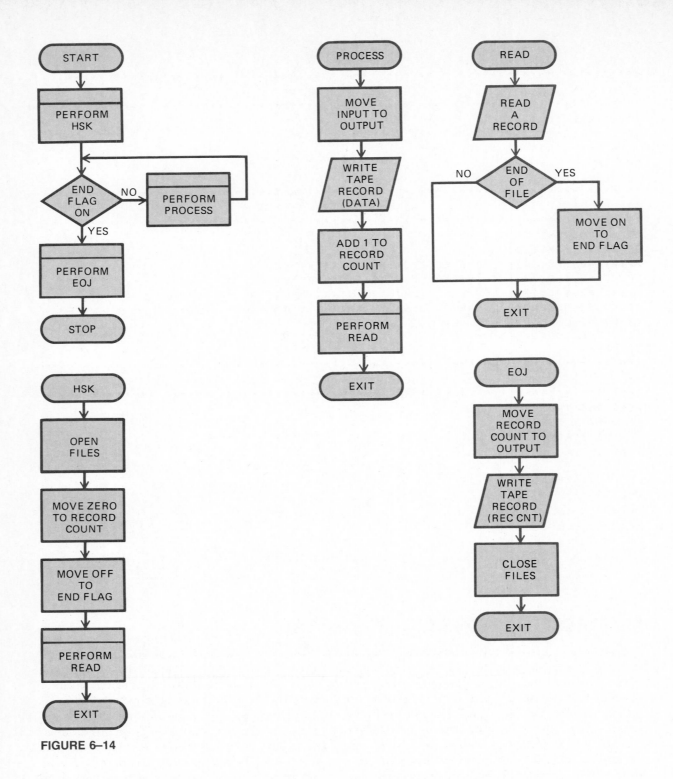

FIGURE 6–14

from the HEADS routine is shown in Figure 6–16. The pseudocode is shown in Figure 6–17. Page count is a type of progressive total that is printed out at given intervals during the processing (that is, at the top of each new page).

Progressive totals are not limited to record counts and page numbers. Let's take a look at a program which processes a payroll summary file. At the end of the report a separate page will be produced showing the totals for the entire company. No more than 50 detail lines will be printed on a single page. Figure 6–18 shows the format of the records in the payroll summary file and a printer layout of the report to be produced. The asterisks indicate fields for which

MAINLINE ROUTINE

PERFORM hsk routine
PERFORM process routine until end flag = on
PERFORM eoj routine
STOP

HSK ROUTINE

OPEN files
MOVE zero to record count
MOVE off to end flag
PERFORM read routine

PROCESS ROUTINE

MOVE input to output
WRITE tape record (data)
ADD 1 to record count
PERFORM read routine

EOJ ROUTINE

MOVE record count to output
WRITE tape record (record count)
CLOSE files

READ ROUTINE

READ a record
AT END of file
MOVE on to end flag

FIGURE 6–15

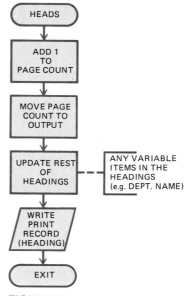

FIGURE 6–16

HEADS ROUTINE

ADD 1 to page count
MOVE page count to output
MOVE other new data to headings (e.g., department name)
WRITE print record (heads)

FIGURE 6–17

RECORD CODE EMPLOYEE NUMBER	GROSS PAY *	FED. TAX *	STATE TAX *	FICA *	CREDIT UNION *	HOSP INS. *	NET PAY *	DIVISION DEPARTMENT	UNUSED

```
9 9 9 9 9 9 9 9 9 9 9 9 9 9 9 9 9 9 9 9 9 9 9 9 9 9 9 9 9 9 9 9 9 9 9 9 9 9 9 9 9 9 9 9 9 9 9 9 9 9 9 9 9 9 9 9 9 9 9 9 9 9 9 9   9 9 9 9 9
1 2 3 4 5 6 7 8 9 10 11 12 13 14 15 16 17 18 19 20 21 22 23 24 25 26 27 28 29 30 31 32 33 34 35 36 37 38 39 40 41 42 43 44 45 46 47 48 49 50 51 52 53 54 55 56 57 58 59 60 61 62 63 64   75 76 77 78 79 80
```

PRINTER LAYOUT

```
         111111111122222222223333333333444444444455555555556666666666777777777788888888889
1234567890123456789012345678901234567890123456789012345678901234567890123456789012345678901234567890
1
2                PAYROLL  SUMMARY  REPORT
3
4                         DIVISION X                                  PAGE XXX
5
6        EMPLOYEE      GROSS        FED        STATE              CREDIT      HOSP         NET
7  DEPT    NUMBER       PAY         TAX         TAX        FICA    UNION       INS         PAY
8
9     X   XXX-XX-XXXX  XXXX.XX    XXXX.XX    XXX.XX     XXX.XX   XXX.XX     XXX.XX     XXXX.XX
10    X   XXX-XX-XXXX  XXXX.XX    XXXX.XX    XXX.XX     XXX.XX   XXX.XX     XXX.XX     XXXX.XX
11
12
13                PAYROLL  SUMMARY  TOTALS
14
15               GROSS  PAY        XXX,XXX.XX
16               FEDERAL  TAX      XXX,XXX.XX
17               STATE  TAX         XX,XXX.XX
18               FICA               XX,XXX.XX
19               CREDIT  UNION      XX,XXX.XX
20               HOSPITAL  INSURANCE XX,XXX.XX
21               NET  PAY          XXX,XXX.XX
22
```

FIGURE 6–18

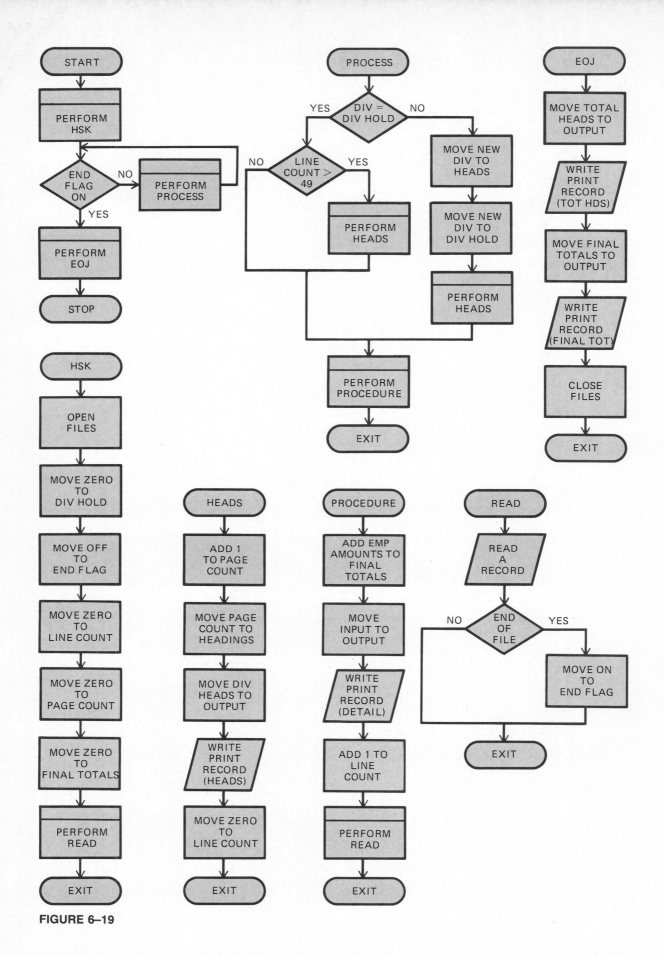

FIGURE 6–19

totals are to be accumulated. Figure 6–19 shows the logic necessary to produce the report and Figure 6–20 is the corresponding pseudocode. The totals are accumulated in the PROCEDURE routine at the same time that the data is being moved to the output record area. The actual printing of the totals is done in the EOJ routine. It is important to note that none of these totals was ever reset to zero anytime after being initialized to zero in the HSK routine.

MAINLINE LOGIC

```
PERFORM hsk routine
PERFORM process routine until end flag = on
PERFORM eoj routine
STOP
```

HSK ROUTINE

```
OPEN files
MOVE zero to division hold
MOVE off to end flag
MOVE zero to line count
MOVE zero to page count
MOVE zero to final totals
PERFORM read routine
```

PROCESS ROUTINE

```
IF division = division hold
      IF line count > 49
            PERFORM heads routine
      ENDIF
ELSE
      MOVE new data to heads (division number)
      MOVE new division to division hold
      PERFORM heads routine
ENDIF
PERFORM procedure routine
```

EOJ ROUTINE

```
MOVE total heads to output
WRITE print record (total heads)
MOVE final totals to output
WRITE print record (final totals)
CLOSE files
```

HEADS ROUTINE

```
ADD 1 to page count
MOVE page count to headings
MOVE division headings to output
WRITE print record (heads)
MOVE zero to line count
```

PROCEDURE ROUTINE

```
ADD employee amounts to final totals
MOVE input to output
WRITE input record (detail)
ADD 1 to line count
PERFORM read routine
```

FIGURE 6–20

CONTROL-BREAK TOTALS

It is also quite common to produce totals at the time that a control break occurs. This means that when a new group is encountered it is necessary to print a total for the group that just ended before starting a new group. This type of single-level total is called a **control-break total.** It requires the total area to be reset to zero each time a control break occurs, after printing the total for the group that just ended. If the total were not reset to zero after being printed then the total would become cumulative until the end-of-file condition was reached. In order to discuss this type of total let's switch our problem around a little and produce the listing by division, with the totals of the deductions being printed at the end of each division. The accumulation of the total still takes place as each record is processed, but the printing of the total takes place when there is a change in division. There will be no final totals produced at this time and there will be no more than 50 detail lines (not including totals) per page. Figure 6–21 shows the record layout and printer layout for the problem. Figure 6–22 is the flowchart of the logic for this problem and Figure 6–23 is the pseudocode for this logic. Totals are being kept for the fields indicated by the asterisk in Figure 6–21.

Notice in Figure 6–22 that the TOTALS routine is done as each new division (DIV) is encountered and also at the end of job. The end-of-job execution of the TOTALS routine is necessary to obtain the totals for the last division. When the end-of-file indicator has been read, there is no opportunity to test for a new division, because the YES branch was taken to terminate processing. Therefore the totals routine needs to be included for the last division in the EOJ routine before the files are closed and processing is terminated.

There is still one problem present in the flowchart. What happens when the first record is read? Following it through the flowchart, a new division is found and therefore the totals are to be printed for the previous division. Whoops—there is no previous division. While there are several ways out of this dilemma, a very common method is the use of first-record switch to prevent totals on the first record read. This would change our TOTALS routine flowchart, as shown in Figure 6–24. The pseudocode is shown in Figure 6–25.

Now when the TOTALS routine is executed on the first record, it will find that the first-record switch is on, and instead of printing totals it will turn off the first-record switch and exit the routine. Now, you ask, just where did this switch get turned on? It was turned on in a portion of the housekeeping routine at the same point that we opened the files. The segment of the housekeeping routine in Figure 6–26 shows this being done.

Another method of preventing a set of totals from printing before the first set of headings is to set the line count to a value high enough to force heads and update the hold area in the HSK routine after reading the first record. The logic and pseudocode for the routines that are affected by this method is shown in Figure 6–27.

RECORD CODE		GROSS PAY *	FED. TAX *	STATE TAX *	FICA *	CREDIT UNION *	HOSP. INS. *	NET PAY *	DIVISION			
	EMPLOYEE NUMBER									DEPARTMENT		
											REGION	
												UNUSED

FIGURE 6–21

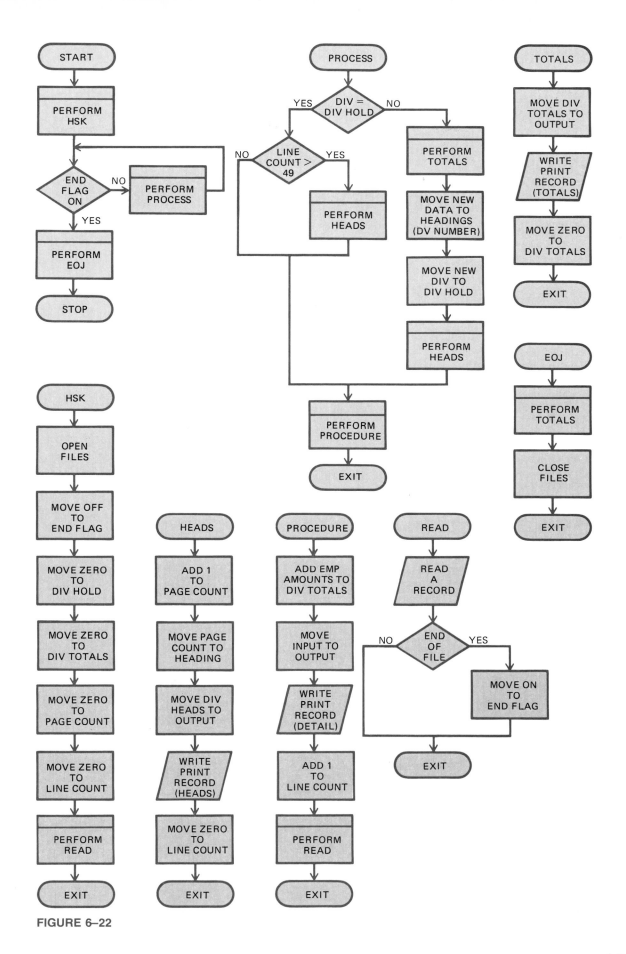

FIGURE 6–22

MAINLINE LOGIC

PERFORM hsk routine
PERFORM process routine until end flag = on
PERFORM eoj routine
STOP

HSK ROUTINE

OPEN files
MOVE off to end flag
MOVE zero to division hold
MOVE zero to division totals
MOVE zero to page count
MOVE zero to line count
PERFORM read routine

PROCESS ROUTINE

IF division = division hold
    IF line count > 49
        PERFORM heads routine
    ENDIF
ELSE
    PERFORM totals routine
    MOVE new data to headings (division number)
    MOVE new division to division hold
    PERFORM heads routine
ENDIF
PERFORM procedure routine

EOJ ROUTINE

PERFORM totals routine
CLOSE files

PROCEDURE ROUTINE

ADD employee amounts to division totals (fields with * in Figure 6–21)
MOVE input to output
WRITE print record (detail)
ADD 1 to line count
PERFORM read routine

TOTALS ROUTINE

MOVE division totals to output
WRITE print record (division totals)
MOVE zeros to division totals

HEADS ROUTINE

ADD 1 to page count
MOVE page count to headings
MOVE division headings to output
WRITE print record (headings)
MOVE zero to line count

READ ROUTINE

READ a record
    AT END of file
        MOVE on to end flag

FIGURE 6–23

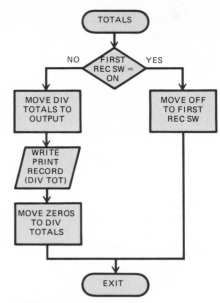

FIGURE 6–24

TOTALS ROUTINE

IF first-record switch = on
    MOVE off to first-record switch
ELSE
    MOVE division totals to output
    WRITE print record (division totals)
    MOVE zeros to division totals
ENDIF

FIGURE 6–25

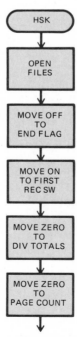

FIGURE 6–26

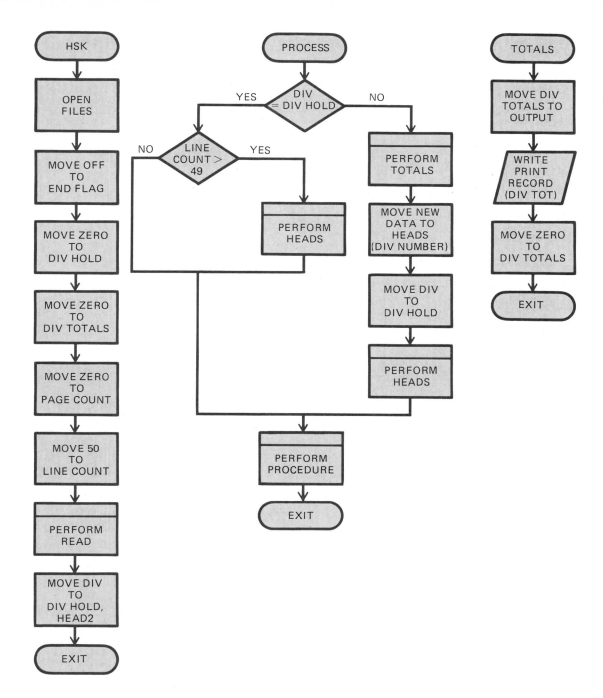

MAINLINE LOGIC

PERFORM hsk routine
PERFORM process routine until end flag = on
PERFORM eoj routine
STOP

HSK ROUTINE

OPEN files
MOVE off to end flag
MOVE zero to division hold
MOVE zero to division totals
MOVE zero to page count
MOVE 50 to line count

FIGURE 6–27

PERFORM read routine
MOVE division to division hold

PROCESS ROUTINE

```
IF division = to division hold
        IF line count > 49
                PERFORM heads routine
        ENDIF
ELSE
        PERFORM totals routine
        MOVE new data to headings (division number)
        MOVE new division to division hold
        PERFORM heads routine
ENDIF
PERFORM procedure routine
```

TOTALS ROUTINE

```
MOVE division totals to output
WRITE print record (division totals)
MOVE zeros to division totals
```

FIGURE 6–27 (continued)

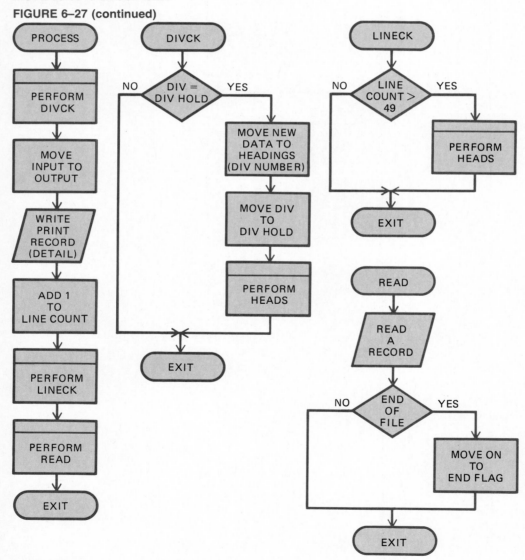

FIGURE 6–28

There is one point that needs to be emphasized. Suppose the test for line count came after building and writing a line and incrementing the line counter (as shown in Figure 6–28). The pseudocode is shown in Figure 6–29. The effect of this is to put the check for forms overflow before the check for a new division. What would happen if we had forms overflow occurring just before a control break?

PROCESS ROUTINE

PERFORM divck routine
MOVE input fields to output
WRITE print record (detail)
ADD 1 to line count
PERFORM lineck
PERFORM read routine

DIVCK ROUTINE

IF division not = division hold
    MOVE new data to headings (division number)
    MOVE division to division hold
    PERFORM heads routine
ENDIF

LINECK ROUTINE

IF line count > 49
    PERFORM heads routine
ENDIF

READ ROUTINE

READ a record
    AT END of file
        MOVE on to end flag

FIGURE 6–29

Suppose that the two records shown in Figure 6–30 are the 50th and 51st records to be processed. As record number 50 (the last record in division 1) is read, a check is made to see whether it is a new division; it is not. Therefore the information from record 50 is read and printed and add 1 is added to the line counter. Next, LINE COUNT is checked to see if it is greater than 49. The value in LINE COUNT is now 50, so the paper is ejected to a new page, the headings are printed, the line counter is reset to zero, and the next record is read.

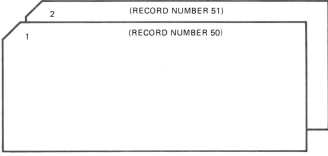

FIGURE 6–30

When record number 51 is read (the first record in division 2), a check is made to see if it is a new division. It is, so the headings are updated, the hold area is updated, the paper is ejected to a new page, new heads are printed, and processing continues with moving and printing the data from record number 51. There is now an extra, and useless, set of headings for division 1. This is why it is usually better to check for overflow before building and printing a detail line.

Chapter 7 will introduce the concepts of rolling totals and producing various levels of control-break totals. Headings on the various levels of breaks will also be presented.

CHAPTER VOCABULARY

Control breaks
Control-break headings
Control-break totals

End-of-job totals
First-record switch

Hold area
Progressive totals

REVIEW QUESTIONS

MATCHING

Control break
End-of-job total
First-record switch

Hold area
Progressive total

1st-record switch **1.** A storage area whose contents determine whether control-break totals are to be printed and thereby prevent totals from printing prior to the first group.

Control break **2.** A method of breaking reports down into smaller units to make the data more meaningful.

Progressive totals **3.** Totals which are incremented but never reset to zero.

EOJ totals **4.** Totals which are only printed after all of the data has been processed.

Hold area **5.** A storage area which facilitates comparing a value in the current record being processed with a value in the previous record processed.

TRUE/FALSE

T **(F)** **1.** Once initialized in housekeeping the control-break hold area is not altered until entering the end-of-job routine.

T **(F)** **2.** Progressive totals are never printed until all of the data has been processed.

(T) F **3.** A first-record switch is initialized in housekeeping.

(T) F **4.** Headings are normally produced on both forms-overflow and control breaks.

(T) F **5.** Control-break totals are printed as a part of the end-of-job routine.

(T) F **6.** There are several ways to avoid totals printing prior to the first group on a report.

T **(F)** **7.** End-of-job totals are accumulated in the housekeeping routine.

T **(F)** **8.** First record switches are used to determine whether end-of-job totals should be printed after all of the data has been processed.

EXERCISES

1. Draw a flowchart to produce a departmentalized listing of the records in a file. The file is in sequence by department. The pages should be numbered sequentially for each department with each department starting at page 1. Each new department should start on a new page. The department name and number should appear in the headings but not in the columns.

2. Draw a flowchart to read and print the contents of the records in a file. At the end of the report print the total number of records read as well as the total sales for the period (sales is one of the fields on each record).

3. Same as exercise number 2 except print the totals at the end of each division. The file is in sequence by division.

DISCUSSION QUESTIONS

1. Describe what control breaks are and indicate their usefulness.
2. Describe the use of a control-break hold area including when to initialize and update its contents.
3. Describe the use of a first-record switch and indicate other methods of accomplishing the same result.
4. Differentiate between control-break, end-of-job and progressive totals.
5. Describe when and how headings are produced.

PROJECTS

Project 1

Draw a flowchart for the following specifications.

INPUT

SALESMAN ACTIVITY FILE

    01–05   Salesman number
    06–07   Region number
    08–09   Division number
    10–16   Sales amount
    17–21   Product number
    22–45   Salesman name

The file is in sequence by region number. All of the data has been previously edited so that the errors have been removed. There is only one record for any given salesman.

PROCESSING

Produce a listing by region of the sales data. All input fields should be included on the output.

OUTPUT

Produce a regional list from the data in the salesman activity file.

1. All of the input fields except region number should be included on the output.
2. Double space the detail lines.
3. No more than 50 detail lines should be on a page.
4. The current data should be included in the headings.
5. Page and column heads should be provided.
6. The region number should be included in the heads and not in the columns.
7. There are 132 print spaces available.

Project 2

Draw a flowchart for the following specifications.

INPUT

Same as project 1

PROCESSING

Produce a regional listing of the data in the salesman activity file. The total sales for a region should be printed at the end of each region. All of the data has been edited to remove errors. There is only one record for any given salesman.

OUTPUT

Same as project 1 with the following additions.

1. Regional totals should be printed at the end of each region.
2. Double space before printing the regional total.
3. The twenty lines per page should include the regional totals.

7

MULTIPLE LEVEL CONTROL BREAKS AND TOTALS

OBJECTIVES

As a result of studying this chapter the student should be able to perform the following activities:

1. Describe what it means to roll totals, and show how this is accomplished.
2. Describe multiple-level control breaks.
3. Describe the difference between single- and multiple-level control breaks and control-break totals.
4. Describe the difference between minor-, intermediate-, and major-level breaks, including the order in which they should be checked.
5. Describe how a first-record switch or indicator is used in conjunction with control-break totals.

6. Describe what is meant by higher-level breaks always forcing all lower-level breaks.
7. Describe an alternative method, other than the use of a first-record switch, for preventing totals from printing prior to the first group on a report.
8. Describe the importance of performing the BREAK routine as a part of the EOJ routine.
9. Indicate what actions are performed on each level of break for a situation where there are three or more levels of control breaks.

INTRODUCTION

It is very common for a program to have provisions for multiple levels of control breaks. In talking about the various levels of control breaks there is a tendency to simply produce a list of items (such as hold-area processing, rolling totals, producing headings, and the sequence in which control breaks should be checked) which must be done. Such a list is to a certain extent unavoidable, but it is important to understand the whys that exist behind the lists in order to be able to produce efficient programs that are structured in their approach.

ROLLING TOTALS

The next topic to be considered is that of handling totals when there is more than one level of total being produced. An easy way of doing this is to deal with accumulating a final total with only one level of control break present in the problem. This process incorporates the concept of rolling totals at the time of a control break. To illustrate this concept let's return to the example where totals were being produced for each division. This time, however, there will also be a final total generated. Figure 7–1 contains the logic for this process. The pseudocode is shown in Figure 7–2.

Notice in the BREAK routine that after the division totals have been moved and printed, they are added to the final totals, thus rolling the division totals into the final totals. **Rolling totals** is adding the total(s) at one level of break to a higher level break total or to a final total.

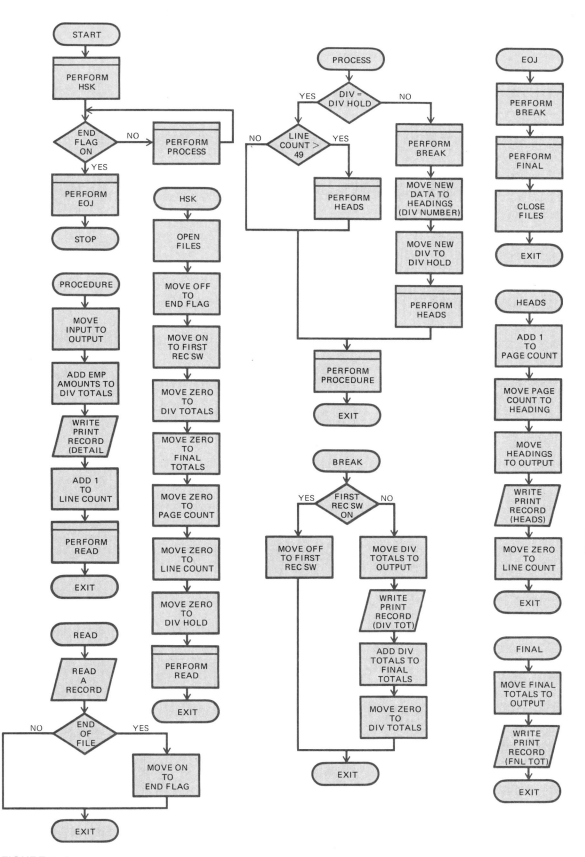

FIGURE 7–1

MAINLINE LOGIC

PERFORM hsk routine
PERFORM process routine until end-flag = on
PERFORM eoj routine
STOP

HSK ROUTINE

OPEN files
MOVE off to end-flag
MOVE on to first-record switch
MOVE zero to division totals
MOVE zero to final totals
MOVE zero to page count
MOVE zero to line count
MOVE zero to division hold
PERFORM read routine

PROCESS ROUTINE

IF division = to division hold
    IF line count > 49
       PERFORM heads routine
    ENDIF
ELSE
    PERFORM break routine
    MOVE new data to headings (division number)
    MOVE new division to division hold
    PERFORM heads routine
ENDIF
PERFORM procedure routine

EOJ ROUTINE

PERFORM break routine
PERFORM final routine
CLOSE files

BREAK ROUTINE

IF first record switch = on
    MOVE off to first-record switch
ELSE
    MOVE division totals to output
    WRITE print record (division totals)
    ADD division totals to final totals
    MOVE zeros to division totals
ENDIF

PROCEDURE ROUTINE

MOVE input to output
ADD employee amounts to division totals
WRITE print record (detail)
    ADD 1 to line count
PERFORM read routine

HEADS ROUTINE

ADD 1 to page count
MOVE page count to heading
MOVE headings to output
WRITE print records (heads)
MOVE zero to line count

FIGURE 7–2

MOVE final totals to output
WRITE print record (final totals)

READ ROUTINE

READ a record
    AT END of file
        MOVE on to end-flag

FIGURE 7–2 (continued)

After being added to the final totals, the division totals are set to zero to prepare for the totals for the next division. It is very important to notice that when the end of the input file is reached, the BREAK routine is invoked in the EOJ routine in order to print the totals for the last group and add them to the final totals. Without performing the BREAK routine at this point the totals for the last group would be missing. We could, however, have done this differently by placing BREAK routine in the FINAL routine (see Figure 7–3). The difference between the two approaches is not as important as realizing what needs to be accomplished.

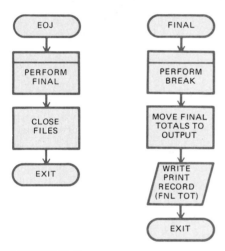

FIGURE 7–3

MULTIPLE-LEVEL CONTROL BREAKS/TOTALS

Up to now only single level control breaks/totals have been discussed. These are control breaks/totals where the contents of a single control field are checked for a change in value. It is possible to have multiple control fields, the contents of which are being checked for a change in value, and therefore have multiple levels of control breaks/totals. The various types of control breaks/totals can be grouped into three categories: major, intermediate, and minor-level control breaks/totals. Final (or grand) totals are not included in these three categories. Final totals are not a type of control-break total.

    If only one control-break field is present then only one type of control-break total is being produced (let's say division totals). When this is true then the totals are referred to as major-level totals or major break totals. If two levels of control-break fields exist and two levels of totals are being produced, such as department totals within division totals, then the one that happens the most often (department totals in our example) is the minor-break total and the one that occurs least often (division totals) is the major-break total. With three levels of control-break fields and three levels of totals, the most frequent is the minor-break total, the least frequent is the major-break total, and the one in the middle is the intermediate-break total. Four or more levels of control-break fields and four or more levels of totals produce multiple intermediate-level totals, such as intermediate-1, intermediate-2, intermediate-3. When there is more than one level of intermediate-level break the lower the number on the break the higher the level. That is intermediate-2 is a higher level break than intermediate-3.

To check for control breaks when there are multiple levels of breaks present it is most efficient to check first for the highest-level break (major) and work down to the lowest-level break (minor). The reason for this is that a break on any level (except minor) always forces a break to occur for all lower-level control fields. In our example this means that when a change in division occurs, there is also a change in department. It is very likely that the new division is going to start on a new page, however before that is done, both the department totals and division totals need to be produced for the department and division that just ended.

If we have a problem which has all three levels of totals (major, intermediate, and minor) as well as final (grand) totals, the logic is merely expanded. The following items are normally performed on each level of break.

MINOR-LEVEL BREAK
1. Move and print minor-level totals.
2. Accumulate (roll) minor-level totals to intermediate- (or next higher) level totals.
3. Zero out minor-level totals in order to allow accumulation of the next minor-level group.
4. Update the minor-level control break hold area.

INTERMEDIATE-LEVEL BREAK
1. Perform minor-level (or next lower intermediate-level) break.
2. Move and print intermediate-level totals.
3. Accumulate (roll) intermediate-level totals to major-level (or next higher intermediate-level) totals.
4. Zero out intermediate-level totals in order to allow accumulation of the next intermediate-level group.
5. Update intermediate-level control break hold area.

MAJOR-LEVEL BREAK
1. Perform intermediate-level (or next lower level) break.
2. Move and print major-level totals.
3. Accumulate (roll) major-level totals to final or grand totals (if final totals are called for in the problem).
4. Zero out major-level totals in order to allow accumulation of the next major-level group.
5. Update the major-level control break hold area.

In order to be able to discuss this let's expand a previous example so that there are several regions, each of which contains several divisions, each of which contains several departments. A listing is to be produced of the employee data in such a way that there will be totals generated for each department within a division, for each division within a region, and for each region. There will also be final totals at the end of the report. The input record format and printer layout are as shown in Figure 7–4. The details of this logic are shown in Figure 7–5, and the pseudocode is shown in Figure 7–6.

Notice that the routine performed on each level of break first performs the routine for the next lower-level break. That is, if a major-break (change in region) occurs, the major-break routine (called MAJOR) performs the intermediate-level break routine (called INTER) for an implied change in division. The intermediate-level break routine in turn performs the minor-level break routine (called MINOR) for an implied change in the department. This is the process by which lower-level breaks are forced by higher-level breaks.

At the end of job the FINAL routine is performed. The first step in the FINAL routine is to perform a major-break. After all the minor-, intermediate-, and major-level totals have been processed, the final totals are moved and printed, and processing is terminated.

If multiple intermediate-level breaks are present, the process is simply expanded to handle more levels of totals. The steps would be the same as already exist for intermediate-level breaks.

RECORD CODE | EMPLOYEE NUMBER | GROSS PAY * | FED. TAX * | STATE TAX * | FICA * | CREDIT UNION * | HOSP. INS. * | NET PAY * | DIVISION / DEPARTMENT / REGION / UNUSED

```
PAYROLL  SUMMARY  REPORT

REGION - X        DIVISION - X         DEPARTMENT - X              PAGE XXX

EMPLOYEE     GROSS      FED        STATE               CREDIT    HOSP      NET
NUMBER       PAY        TAX         TAX      FICA       UNION     INS       PAY

XXX-XX-XXXX  XXXX.XX  XXXX.XX  XXX.XX  XXX.XX  XXX.XX  XXX.XX  XXX.XX
XXX-XX-XXXX  XXXX.XX  XXXX.XX  XXX.XX  XXX.XX  XXX.XX  XXX.XX  XXX.XX

DEPT X TOTALS  XXXXX.XX  XXXXXX.XX  XXXX.XX  XXXX.XX  XXXX.XX  XXXX.XX  XXXX.XX

DIV X TOTALS   XXXXX.XX  XXXXXX.XX  XXXX.XX  XXXX.XX  XXXX.XX  XXXX.XX  XXXX.XX

REG X TOTALS   XXXXX.XX  XXXXXX.XX  XXXX.XX  XXXX.XX  XXXX.XX  XXXX.XX  XXXX.XX


PAYROLL  SUMMARY  REPORT

EMPLOYEE     GROSS      FED        STATE               CREDIT    HOSP      NET
NUMBER       PAY        TAX         TAX      FICA       UNION     INS       PAY

FINAL TOTALS   XXXXX.XX  XXXXXX.XX  XXXX.XX  XXXX.XX  XXXX.XX  XXXX.XX  XXXX.XX
```

FIGURE 7–4

If an intermediate-level break does not exist, then the process is shortened by eliminating the intermediate-level break and modifying where the items being totaled are rolled and what lower-level break is performed. The COBOL and BASIC for the flowchart in Figure 7–5 are shown in Figures 7–7 and 7–8, respectively.

When dealing with multiple-level breaks there is perhaps no better place to see the importance of structuring. One of the strengths of using structured concepts is that logic modules become "pluggable." That is, they can be added or deleted as needed by the requirements of the given problem. Adding or subtracting the logic for more or less levels of control breaks is a natural for the structured concepts. As many levels as needed are included and the only change is what the name of the next lower level item is to be performed and what the next higher level name is where any totals that are being generated should be rolled. In the control-break steps listed above, this is indicated by the use of "or next higher" or "or next lower." It becomes a simple matter to expand or contract the number of levels.

To a certain extent it is a mechanical process to determine what needs to be done to be able to handle multiple-level control breaks. There are, however, some points that need to be emphasized in regard to the process. One of these is the concept of rolling totals. Why is it

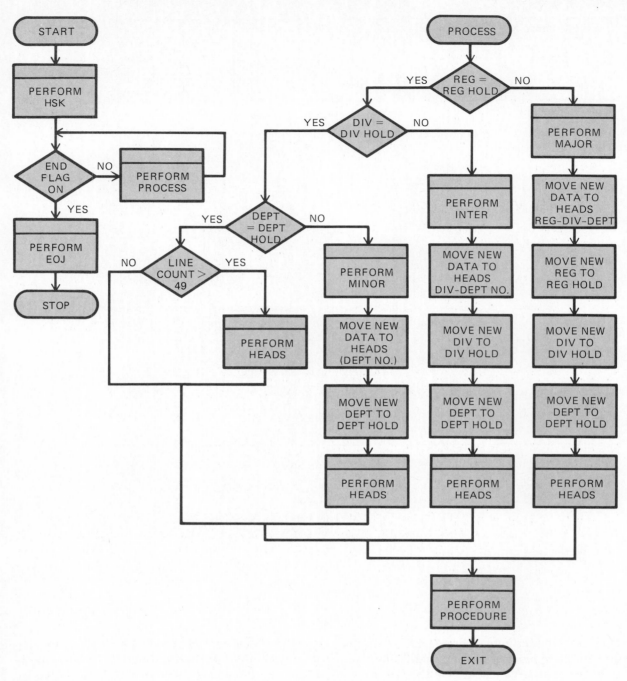

FIGURE 7–5

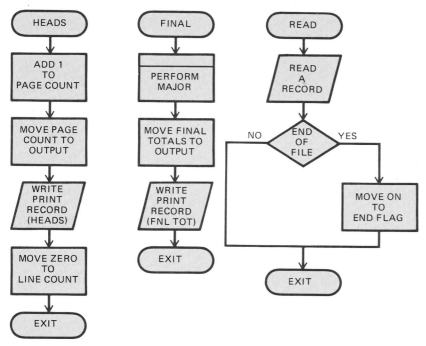

FIGURE 7–5 (continued)

realistic to roll totals rather than do it some other way? Couldn't it be done just as easily by adding the items that are being accumulated to each of the total areas instead of just to the minor-level totals and rolling them on breaks to the next higher-level total?

The answer to both the questions is that it saves processing time and that saves money. The fewer addition operations that are performed the faster the program will run. If all of the jobs on a given computer system are designed in a haphazard manner without any regard to efficiency then there is going to be a lot of wasted time and money going down the tubes.

It should also be noted that the use of a first-record switch here is the same as it was in the previous chapter. That is, a first-record switch is one manner of avoiding totals from being printed prior to the first group. There are other ways out of the situation such as updating the hold areas in the HSK routine or checking the value in a record counter (if one is being used) to see if it is still set to zero. The point is that the process was not unique to the material in Chapter 6. It is one more "pluggable" item that is used when it is needed and left out when it is not needed.

Another concept that needs to be restated is that of when hold areas are updated. Whenever a control break occurs there is updating of hold area(s) to be done. If there is only one level of control break then the only area that needs to be updated when a control break occurs is the one which is being used for comparison. When there are multiple levels of control breaks then the hold areas for the control field that broke as well as all lower-level hold areas need to be updated. When headings are to be produced in the HSK routine after the first record has been read then all of the hold areas need to be updated within the HSK routine in order to prevent an extra set of headings from being produced at the beginning of the PROCESS routine when the control-break fields are checked.

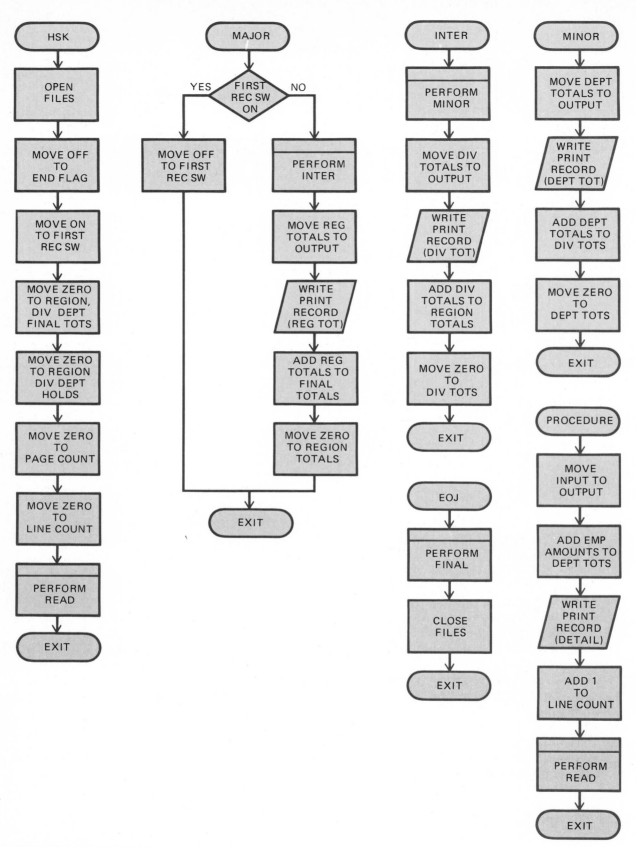

FIGURE 7–5 (continued)

MAINLINE LOGIC

PERFORM hsk routine
PERFORM process routine until end-flag = on
PERFORM eoj routine
STOP

HSK ROUTINE

OPEN files
MOVE off to end-flag
MOVE on to first-record switch
MOVE zeros to region, division, department, and final totals
MOVE zeros to region, division, and department holds
MOVE zeros to page count
MOVE zero to line count
PERFORM read routine

PROCESS ROUTINE

IF region = region hold
    IF division = division hold
        IF department = department hold
            IF line count > 49
                PERFORM heads routine
            ENDIF
        ELSE
            PERFORM minor routine
            MOVE new data to headings (department number)
            MOVE new department to department hold
            PERFORM heads routine
        ENDIF
    ELSE
        PERFORM inter routine
        MOVE new data to headings (division and department numbers)
        MOVE new division to division hold
        MOVE new department to department hold
        PERFORM heads routine
    ENDIF
ELSE
    PERFORM major routine
    MOVE new data to headings (region, division, and department numbers)
    MOVE new region to region hold
    MOVE new division to division hold
    MOVE new department to department hold
    PERFORM heads routine
ENDIF
PERFORM procedure routine

EOJ ROUTINE

PERFORM final routine
CLOSE files

MAJOR ROUTINE

IF first-record switch = on
    MOVE off to first-record switch
ELSE
    PERFORM inter routine
    MOVE Region totals to output
    WRITE print record (region totals)

FIGURE 7–6

        ADD region totals to final totals
        MOVE zeros to region totals
ENDIF

INTER ROUTINE

PERFORM minor routine
MOVE division totals to output
WRITE print record (division totals)
ADD division totals to region totals
MOVE zeros to division totals

MINOR ROUTINE

MOVE department totals to output
WRITE print record (department totals)
ADD department totals to division totals
MOVE zeros to department totals

PROCEDURE ROUTINE

MOVE input to output
ADD employee amounts to department totals
WRITE print record (detail)
ADD 1 to line count
PERFORM read routine

HEADS ROUTINE

ADD 1 to page count
MOVE page count to output
WRITE print record (heads)
MOVE zero to line count

FINAL ROUTINE

PERFORM major routine
MOVE final totals to output
WRITE print record (final totals)

READ ROUTINE

READ a record
        AT END of file
                MOVE on to end-flag

FIGURE 7–6 (continued)

COBOL VERSION:

PROCEDURE DIVISION.

MAINLINE-LOGIC.

PERFORM HSK-ROUTINE
PERFORM PROCESS-ROUTINE UNTIL END-FLAG = 'YES'.
PERFORM EOJ-ROUTINE.
STOP RUN.

FIGURE 7–7

```
HSK-ROUTINE.

    OPEN INPUT EMP-MASTER
        OUTPUT PAYROLL-LIST.
    MOVE 'OFF' TO END-FLAG.
    MOVE 'ON' TO FIRST-REC.
    MOVE ZERO TO FN-GROSS      FIN-FED      FIN-STATE FIN-FICA
                 FIN-CR        FIN-HOSP     FIN-NET
                 REG-GROSS     REG-FED      REG-STATE REG-FICA
                 REG-CR        REG-HOSP     REG-NET
                 DIV-GROSS     DIV-FED      DIV-STATE DIV-FICA
                 DIV-CR        DIV HOSP     DIV-NET
                 DEP-GROSS     DEP-FED      DEP-STATE DEP-FICA
                 DEP-CR        DEP-HOSP     DEP-NET
                 REG-HOLD      DIV-HOLD     DEP-HOLD
                 PAGE-CNT      LINE-CNT.
    PERFORM READ-ROUTINE.


PROCESS-ROUTINE.

IF REG = REG-HOLD
    IF DIV = DIV-HOLD
        IF DEP = DEP-HOLD
            IF LINE-COUNT > 49
                    PERFORM HEADS-ROUTINE
            ELSE
                    NEXT SENTENCE
        ELSE
                PERFORM MINOR-ROUTINE-DEP
                MOVE DEP TO DEP-PRINT
                MOVE DEPT TO DEP-HOLD
                PERFORM HEADS-ROUTINE
    ELSE
            PERFORM INTER-ROUTINE-DEP
            MOVE DEP TO DEP-PRINT
            MOVE DIV TO DIV-PRINT
            MOVE DIV TO DIV-HOLD
            MOVE DEP TO DEP-HOLD
            PERFORM HEADS-ROUTINE
ELSE
        PERFORM MAJOR-ROUTINE-REG
        MOVE DEP TO DEP-PRINT
        MOVE DIV TO DIV-PRINT
        MOVE REG TO REG-PRINT
        MOVE REG TO REG-HOLD
        MOVE DEP TO DEP-HOLD
        MOVE DIV TO DIV-HOLD
        PERFORM HEADS-ROUTINE.
PERFORM PROCEDURE-ROUTINE.


EOJ-ROUTINE.

PERFORM FINAL-ROUTINE.
CLOSE EMP-MASTER
      PAYROLL-LIST.


MAJOR-ROUTINE-REG.

IF FIRST-REC = 'ON'
        MOVE 'OFF' TO FIRST-REC
ELSE
        PERFORM INTER-ROUTINE-DIV
        MOVE REG-GROSS      TO REG-GROSS-PRT
        MOVE REG-FED        TO REG-FED-PRT
        MOVE REG-STATE      TO REG-STATE-PRT
```

FIGURE 7–7 (continued)

```
        MOVE REG-FICA          TO REG-FICA-PRT
        MOVE REG-CR            TO REG-CR-PRT
        MOVE REG-HOSP          TO REG-HOSP-PRT
        MOVE REG-NET           TO REG-NET-PRT
        WRITE PRINT-RECORD FROM REGION-TOTALS-LINE
            AFTER ADVANCING 2 LINES
        ADD REG-GROSS          TO FIN-GROSS
        ADD REG-FED            TO FIN-FED
        ADD REG-STATE          TO FIN-STATE
        ADD REG-FICA           TO FIN-FICA
        ADD REG-CR             TO FIN-CR
        ADD REG-HOSP           TO FIN-HOSP
        ADD REG-NET            TO FIN-NET
        MOVE ZERO              TO REG-GROSS    REG-FED     REG-STATE
                                  REG-FICA     REG-CR      REG-HOSP
                                  REG-NET.
```

INTER-ROUTINE-DIV.

```
    PERFORM MINOR-ROUTINE-DEP.
    MOVE DIV-GROSS        TO DIV-GROSS-PRT.
    MOVE DIV-FED          TO DIV-FED-PRT.
    MOVE DIV-STATE        TO DIV-STATE-PRT.
    MOVE DIV-FICA         TO DIV-FICA-PRT.
    MOVE DIV-CR           TO DIV-CR-PRT.
    MOVE DIV-HOSP         TO DIV-HOSP-PRT.
    MOVE DIV-NET          TO DIV-NET-PRT.
        WRITE PRINT-RECORD FROM DIVISION-TOTALS-LINE
            AFTER ADVANCING 2 LINES.
    ADD DIV-GROSS         TO REG-GROSS.
    ADD DIV-FED           TO REG-FED.
    ADD DIV-STATE         TO REG-STATE.
    ADD DIV-FICA          TO REG-FICA.
    ADD DIV-CR            TO REG-CR.
    ADD DIV-HOSP          TO REG-HOSP.
    ADD DIV-NET           TO REG-NET.
    MOVE ZERO TO DIV-GROSS      DIV-FED     DIV-STATE    DIV-FICA
                                DIV-CR      DIV-HOSP     DIV-NET.
```

MINOR-ROUTINE-DEP.

```
    MOVE DEP-GROSS        TO DEP-GROSS-PRT.
    MOVE DEP-FED          TO DEP-FED-PRT.
    MOVE DEP-STATE        TO DEP-STATE-PRT.
    MOVE DEP-FICA         TO DEP-FICA-PRT.
    MOVE DEP-CR           TO DEP-CR-PRT.
    MOVE DEP-HOSP         TO DEP-HOSP-PRT.
    MOVE DEP-NET          TO DEP-NET-PRT.
    WRITE PRINT-RECORD FROM DEPARTMENT-TOTALS-LINE
        AFTER ADVANCING 2 LINES.
    ADD DEP-GROSS         TO DIV-GROSS.
    ADD DEP-FED           TO DIV-FED.
    ADD DEP-STATE         TO DIV-STATE.
    ADD DEP-FICA          TO DIV-FICA.
    ADD DEP-CR            TO DIV-CR.
    ADD DEP-HOSP          TO DIV-HOSP.
    ADD DEP-NET           TO DIV-NET.
    MOVE ZERO TO    DEP-GROSS    DEP-FED      DEP-STATE    DEP-FICA
                    DEP-CR       DEP-HOSP     DEP-NET.
```

PROCEDURE-ROUTINE

```
    MOVE GROSS-IN        TO GROSS-PRT.
    MOVE FED-IN          TO FED-PRT.
    MOVE STATE-IN        TO STATE-PRT.
```

FIGURE 7–7 (continued)

```
        MOVE FICA-IN        TO FICA-PRT.
        MOVE CR-IN          TO CR-PRT.
        MOVE HOSP-IN        TO HOSP-PRT.
        MOVE NET-IN         TO NET-PRT.
        ADD GROSS-IN        TO DEP-GROSS.
        ADD FED-IN          TO DEP-FED.
        ADD STATE-IN        TO DEP-STATE.
        ADD FICA-IN         TO DEP-FICA.
        ADD CR-IN           TO DEP-CR.
        ADD HOSP-IN         TO DEP-HOSP.
        ADD NET-IN          TO DEP-NET.
        WRITE PRINT-RECORD FROM DETAIL-LINE
              AFTER ADVANCING 1 LINES.
        ADD 1 TO LINE-COUNT.
        PERFORM READ-ROUTINE.

    HEADS-ROUTINE.

        ADD 1 TO PAGE-CNT.
        MOVE PAGE-CNT TO PAGE-PRINT.
        WRITE PRINT-RECORD FROM HEAD-1 AFTER ADVANCING PAGE.
        WRITE PRINT RECORD FROM HEAD-2 AFTER ADVANCING 2 LINES.
        WRITE PRINT-RECORD FROM HEAD-3 AFTER ADVANCING 2 LINES.
        WRITE PRINT-RECORD FROM HEAD-4 AFTER ADVANCING 1 LINES.
        MOVE ZERO TO LINE-CNT.

    FINAL-ROUTINE

        PERFORM MAJOR-ROUTINE-REG.
        MOVE FIN-GROSS      TO FIN-GROSS-PRT.
        MOVE FIN-FED        TO FIN-FED-PRT.
        MOVE FIN-STATE      TO FIN-STATE-PRT.
        MOVE FIN-FICA       TO FIN-FICA-PRT.
        MOVE FIN-CR         TO FIN-CR-PRT.
        MOVE FIN-HOSP       TO FIN-HOSP-PRT.
        MOVE FIN-NET        TO FIN-NET-PRT.
        WRITE PRINT-RECORD FROM HEAD-1 AFTER ADVANCING TOP-OF-PAGE.
        WRITE PRINT-RECORD FROM HEAD-3 AFTER ADVANCING 2 LINES.
        WRITE PRINT-RECORD FROM HEAD-4 AFTER ADVANCING 1 LINES.
        WRITE PRINT-RECORD FROM FINAL-TOTALS-LINE
              AFTER ADVANCING 2 LINES.

    READ-ROUTINE.

        READ EMP-MASTER
             AT END
                  MOVE 'ON' TO END-FLAG.
```

FIGURE 7–7 (continued)

BASIC VERSION:

```
'PROGRAMMERS: J AND J, INC.
'DATE: 10/11/89
'PROGRAM NAME: CASE 7
'*************************************************************************
LET FINAL$ = " FINAL TOTALS  " + "#####.##" + SPACES(1) + "######.##" +
    SPACE$(1) + "####.##" + SPACES(1) + "####.##" + SPACE$(1) + "####.##"
  + SPACE$(1) + "####.##" + SPACES(1) + "####.##"
LET REGIONS$ = " REG # TOTALS  " + "#####.##" + SPACES(1) + "######.##" +
    SPACE$(1) + "####.##" + SPACES(1) + "####.##" + SPACE$(1) + "####.##"
    + SPACE$(1) + "####.##" + SPACES(1) + "####.##"
```

FIGURE 7–8

```
LET DIVIS$ = SPACE$(1) + "&" + SPACE$(1) + "#" + SPACE$(1) +   "&"
LET DIVIS2$  =  SPACE$(2)  +  "#####.##"  +  SPACE$(1)  +  "######.##" +
    SPACE$(1)  +  "####.##"  +  SPACE$(1)  +  "####.##"  +  SPACE$(1)  +
    "####.##" +  SPACE$(1) + "####.##" + SPACE$(1) + "####.##"
LET DETAIL$=SPACE$(2) + "&-&-&"
LET DETAIL2$=SPACE$(3) + "####.##" + SPACE$(3) + "####.##" + SPACE$(2) +
    "###.##" +  SPACE$(2) + "###.##" + SPACE$(2) + "###.##" + SPACE$(2) +
    "###.##" + SPACE$(2) + "###.##"
LET DEPT$ = " DEPT # TOTALS "
LET DEPT2$  =  "#####.##"  +  SPACE$(1)  +  "######.##"  +  SPACE$(1)  +
    "####.##"  +  SPACE$(1)  +  "####.##"  +  SPACE$(1)  +  "####.##"  +
    SPACE$(1) + "####.##" + SPACE$(1) + "####.##"
'********************************************************************
'*                        MAINLINE LOGIC                           *
'********************************************************************
GOSUB HOUSEKEEPING.ROUTINE
WHILE END.FLAG$ = "OFF"
    GOSUB PROCESS.ROUTINE
WEND
GOSUB EOJ.ROUTINE
END
'********************************************************************
'*                      HOUSEKEEPING ROUTINE                       *
'********************************************************************
HOUSEKEEPING.ROUTINE:
OPEN "A:C6B1DATA" FOR INPUT AS #2
FIRST.RECORD.SWITCH$ = "YES"
INPUT "DO YOU WANT THE OUTPUT TO BE PRINTED - ENTER Y OR N",ANSWER$
IF ANSWER$ = "Y" OR ANSWER$ = "y" THEN
    DEVICE$ = "LPT1:"
ELSE
    DEVICE$ = "SCRN:"
END IF
OPEN DEVICE$ FOR OUTPUT AS #1
END.FLAG$ = "OFF"
DIVISION.HOLD = 0
DEPARTMENT.HOLD = 0
PAGE.COUNT = 0
LINE.COUNT = 50
GOSUB READ.ROUTINE
RETURN
'********************************************************************
'*                        PROCESS ROUTINE                          *
'********************************************************************
PROCESS.ROUTINE:
IF REGION.NUMBER <> REGION.HOLD THEN
    GOSUB MAJOR.BREAK.ROUTINE
    GOSUB HEADS.ROUTINE
    GOTO CONTINU
ELSE
    IF DIVISION.NUMBER <> DIVISION.HOLD THEN
        GOSUB INTERMEDIATE.BREAK.ROUTINE
        GOSUB HEADS.ROUTINE
        GOTO CONTINU
    ELSE
        IF DEPARTMENT.NUMBER <> DEPARTMENT.HOLD THEN
            GOSUB MINOR.BREAK.ROUTINE
            GOSUB HEADS.ROUTINE
            GOTO CONTINU
```

FIGURE 7–8 (continued)

```
        ELSE
        END IF
      END IF
    END IF
END IF
IF LINE.COUNT > 49 THEN
    GOSUB HEADS.ROUTINE
ELSE
END IF
CONTINU:
GOSUB PROCEDURE.ROUTINE
RETURN
/***********************************************************************
/*                        EOJ ROUTINE                                  *
/***********************************************************************
EOJ.ROUTINE:
GOSUB MAJOR.BREAK.ROUTINE
LET PAGE.COUNT = PAGE.COUNT + 1
PRINT #1,CHR$(12)
PRINT #1,SPC(26);"PAYROLL SUMMARY REPORT"
PRINT #1,
PRINT #1,"    EMPLOYEE      GROSS      FED      STATE          CREDIT
    HOSP      NET"
PRINT #1,"     NUMBER       PAY        TAX      TAX     FICA   UNION
    INS      PAY"
PRINT #1,
PRINT #1,  USING     FINAL$;    FINAL.GROSS.TOTAL,   FINAL.FEDERAL.TOTAL,
    FINAL.STATE.TOTAL ,    FINAL.FICA.TOTAL ,    FINAL.CREDITUNION.TOTAL ,
    FINAL.HOSPINS.TOTAL,FINAL.NET.TOTAL
CLOSE #1
RETURN
/***********************************************************************
/*                     MAJOR BREAK ROUTINE                             *
/***********************************************************************
MAJOR.BREAK.ROUTINE:
IF FIRST.RECORD.SWITCH$="YES" THEN
    GOSUB SET.RECORD.SWITCH
    GOTO UPDATE.HOLD
ELSE
    GOSUB INTERMEDIATE.BREAK.ROUTINE
    GOSUB FORMAT.REGION
    PRINT #1,   USING     REGION$;   REGION.HOLD,    REGION.GROSS.TOTAL,
      REGION.FEDERAL.TOTAL,    REGION.STATE.TOTAL,    REGION.FICA.TOTAL,
      REGION.CREDITUNION.TOTAL, REGION.HOSPINS.TOTAL, REGION.NET.TOTAL
    LET FINAL.GROSS.TOTAL = FINAL.GROSS.TOTAL + REGION.GROSS.TOTAL
    LET REGION.GROSS.TOTAL = 0
    LET FINAL.FEDERAL.TOTAL = FINAL.FEDERAL.TOTAL + REGION.FEDERAL.TOTAL
    LET REGION.FEDERAL.TOTAL = 0
    LET FINAL.STATE.TOTAL = FINAL.STATE.TOTAL + REGION.STATE.TOTAL
    LET REGION.STATE.TOTAL = 0
    LET FINAL.FICA.TOTAL = FINAL.FICA.TOTAL + REGION.FICA.TOTAL
    LET REGION.FICA.TOTAL = 0
    LET FINAL.CREDITUNION.TOTAL  =  FINAL.CREDITUNION.TOTAL  +
        REGION.CREDITUNION.TOTAL
    LET REGION.CREDITUNION = 0
    LET FINAL.HOSPINS.TOTAL = FINAL.HOSPINS.TOTAL + REGION.HOSPINS.TOTAL
    LET REGION.HOSPINS.TOTAL = 0
    LET FINAL.NET.TOTAL = FINAL.NET.TOTAL + REGION.NET.TOTAL
    LET REGION.NET.TOTAL = 0
END IF
```

FIGURE 7–8 (continued)

```
UPDATE.HOLD:
LET REGION.HOLD = REGION.NUMBER
RETURN
/********************************************************************
/*                    INTERMEDIATE BREAK ROUTINE                   *
/********************************************************************
INTERMEDIATE.BREAK.ROUTINE:
DIV$ = "DIV":TOT$="TOTALS"
GOSUB MINOR.BREAK.ROUTINE
PRINT #1,USING DIVIS$;DIV$,DIVISION.HOLD,TOT$;
PRINT #1, USING  DIVIS2$;  DIVISION.GROSS.TOTAL,  DIVISION.FEDERAL.TOTAL,
    DIVISION.STATE.TOTAL, DIVISION.FICA.TOTAL, DIVISION.CREDITUNION.TOTAL,
    DIVISION.HOSPINS.TOTAL,DIVISION.NET.TOTAL
PRINT #1,
LET REGION.GROSS.TOTAL = REGION.GROSS.TOTAL + DIVISION.GROSS.TOTAL
LET DIVISION.GROSS.TOTAL = 0
LET REGION.FEDERAL.TOTAL = REGION.FEDERAL.TOTAL + DIVISION.FEDERAL.TOTAL
LET DIVISION.FEDERAL.TOTAL = 0
LET REGION.STATE.TOTAL = REGION.STATE.TOTAL + DIVISION.STATE.TOTAL
LET DIVISION.STATE.TOTAL = 0
LET REGION.FICA.TOTAL = REGION.FICA.TOTAL + DIVISION.FICA.TOTAL
LET DIVISION.FICA.TOTAL = 0
LET REGION.CREDITUNION.TOTAL = REGION.CREDITUNION.TOTAL +
    DIVISION.CREDITUNION.TOTAL
LET DIVISION.CREDOTUNION.TOTAL = 0
LET REGION.HOSPINS.TOTAL = REGION.HOSPINS.TOTAL + DIVISION.HOSPINS.TOTAL
LET DIVISION.HOSPINS.TOTAL = 0
LET REGION.NET.TOTAL = REGION.NET.TOTAL + DIVISION.NET.TOTAL
LET DIVISION.NET.TOTAL = 0
LET DIVISION.HOLD = DIVISION.NUMBER
RETURN
/********************************************************************
/*                      MINOR BREAK ROUTINE                        *
/********************************************************************
MINOR.BREAK.ROUTINE:
PRINT #1,
PRINT #1,USING DEPT$;DEPARTMENT.HOLD;
PRINT #1,USING DEPT2$; DEPARTMENT.GROSS.TOTAL, DEPARTMENT.FEDERAL.TOTAL,
    DEPARTMENT.STATE.TOTAL        ,        DEPARTMENT.FICA.TOTAL        ,
    DEPARTMENT.CREDITUNION.TOTAL   ,    DEPARTMENT.HOSPINS.TOTAL    ,
    DEPARTMENT.NET.TOTAL
PRINT #1,
LET DIVISION.GROSS.TOTAL = DIVISION.GROSS.TOTAL + DEPARTMENT.GROSS.TOTAL
LET DEPARTMENT.GROSS.TOTAL = 0
LET DIVISION.FEDERAL.TOTAL    =    DIVISION.FEDERAL.TOTAL     +
    DEPARTMENT.FEDERAL.TOTAL
LET DEPARTMENT.FEDERAL.TOTAL = 0
LET DIVISION.STATE.TOTAL = DIVISION.STATE.TOTAL + DEPARTMENT.STATE.TOTAL
LET DEPARTMENT.STATE.TOTAL = 0
LET DIVISION.FICA.TOTAL = DIVISION.FICA.TOTAL + DEPARTMENT.FICA.TOTAL
LET DEPARTMENT.FICA.TOTAL = 0
LET DIVISION.CREDITUNION.TOTAL   =   DIVISION.CREDITUNION.TOTAL    +
    DEPARTMENT.CREDITUNION.TOTAL
LET DEPARTMENT.CREDITUNION.TOTAL = 0
LET DIVISION.HOSPINS.TOTAL     =      DIVISION.HOSPINS.TOTAL     +
    DEPARTMENT.HOSPINS.TOTAL
LET DEPARTMENT.HOSPINS.TOTAL = 0
LET DIVISION.NET.TOTAL = DIVISION.NET.TOTAL + DEPARTMENT.NET.TOTAL
LET DEPARTMENT.NET.TOTAL = 0
```

FIGURE 7–8 (continued)

```
LET DEPARTMENT.HOLD = DEPARTMENT.NUMBER
RETURN
'******************************************************************************
'*                            PROCEDURE ROUTINE                              *
'******************************************************************************
PROCEDURE.ROUTINE:
LET DEPARTMENT.GROSS.TOTAL = DEPARTMENT.GROSS.TOTAL + GROSS.PAY
LET DEPARTMENT.FEDERAL.TOTAL = DEPARTMENT.FEDERAL.TOTAL + FEDERAL.TAX
LET DEPARTMENT.STATE.TOTAL = DEPARTMENT.STATE.TOTAL + STATE.TAX
LET DEPARTMENT.FICA.TOTAL = DEPARTMENT.FICA.TOTAL + FICA
LET DEPARTMENT.CREDITUNION.TOTAL   =   DEPARTMENT.CREDITUNION.TOTAL   +
    CREDIT.UNION
LET DEPARTMENT.HOSPINS.TOTAL = DEPARTMENT.HOSPINS.TOTAL + HOSP.INS
LET DEPARTMENT.NET.TOTAL = DEPARTMENT.NET.TOTAL + NET.PAY
PRINT #1,      USING      DETAIL$;      MID$(EMPLOYEE.NUMBER$,1,3)    ,
    MID$(EMPLOYEE.NUMBER$,4,2),MID$(EMPLOYEE.NUMBER$,6,4);
PRINT #1,  USING  DETAIL2$; GROSS.PAY,  FEDERAL.TAX,  STATE.TAX, FICA,
    CREDIT.UNION,HOSP.INS,NET.PAY
LET LINE.COUNT = LINE.COUNT + 1
GOSUB READ.ROUTINE
RETURN
'******************************************************************************
'*                            HEADS ROUTINE                                  *
'******************************************************************************
HEADS.ROUTINE:
LET PAGE.COUNT = PAGE.COUNT + 1
PRINT #1,CHR$(12)
PRINT #1,SPC(26);"PAYROLL SUMMARY REPORT"
PRINT #1,
PRINT #1,  SPC(2);  "REGION - ";REGION.NUMBER;SPC(7);"DIVISION - ";
    DIVISION.NUMBER; SPC(7); "DEPARTMENT - "; DEPARTMENT.NUMBER; SPC(13);
    "PAGE ";
LET PAGE$ = "###"
PRINT #1,USING PAGE$; PAGE.COUNT
PRINT#1,
PRINT #1,"    EMPLOYEE" ; SPC(5) ; "GROSS";SPC(6) ; "FED        STATE
    CREDIT     HOSP        NET"
PRINT #1,"     NUMBER         PAY        TAX        TAX      FICA     UNION
    INS        PAY"
PRINT #1,
LET LINE.COUNT = 0
RETURN
'******************************************************************************
'*                            READ ROUTINE                                   *
'******************************************************************************
READ.ROUTINE:
IF EOF(2) THEN
    END.FLAG$ = "ON"
ELSE
    INPUT #2, EMPLOYEE.NUMBER$, GROSS.PAY, FEDERAL.TAX, STATE.TAX, FICA,
    CREDIT.UNION, HOSP.INS, NET.PAY, DIVISION.NUMBER, DEPARTMENT.NUMBER,
    REGION.NUMBER
END IF
RETURN
'******************************************************************************
'*                            WORK ROUTINES                                  *
'******************************************************************************
FORMAT.REGION:
LET REGION$ = " REG # TOTALS  " + "#####.##" + SPACES$(1) + "######.##" +
```

FIGURE 7–8 (continued)

```
          SPACES(1) + "####.##" + SPACES(1) + "####.##" + SPACES(1) + "####.##"
       + SPACES(1) + "####.##" + SPACES(1) + "####.##"
RETURN
SET.RECORD.SWITCH:
LET FIRST.RECORD.SWITCH$ = "NO"
LET DIVISION.HOLD = DIVISION.NUMBER
LET DEPARTMENT.HOLD = DEPARTMENT.NUMBER
RETURN
```

FIGURE 7–8 (continued)

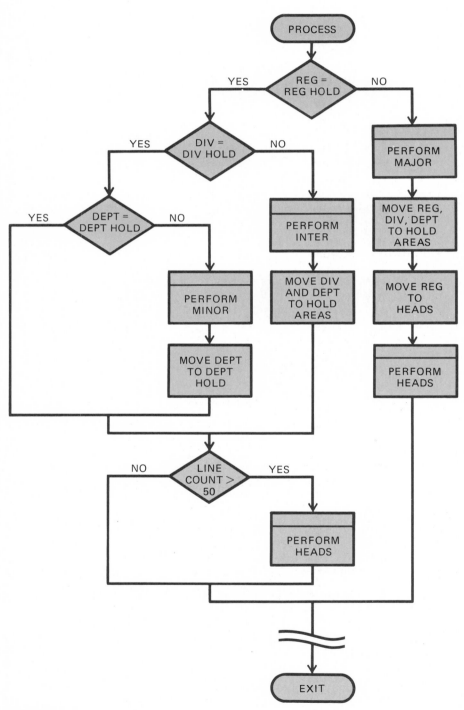

FIGURE 7–9

Another item is when headings need to be produced. When there is only one level of control break, headings are typically going to be needed when there is either an overflow condition or when a control break exists. When there are multiple levels of control breaks the problem becomes a little harder to describe but it is not all that difficult. There will most likely still be headings on an overflow condition, but what about on control breaks? It depends on the specifications of the problem but it is safe to say that if there are three levels of breaks then headings could be provided for any of the following conditions:

1. Overflow conditions
2. Major break and overflow
3. Major, intermediate, and overflow conditions
4. Major, intermediate, minor, and overflow conditions

It is highly unlikely though that headings would be provided for major, minor, and overflow conditions and not for intermediate-level breaks. If the heading routine is only being performed when a major break occurs and on overflow conditions then the test for an overflow condition needs to be included in such a way that overflow conditions are tested for regardless of whether there is (or is not) an intermediate- or minor-level break. This is indicated in Figure 7–9. The pseudocode for the logic is in Figure 7–10.

The moves in the flowchart to the hold areas have been combined into one block when there was more than one move to be done in order to save space in the flowchart but are shown as separate moves in the pseudocode. It should also be noted that if this were being implemented in COBOL without the 85 standard which includes an ENDIF, the test for line count would need to be revamped. Without the 85 standard the line count test would need to be made a subroutine and performed in two places. The first is below MOVE dept to dept hold and the second is below MOVE div and dept to div and dept hold.

By putting the line count check where it is (or separately on both paths), the overflow condition is tested for all situations except a change in region. In that way it is not possible to overlook a situation where it is necessary to eject to a new page and produce another set of heads.

PROCESS ROUTINE

```
IF region = region hold
     IF division = division hold
          IF department = department hold
          ELSE
               PERFORM minor routine
               Move department number to department hold
          ENDIF
     ELSE
          PERFORM inter routine
          MOVE division number to division hold
          MOVE department number to department hold
     ENDIF
     IF line count > 49
          PERFORM heads routine
     ENDIF
ELSE
     PERFORM major routine
     MOVE region to region hold
     MOVE division number to division hold
     MOVE department number to department hold
     MOVE region number to headings
     PERFORM heads routine
ENDIF
```

FIGURE 7–10

CHAPTER VOCABULARY _____

Final totals
First-record switch
Intermediate-break/total

Major-break/total
Minor-break/total
Multiple-level totals

Resetting totals
Rolling totals
Single-level break/totals

REVIEW QUESTIONS _____

MATCHING

Indicate in which routines the following items are usually found. One or more of the lettered items may be used for any item, and the lettered items may be used in more than one place.

A. Housekeeping routine
B. Major-break routine
C. End-of-job routine (final routine)

D. Heading routine (including updating processes)
E. Minor-break routine

_A_ **1.** Opening files.
_E,B_ **2.** Turning off a first-record switch.
_D_ **3.** Incrementing the page number.
_B,C_ **4.** Printing major-level totals.
_A_ **5.** Turning on a first-record switch.
_E,B_ **6.** Updating the minor-break hold area.
_D_ **7.** Ejecting to a new page.
_B_ **8.** Updating the major-break hold area.
_C_ **9.** Closing files.
_E,B_ **10.** Printing minor-level totals.
_C_ **11.** Printing grand totals.
_E,B_ **12.** Rolling minor-level totals to intermediate-level totals.

TRUE/FALSE

T F **1.** First-record switches are typically used to prevent control-break totals as the first record is processed.
T **F** **2.** A first-record switch is usually turned on in the major-break routine.
T **F** **3.** Final totals are usually set to zero in the intermediate-level control-break routine.
T F **4.** Minor totals are printed and reset to zero on both minor- and major-control breaks.
T F **5.** The process of rolling totals can be a time-saver.
T F **6.** Final totals are a type of intermediate-level total.
T F **7.** When only one level of control-break total is being produced, it is called a major-level total.
T **F** **8.** Lower-level control breaks always force higher-level control breaks.
T **F** **9.** The maximum number of levels of control breaks is three.
T F **10.** It is presumed that if a major control break occurs, an intermediate- (if one is present) and a minor-break also occur.
T **F** **11.** First-record switches are normally turned off in the housekeeping routine.
T F **12.** If control-break totals were not reset to zero when breaks occurred, the result would be to produce cumulative totals.
T **F** **13.** First-record switches are the only method of preventing control-break totals prior to the first group.

EXERCISES

1. Draw a flowchart to read a file and accumulate the total sales for each salesman as well as the total sales for the company. There may be multiple records for each salesman. The file is in sequence by salesman number. Each record is to be listed on the report and the total sales for a given salesman should be listed after all of the records for that salesman have been processed. The total sales for the company should be listed on a separate page at the end of the report.

2. Repeat Exercise 1, except that totals are to be generated for salesman, division, and the entire company. The file is in sequence by salesman within division. Each new division should start on a new page and provision should be made for forms overflow.

3. Draw a flowchart to produce a listing of the assets in a company. The file is maintained on tape with each record containing the information about one of the asset types in a given department of a division. The file is in sequence by department within division. The information on each record includes the following items:
   a. The number of the asset
   b. The quantity on hand
   c. The cost per unit
   d. The description of the asset
   e. The department number where the asset is located
   f. The division number where the asset is located
   Each line printed should include the extended cost of the item (quantity * cost). Total extended asset costs are to be developed and printed for each department, division, and for the entire company. The flowchart should incorporate rolling totals from department to division and from division to final totals. The input record format and printer layout are shown below. Headings should appear at the top of each page and should include the department and division numbers. Each new department and division should start at the top of a new page. Page numbers should be restarted for each new division.

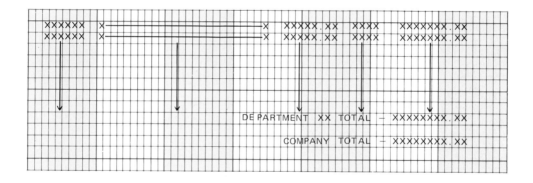

DISCUSSION QUESTIONS

1. Describe what is meant by rolling totals.
2. Describe why and how higher-level breaks force lower-level breaks.
3. Describe the activities that take place on:
   a. Minor-breaks
   b. Intermediate-breaks
   c. Major-breaks
   d. End-of-job.
4. Describe the use of a first-record switch in relation to control-break totals, including when it is turned on and off.
5. Discuss how the process of rolling totals can save processing time in a program.
6. Describe the effect of not setting control-break total areas to zero when control breaks occur. In your description specify which items should be reset to zero on which type of breaks.

PROJECTS

Project 1

Prepare a print chart and a flowchart for the following specifications:

INPUT

MASTER PERSONNEL FILE

01–02	Personnel Record Code	has a range of 1–5
03–03	Personnel Division	has a range of 01–05
04–05	Personnel Department	
	Personnel Employee ID	
06–08	Personnel ID-1	
09–10	Personnel ID-2	
11–14	Personnel ID-3	
15–34	Personnel Name	
35–50	Personnel Street Address	
51–52	Personnel State	
53–57	Personnel Zip	
	Personnel Date of Employment	
58–59	Personnel Month	
60–61	Personnel Day	
62–63	Personnel Year	
64–64	Personnel Experience Code	
65–65	Personnel Responsibility Code	
66–67	Personnel Skill Code	
68–71	Personnel Vacation Days	(4.1)
72–75	Personnel Sick Days	(4.1)
76–80	Personnel Daily Rate	(5.2)

PROCESSING

1. Compute Leave Days (Personnel Vacation Days + Personnel Sick Days).
2. Compute Leave Liability (Leave Days * Personnel Daily Rate).
3. Take a control break on Personnel Division and print the totals of Personnel Vacation Days, Personnel Sick Days, Leave Days, and Leave Liability for each division.
4. Totals for the items listed in number 3 for the company should be printed on a separate page at the end of the report.

OUTPUT

A printed listing of the data from the master file. Include the following:

1. Use 132 print positions.
2. Double-space the detail lines output.
3. Provide report headings, including report title, page numbers, and current date.
4. Provide appropriate column headings.
5. Include all input fields (except record code) on the output. Also, include any computed fields.
6. Use a line count of greater than 50 for overflow.
7. Each new division should start on a new page.

Project 2

Prepare a print chart and a flowchart for the following specifications:

MASTER PERSONNEL FILE

01–02	Personnel Record Code	
03–03	Personnel Division	has a range of 1–5
04–05	Personnel Department	has a range of 01–05
	Personnel Employee ID	
06–08	Personnel ID-1	
09–10	Personnel ID-2	
11–14	Personnel ID-3	
15–34	Personnel Name	
35–50	Personnel Street Address	
51–52	Personnel State	
53–57	Personnel Zip	
	Personnel Date of Employment	
58–59	Personnel Month	
60–61	Personnel Day	

62–63	Personnel Year	
64–64	Personnel Experience Code	
65–65	Personnel Responsibility Code	
66–67	Personnel Skill Code	
68–71	Personnel Vacation Days	(4.1)
72–75	Personnel Sick Days	(4.1)
76–80	Personnel Daily Rate	(5.2)

PROCESSING

1. Using Personnel Date of Employment and the current date, compute the number of full months a person has been employed. (Do not print this field.)
2. Find the average number of sick days an employee has accumulated per month of employment. Print this field.
3. Compute totals for division, department, and final totals for average sick days, and vacation days.

OUTPUT

1. Use 132 print positions.
2. Double-space the output.
3. Provide report headings including report title, page numbers, and current date.
4. Provide appropriate column headings.
5. Output the input fields (except record code).
6. Use a line count of greater than 50 for overflow.
7. Change pages when you begin a new division but not for a new department.
8. Leave 1 blank line before printing department totals.
9. Put the final totals on a separate page at the end of the report.

Project 3

Prepare a print chart and a flow chart for the following specifications:

INPUT

MASTER INVENTORY FILE

1–2	Inventory Record Code	
	Inventory Stock Number	
3–3	Inventory Type	has a range of 1–5
4–5	Inventory Class	has a range of 01–10
6–9	Inventory Part	
10–29	Inventory Description	
30–30	Inventory Location Code	
31–34	Inventory Quantity on Hand	
35–38	Inventory Quantity on Order	
39–42	Inventory Reorder Level	
43–43	Inventory Unit Size Code	
44–48	Inventory Unit Price	(5.2)
49–49	Inventory Discount Code	
50–55	Inventory Annual Usage (Units)	
56–58	Inventory Vendor Code	
	Inventory Transportation Code	
59–59	Inventory Category	
60–60	Inventory Distance	
61–80	Unused	

PROCESSING

1. Compute total inventory quantity (inventory quantity on hand plus inventory quantity on order) and compare it with the inventory reorder level to see if reordering is necessary. If the total inventory quantity is less than, or equal to, inventory reorder level, order one-half (rounded up if needed for actual programming) of the inventory reorder level. If there is no order for a stock number, print asterisks under the appropriate column.
2. Price the order quantity using inventory unit price (gross order amount) and apply a discount, giving net order amount. If the inventory discount code = 1, subtract 5%. If inventory discount code = 2, subtract 10%.
3. Compute inventory type, inventory class, and final totals of gross order amount, net order amount, and discount amount.

OUTPUT

1. Use 132 print positions.
2. Double-space the output.
3. Provide report headings, including report title, page numbers, and current date.
4. Provide appropriate column headings.
5. Print all input fields (except inventory record code) as well as order quantity, gross order amount, net order amount, and discount amount.
6. Use a line count of greater than 50 for page overflow.
7. Change pages after printing type totals but not class totals.
8. Leave a blank line before printing class and type totals.
9. Put the final totals on a separate page at the end of the report with appropriate heads.

TABLES

8

OBJECTIVES

As a result of studying this chapter the student should be able to perform the following activities:

1. Explain what the term dimension means in relation to a table.
2. Describe how a table is subdivided to make each new dimension.
3. Diagram a table given the dimensions and element size.

4. Explain the term subscript.
5. Calculate displacement for a table element.
6. Describe three methods for loading a table.
7. Describe three methods for accessing a table.
8. Describe logic for printing a table.

TABLE STRUCTURE

A table is a set of data items that share a common name and data description. Items are combined into a table because they can be treated in a similar manner. To create a table an area of memory is given a name and then subdivided into table elements. Each data item that can be treated in a similar matter is stored as an element in the table. For example, a student usually takes a number of courses at one school. The data about each course will be treated in a similar manner by any program processing the student's record. Therefore, it is helpful to group the courses together as a table. In the previous chapter totals were kept for departments and divisions. Each time a total was printed the area was zeroed out so a new accumulation could begin. When it is desirable to print all of the totals on one page as a summary of the report, the totals are often kept in a table since all totals must be retained until the end of the program and the total for any one department or division can be treated in the same manner by a computer program as any other total for a department or division.

The terminology applied to tables varies with the programming language used to implement them. In this text we will use the general term table to include tables and arrays and the term subscript to include subscripts and indices. Some examples will be given in both COBOL and BASIC. It is not our intent to teach either language, it simply gives us the opportunity to explain some things that must be taken into consideration when tables are used.

One-Dimensional Tables

In structure, the simplest of tables has only one dimension. This means there is only one level of subdivision. If there are ten data items which require storage then an area of memory can be divided into ten equal parts. Each programming language has its own method of providing storage in memory for a table. COBOL uses an OCCURS clause to specify the number of elements in a table, BASIC uses a DIMENSION statement.

```
COBOL    05  EMP-NBR-TABLE  OCCURS 10 TIMES    PIC 9(4).
BASIC    10  DIMENSION EMP.NBR.TABLE (10)
```

EMP-NBR TABLE is a one-dimensional table. The OCCURS clause or the DIMENSION statement indicates there are ten elements in the table. EMP-NBR-TABLE reserves storage for ten elements, each of which is a numeric data item. In the BASIC programming language the choice of variable name determines the amount of storage each table element will use, COBOL requires the programmer to specify the number of bytes. In our examples we will use the storage requirement specified by the COBOL statements in order to make the amount of storage used more obvious.

Let us assume that the table already contains data. An example of data for a table would be a list of employee numbers. In this example each group of four digits is considered to be an element in the table. In memory the numbers are stored one after another in the order shown below.

1274128513061356137414861590165017761887

While table elements are stored in consecutive memory locations, it is easier to work with a table if the table is arranged on paper to suit our normal reading style. Since we are accustomed to reading lists of things, the table elements can be arranged in ten rows, each of which contains one column, as shown in Figure 8–1.

EMP-NBR-TABLE

1274
1285
1306
1356
1374
1486
1590
1650
1776
1887

FIGURE 8–1

All ten elements of EMP-NBR-TABLE share the same name, so there needs to be a way to tell them apart. Since there is only one column, there can be no confusion about which column is being referenced; therefore, only one number (a row number) is needed to identify a particular element in the table. The usual way of specifying this is to use the table name and enclose in parentheses the number of the element we are interested in. The number in parentheses is called a subscript. A subscript is a constant or a variable which has an integer value indicating an occurrence of an element in the table, first, second, third, and so on. The values for the ten table elements are shown below using a numeric literal as the subscript for each element. For example EMP-NBR-TABLE (5) refers to the fifth element in the table. The fifth element has a value of 1374. Five is the value of the subscript. See Figure 8–2 for the table elements with their values.

Table Element	Value
EMP-NBR-TABLE (1)	1274
EMP-NBR-TABLE (2)	1285
EMP-NBR-TABLE (3)	1306
EMP-NBR-TABLE (4)	1356
EMP-NBR-TABLE (5)	1374
EMP-NBR-TABLE (6)	1486
EMP-NBR-TABLE (7)	1590
EMP-NBR-TABLE (8)	1650
EMP-NBR-TABLE (9)	1776
EMP-NBR-TABLE (10)	1887

FIGURE 8–2

A diagram of memory in Figure 8–3 shows how the 40 bytes of memory reserved by the table is divided into elements.

EMP-NBR-TABLE									
(1)	(2)	(3)	(4)	(5)	(6)	(7)	(8)	(9)	(10)
1274	1285	1306	1356	1374	1486	1590	1650	1776	1887

FIGURE 8–3

Notice that the value of the subscript ranges from one to ten. The lowest possible subscript in COBOL is a +1 while some versions of BASIC allow a zero subscript; the highest subscript should be equal to the number specified in the COBOL OCCURS clause or the BASIC DIMENSION statement for the particular table.

Since a storage area becomes a table when it includes an OCCURS clause or a DIMENSION statement in its description, any item described this way must have a subscript when an individual element is referenced in a program in order to indicate which of the elements is being referenced. If the subscript is left off, a diagnostic will be generated.

If the subscript is always a numeric literal as in Figure 8–2, much of the advantage of having grouped like data items together as a table is lost. As long as the first element of the table must be coded as EMP-NBR-TABLE (1) and the second as EMP-NBR-TABLE (2) and so on, it will require as many lines of code to use the table elements as it would if they were simply ten different variables each with a unique name.

Using a variable as a subscript allows the programmer to reduce the number of statements required to accomplish a task. Let's assume that we wish to add QUANTITY from an input file to a table named QTY-TABLE in such a way that the first element of the table (QTY-TABLE (1)) will contain the total quantity for the first branch of a company, the second table element (QTY-TABLE (2)) will contain the total quantity for the second branch and so on. The definition of the storage for the table would be:

```
COBOL      05  QTY-ROW     OCCURS 5 TIMES    PIC 9(6).
BASIC      10  DIMENSION QTY.TABLE (5)
```

Each input record contains a QUANTITY and a BRANCH. Each time a record is read and processed an instruction like the following may be executed. (COBOL has an ADD statement; we will, however, use the COMPUTE in our examples because it is so similar to the BASIC LET statement).

```
COBOL      COMPUTE QTY-ROW (BRANCH) = QTY-ROW (BRANCH) + QUANTITY
BASIC      LET QTY.TABLE (BRANCH) = QTY.TABLE (BRANCH) + QUANTITY
```

Since each input record contains a value for QUANTITY, it is available to be added to the table. The branch field from the input record will be used to determine which table element the quantity will be added to. In other words the value in BRANCH will act as the subscript. Some sample input data is shown in Figure 8–4. Using the COMPUTE statement above, substitute the sample input values for the variables in COMPUTE QTY-ROW (BRANCH) = QTY-ROW (BRANCH) + QUANTITY and observe in Figure 8–5 how the contents of the table change each time the COMPUTE is executed. The storage area for the table was set to zeros in HSK before the addition began.

```
          INPUT DATA
   QUANTITY      BRANCH
      40            1
      80            1
     300            1
      60            2
      10            3
     500            3
      50            4
      40            4
      90            4
      75            5
      50            5
```

FIGURE 8–4

ADDITION WITH INPUT VALUES SUBSTITUTED FOR THE   TABLE
VARIABLES QUANTITY AND BRANCH

COMPUTE QTY-ROW (BRANCH) = QTY-ROW (BRANCH) + QUANTITY

| THE TABLE BEFORE ANY ADDITIONS | 000000 | 000000 | 000000 | 000000 | 000000 |

COMPUTE QTY-ROW (1) =
    QTY-ROW (1) + 40

| | 000040 | 000000 | 000000 | 000000 | 000000 |

COMPUTE QTY-ROW (1) =
    QTY-ROW (1) + 80

| | 000120 | 000000 | 000000 | 000000 | 000000 |

COMPUTE QTY-ROW (1) =
    QTY-ROW (1) + 300

| | 000420 | 000000 | 000000 | 000000 | 000000 |

COMPUTE QTY-ROW (2) =
    QTY-ROW (2) + 60

| | 000420 | 000060 | 000000 | 000000 | 000000 |

COMPUTE QTY-ROW (3 =
    QTY-ROW (3) + 10

| | 000420 | 000060 | 000010 | 000000 | 000000 |

COMPUTE QTY-ROW (3) =
    QTY-ROW (3) + 500

| | 000420 | 000060 | 000510 | 000000 | 000000 |

COMPUTE QTY-ROW (4) =
    QTY-ROW (4) + 50

| | 000420 | 000060 | 000510 | 000050 | 000000 |

COMPUTE QTY-ROW (4) =
    QTY-ROW (4) + 40

| | 000420 | 000060 | 000510 | 000090 | 000000 |

COMPUTE QTY-ROW (4) =
    QTY-ROW (4) + 90

| | 000420 | 000060 | 000510 | 000180 | 000000 |

COMPUTE QTY-ROW (5) =
    QTY-ROW (5) + 75

| | 000420 | 000060 | 000510 | 000180 | 000075 |

COMPUTE QTY-ROW (5) =
    QTY-ROW (5) + 50

| | 000420 | 000060 | 000510 | 000180 | 000125 |

FIGURE 8–5

If you were to rearrange the input data so that the records were not in sequence by BRANCH and add the input data into the table again, you would see that using BRANCH as a subscript will fill the table properly whether the data is in sequence by BRANCH or not. Each input record provides the data needed (BRANCH) to identify the proper table element. With one add statement included in a loop any number of records in a file may be processed and, if the number of elements in the table is expanded, any number of branches may be present within an organization. In order to accumulate proper totals in a table, the elements of the table must be initialized to zero before the addition starts. Based on the programming language and its method of storing numbers the zeroing may either be done with a single statement which moves zeros to the entire table or it will require a loop which is executed multiple times zeroing one element on each pass.

If a loop is required it can be patterned after the logic shown in Figure 8–6. This routine uses a subscript to determine which element is being zeroed. The subscript is given an initial value of 1. As long as the value of the subscript does not exceed the number of table elements zero is moved to each table element in turn and 1 is added to the subscript. When the subscript exceeds the number of table elements the loop is terminated.

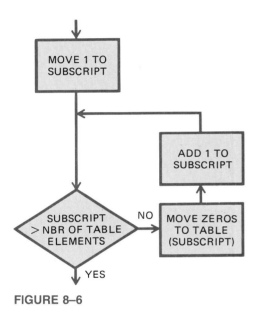

FIGURE 8–6

Two-Dimensional Tables

In many instances, a one-dimensional table will not be adequate to store a particular set of data. The data may be easier to manipulate if it is stored in a two-dimensional table. The naming conventions for tables with more than one dimension are different in COBOL and BASIC. When a table has multiple dimensions it is like having a table inside a table. The area is subdivided into a given number of elements (first dimension) then each of those elements is subdivided again (second dimension). COBOL assigns a new name to each dimension. BASIC uses one name to include all dimensions of a table. See Figure 8–7 for an example of a two-dimensional table.

```
COBOL    01 QTY-TABLE.
               05   QTY-ROW   OCCURS 4 TIMES.
                    10   QTY-COLUMN   OCCURS 3 TIMES          PIC 9(4).
BASIC    10   DIMENSION QTY.TABLE (4, 3)
```

Table structure

QTY-TABLE											
QTY-ROW (1)			QTY-ROW (2)			QTY-ROW (3)			QTY-ROW (4)		
(1, 1)	(1, 2)	(1, 3)	(2, 1)	(2, 2)	(2, 3)	(3, 1)	(3, 2)	(3, 3)	(4, 1)	(4, 2)	(4, 3)

QTY-COLUMN

FIGURE 8–7

In COBOL QTY-TABLE is called a group item, it contains both QTY-ROW and QTY-COLUMN and encompasses 48 bytes of storage. Any reference to QTY-TABLE in COBOL references all 48 bytes. No subscript is allowed when referring to QTY-TABLE in COBOL. QTY-ROW consists of four elements (OCCURS 4 TIMES). Each element of QTY-ROW is 12 bytes. Each element of QTY-ROW is also called a group item since each element of QTY-ROW contains elements of QTY-COLUMN. Any reference to QTY-ROW is a reference to 12 bytes of storage and requires one subscript. Each element of QTY-COLUMN is called an elementary item because it will not be subdivided further. QTY-COLUMN has three four-byte elements for each occurrence of QTY-ROW or a total of 12 elements. Each element of QTY-COLUMN is four bytes. Two subscripts are required to identify an element of QTY-COLUMN. The first subscript identifies which element of QTY-ROW. The second subscript identifies which element of QTY-COLUMN. BASIC tables are structured in the same manner, however only one variable name is used in all references to the table.

Let's store a quantity in the two-dimensional table. Data coming from an input record will contain both the amount to be added (QUANTITY) and the fields to be used as subscripts (REGION and BRANCH). In the example below, a comma (,) followed by a space is used to separate the two subscripts. The input data is shown in Figure 8–8 and compute statements with the values substituted for the variables are shown in Figure 8–9. Notice the difference in variable names used when referencing tables in COBOL and BASIC.

```
COBOL     COMPUTE QTY-COLUMN (REGION, BRANCH) =
                  QTY-COLUMN (REGION, BRANCH) + QUANTITY
BASIC
          LET QTY.TABLE (REGION, BRANCH) =
              QTY.TABLE (REGION, BRANCH) + QUANTITY
```

INPUT DATA

QUANTITY	REGION	BRANCH
10	1	1
15	1	1
25	1	2
15	1	2
5	1	3
20	2	1
10	2	2
25	2	2
50	2	3
5	3	2
40	3	2
20	3	3
15	4	1
25	4	1
10	4	2
55	4	3
15	4	3

FIGURE 8–8

CONTENTS OF TABLE BEFORE ANY ADDS

0000	0000	0000	0000	0000	0000	0000	0000	0000	0000	0000	0000

COMPUTE QTY-COLUMN (1, 1) = QTY-COLUMN (1, 1) + 10.

0010	0000	0000	0000	0000	0000	0000	0000	0000	0000	0000	0000

COMPUTE QTY-COLUMN (1, 1) = QTY-COLUMN (1, 1) + 15.

0025	0000	0000	0000	0000	0000	0000	0000	0000	0000	0000	0000

COMPUTE QTY-COLUMN (1, 2) = QTY-COLUMN (1, 2) + 25.

0025	0025	0000	0000	0000	0000	0000	0000	0000	0000	0000	0000

COMPUTE QTY-COLUMN (1, 2) = QTY-COLUMN (1, 2) + 15.

0025	0040	0000	0000	0000	0000	0000	0000	0000	0000	0000	0000

COMPUTE QTY-COLUMN (1, 3) = QTY-COLUMN (1, 3) + 5.

0025	0040	0005	0000	0000	0000	0000	0000	0000	0000	0000	0000

COMPUTE QTY-COLUMN (2, 1) = QTY-COLUMN (2, 1) + 20.

0025	0040	0005	0020	0000	0000	0000	0000	0000	0000	0000	0000

COMPUTE QTY-COLUMN (2, 2) = QTY-COLUMN (2, 2) + 10.

0025	0040	0005	0020	0010	0000	0000	0000	0000	0000	0000	0000

COMPUTE QTY-COLUMN (2, 2) = QTY-COLUMN (2, 2) + 25.

0025	0040	0005	0020	0035	0000	0000	0000	0000	0000	0000	0000

COMPUTE QTY-COLUMN (2, 3) = QTY-COLUMN (2, 3) + 50.

0025	0040	0005	0020	0035	0050	0000	0000	0000	0000	0000	0000

COMPUTE QTY-COLUMN (3, 2) = QTY-COLUMN (3, 2) + 5.

0025	0040	0005	0020	0035	0050	0000	0005	0000	0000	0000	0000

COMPUTE QTY-COLUMN (3, 2) = QTY-COLUMN (3, 2) + 40.

0025	0040	0005	0020	0035	0050	0000	0045	0000	0000	0000	0000

COMPUTE QTY-COLUMN (3, 3) = QTY-COLUMN (3, 3) + 20.

0025	0040	0005	0020	0035	0050	0000	0045	0020	0000	0000	0000

COMPUTE QTY-COLUMN (4, 1) = QTY-COLUMN (4, 1) + 15.

0025	0040	0005	0020	0035	0050	0000	0045	0020	0015	0000	0000

COMPUTE QTY-COLUMN (4, 1) = QTY-COLUMN (4, 1) + 25.

0025	0040	0005	0020	0035	0050	0000	0045	0020	0040	0000	0000

FIGURE 8–9

COMPUTE QTY-COLUMN (4, 2) = QTY-COLUMN (4, 2) + 10.

0025	0040	0005	0020	0035	0050	0000	0045	0020	0040	0010	0000

COMPUTE QTY-COLUMN (4, 3) = QTY-COLUMN (4, 3) + 55.

0025	0040	0005	0020	0035	0050	0000	0045	0020	0040	0010	0055

COMPUTE QTY-COLUMN (4, 3) = QTY-COLUMN (4, 3) + 15.

0025	0040	0005	0020	0035	0050	0000	0045	0020	0040	0010	0070

FIGURE 8–9 (continued)

Three-Dimensional Table

When an additional dimension is added to a table the lowest subdivision from a two-dimensional table is divided again. Figure 8–10 shows the same 72 bytes divided first as a one-, then two-, then three-dimensional table. The 1985 standard of COBOL will allow seven such subdivisions (seven dimensions). A commonly used version of BASIC allows 256 dimensions.

```
COBOL    01   QTR-TABLE.
              05   QTR-QTY                OCCURS 4 TIMES.
                   10   MONTH-QTY         OCCURS 3 TIMES.
                        15   SEMI-MONTH-QTY   OCCURS 2 TIMES   PIC 9(3).
BASIC    QTR.TABLE (4, 3, 2)
```

FIGURE 8–10

ACCESSING TABLE DATA

Up to this point COMPUTE statements have been used to demonstrate putting data into a table. A reference to a table element may be used in a program in most places that a variable of the same type could be used. Some examples are shown in Figure 8–11. Although we have used numeric literals as subscripts, variables are more likely to be used in an actual program.

COBOL   MOVE ZEROS TO QTY-TABLE.
         COMPUTE QTY-COLUMN (1, 3) = QUANTITY * RATE.
         MOVE QUANTITY TO QTY-COLUMN (2, 1).
         MOVE QTY-COLUMN (2, 1) TO QUANTITY-OUT.
         MULTIPLY PRICE BY QTY-COLUMN (3, 3).
         IF QTY-COLUMN (2, 2) = ZERO . . .

BASIC   LET QTY.TABLE (3, 2) = 0
         IF QTY.TABLE (1, 3) = QTY.TABLE (1, 2) . . .
         LET QTY.TABLE (1, 1) = QTY.ON.HAND * QTY.ON.ORDER
         LET AMOUNT = QTY.TABLE (1, 2) * COST
         LET QTY.HOLD = QTY.TABLE (2, 3)
         LET QTY.TABLE (3, 1) = QTY.TABLE (3, 1) + QUANTITY

FIGURE 8–11

Locating a Table Element

To locate a table element in memory, the computer uses two pieces of data.

1. The memory location where the table begins.
2. The distance into the table where the particular element is located.

The second item is referred to as displacement within the table and is calculated using the subscripts. Displacement indicates how many bytes there are prior to a given element. As a programmer we seldom need to calculate a displacement. However, doing it helps us to understand how tables are structured.

For an example we will first use the one-dimensional table called QTY-TABLE. Assume that QTY-TABLE begins at memory location 8000. QTY-ROW (1) has a displacement of zero. Given that the table begins at memory location 8000, then both QTY-TABLE (the group item) and QTY-ROW (1) begin at memory location 8000. They both have a displacement of zero. QTY-ROW (2) begins at memory location 8006 and has a displacement of 6, meaning there are six bytes before it in the table. QTY-ROW (3) begins at memory location 8012 and has a displacement of 12. See Figure 8–12.

Programming languages use the description of the table and the subscripts to calculate a displacement. The calculated displacement is then added to the memory location for the beginning

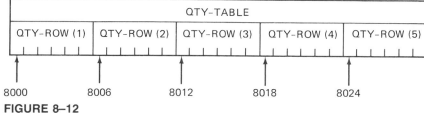

FIGURE 8–12

of the table. This gives the location for the table element. Let's use QTY-ROW (4) as our example. See Figure 8–13.

The steps are:

1) Subtract 1 from the subscript		4
		$-\ 1$
		3
2) Multiply by the size of an element		$*\ 6$
		18
3) Add the table location		$+\ 8000$
		8018

FIGURE 8–13

One is subtracted from the subscript so that the element to be located is not included in the calculation. The number of bytes prior to the element is the result desired.

SUBSCRIPT RANGE

COBOL will not create a diagnostic message if the subscript is too small or too large for the number of elements in the table. It proceeds with the displacement calculation and points to an area of memory outside the table. BASIC on the other hand will generate a diagnostic if the subscript is not in the range of the table. Using the table in Figure 8–12, let's execute the instruction below when **BRANCH** has a value of 8 (remember, QTY-TABLE has only 5 elements). Figure 8–14 shows the calculation.

COMPUTE QTY-ROW (BRANCH) = QTY-ROW (BRANCH) + QUANTITY.

8	(subscript)
$-\ 1$	
7	
$*\ 6$	(size of 1 element)
42	
$+\ 8000$	(beginning of TABLE -B)
8042	

FIGURE 8–14

The last byte in the table is at location 8029, therefore, COBOL will try to add QUANTITY to an area outside the table. Here are some of the possible results:

1) The area will be alphanumeric or have a different usage of numeric data and the program will fail trying to use the data.
2) The area will contain numeric data of the same usage. It will produce the wrong answer in the wrong place. The value of the data item at that location will have been destroyed.

The programmer cannot depend on COBOL as they can BASIC to use only subscripts that are in the proper range for the table. The value should be checked to see if it is within the range of the number of table elements before using it as a subscript.

Let's repeat the process of locating an element in a table with the two-dimensional table in Figure 8–15. See Figure 8–16 for the calculations.

The technique is the same for a three-dimensional table. There is one more subscript from which to subtract 1. The result is then multiplied by the size of an element for the table the subscript represents. This product is added to the beginning location of the table along with the other two. Try a few combinations of subscripts to satisfy yourself that the technique works.

QTY-TABLE											
QTY-ROW (1)			QTY-ROW (2)			QTY-ROW (3)			QTY-ROW (4)		
(1, 1)	(1, 2)	(1, 3)	(2, 1)	(2, 2)	(2, 3)	(3, 1)	(3, 2)	(3, 3)	(4, 1)	(4, 2)	(4, 3)

QTY-COLUMN (label for the bottom row)

FIGURE 8–15

```
01   QTY-TABLE.
     05   QTY-ROW   OCCURS 4 TIMES.
          10   QTY-COLUMN   OCCURS 3 TIMES     PIC 9(4).

     COMPUTE QTY-COLUMN (REGION, BRANCH) =
              QTY-COLUMN (REGION, BRANCH) + QUANTITY

          REGION = 3
          BRANCH = 2
```

1) Subtract 1 from first subscript

$$\begin{array}{r} 3 \\ -\,1 \\ \hline 2 \end{array}$$

2) Multiply by the size of an element (for QTY-ROW)

$$\begin{array}{r} *\,12 \\ \hline 24 \end{array}$$

3) Subtract 1 from second subscript

$$\begin{array}{r} 2 \\ -\,1 \\ \hline 1 \end{array}$$

4) Multiply by the size of an element (for QTY-COLUMN)

$$\begin{array}{r} *\,4 \\ \hline 4 \end{array}$$

5) Add both answers to table location

$$\begin{array}{r} 8000 \\ +\quad 24 \\ +\quad\ \ 4 \\ \hline 8028 \end{array}$$

FIGURE 8–16

OVERVIEW OF TABLE HANDLING

There are three general methods for loading (filling) a table with data and three common methods for accessing data in a table. The following is an overview of these methods so that you can compare them before we start a detailed description of each method.

Compile-Time Table

COBOL is one programming language where the table data can be coded as a part of the source code (in the DATA DIVISION using VALUE clauses). The table data is compiled along with the rest of the program and becomes a part of the object code. The table data loaded this way should be of a permanent nature so that the program does not have to be recompiled to change the table data. An example of data of a permanent type would be the names of the months.

Pre-Process Table

Data for this type of table is input from a keyboard or file, usually in the HSK routine. A loop is used to read each set of data and move it to one of the elements in the area reserved for the table. This technique is used when the data is of a less permanent nature; it provides the option of changing the data each time the program executes. The table data is loaded in the HSK routine so that it will be available as each record of the regular file(s) is processed. Examples would be freight rates, interest rates, and commission rates.

Execution-Time Table

Data for this table is developed as records are processed. The data for the table is often the result of calculations made in the processing of input records. The result is then stored in the appropriate element of the table. Normally this table will be printed as a part of a report.

Direct Access

This method is dependent on location. Subscripts are used to pinpoint the element required. Their value identifies the element by location regardless of its value.

```
COBOL    COMPUTE QTY-ROW (BRANCH) = QTY-ROW (BRANCH) + QUANTITY.
BASIC    LET QTY.ROW (BRANCH) = QTY.ROW (BRANCH) + QUANTITY
```

In the COMPUTE statement, BRANCH from the input was used to select the element to which QUANTITY will be added. The amount is added *directly* to the proper element without considering other elements.

Linear or Serial Search

In order to search, a search argument (the value we are looking for) is needed. A linear search is started at some point in the table and the search argument is compared against each element of the table one after another until a match is found. The matching element in the table is called the search function. A subscript is initialized with a value corresponding to the point in the table where the search should start. The programmer compares the search argument with that table element. If they are equal, the search is over; if not, 1 is added to the subscript and the comparison is made again. This continues until a match is found for the search argument or the end of the table is reached.

Binary Search

This search must be performed on a table which is in ascending or descending order on the search function. It is a very efficient method when used with large tables. The fact that the table is in order by search function, allows the elimination of one-half of the table from the search after each attempt to match a search argument and a search function. Assume the table is in ascending order. The search is started at a table entry in the middle of the table. There are three possible results based on the comparison.

1) The table entries prior to the item being compared are eliminated because their search functions are too low.
2) The table entries prior to the item being compared are eliminated because their search functions are too high.
3) The search function of the compared entry matches the search argument. The compared entry is the entry we are looking for.

If a match is not found the process is repeated by going to the middle of the remaining entries until a match is found or there are no more entries to try.

LOADING TABLES

Loading Compile-Time Tables

A compile-time table describes the contents of the table in the program itself. An example of a part of this procedure for the COBOL language is shown in Figure 8–17.

```
01      TABLE1.
        02      FILLER          PICTURE 9(12)   VALUE 050012001400.
        02      FILLER          PICTURE 9(12)   VALUE 100015001800.
        02      FILLER          PICTURE 9(12)   VALUE 170026002800.
        02      FILLER          PICTURE 9(12)   VALUE 200025003000.
        02      FILLER          PICTURE 9(12)   VALUE 290032003500.

01      TABLE2 REDEFINES TABLE1.
        02      PRODUCT         OCCURS 5 TIMES.
                03      SIZE            OCCURS 3 TIMES      PICTURE 9(4).
```

FIGURE 8–17

The important part of this illustration is the assigning of the actual numeric values needed for the table as a part of the storage assignment for the program. TABLE1 sets aside 60 bytes of storage (5 times 12) and stores the number following the words VALUE in those memory locations. TABLE2 causes those same 60 bytes of storage to be defined in a different way. 02 PRODUCT causes the 60 bytes to be split into five equal parts (OCCURS 5 TIMES). PRODUCT (1) would have a value of 050010001500. See Figure 8–18.

```
050012001400          PRODUCT (1)
100015001800          PRODUCT (2)
170026002800          PRODUCT (3)
200025003000          PRODUCT (4)
290032003500          PRODUCT (5)
```

FIGURE 8–18

Since they represent prices for three different-sized products, the numbers are not directly useful in this form. In order to get at a single price we inform the computer that the group should be subdivided again (OCCURS 3 TIMES). Now to access a price we could use SIZE (3, 2). The 3 indicates which group of 12 bytes, and the 2 indicates which one-third of that group (2000). This redefinition of storage is necessary because of the limitation of the programming language used (COBOL 1974 standard).

Entering the table data as a part of the program causes the information to be stored at the time the program is compiled. If the table information is of a rather permanent nature, this approach is suitable. Any change to the table data, however, will mean that the table data in the program must be changed and the program recompiled.

With a compile-time table no flowcharting is shown, because the data is loaded automatically when the program compiles. We normally flowchart only the steps in the execution of a program.

BASIC can store the data for a table within the program in one or more DATA statements. This data can then be placed in a table using a READ statement as a part of a loop after the program begins execution.

LOADING PRE-PROCESS TABLES

The second way of loading a table is to reserve the storage for the table but not assign the values. In this way the data in the table can be read from an input file. Table data of this type would be read near the beginning of the program (HSK), so that the table data can be used for comparisons and calculations as the other data records are processed. Normally the table data read as input is of a less permanent nature and needs to be changed often. This type of execution-time table we call PRE-PROCESS, because it is loaded prior to PROCESS in the mainline logic (which is divided into HSK, PROCESS, and EOJ.) The logic for this type of load is presented in Figure 8–19. The pseudocode is in Figure 8–20.

In Figure 8–19 the table load is a portion of the HSK routine. All other functions of HSK for a particular program would remain the same (including the initial read of the regular input

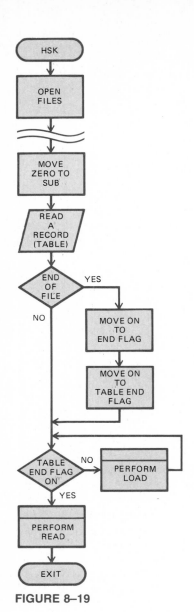

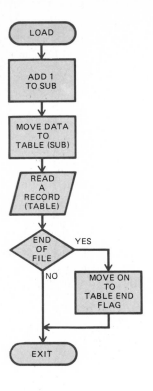

FIGURE 8–19

HSK ROUTINE

OPEN files
MOVE zero to load subscript
READ table file
    AT END of table file
        MOVE on to end flag
        MOVE on to table end flag
PERFORM load table routine until table end flag = on
PERFORM read routine

LOAD TABLE ROUTINE

ADD 1 to load subscript
MOVE table data to table (load subscript)
READ table data
    AT END of table file
        MOVE on to table end flag

FIGURE 8–20

files). First a table record is read. If an end-of-file condition is encountered on the first read, a special end flag called TABLE END FLAG is turned on as well as the regular end FLAG. Since the main processing of the program will depend on the use of the data in this table, we want to know if anything went wrong with the table load. Turning the regular END FLAG on will not allow the logic to proceed with the PROCESS routine. If a table record is present, neither flag is turned on.

Having read the first record, the TABLE END FLAG is tested. If it is off the LOAD-TABLE routine is performed until the flag is turned on. When it is on, logic passes to perform READ.

In LOAD TABLE we ADD to the load subscript in order to identify the proper element in the table in which to place the data. In a one-dimensional table we could initialize the subscript at zero. We would start the load by adding 1 to the subscript. This would allow the first table record to be placed in the first table element. Next, we move the record to the appropriate element and then read the record from the table file again. Data can be loaded in a table an element at a time, a dimension at a time, or the whole table at one time, depending on the amount of data required. The restriction is the size of our input record.

Data loaded in this way could come from an existing file, from keyboard input, or, in the case of BASIC, from DATA statements. Remember, if the table data comes from DATA statements in a BASIC program, the program must be revised in order to change the data.

LOADING EXECUTION-TIME TABLES

A third way of loading a table is to reserve storage without assigning values other than blanks or zeros and then create the specific values for the table by calculations or data movement within the program. Often information is created during processing that lends itself to storage in a table. Imagine a company with 10 divisions and four departments within each division. We are interested in keeping totals of some amount for each department and printing them out as a summary at the end of the program.

We can no longer use the technique in Chapter 7, where the total areas were printed, zeroed out, and then **reused** for the next group of totals. When the program finished, the total areas held only the last set accumulated. This time we want all the totals available at the same time in order to print them out at EOJ time. We can keep all of the totals for the summarization by establishing 40 separate counters, or we can use a 10-by-4 table (see Figure 8–21) subscripted as follows:

TABLE (DIVISION, DEPARTMENT)

When putting data in the table, the proper table element is easy to identify. In this case there is an input record which supplies the values for DIVISION and DEPARTMENT. Assume

DIVISION	DEPARTMENT 1	2	3	4
1	0984323	1290928	0943940	2909828
2	0789378	0345781	0123578	0347812
3	8903730	0378291	0782973	0723482
4	0348927	0278921	1287495	1874902
5	0347864	0347893	0237784	0984732
6	0982674	0487632	0578391	0283746
7	0785326	0853847	0895322	0543783
8	0758472	0674653	2947653	0487365
9	0648763	2764585	1847653	1847653
10	0874676	0873652	3774685	2746875

FIGURE 8–21

an input record with a value of 4 for DIVISION and 2 for DEPARTMENT. Then COBOL and BASIC programming statements which say:

    ADD NET PAY TO TABLE (DIVISION, DEPARTMENT)

or

    LET TABLE (DIVISION, DEPARTMENT) = TABLE (DIVISION, DEPARTMENT) + NET PAY

would add NET-PAY to the table element representing the fourth DIVISION and the second DEPARTMENT (see Figure 8–21).

The flowchart for adding data to a table using this direct-access technique is very simple. All that is required is the one process box shown in Figure 8–22. This flowchart is based on the assumptions that net pay can be calculated and that values for division and department are available from the input.

FIGURE 8–22

The alternative to using tables in programming is very cumbersome. First, we would need 40 different counters defined in memory with 40 different names. Then we would need 40 IF and 40 ADD statements in order to test which counter to use and add the net pay to the proper counter—that is:

    IF DIVISION = 1 AND DEPARTMENT = 1
        ADD NET-PAY TO NET-PAY-COUNTER-11.
    IF DIVISION = 1 AND DEPARTMENT = 2
        ADD NET-PAY TO NET-PAY-COUNTER-12.

and so on; when using a table only one statement is needed. The number of elements in a table does not affect the program statement; it would still require one programming statement for a 400-element table or a 4000-element table. Think of the writing required to handle 4000 separate data names.

TABLE ACCESS METHODS

A table can be accessed in two general ways, with a search or with direct access. If the value in the table that we are looking for is known but not its location, a search is appropriate. A search can be linear or binary.

In some high-level languages a relatively automatic table search is possible. Assume an input record which provides the value to be searched for. Some programming languages allow us to specify the value (a search argument) and to state what should be done if the value is located in the table. We are also allowed to state what should be done if the matching value is not in the table. Other programming languages or techniques may require the programmer to compare the search argument with each element of the table and to increment the subscript in a looping process in order to compare the search argument with the next element.

If a position in a table should be accessed irrespective of its value, then the position can be specified through controlling the subscripts (either by input or by an incrementing process) and the computer does the rest. This is the direct access method.

Table Access-Linear Search

In order to use a linear search the search is started (usually at the beginning of the table) and each table element is compared with the search argument. The search can be stopped when a value equal to the search argument is reached or when the end of the table is reached. On average comparisons against one-half of the elements in the table must be made in order to find a match. This would be a reasonable approach, for example, if we had a table of account number against which payroll expenses could be charged. The account number or numbers from each person's pay record would be used to search the table for a match. If no match were found, an error would be indicated, either in preparing the pay record or in maintaining the table. The flowchart for the linear search is shown in Figure 8–23. Figure 8–24 is the pseudocode. We are not assuming any order for the table.

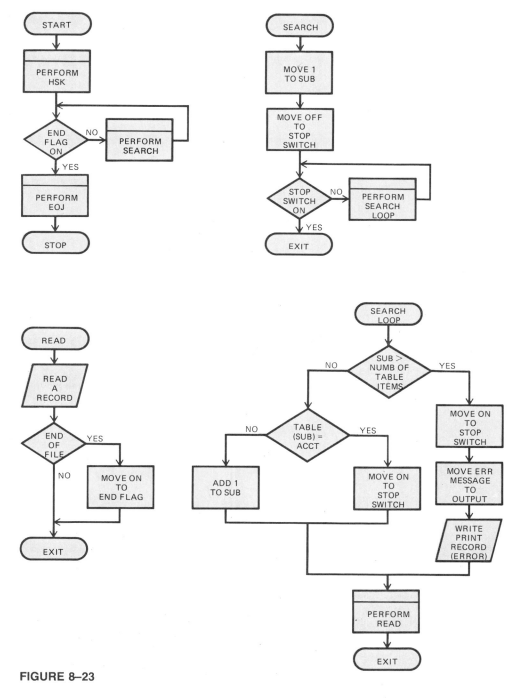

FIGURE 8–23

```
PERFORM hsk routine
PERFORM search routine until end flag = on
PERFORM eoj routine
STOP
```

SEARCH ROUTINE

```
MOVE 1 to search subscript
MOVE off to stop switch
PERFORM search loop routine until stop switch = on
```

SEARCH LOOP ROUTINE

```
IF search subscript > number of table elements
        MOVE on to stop switch
        MOVE error message to output
        WRITE print record (error)
ELSE
        IF table (search subscript) = account number
              MOVE on to stop switch
        ELSE
              ADD 1 to search subscript
        ENDIF
ENDIF
PERFORM read routine
```

FIGURE 8–24

Table Access-Binary Search

The second search method is called a binary search. It is suitable for large ordered tables because it can cut down the number of comparisons necessary to locate an item in a table. Let's first go over the concept in general terms and then develop a flowchart.

Assume a table in ascending order. The first step is to divide the table in half and compare the search argument against an element from the middle of the table. This element will likely be greater or less than the item we are looking for. If it is equal, then the search is over on the first try. If the element is greater than the search argument, then every element following it

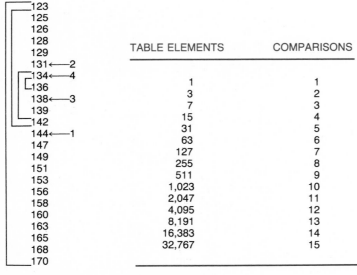

TABLE ELEMENTS	COMPARISONS
1	1
3	2
7	3
15	4
31	5
63	6
127	7
255	8
511	9
1,023	10
2,047	11
4,095	12
8,191	13
16,383	14
32,767	15

FIGURE 8–25 **FIGURE 8–26**

will also be greater and, therefore, not what we are looking for. This allows us to ignore the last half of the table and concentrate on the first half. A second attempt to locate the item is made by splitting the first half of the table in half and comparing against the middle item. If the table element is greater than the search argument, only the first one-fourth of the table can contain the needed match. If they are equal, we have succeeded. If the table element is less only the second one-fourth of the table can contain the needed match. This process continues until the item is found or is determined to be missing.

Assume that we are looking for a value of 134 in a table arranged in ascending order, as shown in Figure 8–25. The middle element is tested first and found to be larger (144) than the search argument. Then the middle element for the first half of the table is tested. It is too small (131). The remaining segment is split and the search argument is compared to 138. This is too large, so the remaining section is split again and the 134 is found. This technique does not seem particularly impressive until we see its application to a large table. Figure 8–26 lists the maximum number of comparisons necessary as the size of the table increases.

The flowchart for this technique is shown in Figure 8–27. Figure 8–28 is the pseudocode.

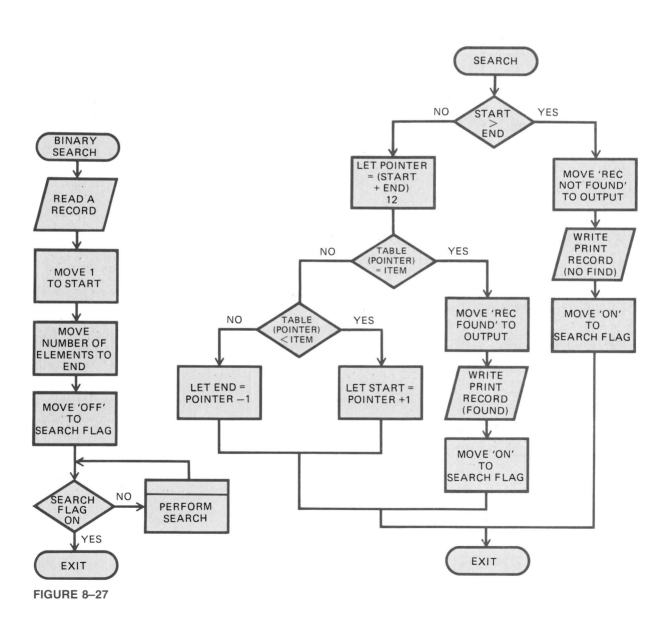

FIGURE 8–27

BINARY SEARCH ROUTINE

```
READ search argument
MOVE 1 to begin
MOVE number of table element to end
MOVE off to end search flag
PERFORM search loop routine until end search flag = on
```

SEARCH LOOP ROUTINE

```
IF start is greater than end
        MOVE 'record not found' to output
        WRITE print record (no find)
        MOVE on to end search flag
ELSE
        COMPUTE pointer = (start + end) / 2
        IF table (pointer) = search argument
                MOVE 'record found' to output
                WRITE print record (found)
                MOVE on to end search flag
        ELSE
                IF table (pointer) < search argument
                        COMPUTE start = pointer + 1
                ELSE
                        COMPUTE end = pointer − 1
                ENDIF
        ENDIF
ENDIF
```

FIGURE 8–28

Table Access-Direct

A table can be accessed in another way when we know the position of the element is more important than its value. This is the case when particular values are assigned to an element in a table because of its position. Figure 8–29 shows a list of product prices arranged in the table so that the first price (10.00) represents product 1, the second price (12.00) represents product 2, and so on.

In this example we are not looking for a specific value. We are looking for the price which corresponds to a product number. For example, whatever value is in the table at TABLE (4) represents the price of product number 4.

```
10.00
12.00
14.00
17.00
19.00
22.00
25.00
28.00
31.00
35.00
```

FIGURE 8–29

To access one of these prices, we use what we know about its position. The product number determines the position of the table element, so the product number is used as the subscript.

The COBOL statement COMPUTE AMOUNT = TABLE (PRODUCT) * UNITS provides direct access to the table element. To change this to a BASIC statement, change the COMPUTE to LET.

WRITING OUT A TABLE

When writing out a table, there are two major things to take into consideration:

1) The number of dimensions in the table.
2) The form the output is to take.

Some of the possible combinations will be demonstrated, starting with one-dimensional tables and working up to three-dimensional tables.

Writing a One-Dimensional Table

A one-dimensional table containing quarterly taxes will be used in the first example. Each quarter's taxes will be printed on a separate line. Figure 8–30 is the print chart, Figure 8–31 shows the structure for the table.

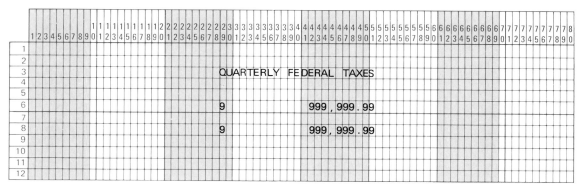

FIGURE 8–30

FIGURE 8–31

The flowchart is in Figure 8–32 and the pseudocode is in Figure 8–33.

The value of QUARTER is initialized to 1. The routine WRITE TAX TABLE prints the heading line for the table. The routine WRITE QUARTER TAX LINE is then performed multiple times. QUARTER is incremented by 1 each time the paragraph is performed. The paragraph is performed until QUARTER exceeds the limit of 4. After performing the paragraph for the fourth time QUARTER is incremented to five. This makes the test condition true and the PERFORM complete.

Let's look at how the ability to vary QUARTER assists in the printing of the table. The variable name QUARTER was chosen as a reminder that each line represents a quarter. QUARTER is being used as a counter. QUARTER is used twice in the WRITE QUARTER TAX LINE routine; first to MOVE the number of the quarter to an area in the print line, and second as a subscript to control which element of QUARTERLY TAXES is being moved to an area in the print line.

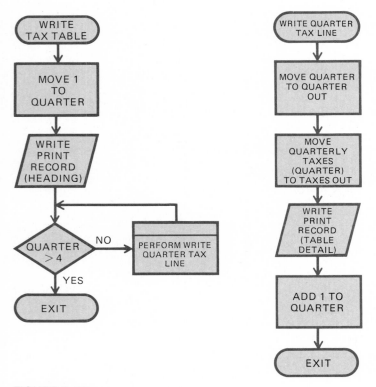

FIGURE 8–32

WRITE TAX TABLE ROUTINE

MOVE 1 to quarter
WRITE print record (heading)
PERFORM write quarter tax line routine until quarter is greater than 4

WRITE QUARTER TAX LINE ROUTINE

MOVE quarter to quarter out
MOVE quarterly taxes (quarter) to taxes out
WRITE print record (table detail line)
ADD 1 to quarter

FIGURE 8–33

WRITING A TWO-DIMENSIONAL TABLE

Net pay is stored in a two-dimensional table by division and department. This table is to be printed in the EOJ routine. The print chart is shown in Figure 8–34 and a diagram of the table structure is shown in Figure 8–35.

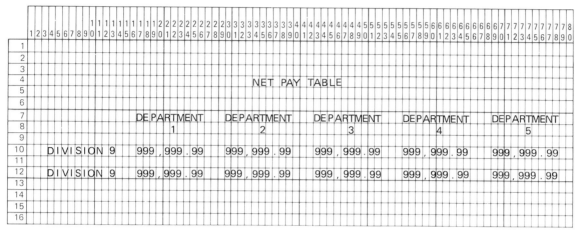

FIGURE 8–34

FIGURE 8–35

Figure 8–36 is the flowchart and Figure 8–37 is the pseudocode.

The word DEPARTMENT and the department numbers are provided in the column headings. The word DIVISION is a literal in the table detail line. The division number is provided by the subscript which is being varied (DIVISION). When the first line is prepared and printed in WRITE NET PAY LINE, DIVISION will have a value of 1. This value is moved to DIVISION OUT and represents the division number of the printed output. The second time WRITE NET PAY LINE is performed, DIVISION will have a value of 2, then 3 and so on.

DIVISION is also used as the first of two subscripts to move data from the table. The first subscript represents the division, and the second the department. DIVISION has a new value each time WRITE NET PAY LINE is performed. This means the data for a new division is transferred each time the routine is performed. The elements for each department within a division are identified by the second subscript which is given as a literal (1 through 5). There are five different variables for table elements on the print line, therefore five moves are required.

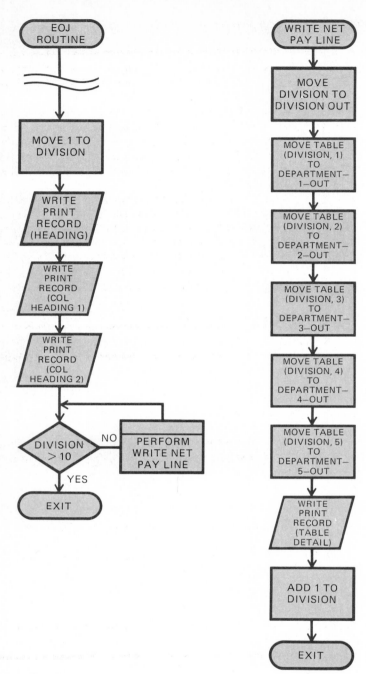

FIGURE 8–36

EOJ ROUTINE

MOVE 1 to division
WRITE print record (table heading)
WRITE print record (column heading 1)
WRITE print record (column heading 2)
PERFORM write net pay line until division is greater than 10

FIGURE 8–37

WRITE NET PAY LINE ROUTINE

MOVE division to division out
MOVE table (division, 1) to department 1 out
MOVE table (division, 2) to department 2 out
MOVE table (division, 3) to department 3 out
MOVE table (division, 4) to department 4 out
MOVE table (division, 5) to department 5 out
WRITE print record (table detail line)
ADD 1 to division

FIGURE 8–37 (continued)

WRITING A THREE-DIMENSIONAL TABLE

When writing a three-dimensional table, one dimension is usually transferred to the headings. Given a three-dimensional table with STATES, COUNTIES and CITIES, the name or number of the state would be incorporated in the heading. The counties and cities would form the rows and columns. This would result in the printing of multiple two-dimensional tables, one for each state. Each table would occupy all or part of a page.

An example of printing a three-dimensional table is provided. It includes payroll data for REGIONS, BRANCHES and SALESPERSONS. REGION is transferred to the headings. In the example, each row of the output represents a branch and each column a salesperson. See Figure 8–38 for the print chart and Figure 8–39 for the table structure.

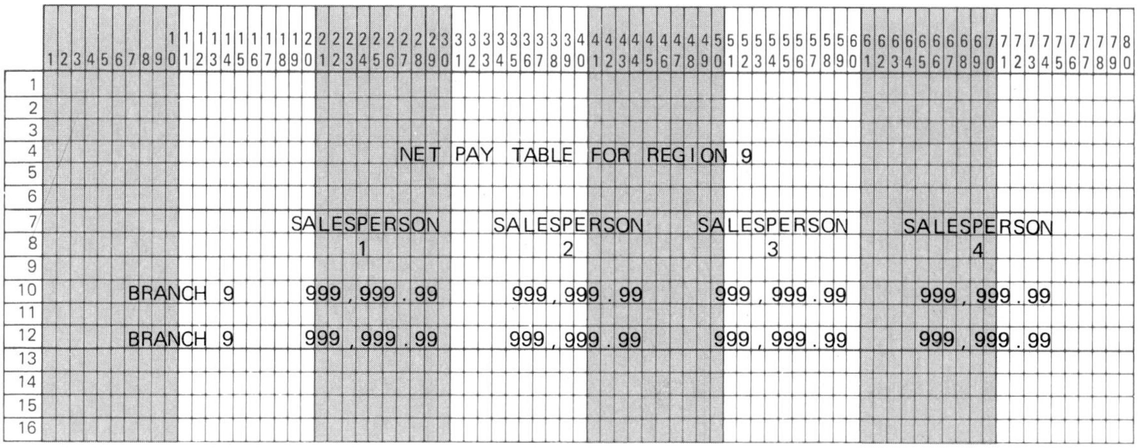

FIGURE 8–38

<table>
<tr><td></td><td colspan="48">NET PAY TABLE</td></tr>
<tr><td>REGION</td><td colspan="16">(1)</td><td colspan="16">(2)</td><td colspan="16">(3)</td></tr>
<tr><td>BRANCH</td><td colspan="4">(1, 1)</td><td colspan="4">(1, 2)</td><td colspan="4">(1, 3)</td><td colspan="4">(1, 4)</td><td colspan="4">(2, 1)</td><td colspan="4">(2, 2)</td><td colspan="4">(2, 3)</td><td colspan="4">(2, 4)</td><td colspan="4">(3, 1)</td><td colspan="4">(3, 2)</td><td colspan="4">(3, 3)</td><td colspan="4">(3, 4)</td></tr>
<tr><td>SALESPERSON</td><td>(1, 1, 1)</td><td>(1, 1, 2)</td><td>(1, 1, 3)</td><td>(1, 1, 4)</td><td>(1, 2, 1)</td><td>(1, 2, 2)</td><td>(1, 2, 3)</td><td>(1, 2, 4)</td><td>(1, 3, 1)</td><td>(1, 3, 2)</td><td>(1, 3, 3)</td><td>(1, 3, 4)</td><td>(1, 4, 1)</td><td>(1, 4, 2)</td><td>(1, 4, 3)</td><td>(1, 4, 4)</td><td>(2, 1, 1)</td><td>(2, 1, 2)</td><td>(2, 1, 3)</td><td>(2, 1, 4)</td><td>(2, 2, 1)</td><td>(2, 2, 2)</td><td>(2, 2, 3)</td><td>(2, 2, 4)</td><td>(2, 3, 1)</td><td>(2, 3, 2)</td><td>(2, 3, 3)</td><td>(2, 3, 4)</td><td>(2, 4, 1)</td><td>(2, 4, 2)</td><td>(2, 4, 3)</td><td>(2, 4, 4)</td><td>(3, 1, 1)</td><td>(3, 1, 2)</td><td>(3, 1, 3)</td><td>(3, 1, 4)</td><td>(3, 2, 1)</td><td>(3, 2, 2)</td><td>(3, 2, 3)</td><td>(3, 2, 4)</td><td>(3, 3, 1)</td><td>(3, 3, 2)</td><td>(3, 3, 3)</td><td>(3, 3, 4)</td><td>(3, 4, 1)</td><td>(3, 4, 2)</td><td>(3, 4, 3)</td><td>(3, 4, 1)</td></tr>
</table>

FIGURE 8–39

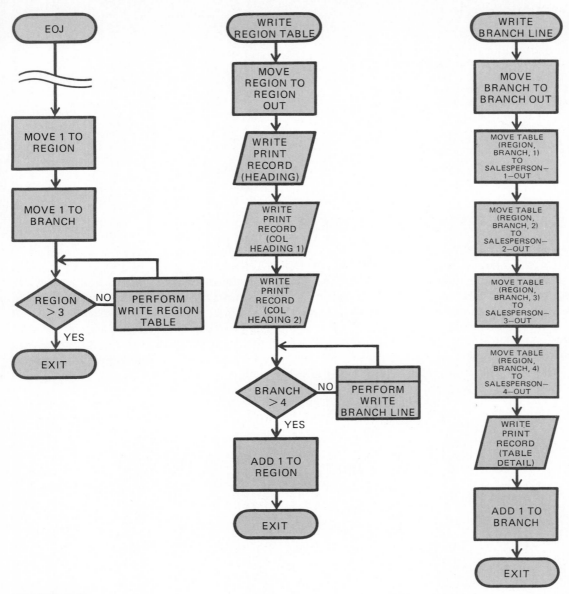

FIGURE 8–40

Figure 8–40 is the flowchart and Figure 8–41 is the pseudocode.

These routines print six two-dimensional tables, one for each occurrence of REGION. This is controlled by a PERFORM in EOJ. WRITE REGION TABLE is performed from EOJ varying the first of three subscripts (REGION).

In WRITE REGION TABLE, REGION is moved to an area in the main heading. This heading and the two column headings are then written. The column headings include the salesperson numbers. Next, the WRITE BRANCH LINE routine is performed varying the second subscript (BRANCH).

EOJ ROUTINE

MOVE 1 to region
MOVE 1 to branch
PERFORM write region table routine until region is greater than 3

WRITE REGION TABLE ROUTINE

MOVE region to region out
WRITE print record (table heading)
WRITE print record (column heading 1)
WRITE print record (column heading 2)
PERFORM write branch line until branch is greater than 4
ADD 1 to region

WRITE BRANCH LINE

MOVE branch to branch out
MOVE table (region, branch, 1) to salesperson 1 out
MOVE table (region, branch, 2) to salesperson 2 out
MOVE table (region, branch, 3) to salesperson 3 out
MOVE table (region, branch, 4) to salesperson 4 out
WRITE print record (table detail line)
ADD 1 to branch

FIGURE 8–41

In WRITE BRANCH LINE, BRANCH is moved to BRANCH OUT to represent the branch number. Then four MOVE statements are used to transfer each of the salesperson elements for that branch. A literal is used as the subscript representing the salesperson. The line representing the salespersons for one branch of one region is then written.

COMPOSITE EXAMPLE

In order to demonstrate some of the table-usage techniques covered in this chapter let's:

1. Load a pre-process table.
2. Use a linear search to access data from the table.
3. Use the table data in a calculation.
4. Store the result of the calculation in a new table using direct access.
5. Write out the table containing the results of the calculations.

In order to do this two types of input are required—data for the table and data which is used to access the table and perform the calculation. The record formats and the actual data for the two files are shown in Figure 8–42. The print chart is shown in Figure 8–43.

In the example each account number is being paid at a different bonus rate. This rate is to be multiplied by the yearly salary in each employee's record. We are to print out the bonus for each employee and save the bonus amount in a table organized by division. The total bonuses paid are to be printed by division in the EOJ routine. The flowchart is shown in Figure 8–44 and the pseudocode in Figure 8–45.

The logic for each of these routines has been discussed at a previous point in the chapter. The COBOL example is Figure 8–46 and the BASIC is Figure 8–47.

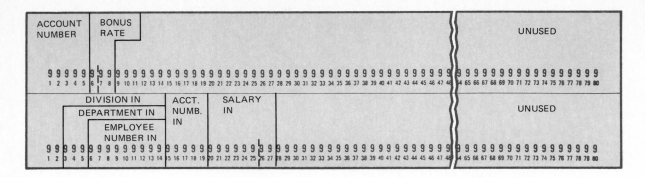

TABLE DATA

12345,.08
12346,.07
12347,.06
12348,.05
12349,.04
12340,.05

REGULAR DATA

01,111,316486794,12345,100000.00
01,111,832836396,12347,90000.00
01,222,382766381,12348,80000.00
02,111,384682697,12345,70000.00
03,111,384745783,12347,60000.00
03,111,398746831,12345,50000.00
04,111,394764824,12340,40000.00
04,222,387547427,12346,30000.00
05,111,397647783,12349,20000.00
05,111,975735273,12347,10000.00

FIGURE 8–42

```
                        LISTING OF BONUSES                    PAGE XX

   DIV     DEPT    EMPLOYEE  NUMB    ACCT         SALARY           BONUS

   XX      XXX     XXXXXXXXX         XXXXX        XXXXXX.XX        XXXXX.XX
   XX      XXX     XXXXXXXXX         XXXXX        XXXXXX.XX        XXXXX.XX
```

```
                        BONUSES  BY  DIVISION

                   DIVISION                        BONUS

                     XX                          XXXXX.XX

                     XX                          XXXXX.XX
```

FIGURE 8–43

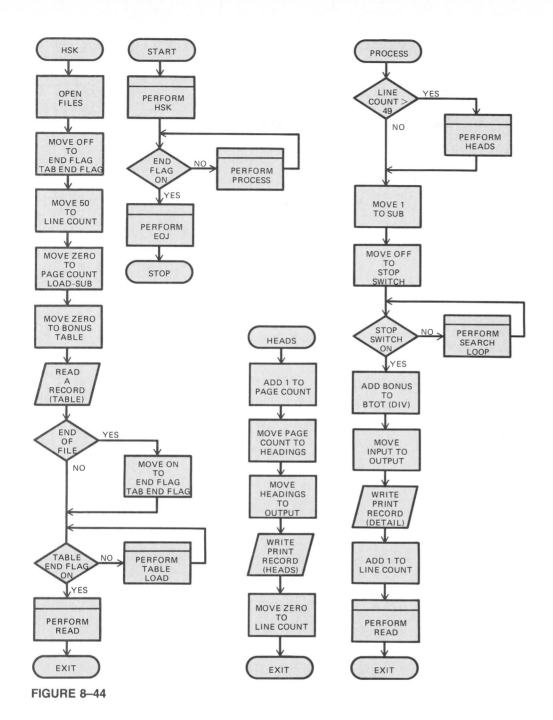

FIGURE 8–44

HSK ROUTINE

OPEN files
MOVE off to end flag
MOVE off to table end flag
MOVE 99 to line count
MOVE zero to page count
MOVE zero to load subscript
MOVE zero to write subscript
MOVE zeros to bonus total table

FIGURE 8–45

READ table file
        AT END of table file
                MOVE on to table end flag
                MOVE on to end flag
PERFORM table load routine until table end flag = on
PERFORM Read routine

PROCESS ROUTINE

IF line count > 49
        PERFORM heads routine
ENDIF
MOVE 1 to search subscript
MOVE off to stop switch
PERFORM search loop until stop switch = on
COMPUTE total bonus (division) = total bonus (division) + bonus
MOVE input to output
WRITE print record (detail)
ADD 1 to line count
PERFORM read routine

EOJ ROUTINE

WRITE print record (table heads)
MOVE 1 to write subscript
PERFORM write table until write subscript > 5
CLOSE files

TABLE LOAD ROUTINE

ADD 1 to load subscript
MOVE account number to table (load subscript)
MOVE bonus rate to table (load subscript)
READ table file
        AT END of table file
                MOVE on to table end flag

READ ROUTINE

READ Data file
        AT END of data file
                MOVE on to end flag

WRITE TABLE LINE ROUTINE

WRITE print record (table detail)
ADD 1 to write subscript

HEADS ROUTINE

ADD 1 to page count
MOVE page count to headings
WRITE print record (heads)
MOVE zero to line count

SEARCH LOOP ROUTINE

IF search subscript > number of table elements
        MOVE on to stop switch
        WRITE print record (error)
ELSE
        IF bonus table (search subscript, 1) = account number
                MOVE on to stop switch
                COMPUTE bonus = bonus table (search subscript, 2) * salary

FIGURE 8–45 (continued)

```
          ELSE
               ADD 1 to search subscript
          END IF
ENDIF
```

FIGURE 8–45 (continued)

COBOL VERSION

PROCEDURE DIVISION.

```
MAINLINE-LOGIC.
     PERFORM HSK-ROUTINE.
     PERFORM PROCESS-ROUTINE UNTIL END-FLAG = 'ON.
     PERFORM EOJ-ROUTINE.
     STOP RUN.
HSK-ROUTINE.
     OPEN INPUT   C8TABLE
                       C8DATA
          OUTPUT PRINT-FILE.
     MOVE 'OFF' to END-FLAG.
     MOVE 'OFF' TO TABLE-END-FLAG.
     MOVE 50 TO LINE-COUNT.
     MOVE ZERO TO PAGE-COUNT.
     MOVE ZERO TO LOAD-SUB.
     MOVE ZEROS TO BONUS-TOTAL-TABLE.
     READ C8 TABLE
          AT END
                MOVE 'ON' TO TABLE-END-FLAG
                MOVE 'ON' TO END-FLAG.
     PERFORM TABLE-LOAD-ROUTINE UNTIL TABLE-END-FLAG = 'ON.'
     PERFORM READ-ROUTINE.
     PROCESS-ROUTINE.
     IF LINE-COUNT > 49
          PERFORM HEADS-ROUTINE.
     SET SEARCH-SUB TO 1.
     SEARCH TABLE-ELEMENT
          AT END
                MOVE ZEROS TO BONUS
                DISPLAY 'ERROR'
          WHEN TABLE-ACCT (SEARCH-SUB) = ACCT-IN
                COMPUTE BONUS = TABLE-BONUS-RATE (SEARCH-SUB) *
                     SALARY-IN.
     MOVE DIV-IN         TO DIV-OUT.
     MOVE DEPT-IN        TO DEPT-OUT.
     MOVE EMPNO-IN       TO EMPNO-OUT.
     MOVE ACCT-IN        TO ACCT-OUT.
     MOVE SALARY-IN      TO SALARY-OUT.
     MOVE BONUS          TO BONUS-OUT.
     ADD BONUS TO BONUS-TOTAL (DIV-IN).
     WRITE PRINT-RECORD FROM DETAIL-LINE
          AFTER ADVANCING 1 LINES.
     ADD 1 TO LINE-COUNT.
     PERFORM READ-ROUTINE.
EOJ-ROUTINE.
     WRITE PRINT-RECORD FROM TAB-HEADS1
          AFTER ADVANCING TOP-OF-PAGE.
     WRITE PRINT-RECORD FROM TAB-HEADS2
          AFTER ADVANCING 2 LINES.
     PERFORM WRITE-TABLE-LINE-ROUTINE VARYING WRITE-SUB
          FROM 1 BY 1 UNTIL WRITE-SUB > 5.
     CLOSE C8TABLE
          C8DATA
          PRINT-FILE.
```

FIGURE 8–46

```
TABLE-LOAD-ROUTINE.
     ADD 1 TO LOAD-SUB.
     MOVE ACCT            TO TABLE-ACCT (LOAD-SUB).
     MOVE BONUS-RATE    TO TABLE-BONUS-RATE (LOAD-SUB).
     READ C8TABLE
          AT END
               MOVE 'ON' TO TABLE-END-FLAG.
READ ROUTINE
     READ C8DATA
          AT END
               MOVE 'ON' TO END-FLAG.
WRITE-TABLE-LINE-ROUTINE.
     MOVE WRITE-SUB TO TAB-DIV-OUT.
     MOVE BONUS-TOTAL (WRITE-SUB) TO TAB-BONUS-OUT.
     WRITE PRINT-RECORD FROM TABLE-DETAIL
          AFTER ADVANCING 2 LINES.
HEADS-ROUTINE.
     ADD 1 TO PAGE-COUNT.
     MOVE PAGE-COUNT TO PAGE-OUT.
     WRITE PRINT-RECORD FROM HEADS1
          AFTER ADVANCING TOP-OF-PAGE.
     WRITE PRINT-RECORD FROM HEADS2
          AFTER ADVANCING 2 LINES.
     MOVE ZERO TO LINE-COUNT.
```

FIGURE 8–46 (continued)

BASIC VERSION

```
'PROGRAMMERS:   J AND J, INC.
'DATE:          8/11/90
'PROGRAM NAME:  CASE8
'*******************************************************************************
'                               MAINLINE LOGIC                                *
'*******************************************************************************
GOSUB HOUSEKEEPING.ROUTINE
WHILE END.FLAG$ = "OFF"
    GOSUB PROCESS.ROUTINE
WEND
GOSUB EOJ.ROUTINE
END
'*******************************************************************************
'                               HOUSEKEEPING ROUTINE                          *
'*******************************************************************************
HOUSEKEEPING.ROUTINE:
OPEN "A:C8TABLE1" FOR INPUT AS #1
OPEN "A:C8DATA1" FOR INPUT AS #3
D$ = "SCRN:":  CLS
INPUT "OUTPUT TO THE PRINTER - ANSWER Y OR N"; ANSWER$
IF ANSWER$ = "y" OR ANSWER$ = "Y" THEN
    D$ = "LPT1:":WIDTH "LPT1:",80:LPRINT CHR$(15)
END IF
OPEN D$ FOR OUTPUT AS #2
LET DETAIL.FORMAT$ = SPACE$(5) + "##" + SPACE$(5) + "###" + SPACE$(5) +
    "#########" + SPACE$(5) + "#####" + SPACE$(5) + "######.##" + SPACE$(5)
    + "#####.##"
LET TABLE.FORMAT$ = SPACE$(19) + "##" + SPACE$(20) + "######.##"
DIM TOTAL.TABLE(5), BONUS.TABLE(7,2)
LET END.FLAG$ = "OFF"
```

FIGURE 8–47

```
LET TABLE.END.FLAG$ = "OFF"
LET LINE.COUNT = 50
LET STOP.SWITCH$ = "N"
INPUT #1, TABLE.ACCT.NBR, TABLE.BONUS.RATE
WHILE TABLE.END.FLAG$ = "OFF"
    GOSUB LOAD.TABLE.ROUTINE
WEND
GOSUB READ.ROUTINE
RETURN
'*********************************************************************
'                          PROCESS ROUTINE                          *
'*********************************************************************
PROCESS.ROUTINE:
LET STOP.SWITCH$ = "N"
LET SEARCH.SUB = 1
IF LINE.COUNT > 49 THEN
    GOSUB HEADS.ROUTINE
END IF
WHILE STOP.SWITCH$ = "N"
    GOSUB SEARCH.ROUTINE
WEND
LET TOTAL.TABLE(DIV) = TOTAL.TABLE(DIV) + BONUS
PRINT #2, USING DETAIL.FORMAT$; DIV,DEPT,EMP.NBR#, ACCOUNT, SALARY, BONUS
GOSUB READ.ROUTINE
RETURN
'*********************************************************************
'                            EOJ ROUTINE                            *
'*********************************************************************
EOJ.ROUTINE:
PRINT #2, CHR$(12)
PRINT #2, TAB(26); "BONUSES BY DIVISION": PRINT #2,
PRINT #2, TAB(18); "DIVISION                    BONUS": PRINT #2,
LET WRITE.SUB = 1
WHILE WRITE.SUB <= 5
    GOSUB WRITE.TABLE.LINE.ROUTINE
WEND
CLOSE
RETURN
'*********************************************************************
'                         LOAD TABLE ROUTINE                        *
'*********************************************************************
LOAD.TABLE.ROUTINE:
LET LOAD.SUB = LOAD.SUB + 1
INPUT #1, TABLE.ACCT.NBR, TABLE.BONUS.RATE
LET BONUS.TABLE(LOAD.SUB, 1) = TABLE.ACCT.NBR
LET BONUS.TABLE(LOAD.SUB, 2) = TABLE.BONUS.RATE
IF EOF(1) THEN
    LET TABLE.END.FLAG$ = "ON"
END IF
RETURN
'*********************************************************************
'                            READ ROUTINE                           *
'*********************************************************************
READ.ROUTINE:
INPUT #3, DIV, DEPT, EMP.NBR#, ACCOUNT, SALARY
IF EOF(3) THEN
    LET END.FLAG$ = "ON"
END IF
RETURN
```

FIGURE 8–47 (continued)

```
/*******************************************************************************
'                         WRITE TABLE LINE ROUTINE                            *
/*******************************************************************************
WRITE.TABLE.LINE.ROUTINE:
PRINT #2, USING TABLE.FORMAT$; WRITE.SUB, TOTAL.TABLE(WRITE.SUB)
LET WRITE.SUB = WRITE.SUB + 1
RETURN
/*******************************************************************************
'                              HEADS ROUTINE                                  *
/*******************************************************************************
HEADS.ROUTINE:
LET PAGE.COUNT = PAGE.COUNT + 1
PRINT #2, CHR$(12)
PRINT #2, TAB(26); "LISTING OF BONUSES";
PRINT #2, TAB(59) USING "PAGE ##"; PAGE.COUNT
PRINT #2,
PRINT #2,
PRINT #2, TAB(5); "DIV    DEPT    EMPLOYEE NUMB    ACCT"; TAB(47); "SALARY          BONUS"
PRINT #2,
LET LINE.COUNT = 0
RETURN
/*******************************************************************************
'                              SEARCH ROUTINE                                 *
/*******************************************************************************
SEARCH.ROUTINE:
IF SEARCH.SUB > 7   THEN
    LET BONUS = 0
    LET STOP.SWITCH$ = "Y"
    PRINT #2, "ERROR"
ELSE
    IF BONUS.TABLE(SEARCH.SUB,1) = ACCOUNT THEN
        LET BONUS = BONUS.TABLE(SEARCH.SUB,2) * SALARY
        LET STOP.SWITCH$ = "Y"
    ELSE
        LET SEARCH.SUB = SEARCH.SUB + 1
    END IF
END IF
RETURN
```

FIGURE 8–47 (continued)

CHAPTER VOCABULARY _____

Binary search	Linear search	Subscript
Compile-time table	Loading	Table access
Dimension	Occurs	Table switch
Direct access	Pre-process table	Tables
Execution-time table		

MATCHING

A. Binary search
B. Linear search
C. Dimension
D. Subscript

E. Compile-time table
F. Execution-time table
G. Pre-process table

_C_ **1.** The number of times a table is subdivided.

_B_ **2.** A table access method which examines each table element in a sequential manner.

_G_ **3.** A table loaded in HSK.

_A_ **4.** A table access method which divides the table in half for each new attempt at locating an element required.

_D_ **5.** Used to identify one element in a table.

_E_ **6.** A table whose values are written as the program is coded in COBOL.

_F_ **7.** A table whose values are established as regular processing is done.

TRUE/FALSE

T **(F)** **1.** Subscripts are always constants.

(T) F **2.** Binary searches are especially suited to large tables.

(T) F **3.** Direct table access is the fastest of all table access methods.

(T) F **4.** For a large table a binary search is faster than a linear search.

T **(F)** **5.** A one-dimensional table could be subscripted as TABLE (5, 2).

(T) F **6.** Tables in which we are looking for a particular value must be loaded in ascending or descending order.

(T) F **7.** A three-dimensional table would need three subscripts to access one element.

(T) F **8.** Pre-process tables should be loaded in HSK.

MATCHING

Indicate whether each of the following tables is most likely to be loaded as a _____ table.

a) COMPILE-TIME
b) PRE-PROCESS
c) EXECUTION

_A_ **1.** The names of the months.

_C_ **2.** NET PAY per pay period.

_A_ **3.** The names of the days of the week.

_B_ **4.** Current interest rates on Treasury Bills.

_A_ **5.** The names of states.

_B_ **6.** Freight rates.

_B_ **7.** Sales tax by month.

_B_ **8.** The Prime Interest Rate.

_C_ **9.** Commissions earned by salespersons.

_A_ **10.** Miles between locations.

EXERCISE

1. Given the table described below for storage, perform the calculations. Place each answer in the proper table element. The results should be cumulative.

```
01   AMOUNT-TABLE          VALUE ZEROS.
     05   ROW-ELEMENT      OCCURS 4 TIMES.
          10   COL-ELEMENT  OCCURS 3 TIMES      PIC 9(5).
```

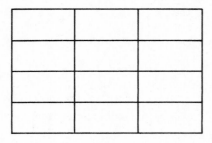

ADD 15 TO COL-ELEMENT (2, 1).
ADD 40 TO COL-ELEMENT (4, 2).
ADD 10 TO COL-ELEMENT (1, 3).
ADD 25 TO COL-ELEMENT (3, 2).
ADD COL-ELEMENT (3, 2) TO COL-ELEMENT (4, 2).
ADD COL-ELEMENT (4, 2) TO COL-ELEMENT (1, 3).
SUBTRACT COL-ELEMENT (3, 2) FROM COL-ELEMENT (1, 3).

2. Construct and label a table for pricing a piece of furniture which comes in two sizes and four grades of upholstery fabric. Use a five-byted element and indicate both subscripts and displacement.
3. Given the taxable wages as input, flowchart a routine to search a tax table for the appropriate row and calculate the tax.

IF THE AMOUNT OF WAGES IS:		THE AMOUNT OF INCOME TAX TO BE WITHHELD SHALL BE:	
OVER:	BUT NOT OVER:	0	OF EXCESS OVER:
Not over $58			
$ 58	$ 171	12&	$ 68
$ 171	$ 396	$ 13.56 plus 15%	$ 171
$ 396	$ 600	$ 47.31 plus 19%	$ 396
$ 600	$ 917	$ 86.07 plus 25%	$ 600
$ 917	$1158	$165.32 plus 30%	$ 917
$1158	$1379	$237.62 plus 34%	$1158
$1379		$312.76 plus 37%	$1379

4. Flowchart a routine to move out and print a table which has five rows and five columns. All items from a single row are to be printed on the same line.

DISCUSSION QUESTIONS

1. What are some advantages of using tables in programs?
2. Name some tables that should be loaded at compile-time, at pre-process or at execution time.
3. When is it better to use a binary search rather than a linear search?

PROJECTS

Project 1

Prepare a print chart and a flowchart for the following specifications:

INPUT

01–02	Personnel Record Code	
03–03	Personnel Division	has a range of 1–5
04–05	Personnel Department	has a range of 1–5
	Personnel Employee ID	
06–08	Personnel ID–1	
09–10	Personnel ID–2	
11–14	Personnel ID–3	
15–34	Personnel Name	
36–50	Personnel Street Address	
51–52	Personnel State	
53–57	Personnel Zip	
	Personnel Date of Employment	
58–59	Personnel Month	
60–61	Personnel Day	
62–63	Personnel Year	
64–64	Personnel Experience Code	
65–65	Personnel Responsibility Code	
66–67	Personnel Skill Code	
68–71	Personnel Vacation Days	(4.1)
72–75	Personnel Sick Days	(4.1)
76–80	Personnel Daily Rate	(5.2)

PROCESSING

1. Search a promotion table (below) for a match on experience, responsibility and skill codes. If a match is found print the job title. If there is no match, print 'none available.'
2. Store in a table, which is to be printed out at end of job, the following items, by Division:
   Vacation days
   Sick days
   Leave days
   Leave liability

PROMOTION TABLE

EXP.	RES.	SKILL	TITLE
1	1	1	elephant trainer
2	1	1	"
1	2	1	"
2	2	1	"
1	1	1	high wire walker
2	1	2	"
1	2	2	"
1	1	3	lion tamer
2	1	3	"
2	2	3	"
1	1	4	clown
2	1	4	"
1	2	4	"
2	2	4	"

OUTPUT

1. Use 132 print positions.
2. Double-space the output.
3. Provide report headings including page numbers and current date.
4. Provide appropriate column headings.
5. Include all input fields (except record-code) on the output. Also, include any computed fields.
6. Use a line count of greater than 50 for overflow.

Project 2

Prepare a print chart and a flowchart for the following specifications:

INPUT

MASTER INVENTORY FILE
```
 1– 2   Inventory Record Code
         Inventory Stock Number
 3– 3        Inventory Type          Has a range of 1–5
 4– 5        Inventory Class         Has a range of 1–5
 6– 9        Inventory Part
10–29   Inventory Description
30–30   Inventory Location Code
31–34   Inventory Quantity on Hand
35–38   INVENTORY Quantity on Order
39–42   Inventory Order Level
43–43   Inventory Unit Size Code
44–48   Inventory Unit Price          (5.2)
49–49   Inventory Discount Code
50–55   Inventory Annual Usage (Units)
56–58   Inventory Vendor Code
         Inventory Transportation Code
59–59        Inventory Category
60–60        Inventory Distance
61–80   Filler
```

PROCESSING

1. Determine whether an item is to be ordered if inventory quantity on hand plus inventory quantity on order is less than or equal to inventory reorder level. Use the following formula to determine the amount to be ordered.

$$\text{EOQ (Units)} = \frac{2*C*A}{I*U}$$

where C = cost of an order in dollars
A = inventory annual usage
I = carrying cost
U = inventory unit price.

2. Values for C and I are to be read from a separate file at the beginning of execution. The formula is shown above. Include transportation when pricing the order. If the inventory transportation code = zero, no transportation is to be added. If the transportation code is not zero use the data in the field to locate a transportation cost per unit in a table whose rows represent category and columns represent distance.

3. The totals of inventory quantity on hand, inventory quantity on order, inventory annual usage, order quantity and net order amount for inventory types are to be stored in a table and printed on a separate page at end of job time.

TRANSPORTATION COST TABLE

		1	2	3	4	5	6	7
				DISTANCE				
	1	1.00	1.10	1.20	1.30	1.40	1.50	1.60
	2	.50	.60	.70	.80	.90	.95	1.00
	3	.75	.80	.85	.90	.95	.95	.90
CATEGORY	4	1.00	.95	.90	.85	.90	.95	.98
	5	.80	.85	.85	.80	1.00	1.25	1.50
	6	1.50	1.60	1.65	1.50	1.40	1.30	1.25
	7	1.25	1.30	1.40	1.50	1.60	1.70	1.75

OUTPUT

1. Use 132 print positions.
2. Double-space the output.
3. Provide report headings including page numbers and current date.

4. Provide appropriate column headings.

5. Include all input fields (except record code) on the output. Also, include any computed fields.

6. Use a line count of greater than 50 for overflow.

RECORD FROM PARAMETER FILE

Cost of an order	Forty-five dollars
Carrying cost	Fifteen percent

9

MISCELLANEOUS ROUTINE

OBJECTIVES

After studying this chapter the student should be able to perform the following activities:

1. Flowchart the logic for a special date record.
2. Flowchart the logic for a parameter record.
3. Explain the function of key fields in sorting.
4. Flowchart the logic for a bubble sort.
5. Flowchart the logic for a Shell sort.

INTRODUCTION

This chapter contains the logic for reading small files (as small as one record) to supplement the data found in the major files used by a program. Two examples of special records in these small files are date records and parameter records. This chapter also contains the logic for two programmer written sorts, the bubble and the Shell sort.

DATE RECORD

Often a single record is read at the beginning of a program run to provide information concerning a single execution of that program. A common example is a date record. While the current date is available on most computers, not all reports carry the current date. Sales and inventory reports in particular often carry a month-ending date, even though these reports may not actually be run until early the following month.

In order to furnish the appropriate data a single record containing the date is prepared and read into memory (a one-record file). The date is then moved to output and usually used as a part of the heading. The date can also be used in calculations such as computing the age of an asset in a depreciation report.

The flowcharting of a special date record is simple. It generally is represented by a read statement in the housekeeping routine (see Figure 9–1). Any further processing of the date record would depend on the needs of a particular program.

PARAMETERS

One definition of a parameter is a fixed limit or guideline. In this sense, parameter records are used to define some processing limit(s) within a program.

First, what is a parameter record in a physical sense? It is an input record generally read at the beginning of the program. The reading of the record occurs as a part of housekeeping in a manner similar to the reading of a date record. It usually is a one-time need. Once the data from the parameter record has been saved, repeated use of the data may be made.

There are three choices for the input of a parameter record or records. It may be the only

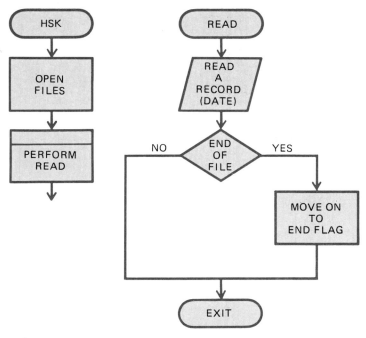

FIGURE 9–1

record in a file of its own, it may be the first record of a file, having a format different from that of the rest of the records, or it may be the result of communications with the operator. As long as the parameter record is the only record in a file of its own, its contents will remain in the input area for its own file and be available to the program throughout its execution. This means that the data need not be moved from the input area to another area in memory in order to save it. The important thing to note here is that each file has its own input/output area. If the parameter record is the first record of a file that contains additional records used for other purposes in the program, the contents of the parameter record must be moved from the input area to another area in memory in order to save them. Otherwise, when additional records are read from that file, the parameter data will be overlayed and destroyed. The third possibility is to have the computer operator enter the parameters for processing through the console keyboard at the beginning of the program execution.

The flowcharts of these three possibilities are shown in a general way in Figure 9–2(a), (b), and (c). These flowcharts represent only a portion of a housekeeping routine. (Any of these three methods could also be used for a date record.)

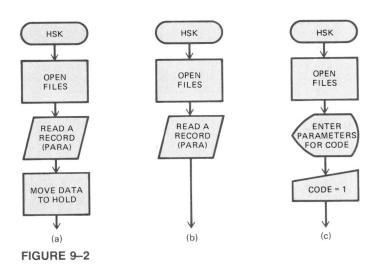

FIGURE 9–2

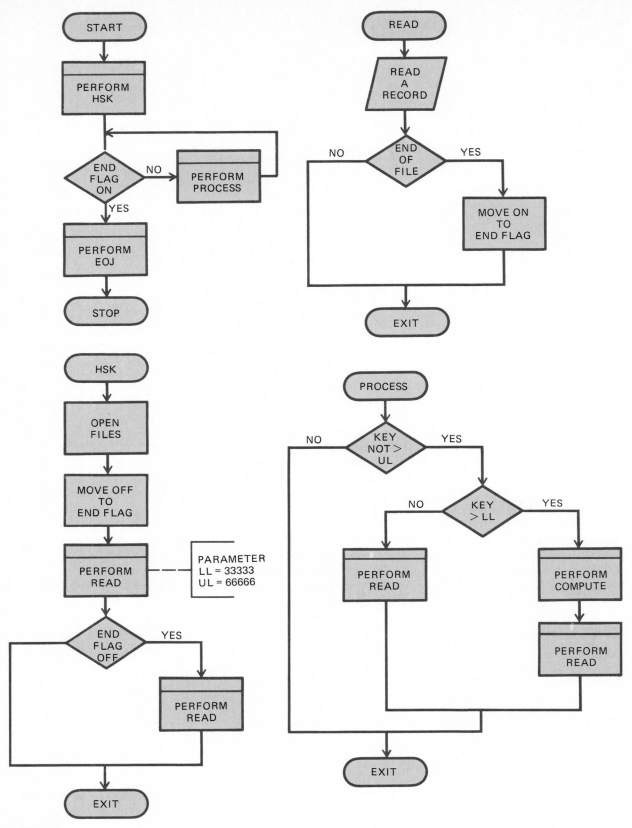

FIGURE 9–3

The uses of parameter records are varied. To make the program more flexible, they may be included as a part of the logic. An interest rate which changes almost daily may be required as a part of a program calculation. Providing the interest rate to the program through a parameter record rather than using it as a constant in the code of the program allows the rate to be changed every time the program is executed. If the rate were used as a constant in the program, we would need to recompile the program every time the interest rate changed.

Sometimes a company may operate under more than one trade name. All of the order, inventory, and billing information may be kept in a single file with only a code to designate the trade name under which it is to be invoiced. Some information is necessary then at the beginning of the program to indicate which records are to be billed in a particular program execution and under what name. The selected code could be entered as a parameter record, and any records with a different code would be bypassed.

Rather than selecting individual records from a file as in the case above, sometimes we want to process a block of records. On a small system in particular some programs may take hours to run and no such uninterrupted stretch of time is available. It is possible to start the program at a specific point in the file (specifying the contents of a key field as the starting point) and stop at a predetermined point. This allows the program to run in segments, making it easier to schedule.

For example, a file might contain part numbers ranging from 00001 through 99999. Not all of the part numbers will necessarily be present. By entering 00000 and 33333 as the beginning and ending limits, we could process approximately one-third of the file. Then, if we wanted to continue the job, 33333 would be the beginning limit and the ending limit would be whatever we wished to make it. Notice in the logic shown in Figure 9–3 (and pseudocoded in Figure 9–4) that the first record to be processed would be 33334. The numbers you would choose when setting the limits would depend on your choice of greater-than or less-than tests in the logic. Equal is not a suitable test for a problem of this kind, because not all part numbers within the range are required to be present. A test for equal might never be successful.

MAINLINE ROUTINE

```
PERFORM hsk routine
PERFORM process routine until end flag = on
PERFORM eoj routine
STOP
```

HSK ROUTINE

```
OPEN files
MOVE off to end flag
PERFORM read routine (parameter)
IF end flag = off
        PERFORM read routine
ENDIF
```

PROCESS ROUTINE

```
IF key not > upper limit
        IF key > lower limit
                PERFORM compute routine
                PERFORM read routine
        ELSE
                PERFORM Read routine
        ENDIF
ELSE
                MOVE on to end flag
ENDIF
```

FIGURE 9–4

```
READ a record
    AT END of file
        MOVE on to end flag
```

FIGURE 9–4 (continued)

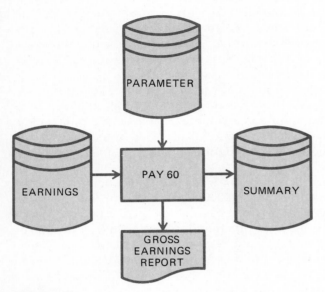

FIGURE 9–5

Another example of parameter record usage can be found in a payroll system. A section of a system flowchart where this might exist is shown in Figure 9–5.

In this system the header record is being used as a parameter record. It is a file containing a single record. The record layout is as follows:

POSITIONS	VARIABLE NAMES
1– 2	RECORD CODE
3– 8	PAY PERIOD ENDING
9–14	CHECK DATE
15–20	TIME CARD DATE
21–21	CREDIT UNION
22–22	HOSPITAL INSURANCE

This record is read near the beginning of the execution of the payroll program and will determine the date printed on the check, the period ending date for the check stub, and the date for any time-card labels produced. It will also determine which of the voluntary deductions will be taken for this pay period. For example, the payroll might be run twice a month but hospital insurance is deducted only once a month. The contents of position 22 (X if yes) in this record would be the determining factor in making payroll deductions for hospital insurance. An X in position 22 indicates only that it is the appropriate pay period to deduct hospital insurance. The individual employee's master record must have an amount allocated for hospital insurance before any deduction for that employee will be made. The same procedure applies to the other voluntary deduction (credit union) on this record.

Assuming that the parameter record was read in housekeeping, Figure 9–6 shows the tests being made for voluntary deductions. Figure 9–7 is the pseudocode. The dates from the parameter record need only be moved to an output area.

The uses of parameter records are varied. The underlying reason for using them is to allow additional flexibility in programs.

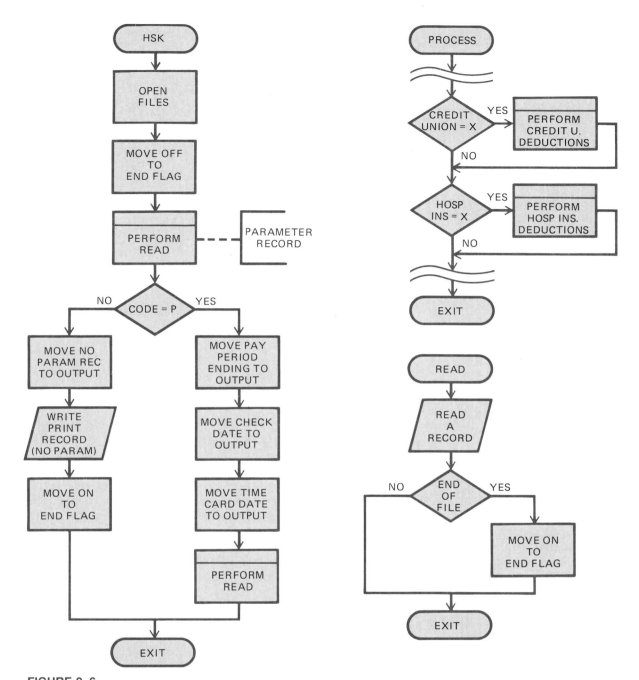

FIGURE 9–6

HSK ROUTINE

OPEN files
MOVE off to end flag
PERFORM read routine (parameter)
IF record is a parameter record
      MOVE pay period ending to output
      MOVE check date to output
      PERFORM Read routine (regular data)

FIGURE 9–7

```
ELSE
      MOVE 'no parameter record' to output
      WRITE print record (error message)
      MOVE on to end flag
ENDIF
```

PROCESS ROUTINE

```
--
IF credit union = X
      PERFORM credit union deductions routine
ENDIF
IF hospital insurance = X
      PERFORM hospital insurance deductions routine
ENDIF
--
```

READ ROUTINE

```
READ a record
      AT END of file
            MOVE on to end flag
```

FIGURE 9–7 (continued)

SORTING

Sorting allows us to change the order in which records are stored in a file. First, a key field or fields are selected from the record. The key field might be a social security number in a payroll file, a name in a file of names and addresses, or a zip code in a direct-mail file. The new order of the records after the sort will be based on the contents of the key field(s). We may opt for ascending or descending for each of the key fields. When there are multiple key fields we have to determine which one is the most important (major), less important (intermediate), and least important (minor). If all of the key fields in a record are to be sorted in the same order (all ascending or all descending), we can combine the key fields into one group field and sort on the combined field. The fields would be combined with the major field first, then any intermediate fields, then the minor field. If there is a change in the direction of the sort (some key fields ascending, some key fields descending) then each time the direction changes a separate sort is required. In this situation the minor field(s) should be sorted first, then the intermediate, then the major.

Figure 9–8 is an example of some records that have been sorted in descending order by pay rate and ascending order by name. Notice how pay rates are listed from highest to lowest (descending) and within each pay rate the names are in alphabetic order (ascending).

The COBOL language has an embedded sort which allows the programmer to request that a file be sorted and not be concerned with programming the individual logic steps to

NAME	EMPLOYEE NUMBER	HIRE DATE	PAY RATE
BABCOCK, RON	519-38-4742	01-03-88	50000.00
EVERETT, PATRICIA	519-32-2061	03-01-86	50000.00
LANE, WILLIAM	518-56-9876	11-09-66	50000.00
SIAVELIS, JOAN	414-88-6539	08-18-76	50000.00
EBNER, JO ELLEN	519-76-8358	09-11-87	45000.00
HALE, DEBBIE	517-98-5793	11-28-88	45000.00
PRELL, JOYCE	519-99-8357	01-22-78	45000.00
BENDER, VIRGINIA	519-89-5238	12-16-88	40000.00
GINTOWT, GEORGE	519-56-6485	01-15-86	40000.00
NOWAKOWSKI, SUE	517-84-9746	04-19-85	40000.00

FIGURE 9–8

accomplish the rearrangement of the records. The COBOL programmer need only specify the file, the key fields and the order desired.

Most versions of BASIC leave it up to the programmer to write the individual logic steps for the rearrangement of records. We will demonstrate two memory sorts, bubble and Shell, as they might be planned for use with a language such as BASIC which has no embedded sort. In order to do a memory sort we need to have all of the records in memory at one time. This is done by reading the records from the file to be sorted and loading them into a table. If there is more than one field in a record a two-dimensional table will be required. Each record then forms one row of the table, the fields of the record form the columns of the table. After the sort is complete the records can be written from the table to a file in their new order. The flowchart of the routine to load the table is shown in Figure 9–9, the pseudocode is in Figure 9–10. The logic assumes that one data item is read at a time and that four data items make one record. Notice that the data is read directly into the table. It could have been read into another area and then been moved to the table.

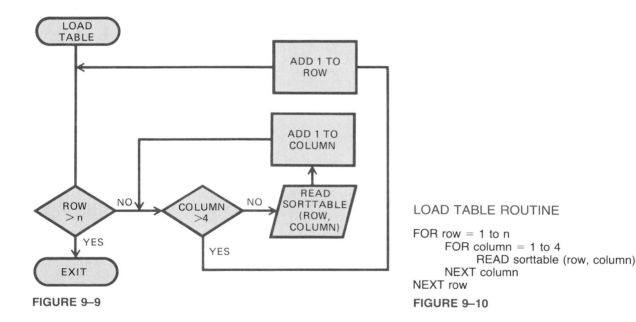

FIGURE 9–9

LOAD TABLE ROUTINE

FOR row = 1 to n
    FOR column = 1 to 4
        READ sorttable (row, column)
    NEXT column
NEXT row

FIGURE 9–10

BUBBLE SORT

The advantage of the bubble sort is its simplicity, the disadvantage is its lack of speed. The bubble sorting technique compares the key field column of adjacent rows to determine if a row requires moving to achieve the desired order (ascending or descending). The movement of the rows is accomplished by exchanging the two records just tested. Some versions of BASIC allow the programmer to make the exchange with only one line of code because the version includes a SWAP statement which can exchange two data items. If no SWAP statement is available the exchange is done in three steps; 1) the first item is moved to a hold area, 2) the second item is moved to the first and, 3) the hold is moved to the second item. The flowchart for the bubble sort is shown in Figure 9–11 and the pseudocode is in Figure 9–12.

Two switches are used in the bubble sort. The first, called SORTED, is used to determine if the sort routine should be executed again. It is set to no before the sort routine is executed for the first time and remains no until a sorting pass through the table result in no records being exchanged. At this point SORTED is changed to yes and the sort is complete. With a bubble sort this may mean as many as n-1 passes where n is the number of records (rows). The second switch (SWAPS) is set to no at the beginning of each pass. If any exchanges are made on the pass SWAPS will be changed to yes. Only when SWAPS remains no at the end of a pass are the records sorted.

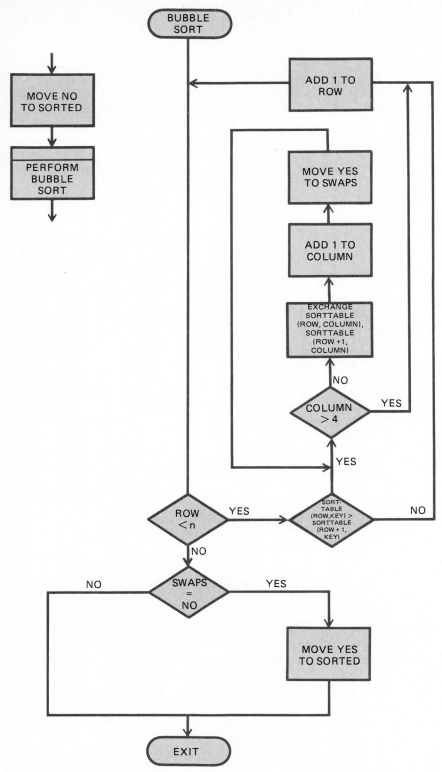

FIGURE 9–11

Notice that each sorting pass starts at row 1 and goes to row n-1. The n represents the number of records (or rows) in the table with n-1 being the next to last row. We compare the key field of a row with the key field of the row following it. When the comparison reaches

```
    .
MOVE no to sorted
PERFORM bubble sort routine until sorted = yes
    .
    .
BUBBLE SORT ROUTINE
MOVE no to swaps
FOR row = 1 to n-1
      If sorttable (row, key) > sorttable (row + 1, key)
            FOR column = 1 to 4
                  EXCHANGE sorttable (row, column), sorttable (row + 1, column)
            NEXT column
            MOVE yes to swaps
NEXT row
IF swaps = no
      MOVE yes to sorted
```

FIGURE 9–12

the next to the last row (n-1) that row will be compared to the last row thereby including all rows in the table in the comparisons.

When the comparisons of the key fields of adjacent rows is made, key is used as the second subscript to identify which column (field) of the record is being compared. Key is being used in a symbolic way in the pseudocode. The data item or constant used here would need to identify the column number of the table where the key field is located.

In the example > is used when comparing the key fields of adjacent rows. This will give an ascending sort. If the key field of a row is greater than the key field of the row below it, an exchange of the rows is appropriate to place the smaller item first. In order to do a descending sort we simply change the relationship to a < so that an exchange is made when the first item in the comparison is less than the second.

The exchange must include not only the key fields but also all fields in the record. This can be done by using a loop which exchanges the fields (columns) one at a time. The example provided assumes four fields in the record.

SHELL SORT

The Shell sort is faster than the bubble sort. Instead of comparing key fields of adjacent records each time, the Shell sort divides the number of table items in half to determine the gap for comparing records on the first pass. If there were 80 records, then the gap for the first pass would be 40. The key fields for records 1 and 41 would be the first comparison, then 2 and 42, then 3 and 43 and so on until 40 and 80 are compared. When this pass is completed the gap is divided in half using integer division. The new gap would be 20. Now item 1 and 21, 2 and 22, 3 and 23 and so on are compared until the key fields for records 60 and 80 are compared. This process is repeated until the gap has reached zero. The last pass then would compare adjacent records since the gap would be 1. Figure 9–13 shows the number of passes required to sort a table of 80 records. It also shows examples of the comparisons made. Notice that integer division is used so that 5 divided by 2 has a result of 2. Figure 9–14 is the flowchart for the Shell sort and Figure 9–15 is the pseudocode.

PASS	GAP	LAST	RANGE OF COMPARISONS
1st	40	40	1:41, 2:42, 3:43 ....40:80
2nd	20	60	1:21, 2:22, 3:23 ....60:80
3rd	10	70	1:11, 2:12, 3:13 ....70:80
4th	5	75	1:6, 2:7, 3:8 ....75:80
5th	2	78	1:3, 2:4, 3:5 ....78:80
6th	1	79	1:2, 2:3, 3:4 ....79:80

FIGURE 9–13

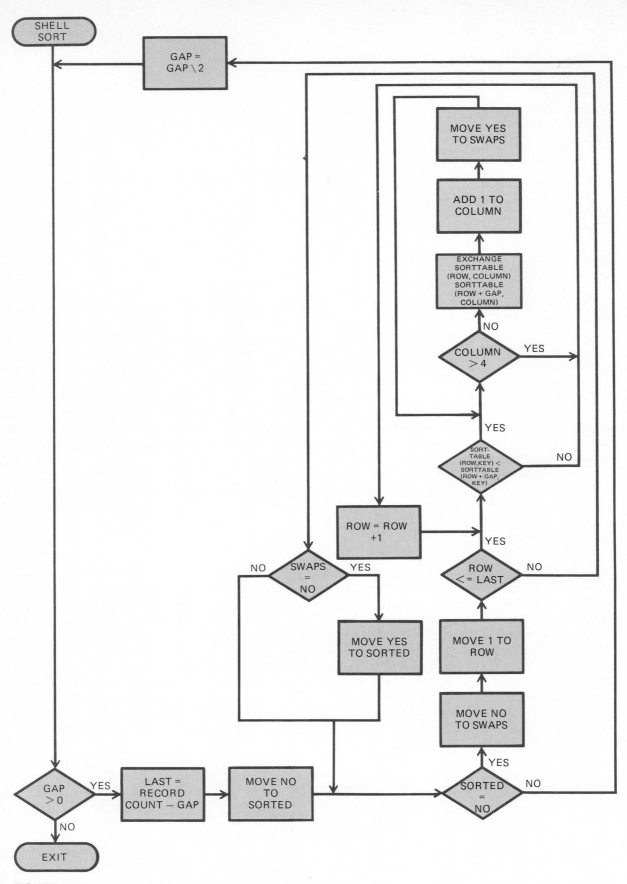

FIGURE 9–14

```
SHELL SORT
CALCULATE gap = record count \ 2
DO WHILE gap greater than 0
      CALCULATE last = record count − gap
      MOVE no to sorted
      DO WHILE sorted = no
            MOVE no to swaps
            MOVE 1 to row
            DO WHILE row less than or equal to last
                  IF sorttable (row, key) < sorttable (row + gap, key)
                        FOR column = 1 to 4
                              EXCHANGE sorttable (row,column),
                                          sorttable (row + gap, column)
                        NEXT column
                        MOVE yes to swaps
                  ADD 1 to row
            ENDDO
            IF swaps = no
                  MOVE yes to sorted
      ENDDO
      CALCULATE Gap = gap \ 2
ENDDO
```

FIGURE 9–15

CHAPTER VOCABULARY

Ascending order
Bubble sort
Date Record
Descending order

Gap
Key field
Major key
Minor key

Parameter record
Shell sort
Swap

REVIEW QUESTIONS

MATCHING

a. Key field
b. Major
c. Descending order
d. Bubble sort

e. Ascending order
f. Parameter record
g. Shell sort
h. Minor

_____ **1.** A sort which compares adjacent records in a file.
_____ **2.** From least to most.
_____ **3.** The most important key field.
_____ **4.** A special record used to allow flexibility in a program.
_____ **5.** From most to least.
_____ **6.** A field(s) used to determine the order of records in a sort.
_____ **7.** The least important key field.
_____ **8.** A sort which compares records that are varying distances apart in the file.

TRUE/FALSE

T **F** **1.** The bubble sort is faster than the Shell sort.
T **F** **2.** Only one field in a record may be the key field for a sort.
T F **3.** Shell sorts compare key field in records that are some distance apart when determining which records to swap.
T F **4.** Files containing parameter records are generally very large files.
T **F** **5.** The current date is the only date used on reports.

T F **6.** When sorting on multiple key fields in one record the fields can be combined and sorted as a group if they should all be sorted in the same direction.

T F **7.** If there are multiple key fields in a record that require sorting in different directions the sorts should be done on the minor key first.

T F **8.** Parameter records are normally read in the EOJ routine.

EXERCISES

1. Prepare a set of sample data with 10 records in a file. List only the key field for each record in a random order. Show the passes required, the comparisons made, and the exchanges made in order to sort the data into ascending order using the bubble sort.
2. Use the set of data from exercise 1 still in random order. Show the passes required, the comparisons made, and the exchanges made in order to sort the data into descending order using the Shell sort.

DISCUSSION QUESTIONS

1. What are some possible applications for the use of parameter records?
2. Compare the number of possible comparisons made using the Shell sort versus the bubble sort when sorting the same file.
3. Why must the data be in memory rather than on disk to accomplish the sorts in this chapter?

PROJECTS

Project 1

Prepare a print chart and a flowchart for the following specifications:

INPUT

MASTER PERSONNEL FILE

01–02	Personnel Record Code	
03–03	Personnel Division	has a range of 1–5
04–05	Personnel Department	has a range of 1–5
	Personnel Employee ID	
06–08	Personnel ID-1	
09–10	Personnel ID-2	
11–14	Personnel ID-3	
15–34	Personnel Name	
35–50	Personnel Street Address	
51–62	Personnel State	
53–57	Personnel Zip	
	Personnel Date of Employment	
58–59	Personnel Month	
60–61	Personnel Day	
62–63	Personnel Year	
64–64	Personnel Experience Code	
65–65	Personnel Responsibility Code	
66–67	Personnel Skill Code	
68–71	Personnel Vacation Days	(4.1)
72–75	Personnel Sick Days	(4.1)
76–80	Personnel Daily Rate	(5.2)

PROCESSING

1. Read the file of 20 records and store them in a table.
2. Sort the records on Personnel experience code and list the newly sorted table.

OUTPUT

1. List the sorted table with appropriate headings.

Project 2

Prepare a print chart and a flowchart for the following specifications:

INPUT

MASTER INVENTORY FILE

```
 1– 2   Inventory Record Code
         Inventory Stock Number
 3– 3          Inventory Type          Has a range of 1–5
 4– 5          Inventory Class         Has a range of 1–10
 6– 9          Inventory Part
10–29   Inventory Description
30–30   Inventory Location Code
31–34   Inventory Quantity on Hand
35–38   Inventory Quantity on Order
39–42   Inventory Reorder Level
43–43   Inventory Unit Size Code
44–48   Inventory Unit Price          (5.2)
49–49   Inventory Discount Code
50–55   Inventory Annual Usage (Units)
56–58   Inventory Vendor Code
         Inventory Transportation Code
59–59          Inventory Category
60–60          Inventory Distance
61–80   Unused
```

PROCESSING

1. Read the file of 20 records and load them into a table. Sort the table in ascending order on Inventory stock number using a Shell sort.
2. Write the table to a file and then list the file.

OUTPUT

1. List the newly sorted file with appropriate headings.

INPUT EDIT PROGRAMS

OBJECTIVES

After studying this chapter the student should be able to perform the following activities:

1. Describe what an input edit program is.
2. List the types of edit tests that can be made on data.
3. Give examples of tests for class, range, presence, existence and consistency.
4. Flowchart an edit program.
5. Flowchart a program which has multiple record types in one file.
6. Flowchart a two-step program where good records from an edit are written to disk file and then read from the new file and listed.

INTRODUCTION

Programming would be simpler if we could depend on all data to be valid. Because of errors and misunderstandings, however, data is often less than perfect. Using bad data in a program can cause a program to interrupt. To avoid this, data is put through an input edit. Input edit programs involve the testing of data to ensure that the data is valid. Before we can write an edit program, we must analyze the data and the programs for which it will be used as input in terms of potential trouble spots. We cannot check for problems without an understanding of what the problems may be.

TYPES OF EDIT TESTS

In an on-line system, testing may be done at the point of entry of the data, allowing for rejection of invalid data and requesting reentry of the data. In a batch system, editing may take place after a file is created but before the file is used in normal production. A special type of program whose only purpose is to edit the file may be executed first. This program will identify errors so that they may be corrected. In an edit program, tests are made on each data item based on the criteria set for the data item. Input edits should be as thorough as possible in order to limit the amount of incorrect data entering the system. Editing may include tests for the following:

1. Class (numeric or alphanumeric)
2. Range
3. Presence
4. Existence
5. Consistency

Class

Testing the class of data allows us to find out whether the contents of a data item are of the class we desire them to be. Describing data in a program as numeric or alphanumeric does not ensure that any data stored in those areas will be of that type. In COBOL for example, the programmer may have specified that a field is numeric by using a PICTURE of 9(3). However, this definition in no way guarantees that the data contained in that field will actually be numeric. This is because, in executing a read statement or moving a group of items, COBOL does not check that data being placed in the individual items to see whether the actual data type matches the data type of the PICTURE clause. Accordingly, it is possible to have nonnumeric data in fields which are described as numeric. It is important then to distinguish between the description of the data (what type of data the field should contain) and the actual data (what type of data the field in fact contains). In order to make sure that the actual data agrees with the description of the data item COBOL allows us to use a class test in which we ask if the field is numeric.

BASIC does its own input edit when data is entered for a particular variable making sure that the data agrees with the type indicated by the variable name. If the types do not agree the program does interrupt to let you know there is a type mismatch. If you can anticipate where the problems may occur BASIC allows you to write error-trapping routines to handle this situation and avoid the program interruption that would otherwise occur.

We especially need to ensure that data items that will be used in calculations, as subscripts, or which require the addition of numeric editing characters when printed, do indeed contain numeric data. Failure to do this will cause a data exception in COBOL or a type mismatch in BASIC. Both of these cause a program interruption. Processing stops and an error message is printed out that will lead us to the instruction in which the error was detected. One or more of the variable names used in this instruction contain data that is unsuitable for the type of instruction we are trying to execute. Since we cannot afford to stop and restart continually, it is better to edit the data, prepare an error list to be corrected, and then run the production program with correct data.

Range

For many data items it is important that the values be within a range. In a high school, the year in school could have a range of 1 through 4 or a range of 9 through 12. The range that will be used is based on a choice made by the school. Most ranges are determined by the organization using the data. A few ranges, such as the date are more widely defined. The components of a data are limited to an acceptable range. The month must be between 1 and 12, the day must be between 1 and 31, the range of the year will depend on the particular application. For example, it could be acceptable to have as a hire year any year that did not exceed the current year. Figure 10–1 checks range for each of the components of the data field. There are still some potential problems with the date that this example does not address. What if the month is a 2 and the day is a 31? Both of these figures are within the general range for months and days, but the numbers are inconsistent. This flowchart will be expanded later under the discussion of consistency.

At times our interest in range is concentrated on the lower or upper limit. A net pay of less than zero is at the very least a reason for concern. A bank balance less than a specified amount may incur service charges. Zero is of particular interest to us since division by zero will cause an error in most programming languages. If there is any possibility the data item will be used as a divisor, we must ensure that it does not have a value of zero. At times we are more interested in the upper limit for a field; an hourly pay rate that can be no larger than $300, regular hours worked per week no greater than 40, or total hours worked per week no greater than 80.

Ranges are especially important when the data item is to be used as a subscript for a table. For many programming languages a zero used as a subscript creates a problem. If a table has ten elements, then a subscript used with that table must be numeric and cannot exceed 10. BASIC will reject a subscript that is not in the range of the table before trying to locate a table element with it. This rejection causes the program to interrupt. COBOL on the other hand will use the subscript in a calculation and locate an area of memory it presumes to be the table element you wanted. If the subscript is too large or too small for the table, the memory area pinpointed by the subscript will be outside the table. If the area pinpointed is numeric you could end up calculating with an area you hadn't intended to use or if the area is alphanumeric a data exception will occur causing the program to stop execution.

Ranges can be checked for alphanumeric fields also. Programming languages can determine if a character is in the range of A through I in the same way it can test for a numeric range.

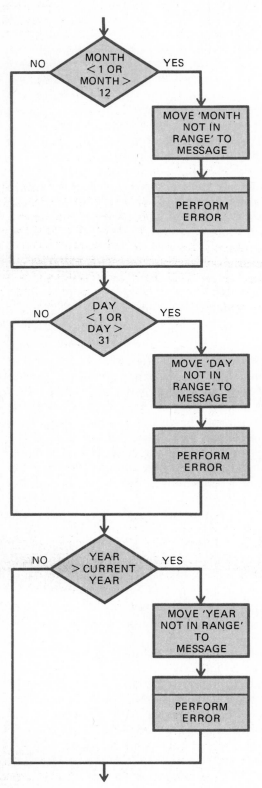

FIGURE 10–1

Presence

Alphanumeric data presents some special editing programs. A class test would be of no value since any and all combinations of characters would pass the test. A range test is possible, there are however fewer occasions to use it than there are with numeric data; in most cases a range test on a street address will prove little. When there is no basis for a range, existence, or consistency test we can still check for presence. If, for example, the field will contain blanks if no data were entered in the field, we could compare the field to blanks. If the field is equal to blanks we have an error condition. If the field is not equal to blanks, we know it contains data; we do not, however, have any idea of the validity of the data. See Figure 10–2.

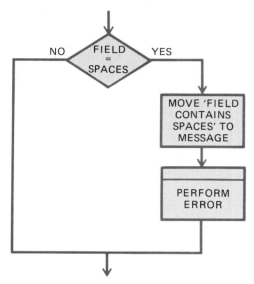

FIGURE 10–2

Existence

A field may contain data that is of the proper class (numeric or alphanumeric), and of the proper range and still contain incorrect data. Let's assume that labor is charged to account numbers that are three digits and have a range of 1 to 999. There are 50 labor accounts. This means that many of the possible numbers in the range are not associated with a labor account.

We need some way of determining if a given number corresponds with a labor account. We can do this by storing the numbers which are associated with a labor account in a table. We can then do a linear or binary search of the table using the account number from the file to be edited as the search argument. If a match is found, the data in the field exists as a labor account number. If no match is found, we have an incorrect labor account number. We can expand the table to include both account numbers and a description of the account so that we can verify the existence of the account number and retrieve an appropriate description of the labor account at the same time. Such a table lookup is shown in Figure 10–3. We use two switches in this search. The stop switch is used to terminate the search. It is turned on if we find the item we are searching for or the end of the table is reached without finding the item. The found switch on the other hand is only turned on when a matching item is located. After completing the search we can test the found switch to make sure a match was found before we attempt to use the item.

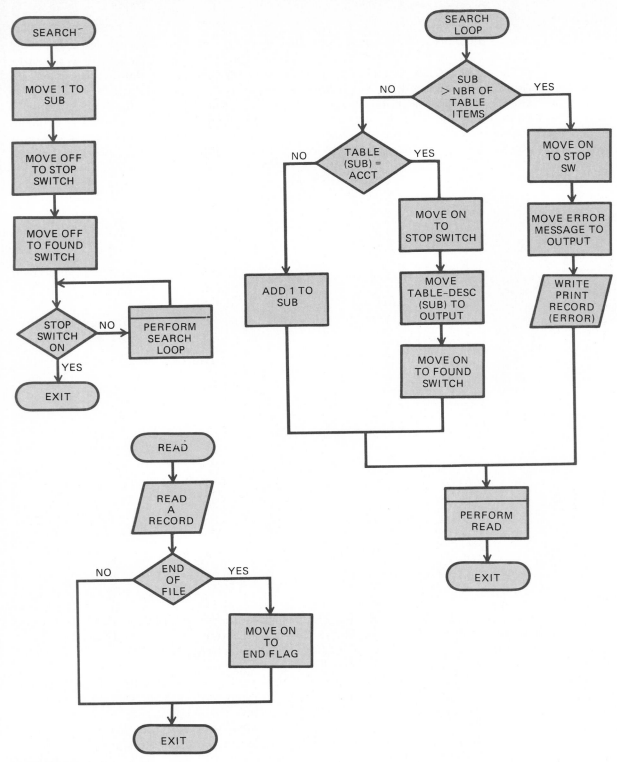

FIGURE 10–3

Consistency

Data may meet all of the other edit tests and still lack consistency. The existence of overtime hours may not be consistent with less than 40 regular hours. A person's department may not be consistent with the labor account number his hours are being changed to.

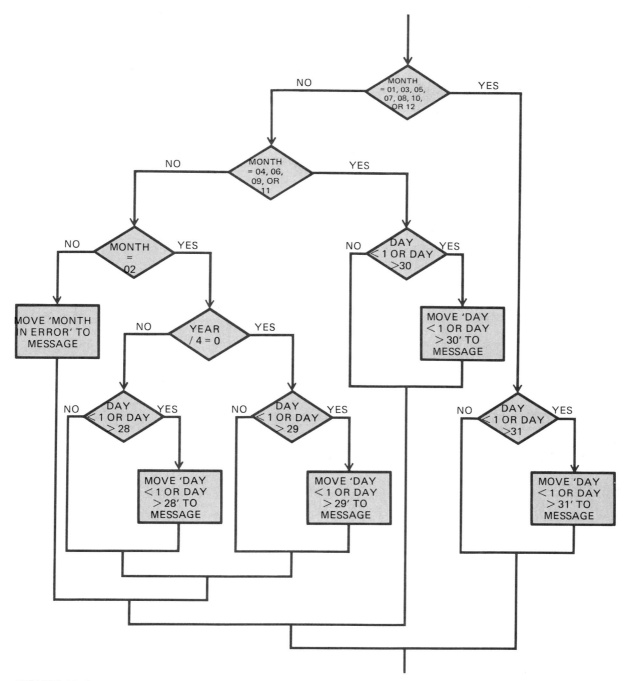

FIGURE 10–4

Dates make a good example of the need to test for consistency. The day portion of a date may be numeric and in a range of 1 to 31, but the value may not be consistent with the month. A 30 would not be consistent with a 02 for February. How about a day of 29 and a month of 02? You will not know if the two are consistent until you check the year to see if it is a leap year. Our test for leap year does not include a test to see if the year is an odd numbered century as in the year 1900 or 2100 which are not leap years. See Figure 10–4 for an example of editing a date for range and consistency.

AN EDIT EXAMPLE

In a sample payroll-system edit the hours could be reported weekly and a record prepared with the following format:

1–2	RECORD CODE
3–11	EMPLOYEE NUMBER
12–16	ACCOUNT NUMBER
17–20	REGULAR HOURS
21–24	OVERTIME HOURS
25–30	PAY RATE

A record layout is shown in Figure 10–5 and a print chart for the error listing is shown in Figure 10–6.

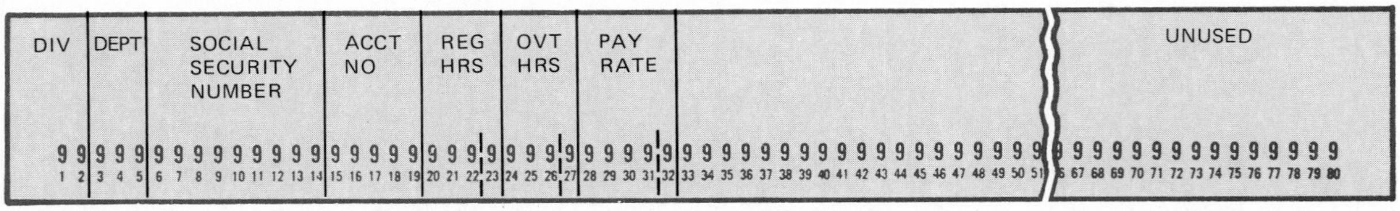

FIGURE 10–5

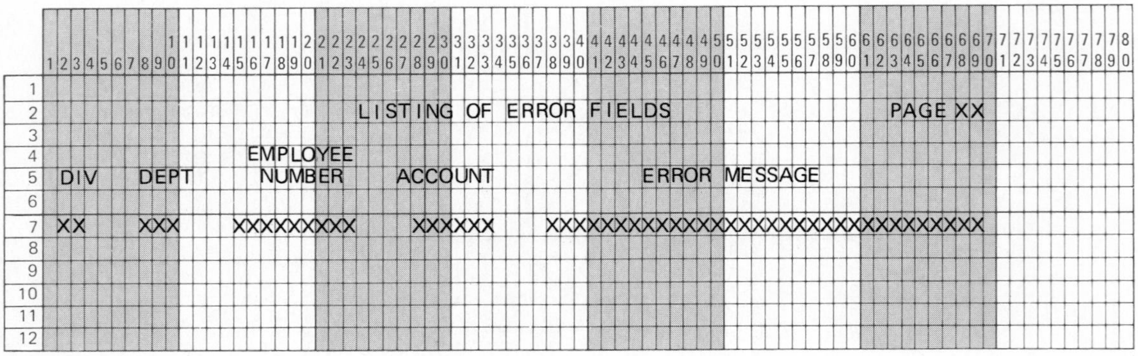

FIGURE 10–6

To avoid data exceptions, the fields called REGULAR HOURS, OVERTIME HOURS, and PAY RATE must all be checked to ensure that they contain numeric data. This is necessary because these fields will be used in calculations. To ensure correct output, other checks can be made:

1. A table of employee numbers can be searched in an effort to find a match for the employee number from the input record.
2. A table of valid account numbers can be searched in an effort to find a match for the account number from the input record.
3. If any overtime hours are present, the REGULAR HOURS can be tested for a minimum number such as 40.
4. The PAY RATE can be tested to make sure that it falls within the range for a particular category of job as indicated by the account number.

Each field is tested; if the data is in error an appropriate message is moved to output and an error routine is performed. If we wish to print multiple errors that appear in one record, then we must continue the testing of the record after any one error has been discovered. The flowchart in Figure 10–7 shows the logic for this type of checking; the pseudocode is in Figure 10–8. The logic for the searches that are performed would be similar to the searches in Figure 10–3. The contents of FOUNDSW after the search is complete will indicate if matching data is found. The objective here is to move the appropriate message to output each time an error is

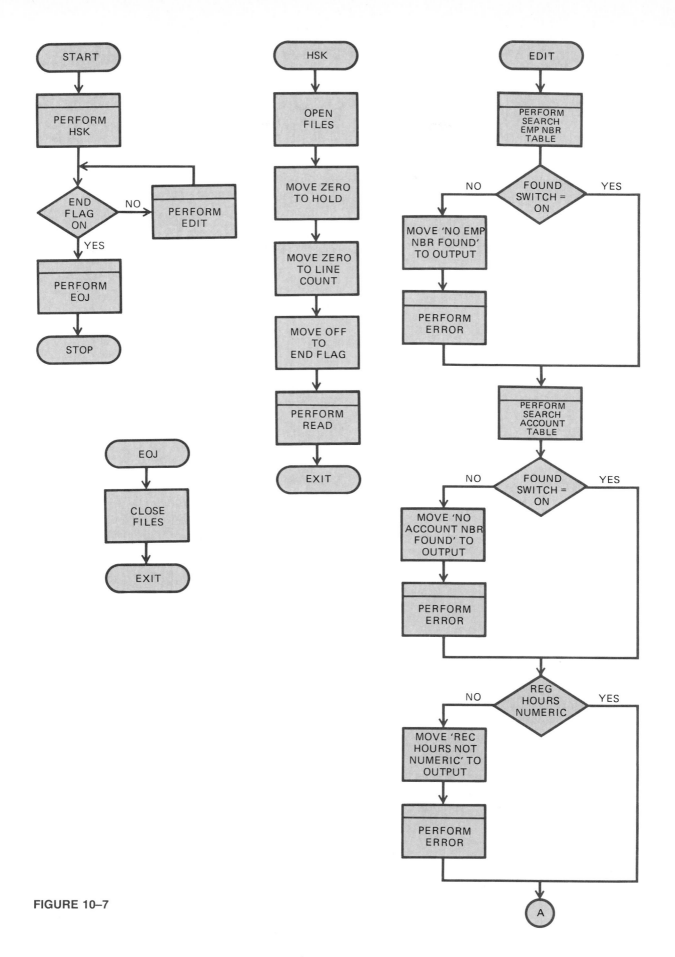

FIGURE 10–7

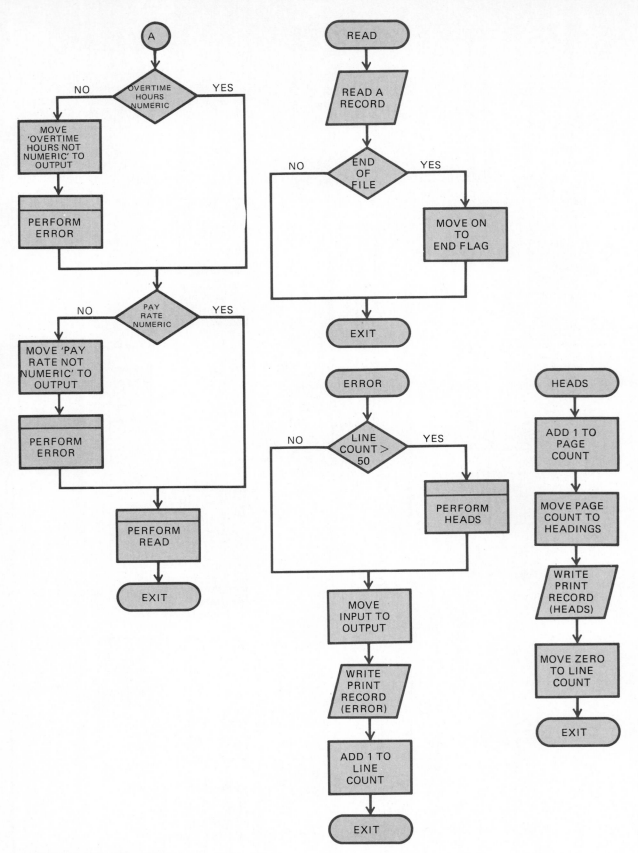

FIGURE 10–7 (continued)

MAINLINE ROUTINE

PERFORM hsk routine
PERFORM edit routine until end flag = on
PERFORM eoj routine
STOP

HSK ROUTINE

OPEN FILES
MOVE zero to hold
MOVE zero to line count
MOVE off to end flag
PERFORM read routine

EDIT ROUTINE

PERFORM search emp nbr table
IF emp number found
ELSE
    MOVE 'no employee number found' to output
    PERFORM error routine
ENDIF
PERFORM search acct table
IF account number found
ELSE
    MOVE 'no account number found' to output
    PERFORM error routine
ENDIF
IF regular hours are numeric
ELSE
    MOVE 'regular hours not numeric' to output
    PERFORM error routine
ENDIF
IF overtime hours are numeric
ELSE
    MOVE 'overtime hours not numeric' to output
    PERFORM error routine
ENDIF
IF pay rate is numeric
ELSE
    MOVE 'pay rate not numeric' to output
    PERFORM error routine
ENDIF
PERFORM read routine

EOJ ROUTINE

CLOSE files

READ ROUTINE

READ a record
    AT END of file
        MOVE on to end flag

ERROR ROUTINE

IF line count > 50
    PERFORM heads routine
ENDIF
MOVE input to output (division, department, employee nbr, account nbr)
WRITE print record (error)
ADD 1 to line count

FIGURE 10–8

ADD 1 to page count
MOVE page count to headings
WRITE print record (heads)
MOVE zero to line count

FIGURE 10–8 (continued)

found and print a line. Notice that the social security number is moved to output with the message in order to identify the problem record.

Let's assume that we want to count the number of good and bad records—not fields, **records.** We could incorporate MOVE 'ON' TO ERROR SWITCH in the ERROR routine and then test the switch just before reading the next record in the EDIT routine, as shown in Figure 10–9. The pseudocode is in Figure 10–10. If the switch is off, we will add 1 to GOOD RECORD COUNT otherwise we will add 1 to BAD RECORD COUNT. The ERROR SWITCH is set off at the beginning of the EDIT routine. With this method we move 'ON' to ERROR SWITCH for every bad field. However, it doesn't matter if we move 'ON' one time or 10 times; we still get the same result when we perform the test.

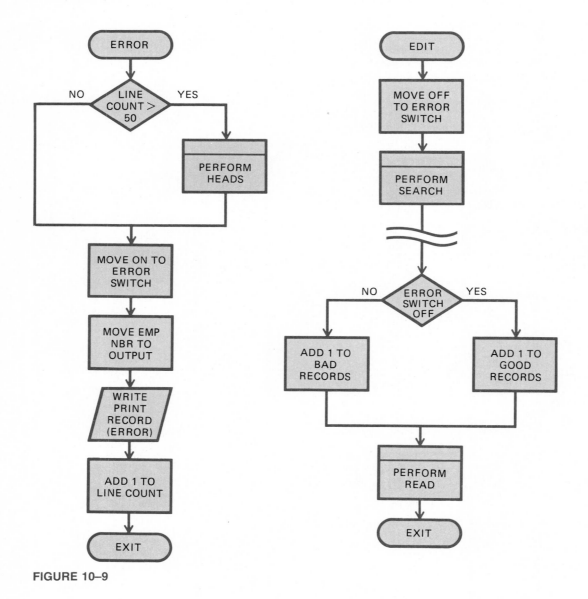

FIGURE 10–9

IF line count > 50
        PERFORM heads routine
ENDIF
MOVE on to error switch
MOVE employee number to output
WRITE print record (error)
ADD 1 to line count

EDIT ROUTINE

MOVE off to error switch
PERFORM search
—

—

IF error switch = off
        ADD 1 to good records
ELSE
        ADD 1 to bad records
ENDIF
PERFORM read routine

FIGURE 10–10

MULTIPLE RECORD TYPES

A complicating factor in edits as well as other types of programming is the presence of more than one type of record in a file. An example is a master record followed by one or more transactions. These record types share the same input area when they are read into storage, because they are part of the same file. The record types must have an identifying characteristic which can be tested after the read so they can be told apart. Since there are one or more transactions, we cannot anticipate in advance which record type will be read.

Assume a disk file as input and an 80-character area reserved for storing input for that file in memory. The programmer would reserve a particular series of memory locations for the storage of the input record. The format of these two records is shown in Figure 10–11. We will use memory locations 4000 to 4079 for our example. Therefore, when any record type is read from our file, it will reside in memory locations 4000–4079. Since we have master records followed by one or more transaction records, the type of record read can be determined only after it is in the input area, where a test can be performed on it. Consequently, the test for the record type should come after the READ and test-for-END-OF-FILE portion of the flowchart. An attempt to edit a field before determining the record type will produce either a data exception or incorrect test results.

When a master record is read into the computer, its contents are stored as follows:

4000–4016	ITEM NAME
4017–4020	ITEM NUMBER M
4021–4024	OLD QUANTITY
4025–4078	UNUSED
4079–4079	CONTROL CODE (0 indicates a master record)

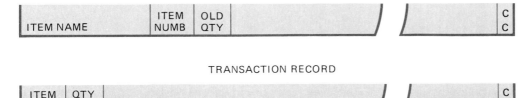

MASTER RECORD

TRANSACTION RECORD

FIGURE 10–11

When a transaction record is read into the computer, its contents are stored as follows:

4000–4003	ITEM NUMBER T
4004–4007	QUANTITY CHANGE
4008–4078	UNUSED
4079–4079	CONTROL CODE (1 indicates a transaction record)

All locations of storage labeled unused will contain blanks. The blanks or spaces as well as the data are transferred from the record when it is read into storage.

If any tests are made on fields before determination of the type of record in the input area (see Figure 10–12), the following may result. The test QUANTITY CHANGE NUMERIC will check the content of memory location 4004–4007 for numeric data. If there is a transaction record in the input area at the time, the test results will be valid. If it is a master record, the master record will be rejected as a transaction with a nonnumeric field. This is because memory location 4004–4007 are a part of the ITEM NAME field on the master record.

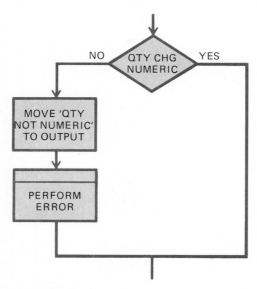

FIGURE 10–12

Another problem may arise if we have read a master record and, upon reading a transaction, ADD QUANTITY CHANGE TO OLD QUANTITY. Since we have just read a transaction, the QUANTITY CHANGE field will be correct, but OLD QUANTITY will be taken from memory locations 4021–4024, which currently contain blanks. Let's put actual data in our record formats (see Figure 10–13) and follow through the explanation above. We have just read a transaction record, and, knowing that we have read a master record previously, we issue the instruction ADD QUANTITY CHANGE TO OLD QUANTITY. QUANTITY CHANGE (4004–4007) contains 0003, an acceptable value for a numeric field. OLD QUANTITY (4021–4024) contains blanks, not an acceptable value for a numeric field. If two fields from different record types must be used together, we will need to transfer the first one that is read to a hold area so that it is still available.

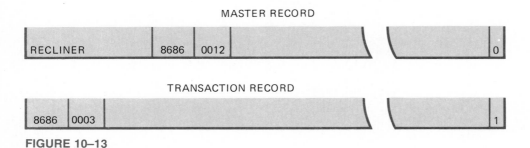

FIGURE 10–13

The flowchart in Figure 10–14 shows the proper method for checking records which share a common area in storage; the pseudocode is in Figure 10–15. The two edit routines would ordinarily contain many more tests than the single test we have shown you.

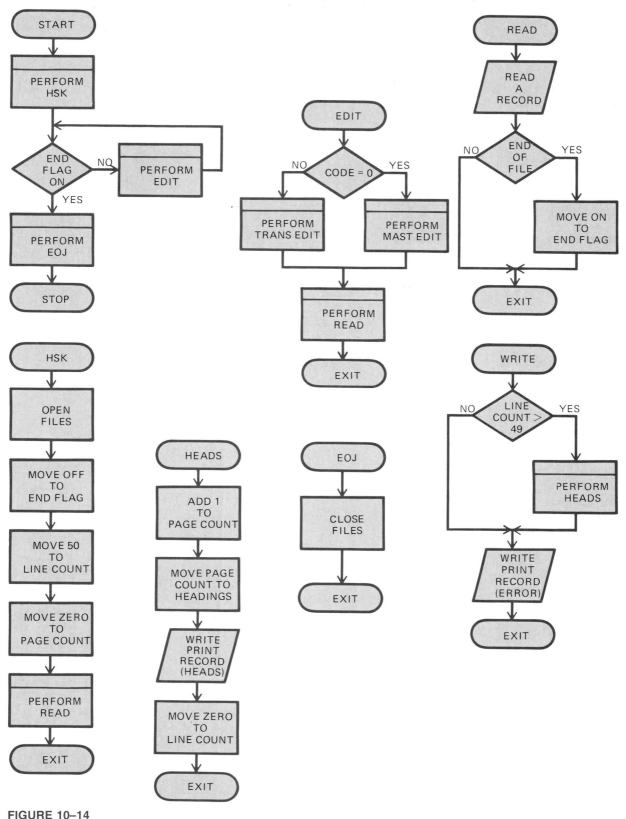

FIGURE 10–14

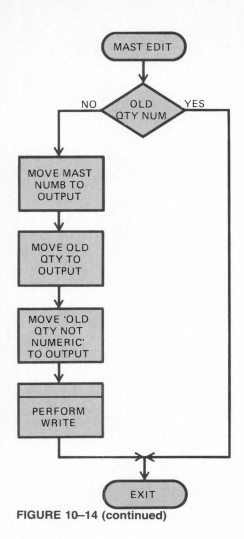

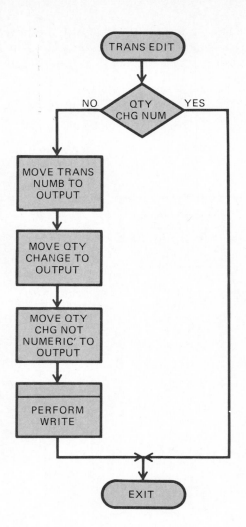

FIGURE 10–14 (continued)

MAINLINE LOGIC

PERFORM hsk routine
PERFORM edit routine until end flag = on
PERFORM eoj routine
STOP

HSK ROUTINE

OPEN files
MOVE off to end flag
MOVE 50 to line count
MOVE zero to page count
PERFORM read routine

EDIT ROUTINE

IF code = zero
      PERFORM mast edit routine
ELSE
      PERFORM trans edit routine
ENDIF
PERFORM read routine

FIGURE 10–15

EOJ ROUTINE

CLOSE files

READ ROUTINE

READ a record
        AT END of file
                MOVE on to end flag

MAST EDIT ROUTINE

IF old quantity is numeric
ELSE
        MOVE item number master to output
        MOVE old quantity to output
        MOVE 'old quantity not numeric' to output
        PERFORM write routine
ENDIF

TRANS EDIT ROUTINE

IF quantity change is numeric
ELSE
        MOVE item number transaction to output
        MOVE quantity change to output
        MOVE 'quantity change not numeric' to output
        PERFORM write routine
ENDIF

WRITE ROUTINE

IF line count > 49
        PERFORM heads routine
ENDIF
WRITE print record (error)

HEADS ROUTINE

ADD 1 to page count
MOVE page count to headings
WRITE print record (heads)
MOVE zero to line count

FIGURE 10–15 (continued)

TWO-PART PROGRAM

A sequential file can be created and then retrieved in the same program; to do this we have created a two-part edit program. In part one a file of unedited data is read, and tests are made on each field. If any field is "bad", an error line is written. If the record passes all edit tests, it is written to a new disk file. In part two the new disk file, which contains only records which passed all edit tests is read and listed. A portion of the system flowchart for this project is shown in Figure 10–16.

Figure 10–17 shows the record layout and the test data used. Figure 10–18 is the printer spacing chart for part one, the error listing. Division, department, employee number, and name are printed for every record which has a bad field to help identify the record. Then the name of the field in the error record and the data in the bad field are printed. The actual output for part one is shown in Figure 10–19.

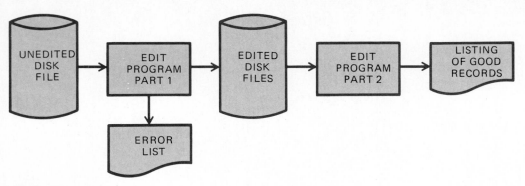

FIGURE 10–16

DIV	DEPT	EMPLOYEE NUMBER	EMPLOYEE NAME	PAY RATE	HRS WORKED	SICK DAYS	VAC. DAYS		UNUSED
9 9	9 9 9	9 9 9 9 9 9 9 9 9	9 9 9 9 9 9 9 9 9 9 9 9 9 9 9 9 9 9	9 9 9 9 9	9 9 9 9 9	9 9 9 9	9 9 9 9	9 9 9 9 9 9 9 9 9	9 9 9 9 9
1 2	3 4 5	6 7 8 9 10 11 12 13 14	15 16 17 18 19 20 21 22 23 24 25 26 27 28 29 30 31 32	33 34 35 36 37	38 39 40 41 42 43	44 45 46 47	48 49 50 51	52 53 54 55 56 57 58 59 60	75 76 77 78 79 80

```
06,001,316486794,SALLY DODD,31.64,86,79,4
01,001,356872384,WAYNE ABBOTT,35.68,7,238,4
01,001,358429773,HARVEY COLLINS,35.84,29,77,3
01,111,483837659,SARAH CUNDIFF,48.38,37,65,9
01,002,564982498,RALPH HOWARD,56.49,82,49,8
01,002,423494864,BILL NESS,42.34,94,86,4
01,002,238763983,LARRY KINGSLEY,23.87,63,98,3
02,001,238764832,,23.87,64,83,2
04,001,349324080,JAMES SEEK,34.93,2408,0,32
04,001,128497352,BILL NEAL,12.84,97,352,23
04,001,297653978,WILLIAM DAVIS,29.76,53,978,78
04,002,397654962,MIKE VERNON,39.76,54,96,2
00,000,000000000,DONE,0,0,0,0
```

FIGURE 10–17

	1 2 3 4 5 6 7 8 9 0	1 1 1 1 1 1 1 1 1 1 2 1 2 3 4 5 6 7 8 9 0	2 2 2 2 2 2 2 2 2 3 1 2 3 4 5 6 7 8 9 0	3 3 3 3 3 3 3 3 3 4 1 2 3 4 5 6 7 8 9 0	4 4 4 4 4 4 4 4 4 5 1 2 3 4 5 6 7 8 9 0	5 5 5 5 5 5 5 5 5 6 1 2 3 4 5 6 7 8 9 0	6 6 6 6 6 6 6 6 6 7 1 2 3 4 5 6 7 8 9 0	7 7 7 7 7 7 7 7 7 8 1 2 3 4 5 6 7 8 9 0
1								
2		LISTING OF ERROR FIELDS				PAGE XX		
3								
4		EMPLOYEE		ERROR		DATA IN		
5	DIV DEPT	NUMBER	NAME	FIELD		ERROR		
6								
7	XX XXX	XXXXXXXXX	XXXXXXXXXXXXXXXXXX	XXXXXXXXX	XXXXXXXXXXXXXXXXXXXX			
8	XX XXX	XXXXXXXXX	XXXXXXXXXXXXXXXXXX	XXXXXXXXX	XXXXXXXXXXXXXXXXXXXX			
9								
10								

FIGURE 10–18

Figure 10–20 is the printer spacing chart for part two. It represents a simple listing of the data from the edited file. This output was produced by reading the disk created in part one and listing the data. The actual output is shown in Figure 10–21.

The logic for this program is developed by putting together two types of programs already covered—the edit and a simple list. Notice that the MAINLINE logic is a combination of two

DIV	DEPT	EMPLOYEE NUMBER	NAME	ERROR FIELD	DATA IN ERROR
6	1	316486794	SALLY DODD	DIV-IN	6
1	1	356872384	WAYNE ABBOTT	SICK-DAYS	238
1	111	483837659	SARAH CUNDIFF	DEPT-IN	111
2	1	238764832		NAME	
4	1	349324080	JAMES SEEK	HOURS-WKD	2408
4	1	349324080	JAMES SEEK	VACN-DAYS	32
4	1	128497352	BILL NEAL	SICK-DAYS	352
4	1	297653978	WILLIAM DAVIS	SICK-DAYS	978
4	1	297653978	WILLIAM DAVIS	VACN-DAYS	78

FIGURE 10–19

FIGURE 10–20

DIV	DEPT	EMPLOYEE NUMBER	NAME	PAY RATE	HOURS WORKED	SICK DAYS	VACN DAYS
1	1	358429773	HARVEY COLLINS	35.84	29.0	77.0	3.0
1	2	564982498	RALPH HOWARD	56.49	82.0	49.0	8.0
1	2	423494864	BILL NESS	42.34	94.0	86.0	4.0
1	2	238763983	LARRY KINGSLEY	23.87	63.0	98.0	3.0

FIGURE 10–21

regular mainlines, instead of having a separate EOJ for part one and a HSK for part two. In part one the unedited file is opened as input and the new disk file is opened as output so that the new file can be created. In EOF1-HSK2 (the transition routine) we close the disk files and reopen the new disk file as input so that it can be read and listed in part two. The print file is left open since a listing is created in both parts. We are using a different end flag for each part, if we were using the same end flag for both disk files we would have to be careful to turn the end flag off again in EOF1-HSK2.

In the EDIT routine we test each field for some condition(s). The conditions we have used here are arbitrary. Realistic conditions would depend on the organization's needs. If the field does not pass the tests, we prepare the error line and write it. In the WRITE ERROR routine the error switch is turned on. This switch is tested at the end of the EDIT routine to determine if the record has any bad fields. If it does, we simply read the next record since any errors that exist have already been listed. If the error switch is still off then the record has no errors and the record is written on disk. Any records written on the new disk will be read and listed in part two. The flowchart is shown in Figure 10–22 and the pseudocode in Figure 10–23.

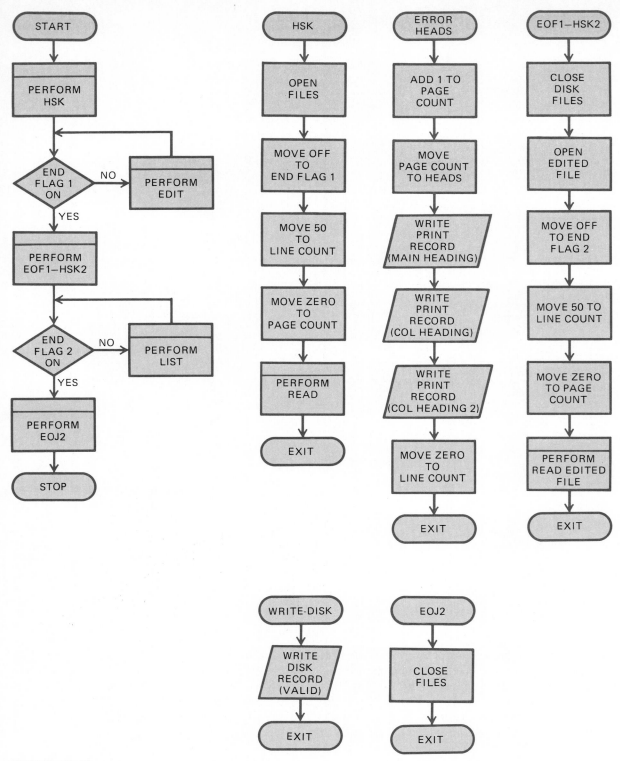

FIGURE 10–22

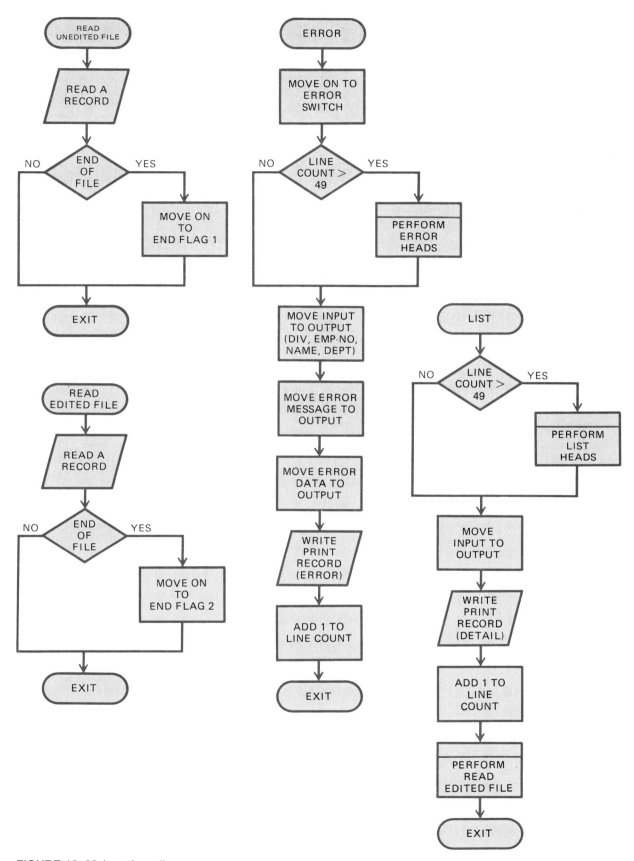

FIGURE 10–22 (continued)

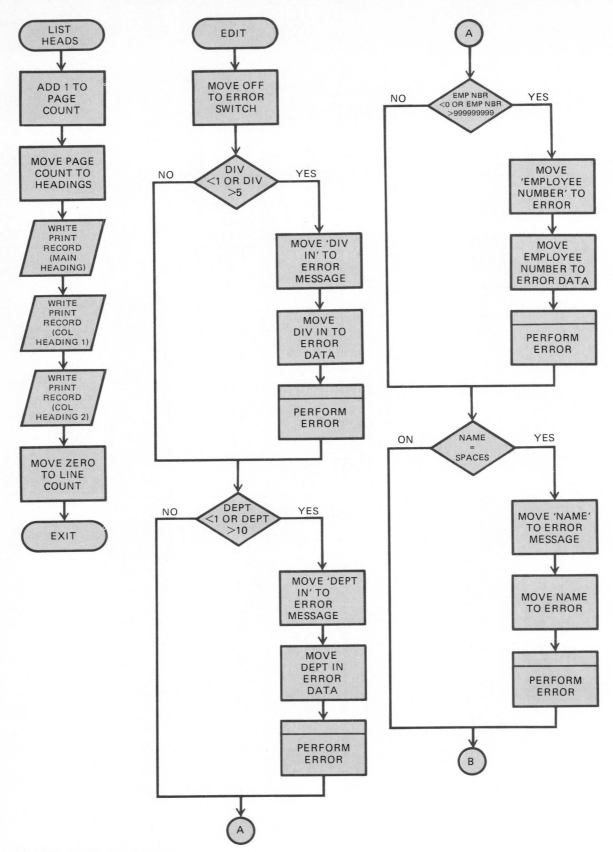

FIGURE 10–22 (continued)

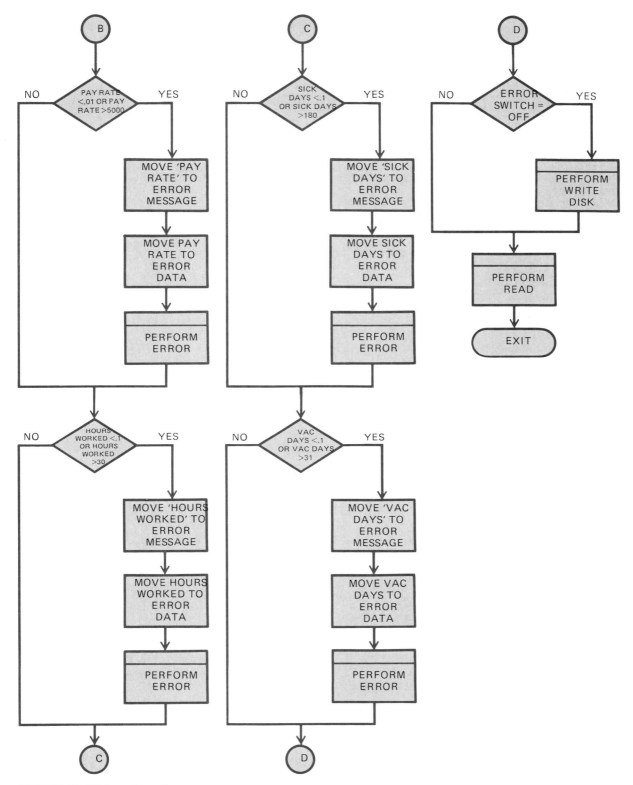

FIGURE 10–22 (continued)

MAINLINE LOGIC

PERFORM hsk routine
PERFORM edit routine until end flag1 = on
PERFORM eof1-hsk2
PERFORM list routine until end flag2 = on
PERFORM eoj routine
STOP

HSK ROUTINE

OPEN files
MOVE off to end flag1
MOVE 50 to line count
MOVE zero to page count
PERFORM read routine

EDIT ROUTINE

MOVE off to error switch
IF division < 1 or division > 5
    MOVE 'division' to error message
    MOVE division to error data
    PERFORM error routine
ENDIF
IF department < 1 or department > 10
    MOVE 'department' to error message
    MOVE department to error data
    PERFORM error routine
ENDIF
IF employee number < 0 or employee number > 999999999
    MOVE 'employee number' to error message
    MOVE employee number to error data
    PERFORM error routine
ENDIF
IF name = spaces
    MOVE 'name' to error message
    MOVE name to error data
    PERFORM error routine
ENDIF
IF pay rate < .01 or pay rate > 5000.00
    MOVE 'pay rate' to error message
    MOVE pay rate to error data
    PERFORM error routine
ENDIF
IF hours worked < .1 or hours worked > 40
    MOVE 'hours worked' to error message
    MOVE hours worked to error data
    PERFORM error routine
ENDIF
IF sick days < .1 or sick days > 180
    MOVE 'sick days' to error message
    MOVE sick days to error data
    PERFORM error routine
ENDIF
IF vacation days < .1 or vacation days > 31
    MOVE 'vacation days' to error message
    MOVE vacation days to error data
    PERFORM error routine
ENDIF
IF error switch = off
    PERFORM write disk routine
ENDIF
PERFORM read routine
EOF1-HSK2
CLOSE files (disk)

FIGURE 10–23

OPEN file (edited disk as input)
MOVE off to end flag2
MOVE 50 to line count
MOVE zero to page count
PERFORM read edited disk routine

LIST ROUTINE

IF line count > 49
       PERFORM edited heading
ENDIF
MOVE input to output
WRITE print record (detail)
ADD 1 to line count
PERFORM read edited file routine

EOJ2 ROUTINE

CLOSE files

WRITE DISK ROUTINE

WRITE disk record (valid records)

ERROR ROUTINE

MOVE on to error switch
IF line count > 49
       PERFORM error heads routine
ENDIF
MOVE input to output (division, department, number, name)
MOVE error message to output
MOVE error data to output
WRITE print record (error)
ADD 1 to line count

ERROR HEADS ROUTINE

ADD 1 to page count
MOVE page count to page out
WRITE print record (main heading)
WRITE print record (col heading 1)
WRITE print record (col heading 2)
MOVE zero to line count

READ UNEDITED FILE ROUTINE

READ a record
     AT end
         MOVE 'on' to end flag

HEADS ROUTINE

ADD 1 to page count
MOVE page count to headings
WRITE print record (main heading)
WRITE print record (col heading 1)
WRITE print record (col heading 2)
MOVE zero to line count

READ EDITED FILE ROUTINE

READ a record
     AT END
         MOVE on to end flag edited file

FIGURE 10–23 (continued)

In preparing the COBOL and BASIC versions we have made some assumptions. In the COBOL program (Figure 10–24) the input data was declared alphanumeric to avoid the need for a numeric test. The original input for the BASIC program (Figure 10–25) was created by a BASIC program that will not allow us to enter alphanumeric data in a numeric field. This eliminated the need to test for numeric data in the BASIC program. These assumptions allowed us to keep the two programs similar.

COBOL VERSION

```
PROCEDURE DIVISION.

MAINLINE-LOGIC.
      PERFORM HSK-ROUTINE
      PERFORM EDIT-ROUTINE UNTIL END-FLAG1 = 'ON'.
      PERFORM EOF1-HSK2-ROUTINE.
      PERFORM LIST-ROUTINE UNTIL END-FLAG2 = 'ON'.
      PERFORM EOJ2-ROUTINE.
      STOP RUN.
HSK-ROUTINE
      OPEN INPUT C10B1DATA
            OUTPUT PRINT-FILE
                 DISK-FILE.
      MOVE 'OFF' TO END-FLAG1.
      MOVE 50 TO LINE-COUNT.
      MOVE ZERO TO PAGE-COUNT.
      PERFORM READ-ROUTINE.
EDIT-ROUTINE
      MOVE 'OFF' TO ERROR-SWITCH.
      IF DIV-IN < 1 or DIV-IN > 5
            MOVE 'DIV-IN' TO ERROR-MESSAGE
            MOVE DIV-IN TO ERROR-DATA
            PERFORM ERROR-WRITE-ROUTINE.
      IF DEPT-IN < OR DEPT-IN > 10
            MOVE 'DEPT-IN' TO ERROR-MESSAGE
            MOVE DEPT-IN TO ERROR-DATA
            PERFORM ERROR-WRITE-ROUTINE.
      IF EMPNO-IN < 1 or EMPNO > 999999999
            MOVE 'EMPNO-IN' TO ERROR-MESSAGE
            MOVE EMPNO-IN TO ERROR-DATA
            PERFORM ERROR WRITE-ROUTINE.
      IF NAME-IN = SPACES
            MOVE 'NAME-IN' TO ERROR-MESSAGE
            MOVE NAME-IN TO ERROR-DATA
            PERFORM ERROR-WRITE-ROUTINE.
      IF PAY-RATE-IN < .01 or PAY-RATE-I < 5000.00
            MOVE 'PAY-RATE' TO ERROR-MESSAGE
            MOVE PAY-RATE-IN TO ERROR-DATA
            PERFORM ERROR-WRITE-ROUTINE.
      IF HOURS-WORKED-IN < .01 OR HOURS-WORKED-IN > 40
            MOVE 'HOURS WKD' TO ERROR-MESSAGE
            MOVE HOURS-WORKED-IN TO ERROR-DATA
            PERFORM ERROR-WRITE-ROUTINE.
      IF SICK-DAYS-IN < .01 OR SICK-DAYS-IN > 180
            MOVE 'SICK-DAYS' TO ERROR-MESSAGE
            MOVE SICK-DAYS-IN TO ERROR-DATA
            PERFORM ERROR-WRITE-ROUTINE.
      IF VACATION-DAYS-IN < .01 OR VACATION-DAYS-IN > 31
            MOVE 'VAC-DAYS' TO ERROR-MESSAGE
            MOVE VACATION-DAYS-IN TO ERROR-DATA
            PERFORM ERROR-WRITE-ROUTINE.
      IF ERROR-SWITCH = 'OFF'
```

FIGURE 10–24

```
            PERFORM WRITE-DISK-ROUTINE.
          PERFORM READ-UNEDITED-FILE.
EOF1-HSK2-ROUTINE
        CLOSE C10B1DATA
              DISK-FILE.
        OPEN INPUT DISK-FILE.
        MOVE 'OFF' to END-FLAG2.
        MOVE 50 TO LINE-COUNT.
        MOVE ZERO TO PAGE-COUNT.
        PERFORM READ2-ROUTINE.
LIST-ROUTINE.
        IF LINE-COUNT > 49
              PERFORM HEADS2-ROUTINE.
        MOVE DIV-IN                  TO DIV-OUT.
        MOVE DEPT-IN                 TO DEPT-OUT.
        MOVE EMPNO-IN                TO EMPNO-OUT.
        MOVE NAME-IN                 TO NAME-OUT.
        MOVE PAY-RATE-IN             TO PAY-RATE-OUT.
        MOVE HOURS-WORKED-IN         TO HOURS-WORKED-OUT.
        MOVE SICK-DAYS-IN            TO SICK-DAYS-OUT.
        MOVE VACATION-DAYS-IN        TO VACATION-DAYS-OUT.
        WRITE PRINT-RECORD FROM DETAIL-LINE
              AFTER ADVANCING 1 LINES.
        ADD 1 TO LINE-COUNT.
        PERFORM READ-EDITED-FILE-ROUTINE.
EOJ2-ROUTINE.
        CLOSE DISK-FILE
              PRINT-FILE.
        WRITE-DISK-ROUTINE.
        WRITE DISK-RECORD FROM DATA-RECORD-IN.
ERROR-WRITE-ROUTINE.
        MOVE 'ON' TO ERROR-SWITCH.
        IF LINE-COUNT > 49
              PERFORM ERROR-HEADS-ROUTINE
        MOVE DIV-IN         TO E-DIV-OUT.
        MOVE DEPT-IN        TO E-DEPT-OUT.
        MOVE EMPNO-IN       TO E-EMPNO-OUT.
        MOVE NAME-IN        TO E-NAME-OUT.
        WRITE PRINT RECORD FROM ERROR-LINE
              AFTER ADVANCING 1 LINES.
        ADD 1 TO LINE-COUNT.
ERROR-HEADS-ROUTINE.
        ADD 1 TO PAGE-COUNT.
        MOVE PAGE-COUNT TO PAGE-OUT.

        WRITE PRINT-RECORD FROM E-HEADS1
              AFTER ADVANCING TOP-OF-PAGE.
        WRITE PRINT-RECORD FROM E-HEADS2
              AFTER ADVANCING 2 LINES.
        WRITE PRINT-RECORD FROM E-HEADS3
              AFTER ADVANCING 1 LINES.
        MOVE ZERO TO LINE-COUNT.
READ-UNEDITED-FILE.
        READ C10B1DATA
              AT END
                    MOVE 'ON' TO END-FLAG.
HEADS2-ROUTINE.
        ADD 1 TO PAGE-COUNT.
        MOVE PAGE-COUNT TO PAGE-OUT2.
        WRITE PRINT-RECORD FROM HEADS 1
              AFTER ADVANCING TOP-OF-PAGE.
        WRITE PRINT-RECORD FROM HEADS2
              AFTER ADVANCING 2 LINES.
        WRITE PRINT-RECORD FROM HEADS3
              AFTER ADVANCING 1 LINES.
        MOVE ZERO TO LINE-COUNT.
```

FIGURE 10–24 (continued)

READ-EDITED-FILE-ROUTINE.

```
        READ DISK-FILE
            AT END
                MOVE 'ON' TO END-FLAG.
```

FIGURE 10–24 (continued)

BASIC VERSION

```
'PROGRAMMERS:    J AND J, INC.
'DATE:           10/11/90
'PROGRAM NAME:   CASE 10
'****************************************************************************
'                              MAINLINE LOGIC                               *
'****************************************************************************
GOSUB HOUSEKEEPING.ROUTINE
WHILE END.FLAG$ = "OFF"
   GOSUB EDIT.ROUTINE
WEND
GOSUB EOJ1.HSK2.ROUTINE
WHILE END.FLAG$ = "OFF"
    GOSUB LIST.ROUTINE
WEND
GOSUB EOJ2.ROUTINE
END
'****************************************************************************
'                            HOUSEKEEPING ROUTINE                           *
'****************************************************************************
HOUSEKEEPING.ROUTINE:
OPEN "A:C10DATA" FOR INPUT AS #1
OPEN "A:C10EDIT" FOR OUTPUT AS #3
D$ = "SCRN:": CLS
INPUT "OUTPUT TO PRINTER - ANSWER Y OR N"; ANSWER$
IF ANSWER$ = "Y" OR ANSWER$ = "y" THEN
   D$ = "LPT1:":WIDTH "LPT1:",80: LPRINT CHR$(15)
END IF
OPEN D$ FOR OUTPUT AS #2
LET DETAIL.FORMAT$ =     SPACE$(1) + "##" + SPACE$(2) + "###" + SPACE$(2) +
   "#########" +    SPACE$(2) + "\              \" + SPACE$(1) + "\         \"
   + SPACE$(1) + "&"
LET EDITED.LINE$ =       SPACE$(1) + "##" + SPACE$(2) + "###" + SPACE$(2) +
   "#########" + SPACE$(2) + "\               \" + SPACE$(2) + "####.##"
   + SPACE$(2) + "####.#"  + SPACE$(2) ' + "###.#" + SPACE$(2) + "###.#"
LET LINE.COUNT = 50
LET END.FLAG$ = "OFF"
GOSUB READ.ROUTINE
RETURN
'****************************************************************************
'                                EDIT ROUTINE                               *
'****************************************************************************
EDIT.ROUTINE:
LET ERR.SWITCH$ = "N"
IF DIV > 0 AND DIV < 6 THEN
ELSE
   LET ERR.MESSAGE$ = "DIV-IN"
   LET ERR.DATA$ = STR$(DIV)
   GOSUB ERROR.WRITE.ROUTINE
END IF
```

FIGURE 10–25

```
IF DEPT > 0 AND DEPT < 11 THEN
ELSE
    LET ERR.MESSAGE$ = "DEPT-IN"
    LET ERR.DATA$ = STR$(DEPT)
    GOSUB ERROR.WRITE.ROUTINE
END IF


IF EMP.NBR# > 0 AND EMP.NBR# < 1000000000# THEN
ELSE
    LET ERR.MESSAGE$ = "EMPNO-IN"
    LET ERR.DATA$ = STR$(EMP.NBR#)
    GOSUB ERROR.WRITE.ROUTINE
END IF


IF EMP.NAME$ <>   "" THEN
ELSE
    LET ERR.MESSAGE$ = "NAME"
    LET ERR.DATA$ = EMP.NAME$
    GOSUB ERROR.WRITE.ROUTINE
END IF


IF PAY.RATE > 0 AND PAY.RATE < 5000! THEN
ELSE
    LET ERR.MESSAGE$ = "PAY-RATE"
    LET ERR.DATA$ = STR$(PAY.RATE)
    GOSUB ERROR.WRITE.ROUTINE
END IF


IF HOURS.WORKED >= 0 AND HOURS.WORKED < 300 THEN
ELSE
    LET ERR.MESSAGE$ = "HOURS-WKD"
    LET ERR.DATA$ = STR$(HOURS.WORKED)
    GOSUB ERROR.WRITE.ROUTINE
END IF


IF SICK.DAYS >= 0 AND SICK.DAYS < 180 THEN
ELSE
    LET ERR.MESSAGE$ = "SICK-DAYS"
    LET ERR.DATA$ = STR$(SICK.DAYS)
    GOSUB ERROR.WRITE.ROUTINE
END IF


IF VACATION.DAYS >= 0 AND VACATION.DAYS < 31   THEN
ELSE
    LET ERR.MESSAGE$ = "VACN-DAYS"
    LET ERR.DATA$ = STR$(VACATION.DAYS)
    GOSUB ERROR.WRITE.ROUTINE
END IF


IF ERR.SWITCH$ = "N" THEN
    GOSUB WRITE.DISK.ROUTINE
END IF
GOSUB READ.ROUTINE
RETURN
'*****************************************************************
'                          EOJ1 HSK2 ROUTINE                     *
'*****************************************************************
EOJ1.HSK2.ROUTINE:
CLOSE #1, #3
```

FIGURE 10–25 (continued)

```
OPEN "A:C10EDIT" FOR INPUT AS #3
LET END.FLAG$ = "OFF"
LET LINE.COUNT = 50
LET PAGE.COUNT = 0
GOSUB READ2.ROUTINE
RETURN
'*******************************************************************************
'                                LIST ROUTINE                                 *
'*******************************************************************************
LIST.ROUTINE:
IF LINE.COUNT > 49 THEN
    GOSUB HEADS2.ROUTINE
END IF
PRINT #2, USING EDITED.LINE$; DIV,  DEPT,  EMP.NBR#,  EMP.NAME$,  PAY.RATE,
    HOURS.WORKED, SICK.DAYS, VACATION.DAYS
LET LINE.COUNT = LINE.COUNT + 1
GOSUB READ2.ROUTINE
RETURN
'*******************************************************************************
'                                EOJ2 ROUTINE                                 *
'*******************************************************************************
EOJ2.ROUTINE:
CLOSE
RETURN
'*******************************************************************************
'                              WRITE DISK ROUTINE                             *
'*******************************************************************************
WRITE.DISK.ROUTINE:
WRITE #3, DIV, DEPT, EMP.NBR#, EMP.NAME$, PAY.RATE, HOURS.WORKED, SICK.DAYS,
    VACATION.DAYS
RETURN
'*******************************************************************************
'                              ERROR WRITE ROUTINE                           *
'*******************************************************************************
ERROR.WRITE.ROUTINE:
LET ERR.SWITCH$ = "Y"
IF LINE.COUNT > 49 THEN
    GOSUB HEADS1.ROUTINE
END IF
PRINT #2, USING DETAIL.FORMAT$; DIV, DEPT, EMP.NBR#, EMP.NAME$, ERR.MESSAGE$,
    ERR.DATA$
LET LINE.COUNT = LINE.COUNT + 1
RETURN
'*******************************************************************************
'                                HEADS1 ROUTINE                              *
'*******************************************************************************
HEADS1.ROUTINE:
LET PAGE.COUNT = PAGE.COUNT + 1
PRINT #2, CHR$(12)
PRINT #2, TAB(24); "LISTING OF ERROR FIELDS";
PRINT #2, TAB(63) USING "PAGE ##"; PAGE.COUNT
PRINT #2,
PRINT #2, TAB(12); "EMPLOYEE"; TAB(43); "ERROR"; TAB(56); "DATA IN"
PRINT #2, TAB(2); "DIV DEPT    NUMBER"; TAB(29); "NAME"; TAB(43); "FIELD";
    TAB(57); "ERROR"
PRINT #2,
LET LINE.COUNT = 0
RETURN
```

FIGURE 10–25 (continued)

```
'*********************************************************************
'                          READ ROUTINE                            *
'*********************************************************************
READ.ROUTINE:
INPUT #1, DIV, DEPT,  EMP.NBR#,  EMP.NAME$,  PAY.RATE, HOURS.WORKED, SICK.DAYS,
    VACATION.DAYS
IF EOF(1) THEN
    END.FLAG$ = "ON"
END IF
RETURN
'*********************************************************************
'                          HEADS2 ROUTINE                          *
'*********************************************************************
HEADS2.ROUTINE:
PRINT #2, CHR$(12)
LET PAGE.COUNT = PAGE.COUNT + 1
PRINT #2, TAB(23); "LISTING OF EDITED RECORDS";
PRINT #2, TAB(64) USING  "PAGE ##"; PAGE.COUNT
PRINT #2,
PRINT #2, TAB(12); "EMPLOYEE"; TAB(44); "PAY    HOURS    SICK    VACN"
PRINT #2, TAB(2); "DIV DEPT    NUMBER"; TAB(29); "NAME"; TAB(44); "RATE    WORKED
    DAYS   DAYS"
PRINT #2,
LET LINE.COUNT = 0
RETURN
'*********************************************************************
'                          READ2 ROUTINE                           *
'*********************************************************************
READ2.ROUTINE:
INPUT #3, DIV, DEPT, EMP.NBR#, EMP.NAME$, PAY.RATE, HOURS.WORKED, SICK.DAYS
    VACATION.DAYS
IF EOF(3) THEN
    END.FLAG$ = "ON"
END IF
RETURN
```

FIGURE 10–25 (continued)

CHAPTER VOCABULARY

Class
Consistency
Data exception
Edit
Error counter

Error switch
Existence
Input edit
Multiple record types
Presence

Program interrupt
Range
Record type
Search

REVIEW QUESTIONS

MATCHING

A. Edit program
B. Program interrupt
C. Range
D. Error list
E. Consistency

F. Multiple record types
G. Existence
H. Class
I. Presence

_____ **1.** Two or more record formats in a single file.
_____ **2.** A test to determine if any data has been entered in a field.

_____ **3.** The premature termination of a program, sometimes caused by incorrect data.

_____ **4.** A test to determine if the value of the data item falls within prescribed limits.

_____ **5.** A program which checks the input in various ways in order to avoid problems at a later point.

_____ **6.** A test to determine if data is numeric.

_____ **7.** A report which indicates those items needing correction prior to the use of the data in subsequent programs.

_____ **8.** The use of a table to determine if a data element is one of a set.

_____ **9.** Comparing two or more items to determine if one is okay in relation to the others.

TRUE/FALSE

T   F   **1.** The most specific of all edit tests is the one for presence.

T   F   **2.** A test for range can be made on numeric or alphanumeric data items.

T   F   **3.** Division by zero is not permissible in most programming languages.

T   F   **4.** Data exceptions are one form of program interrupt.

T   F   **5.** One purpose of an edit program is to check the validity of the data and prepare an error list.

T   F   **6.** When multiple record types are in a file, each type is automatically stored in a separate memory location.

EXERCISES

1. Draw a flowchart to edit the following input in order to avoid incorrect output or program interrupts.
CUSTOMER NUMBER
ORDER NUMBER
STYLE
COLOR (a two-digit number, color name is in a table)
SIZE
QUANTITY ORDERED

2. Draw a flowchart to edit a file which has two record types—a master and a transaction. Indicate the routines needed by performing subroutines, but do not expand the subroutines.

3. Draw a flowchart which edits data about to be used for preparing an invoice. Identify the fields you would expect to be present that require editing.

DISCUSSION QUESTIONS

1. What types of tests would you expect to find in a payroll transaction edit?

2. What types of tests would you expect to find in an order entry edit?

3. What types of tests would you expect to find in an accounts receivable edit of cash receipts?

4. Name other business data processing applications where edits can be usefully applied.

5. What types of problems might arise from not editing input data?

PROJECTS

Project 1

Prepare a print chart and a flowchart for the following specifications:

INPUT

MASTER PERSONNEL FILE

01–02	Personnel Record Code	
03–03	Personnel Division	has a range of 1–5
04–05	Personnel Department	has a range of 1–5
	Personnel Employee ID	
06–08	Personnel ID-1	
09–10	Personnel ID-2	
11–14	Personnel ID-3	
15–34	Personnel Name	
35–50	Personnel Street Address	
51–62	Personnel State	
53–57	Personnel Zip	
	Personnel Date of Employment	

58–59	Personnel Month	
60–61	Personnel Day	
62–63	Personnel Year	
64–64	Personnel Experience Code	
65–65	Personnel Responsibility Code	
66–67	Personnel Skill Code	
68–71	Personnel Vacation Days	(4.1)
72–75	Personnel Sick Days	(4.1)
76–80	Personnel Daily Rate	(5.2)

PROCESSING

1. Inspect the fields of the output for any potential problems. Look for items which may cause incorrect output or data exceptions if you were to use the data for any of the previous projects in the book.
2. Store a count of good and bad records per division.

OUTPUT

1. Records which pass all of the edit tests should be written on disk. There will be multiple errors for some records. Those that fail any of the edit tests should be printed along with an explanation of the error. Print one line for each error.
2. Print the record counts (good, bad) on a separate page.

Project 2

Prepare a print chart and a flowchart for the following specifications:

INPUT

MASTER INVENTORY FILE

1– 2	Inventory Record Code	
	Inventory Stock Number	
3– 3	Inventory Type	Has a range of 1–5
4– 5	Inventory Class	Has a range of 1–10
6– 9	Inventory Part	
10–29	Inventory Description	
30–30	Inventory Location Code	
31–34	Inventory Quantity on Hand	
35–38	Inventory Quantity on Order	
39–42	Inventory Reorder Level	
43–43	Inventory Unit Size Code	
44–48	Inventory Unit Price	(5.2)
49–49	Inventory Discount Code	
50–55	Inventory Annual Usage (Units)	
56–58	Inventory Vendor Code	
	Inventory Transportation Code	
59–59	Inventory Category	
60–60	Inventory Distance	
61–80	Unused	

PROCESSING

1. Inspect the fields of the input for any potential problems. Look for items which may cause incorrect output or data exceptions.
2. Store a count of good and bad records per type.

OUTPUT

1. Records which pass all of the edit tests should be written on disk. There will be multiple errors for some records. Those fields that fail any of the edit tests should be printed along with an explanation of the error. Print one line for each error.
2. Print the record counts (good, bad) on a separate page at the end of the report.

11

TWO INPUT FILES

OBJECTIVES

As a result of studying this chapter the student should be able to perform the following activities.

1. Describe and flowchart the necessary activities in the housekeeping routine of a file-matching program.
2. Describe what situation the high/equal/low paths represent when comparing master and transaction records.
3. Describe and flowchart the necessary processing for the high/equal/low paths when comparing master and transaction records.
4. Describe and flowchart the use of end-master and end-transaction switches.
5. Describe and flowchart the use of an END FLAG switch.
6. Flowchart read-master and read-transaction subroutines for a file-matching program.
7. Describe error handling in terms of why it is needed and what should be done in file-matching programs.
8. Describe the use of the MATCH-SW switch, including when it is initialized and altered.

INTRODUCTION

The input which has been considered up to now has been in the form of a single, sequentially organized file. It is very common to have multiple sequential input files (usually two) coming into a program. The files must be in sequence on the same item, such as part number, division number, or the like.

As an example of this type of processing, a program in a payroll system (see Figure 11–1) might read the employee file for the current period and check to see if the employees who are to be paid actually work for the company. This is done by cross-referencing the current payroll file for employees during a given period with a master file of employee numbers. If there are current earnings for which there is no matching master employee number, doubts are raised as to who is being paid and why. If there are master items for which there are no current

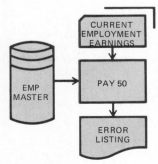

FIGURE 11–1

earnings, it needs to be shown someplace that certain employees are not being paid this period. If the master employee number agrees with the current earnings employee number, things are presumed to be OK at this point.

In order for unmatched situations to be uncovered, both files (employee master number file and employee current earnings file) need to be read and processed at the same time. Our example will presume only one current earnings record for each employee, although there could be more than one.

FIRST-RECORD PROCESSING

The typical way to begin this process is to read the first record from both the master (employee number master) and the transaction (current earnings) files. If an end-of-file condition is reached when trying to read the **first** record of either file, an error condition exists, which should force special processing and the termination of the run. The flowcharting for this is shown in Figure 11–2. The NO MAST and NO TRANS subroutines, as well as END MAST and END TRANS switches, will be detailed later in the chapter; at this point it should be noted that NO MAST

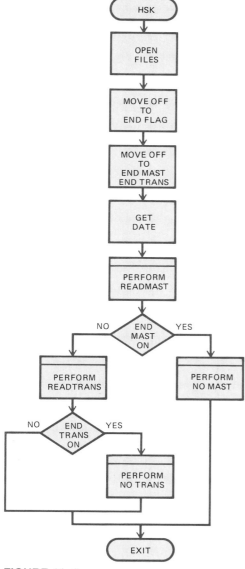

FIGURE 11–2

and NO TRANS will turn on the END FLAG to force the end of the run. (The pseudocode for all parts of the matching process is presented in Figure 11–11.)

MATCHING THE FILES

Once the first record from each of the two files has been read into storage (there is a separate input area for each file), the next step is to see if they match. In our case this means to see if the current earnings employee number has a match on the employee master file. Whenever two items, such a field on a master record and a field on a transaction record, are being compared, there are only three possible outcomes: (1) the master item is higher in value, or (2) the transaction item is higher in value, or (3) the two values are equal. This type of comparison is shown in Figure 11–3.

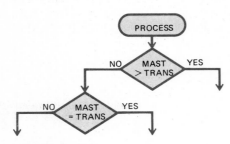

FIGURE 11–3

To show how this works, we need some sample items. The first few employees on both files (at least their numbers) are shown in Figure 11–4. Although in reality the employee number would probably be the social security number, we will use single-digit numbers to make the explanation easier to follow.

MASTER FILE	TRANS FILE
1	1
2	3
3	4
5	5

FIGURE 11–4

Upon entering the master/trans comparison the first record from both files has been read. In comparing the values in the master and transaction records, it is found that the employee numbers are in fact equal (1 = 1). Thus, the first employee in the current earnings file does in fact work for the company. Since we want to know about only the mismatched or unequal situations, no further processing of these items is currently needed. The next step is to read the next record from both files and return to the comparison. The reading of both files is shown in Figure 11–5.

Because of the logic required in reading the next records, two separately performed routines are shown at this point for reading the master and transaction files. Presuming that the files have been read, master employee number 2 and transaction employee number 3 are now in storage when the comparing step is reentered.

When comparing the master and transaction items this time it is found that the transaction item is found to be high (3 > 2). In our case this means that there are no current earnings for employee number 2. This should be noted someplace so that proper records can be maintained. For our purposes a message will be printed on the printer indicating that there are no current earnings for employee number 2 this period. This action is shown in Figure 11–6.

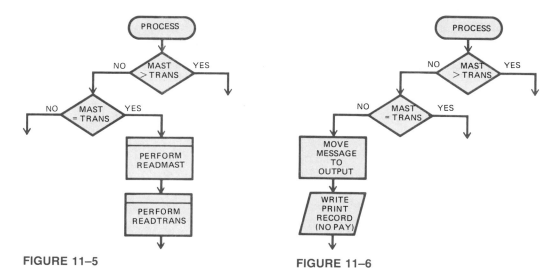

FIGURE 11-5

FIGURE 11-6

After writing the message, processing of the master record is complete, and once again the master file needs to be read before returning to the comparison. It is not necessary to read the transaction file yet, since it has not been verified that employee number 3 exists. The addition to the logic for reading the next master record is shown in Figure 11–7.

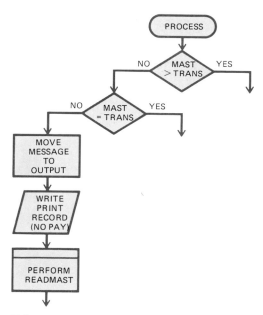

FIGURE 11-7

After reading the next master record (employee number 3) and reentering the comparison, another equal situation (3 = 3) is found. This results in the reading of both files and reentering the comparison. At this point master record number 5 and transaction record number 4 are in storage.

When the comparison is made the master is found to be high (5 > 4). This means there was no 4 on the master file, indicating that either somebody is being paid who does not work for the company or the master file is being poorly maintained. This situation definitely needs to be noted for investigation. An error message is printed on the printer and processing continues.

It is important to observe that processing does continue and the program is not stopped. Since processing of the transaction record is now completed, the next transaction record on the file is read (shown in Figure 11–8) before reentering the comparison.

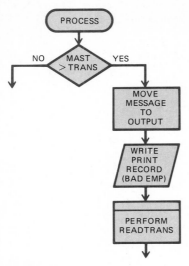

FIGURE 11–8

All three of the possible paths resulting from comparing two numbers have now been presented. These comprise the PROCESS subroutine shown in Figure 11–9.

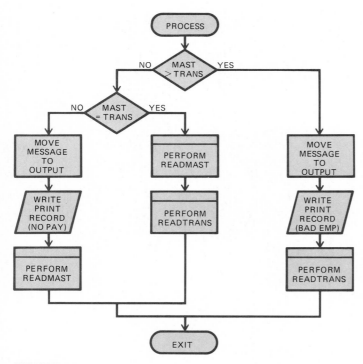

FIGURE 11–9

Before going on to the read routines for master and transaction files, let's put everything we have so far together in the standard format that we have been using. This is shown in Figure 11–10. The pseudocode is shown in Figure 11–11.

Let's walk through this complete version of the flowchart using the same data as before (see Figure 11–4). The first step is to perform the HSK routine. In HSK the files are opened, END FLAG, END MAST, and END TRANS are initialized, the current date is obtained, and the first master record (employee number 1) is read. The use of END MAST, END TRANS, and

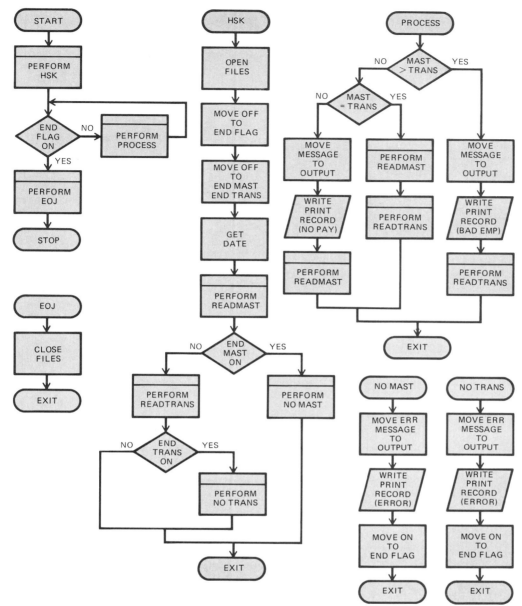

FIGURE 11-10

MAINLINE LOGIC

    PERFORM hsk routine
    PERFORM process routine until end flag = on
    PERFORM eoj routine
    STOP

HSK ROUTINE

    OPEN files
    MOVE off to end flag
    MOVE off to end mast
    MOVE off to end trans
    GET date
    PERFORM readmast routine

FIGURE 11-11

```
    IF end mast = on
          PERFORM no mast routine
    ELSE
          PERFORM readtrans routine
          IF end trans = on
                PERFORM no trans routine
          ENDIF
    ENDIF
```

PROCESS ROUTINE

```
    IF master > trans
          MOVE bad employee message to output
          WRITE print record (error)
          PERFORM readtrans routine
    ELSE
          IF master = trans
                PERFORM readmast routine
                PERFORM readtrans routine
          ELSE
                MOVE no earnings message to output
                WRITE print record (no pay)
                PERFORM readmast routine
          ENDIF
    ENDIF
```

NO MAST ROUTINE

```
    MOVE no master file message to output
    WRITE print record (error)
    MOVE on to end flag
```

NO TRANS ROUTINE

```
    MOVE no trans file message to output
    WRITE print record (error)
    MOVE on to end flag
```

EOJ ROUTINE

```
    CLOSE files
```

FIGURE 11–11 (continued)

END FLAG will be pointed out later. Had the master file contained no records (END MAST would be on), the NO MAST routine would have been performed and processing would have dropped through to the exit in HSK. The NO MAST routine would have printed an error message indicating the absence of any master data and turned on the END FLAG switch.

After reading the first master record, the first transaction record needs to be read (employee number 1). Had the transaction file contained no records (END TRANS would be on), the NO TRANS routine would have been performed and processing would have dropped through to the exit in HSK. The NO TRANS routine would have printed an error message indicating no activity against the master file and turned on the END FLAG switch.

Once the HSK routine is left through the exit, either the first master record and the first transaction record (both number 1 in our case) will have been read or an error message has been printed and END FLAG will have been turned on. The next step is to see if the END FLAG switch has been turned on. If it is on, then one or the other file had no records, so the EOJ routine is performed and the program is terminated.

Since a record from both master and transaction files has been read, when the END FLAG Switch is tested it is found to be off. Thus the PROCESS routine is performed. The first step in the PROCESS routine is to compare the master and transaction values. Both values are equal to 1, so the equal path is followed. In this case no further processing is needed, as we are interested only in unmatched situations. The next master record is then read (employee number 2), the next transaction record is read (employee number 3), and it is time to exit the PROCESS routine.

Upon leaving the PROCESS routine, the logic returns to check the END FLAG switch. Since a record was successfully read from both files, this switch should still be off. The only time END FLAG will be turned on is when both files have reached the end. If both files have ended, the END FLAG switch will have been turned on during the reading process. finding the END FLAG switch off, the PROCESS routine is once again performed.

Upon entering the PROCESS routine this time the master is less than the transaction (2 < 3). This indicates an employee with no earnings this period. After writing an appropriate message on the printer, processing of the master record is completed and the next master needs to be read. In performing READ MAST the record for employee number 3 is read. The logic at this point exits the PROCESS routine and returns to check the END FLAG.

The END FLAG switch is still off, since the end of both files has not been reached. The next step is to reenter the PROCESS routine and compare master and transaction employee numbers. At this point an equal condition (3 = 3) exists, so the next master (employee number 5) and transaction (employee number 4) records on the respective files are read. It is again time to exit the PROCESS routine and return to compare the END FLAG switch. Transaction record 4 will be printed with an appropriate error message and after reading the next transaction record (employee number 5) the logic will return to test the END FLAG switch.

Still finding the END FLAG switch off, the PROCESS routine will again be performed. On this pass through the PROCESS routine the master and transaction values are equal (5 = 5). As before, another master and transaction record will be read. However, as can be seen from the data, both files have reached an end-of-file condition.

END-OF-FILE LOGIC

This brings up the end-of-file logic. How do we handle the reading process when one file or both files have ended? Figure 11–12 shows the logic for reading the master file, and Figure 11–13 is the pseudocode.

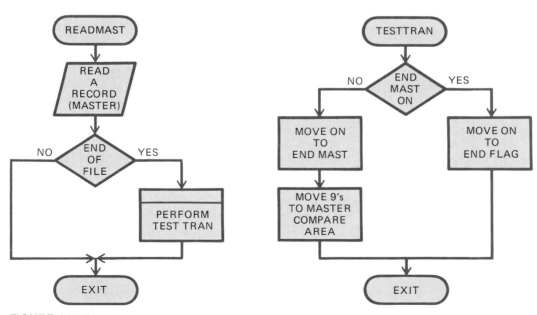

FIGURE 11–12

READMAST ROUTINE

```
READ a record (master)
        AT END of file
                PERFORM test tran routine
ENREAD
```

TEST TRAN ROUTINE

```
IF end trans = on
        MOVE on to end flag
ELSE
        MOVE on end mast
        MOVE 9's to master compare area
ENDIF
```

FIGURE 11–13

Let's take a look at where this fits in the PROCESS routine. There are two places in the PROCESS routine where the READMAST routine is performed. One place is on the master-less-than-transaction path. This path represents those employees who have no earnings this period. Whenever this path is encountered, the master record has been printed along with a message indicating the no-salary status. If, when the READMAST routine is entered, an attempt to read the master file finds the end of the file, then the TEST TRANS routine is performed. If END TRAN is on (it will be on only if the transaction file has already ended), then both files have ended, so END FLAG will be turned on. This portion of the logic is shown in Figure 11–14.

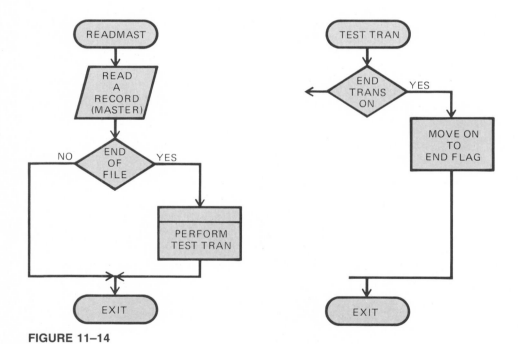

FIGURE 11–14

If an end-of-file condition is not found when reading the master file, the logic will fall through to the exit of the READMAST routine (Figure 11–15); and the TEST TRAN routine will not be performed.

The one remaining path through the READMAST and TEST TRAN routines is when an end-of-file condition is found when reading the master file, and the transaction file has not yet ended. In this case all remaining transaction items represent people being paid who are not on the master file—in other words, MASTER > TRANS conditions. To force this situation 9's are

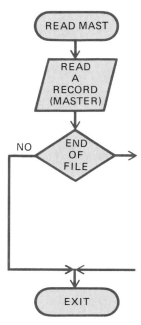

FIGURE 11-15

moved to the master area. In this way any other transaction items will compare low and cause the appropriate error message to be printed. The END MAST switch is turned on at the same time that 9's are moved to the master area. This logic path is shown in Figure 11–16.

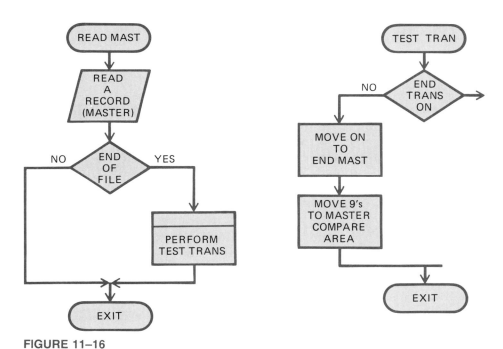

FIGURE 11-16

The other place where the READMAST routine is performed within PROCESS is on the MAST = TRANS path. The explanation given above also fits the equal path execution of READ-MAST.

The logic for reading the transaction file is similar. This and the related pseudocode are shown in Figure 11–17. Notice that the END MAST and END TRANS switches were turned off

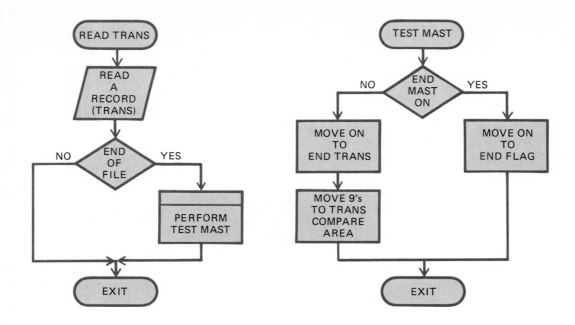

READTRANS ROUTINE
READ a record (transaction)
ATEND OF FILE
PERFORM test mast
ENDREAD

TEST MAST ROUTINE
IF end mast is on
 MOVE on to end flag
ELSE
 MOVE on to end trans
 MOVE 9's to transaction compare area

FIGURE 11–17

initially in the HSK routine. This is important, since they need to be given an initial value or take pot luck with what is left over in storage at their locations.

Let's return to the point where master and transaction number 5 had been processed; the next step was to read the master and transaction files. In READMAST an attempt is made to read the next record. At this point an end-of-file condition on the master file is encountered. Thus the TEST TRANS routine is performed. In so doing a check is made to see if the transaction file has already ended (END TRANS will be on if it has). It has not, so 9's are moved to the master area, the END MAST switch is turned on, and the logic continues on to exist the TEST TRAN and READMAST routines.

The next step is to perform the READTRANS routine. In doing so an attempt is made to read the next record on the transaction file. This produces an end-of-file condition on the transaction file so the TEST MAST routine is performed where a check is made to find out if the master file has ended. Since the master file has ended (that is, END MAST has been turned on), the END FLAG switch is turned on and the logic exits the TEST MAST and READ TRANS routines.

This time when the logic returns to check the END FLAG switch, it is on. Therefore, the EOJ routine is performed and processing is terminated.

TRANSACTION FILE ENDING FIRST

Realistically the odds are very good that both files will not end at the same time. One possibility is that the transaction file will end before the master file.

Assuming that the HSK routine has been executed and that both files do exist, the END FLAG switch is off the first time it is tested; thus the PROCESS routine will be performed. The data presented earlier is shown below, except that we have added a master record (employee number 6) to ensure that the transaction file ends first.

MASTER FILE	TRANSFILE
1	1
2	3
3	4
5	5
6	

Since the housekeeping (HSK) routine is already finished, the first record from both files (employee number 1 in both cases) is already in storage. When the master and transaction items are compared, they are found equal (1 = 1). Therefore the next step is to perform the READMAST routine. READMAST reads the next record (employee number 2), finds no end of file, and exits the routine. The next step is to perform READTRANS.

In performing the READTRANS routine the next transaction record is read (employee number 3) and, finding no end-of-file, the logic proceeds to exit the routine. Having read both a master and a transaction record, it is time to exit the PROCESS routine. The next step in the mainline logic is to test whether the END FLAG switch is on or off. It is off, so the next step is to return to the PROCESS routine. Upon entering the PROCESS routine both master record number 2 and transaction record number 3 have been read.

When the two records are compared, the master is found to be low (2 < 3), so a message is printed showing no earnings this period for employee number 2 and the READMAST routine is performed. The next master record is read (employee number 3) and, finding no end-of-file, the next step is to exit the READMAST routine. It is once again time to exit the PROCESS routine and return to test the END-FLAG switch. Since it is still off, the logic returns to performing the PROCESS routine.

This time when the comparison is made the results are equal (3 = 3), so the READMAST routine is performed. In reading the next master record (employee number 5) no end-of-file condition is found, so the next step is to exit the READMAST routine. Next the READTRANS routine is performed. This causes employee number 4 to be read in from the transaction file. Since no end-of-file condition exists, the next step is to exit the READTRANS routine after reading the record. At this point it is again time to exit the PROCESS routine and return to check the END-FLAG switch.

END-FLAG is still off, so the PROCESS routine is again entered and the master and transaction records are compared. This time the master is high (5. > 4), so a message is printed indicating that there are current earnings for a nonexistent employee and the READTRANS routine is performed. Employee number 5's record is read into storage and, finding no end-of-file, it is again time to exit the routine. It is also time to exit the PROCESS routine and return to check the END-FLAG switch. Finding it still off, it is once again time to enter the PROCESS routine.

When comparing the master and transaction items this time they are found to be equal (5 = 5) and therefore the logic proceeds to performing the READMAST routine. Employee number 6's record is read without finding an end-of-file, so it is time to exit the READMAST routine. The READTRANS routine is then performed. This time an end-of-file condition is found. In performing the TEST MAST routine it is found that the END MAST switch is not on, so the END TRANS switch is turned on, 9's are moved to the transaction area, and the logic proceeds to exit the TEST MAST and READTRANS routines.

The logic also exits the PROCESS routine and returns to check the END-FLAG switch. END-FLAG is still off, so the PROCESS routine is again entered. This time, when comparing the master and transaction values, the master is found to be low (6 < 9's). A message indicating no current salary for employee number 6 is printed, and the READMAST routine is performed. Notice the importance of having moved 9's to the transaction area when the transaction file ended. This allowed the extra master record (number 6) to compare low and the proper path in the PROCESS routine to be followed.

On this performance of READMAST an end-of-file condition is found on the master file.

Since, in the TEST TRAN routine, the END TRANS switch is found to be on, the END-FLAG switch is turned on (both files have now ended) and the logic will exit the TEST TRAN, READ-MAST, and PROCESS routines. The next step is to check END-FLAG and this time, it is found to be on, so it is time to perform EOJ and terminate processing.

MASTER FILE ENDING FIRST

Now let's switch the data around just a little so that the master file ends first.

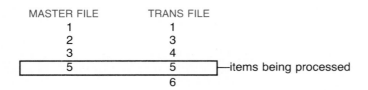

Assume that the records for employee number 5 from both files have been read. The master record will be compared with the transaction record within the PROCESS routine and they will be found to be equal. The logic will fall through on the equal path to perform the READMAST routine. In trying to read a master record an end-of-file condition is found on the master file. Since the END TRANS switch in the TEST TRAN routine is not on, the END MAST switch is turned on, 9's are moved to the master area, and the logic proceeds to exit the READMAST routine. After reading the next transaction record (employee number 6) it is time to exit the PROCESS routine and return to checking END-FLAG. END-FLAG is still off, so the PROCESS routine will be performed.

When comparing the master and transaction values the master is found to be high (9's > 6). Accordingly, a message is printed to indicate that employee number 6 is being paid but is not on the master file, and READTRANS is performed. When attempting to read the next transaction record an end-of-file condition occurs on the transaction file. Since the END MAST switch is on, the END-FLAG switch is turned on and the logic proceeds to exit the TEST MAST, READ-TRANS, and PROCESS routines. Returning to check the END-FLAG, it is now found to be on, so the EOJ routine is performed and processing is terminated. Once again the importance of moving 9's to the master area when the master file ended should be noted. It allowed the master to compare high when the record for employee number 6 was being compared and the processing to proceed properly.

Figure 11–18 shows the format of the report produced by such a file-matching program. Although it was not in the previous example, a message "EMPLOYEE NUMBERS MATCH" has been added so that we will know when the equal path has been executed. COBOL and BASIC programs are shown in Figure 11–19 and 11–20 to help put this in perspective.

	S AND L PROGRAMMING SERVICES
	FILE MATCHING REPORT PAGE XX
	EMPLOYEE STATUS
	NUMBER MESSAGE
	XXX–XX–XXXX NO EARNINGS THIS PERIOD
	XXX–XX–XXXX NO SUCH EMPLOYEE FOUND
	XXX–XX–XXXX EMPLOYEE NUMBERS MATCH

FIGURE 11–18

COBOL VERSION

```
        PROCEDURE DIVISION.
        MAINLINE-LOGIC.
            PERFORM HSK-ROUTINE.
            PERFORM PROCESS-ROUTINE UNTIL END-FLAG = 'ON'.
            PERFORM EOJ-ROUTINE.
            STOP RUN.
        HSK ROUTINE.
            OPEN INPUT EMP-MAST
                        EMP-TRANS
                OUTPUT MATCHING-REPORT.
            MOVE 'OFF' TO END-FLAG.
            MOVE 'OFF' TO END-MAST.
            MOVE 'OFF' TO END-TRANS.
            PERFORM READ-MAST-ROUTINE.
            IF END-MAST = 'ON'
                PERFORM NO-MAST-ROUTINE
            ELSE
                PERFORM READ-TRANS-ROUTINE
                IF END-TRANS = 'ON'
                    PERFORM NO-TRANS-ROUTINE.
        PROCESS-ROUTINE.
            IF MAST-EMPNUM > TRANS-EMPNUM
                MOVE TRANS-EMPNUM TO NUM-PRT
                MOVE 'NO MATCHING EMPLOYEE FOUND' TO MESSAGE-PRT
                WRITE PRINT-RECORD FROM DETAIL-LINE
                    AFTER ADVANCING 1 LINES
                PERFORM READ-TRANS = ROUTINE
            ELSE
                IFMAST-EMPNOM = TRANS-EMPNUM
                    MOVE 'EMPLOYEE NUMBERS MATCH' TO MESSAGE-PRT
                    MOVE MAST-EMPNUM TO NUM-PRT
                    WRITE PRINT RECORD FROM DETAIL-LINE
                        AFTER ADVANCING 1 LINES
                    PERFORM READ-MAST-ROUTINE
                    PERFORM READ-TRANS-ROUTINE
                ELSE
                    MOVE 'NO EARNINGS THIS PERIOD' TO MESSAGE-PRT
                    MOVE MAST-EMPNUM TO NUM-PRT
                    WRITE PRINT-RECORD FROM DETAIL-LINE
                        AFTER ADVANCING 1 LINES
                    PERFORM READ-MAST-ROUTINE.


    EOJ ROUTINE.

        CLOSE EMP-MAST
            EMP-TRANS
            MATCHING-REPORT.


    NO-MAST-ROUTINE.

        MOVE 'MASTER FILE NOT PRESENT' TO ERROR-MSG.
        WRITE PRINT-RECORD FROM ERROR-LINE
            AFTER ADVANCING TOP-OF-PAGE.
        MOVE 'ON' TO END-FLAG.


    NO-TRANS-ROUTINE

        MOVE 'TRANSACTION FILE NOT PRESENT' TO ERROR-MSG.
        WRITE PRINT-RECORD FROM ERROR-LINE
            AFTER ADVANCING TOP-OF-PAGE.
        MOVE 'ON' TO END-FLAG.
```

FIGURE 11–19

READ-MAST-ROUTINE.

        READ EMP-MAST
           AT END
               PERFORM TEST-TRAN-ROUTINE.

TEST-TRAN-ROUTINE.

    IF END-TRANS = 'ON'
        MOVE 'ON' TO END-FLAG
    ELSE
        MOVE 'ON' TO END-MAST
        MOVE HIGH-VALUES TO MAST-EMPNUM.

READ-TRANS-ROUTINE.

    READ EMP-TRANS
        AT END
           PERFORM TEST-MAST-ROUTINE.

TEST-MAST-ROUTINE.

    IF END-MAST = 'ON'
        MOVE 'ON' TO END-FLAG
    ELSE
        MOVE 'ON' TO END-TRANS
        MOVE HIGH-VALUES TO TRANS-EMPNUM.

FIGURE 11–19 (continued)

BASIC VERSION

```
'PROGRAMMERS: J AND J, INC.
'DATE: 10-11-89
'PROGRAM NAME CASE 11
'******************************************************************************
'*                         MAINLINE LOGIC                                     *
'******************************************************************************
GOSUB HOUSEKEEPING.ROUTINE
WHILE END.FLAG$ = "OFF"
    GOSUB PROCESS.ROUTINE
WEND
GOSUB EOJ.ROUTINE
END
'******************************************************************************
'*                       HOUSEKEEPING ROUTINE                                 *
'******************************************************************************
HOUSEKEEPING.ROUTINE:
OPEN "A:C11B1DATA" FOR INPUT AS #2
OPEN "A:C11B2DATA" FOR INPUT AS #3
INPUT "DO YOU WANT THE OUTPUT TO BE PRINTED.- ENTER Y OR N",ANSWER$
IF ANSWER$ = "Y" OR ANSWER$ ="y" THEN
    DEVICE$ = "LPT1:"
ELSE
    DEVICE$ = "SCRN:"
END IF
OPEN DEVICE$ FOR OUTPUT AS #1
LET END.FLAG$ = "OFF"
LET END.MAST$ = "OFF"
LET END.TRAN$ = "OFF"
LET LINE.COUNT = 50
LET PAGE.COUNT = 0
```
FIGURE 11–20

```
GOSUB READ.MASTER.ROUTINE
IF END.MAST$ = "ON" THEN
    GOSUB NO.MASTER.ROUTINE
    GO TO EXIT.HOUSEKEEPING
ELSE
    GOSUB READ.TRANSACTION.ROUTINE
END IF
IF END.TRAN$ = "ON" THEN
    GOSUB NO.TRANSACTION.ROUTINE
ELSE
END IF
EXIT.HOUSEKEEPING:
RETURN
'*********************************************************************
'*                         PROCESS ROUTINE                         *
'*********************************************************************
PROCESS.ROUTINE:
IF LINE.COUNT > 49 THEN GOSUB HEADS.ROUTINE
IF MASTER.NUMBER$ <= TRANSACTION.NUMBER$ THEN
    GO TO CHECK.LOW
ELSE
END IF
LET MESSAGE1$ = "NO SUCH EMPLOYEE FOUND"
LET MESSAGE2$ = SPACES$(6) + "&-&-&" + SPACES$(7) + "&"
PRINT #1,      USING MESSAGE2$;      MID$(TRANSACTION.NUMBER$,1,3)     ,
    MID$(TRANSACTION.NUMBER$,4,2)   ,   MID$(TRANSACTION.NUMBER$,6,4)   ,
    MID$(MESSAGE1$,1,22)
GOSUB READ.TRANSACTION.ROUTINE
GO TO EXIT.ROUTINE
CHECK.LOW:
IF MASTER.NUMBER$ < TRANSACTION.NUMBER$ THEN
    GO TO PROCESS.LOW
ELSE
    LET MESSAGE1$ = "EMPLOYEE NUMBERS MATCH"
    LET MESSAGE2$ = SPACES$(6) + "&-&-&" + SPACES$(7) + "&"
    PRINT #1,     USING      MESSAGE2$;      MID$(MASTER.NUMBER$,1,3)     ,
        MID$(MASTER.NUMBER$,4,2)       ,      MID$(MASTER.NUMBER$,6,4)      ,
        MID$(MESSAGE1$,1,22)
    GOSUB READ.MASTER.ROUTINE
    GOSUB READ.TRANSACTION.ROUTINE
    GOTO EXIT.ROUTINE
END IF
PROCESS.LOW:
LET MESSAGE1$ = "NO EARNINGS THIS PERIOD"
LET MESSAGE2$ = SPACES$(6) + "&-&-&" +SPACES$(7) + "&"
PRINT #1,      USING      MESSAGE2$;      MID$(MASTER.NUMBER$,1,3)      ,
    MID$(MASTER.NUMBER$,4,2),MID$(MASTER.NUMBER$,6,4),MID$(MESSAGE1$,1,23)
GOSUB READ.MASTER.ROUTINE
EXIT.ROUTINE:
RETURN
'*********************************************************************
'*                           EOJ ROUTINE                           *
'*********************************************************************
EOJ.ROUTINE:
CLOSE #1,#2,#3
RETURN
'*********************************************************************
'*                        NO MASTER ROUTINE                        *
'*********************************************************************
```

FIGURE 11–20 (continued)

```
NO.MASTER.ROUTINE:
PRINT #1,"        MASTER FILE NOT PRESENT"
LET END.FLAG$ = "ON"
RETURN
/*****************************************************************
/*                      NO TRANSACTION ROUTINE                  *
/*****************************************************************
NO.TRANSACTION.ROUTINE:
PRINT #1,"        TRANSACTION FILE NOT PRESENT"
LET END.FLAG$ = "ON"
RETURN
/*****************************************************************
/*                      READ MASTER ROUTINE                     *
/*****************************************************************
READ.MASTER.ROUTINE:
IF EOF(2) THEN
    GOSUB TEST.TRANSACTION.ROUTINE
ELSE
    INPUT #2,MASTER.NUMBER$
END IF
RETURN
/*****************************************************************
/*                      TEST TRANSACTION ROUTINE               *
/*****************************************************************
TEST.TRANSACTION.ROUTINE:
IF END.TRAN$ = "ON" THEN
    LET END.FLAG$ = "ON"
ELSE
    LET END.MAST$ = "ON"
    LET MAST.NUM$ = "999999999"
END IF
RETURN
/*****************************************************************
/*                      READ TRANSACTION ROUTINE               *
/*****************************************************************
READ.TRANSACTION.ROUTINE:
IF EOF(3) THEN
    GOSUB TEST.MASTER.ROUTINE
ELSE
    INPUT #3,TRANSACTION.NUMBER$
END IF
RETURN
/
/*****************************************************************
/*                      TEST MASTER ROUTINE                     *
/*****************************************************************
TEST.MASTER.ROUTINE:
IF END.MAST$ = "ON" THEN
    LET END.FLAG$ = "ON"
ELSE
    LET END.TRAN$ = "ON"
    LET TRAN.NUM$ = "999999999"
END IF
RETURN
/*****************************************************************
/*                      HEADS ROUTINE                           *
/*****************************************************************
HEADS.ROUTINE:
LET PAGE.COUNT = PAGE.COUNT + 1
```

FIGURE 11–20 (continued)

```
PRINT #1,CHR$(12)
PRINT #1,SPC(16);"S AND L PROGRAMMING SERVICES"
PRINT #1,
PRINT #1,SPC(10);"FILE MATCHING REPORT";SPC(12);"PAGE ";PAGE.COUNT
PRINT #1,
PRINT #1,SPC(8);"EMPLOYEE";SPC(17);"STATUS"
PRINT #1,SPC(9);"NUMBER";SPC(17);"MESSAGE"
PRINT #1,
LET LINE.COUNT = 0
RETURN
```

FIGURE 11–20 (continued)

ERROR PROCESSING

Errors found when two input files are matched may be handled in various ways, depending on the severity of the error and on company practices. In our examples the initial file reading in the HSK routine was the only place where an error caused the program to be terminated. The error here was the absence of one of the files, which obviously would prevent any reasonable processing from being done.

The rest of the errors, which were basically unmatched master or transaction records, caused a message to be printed, and processing continued. While a nonexistent employee may seem to be a drastic enough error to stop processing, this program's function was to find these types of errors. We want to know what all the errors are so that they can be checked, corrected, and made ready for future processing. In general most errors in a program of this type are not enough to cause termination of the program.

MULTIPLE TRANSACTIONS PER MASTER

It is quite possible that when two sequential files are being matched that there will be multiple transaction records present for each master record that is present. When this type of situation is true there are some minor changes needed in the HSK and PROCESS routines. Figure 11–21 shows the HSK and PROCESS routines which will be needed to handle this situation.

Figure 11–22 shows the data that will be used to describe this process. This program will identify all masters with no matching transactions (number 1 in the example), transactions with no matching master (number 4 in the example), and matching records (numbers 2, 3, and 5 in the example). The MATCH SW was set to an off condition in the HSK routine. The first record from both files was also read in the HSK routine.

When entering the PROCESS routine the master and transaction records are compared and the master is found to be low (1 < 2). The MATCH SW is off so a message is printed indicating that master record 1 is an unmatched master record and the next master record (number 2) is read.

Since END FLAG is off the PROCESS routine is again executed. This time the comparison yields an equal (2 = 2) condition. As a result a matching record message is printed, MATCH SW, is set on, and the next transaction record (number 2) is read. END FLAG is still off so the logic once again will return to the PROCESS routine.

Another equal condition is present this time (2 = 2) so another matching record message is printed, MATCH SW is set on (even though it is already on), and the next transaction record (number 3) is read. END FLAG is still off so the logic will proceed to the PROCESS routine.

This time when performing the comparison the master record is found to be low (2 < 3). Since the MATCH SW is on, the next steps are to turn off MATCH SW and read the next master record (number 3). It should be noted that since MATCH SW was on no message for an unmatched master was printed. This is the function of the MATCH SW.

Since END FLAG is not yet on, the logic will again proceed to performing the PROCESS routine. Another equal condition (3 = 3) at this point so another matching record message is printed. The MATCH SW is again turned on and the next transaction record (number 4) is read.

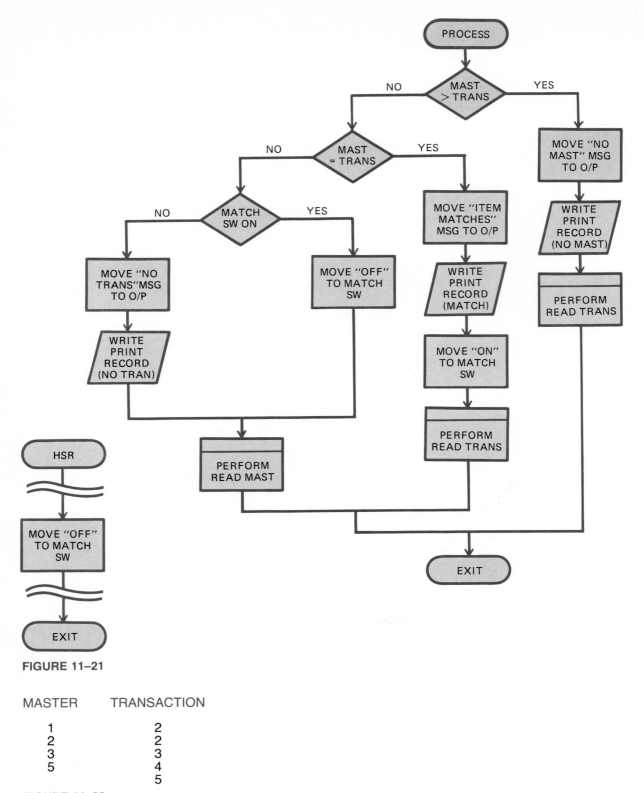

FIGURE 11-21

MASTER	TRANSACTION
1	2
2	2
3	3
5	4
	5

FIGURE 11-22

Still finding the END FLAG off it is once again time to perform the PROCESS routine. The comparison yields a master less than transaction (3 < 4) situation. Since MATCH SW is on, the only steps left to do are to turn off MATCH SW and read the next master record (number 5).

Since END FLAG has yet to be turned on the PROCESS routine is once again performed. This time the master record is high (5 > 4) so a message indicating a transaction record without a matching master is printed and the next transaction record (number 5) is read.

Returning once more to the PROCESS routine an equal condition is encountered. As a result a matching record message is printed, MATCH SW is turned on, and an attempt is made to read the next transaction record. In attempting to read another transaction an end-of-file condition is encountered. This in turn causes the TEST MAST routine (previously described) to be executed. Since the master file has not yet ended the END TRANS switch is turned on and 9's are moved to the transaction comparing area.

END FLAG is still off so the PROCESS routine is again executed. This time the master record is found to be low (5 < 9's). As a result the MATCH SW is tested. Since it is on, the next steps are to turn off MATCH SW and attempt to read another master record.

This time when an attempt is made to read another master record an end-of-file condition is encountered on the master file. As a result the TEST TRAN routine (also presented earlier) is executed. Since END TRANS is on it is time to turn on END-FLAG and exit the TEST TRAN and PROCESS routines. Since END-FLAG is now on it is time to execute the EOJ routine and terminate processing.

There are some items which need to be discussed at this point. First is the fact that only the transaction file is read on the master equal transaction path of the PROCESS routine. This is true since there may be several transactions for a given master record.

Second is the use of the MATCH SW switch. This switch is used to prevent the printing of an unmatched master message on the master less than transaction path of the PROCESS routine when there are matching records. This switch needs to have been initialized in the HSK routine.

The process of matching multiple sequential input files will be further explained in Chapter 12. Chapter 12 covers the updating process for sequential files.

CHAPTER VOCABULARY

END MAST switch	File matching	NO TRANS routine
End-of-file logic on matching	First-record processing	READMAST
END TRANS switch	NO MAST routine	READTRANS

REVIEW QUESTIONS

MATCHING

A. Causes processing to be terminated
B. Handled in the houskeeping routine
C. Master > transaction
D. Master < transaction

E. END MAST switch
F. END FLAG switch
G. READTRANS
H. READMAST

_____ **1.** Indicates that there is a master record with no matching transaction record.
_____ **2.** Reading the first record from both master and transaction files.
_____ **3.** Set on when both files have ended.
_____ **4.** No master or no transaction file present.
_____ **5.** Indicates that there is a transaction record with no matching master record.
_____ **6.** Done on both the equal and master-greater-than-transaction paths of the PROCESS routine.
_____ **7.** Set on in the TEST TRAN routine when END TRANS is not on.
_____ **8.** Done on both the equal and master-less-than transaction paths of the PROCESS routine.

TRUE/FALSE

T   F   **1.** It is very uncommon to find two sequential files being used as input to the same program.
T   F   **2.** It is valid to have multiple transactions for a single master in a file-matching program.
T   F   **3.** The first master and transaction records are usually read in the READMAST routine.

T	F	**4.** An error condition is usually indicated when the master and transaction records are equal.
T	F	**5.** Master records for which there are no transactions during the period usually represent a master greater than-transaction situation.
T	F	**6.** The END FLAG switch is typically turned off in the housekeeping routine.
T	F	**7.** Whenever the master file ends before the transaction file in a file-matching program, the remaining transactions are in error.
T	F	**8.** The END MAST and END TRANS switches, if used, must be turned off in the housekeeping routine.
T	F	**9.** End-of-job (EOJ) processing is done only when the END FLAG switch is off.
T	F	**10.** The END FLAG switch is turned on after only the master file has ended.
T	F	**11.** Any error condition usually causes the job to be terminated.
T	F	**12.** Files are opened and closed in the housekeeping (HSK) routine.
T	F	**13.** It is possible for both the END MAST and END TRANS switches to be turned on in a file matching program.

EXERCISES

1. Flowchart the routines for reading the master and transaction files in a two-input file program.
2. Flowchart the housekeeping routine for a two-file matching program.
3. Flowchart the entire program for reading two sequential input files with the following requirements. Each record on the transaction file is to be checked to see if there is a corresponding record on the master file. Unmatched masters should cause the message "NO TRANSACTION FOR MASTER NUMBER X" to be printed. Matching master and transaction records should cause the message "MASTER AND TRANS NUMBERS X FOUND EQUAL" to be printed. Unmatched transactions should cause the message "NO MASTER FOR TRANSACTION NUMBER X" to be printed.

DISCUSSION QUESTIONS

1. Describe the use of the END MAST and END TRANS switches including why they are used, when they are initialized and when they are modified.
2. Describe how the first records from the master and transaction files are read and how end-of-file conditions are handled in the housekeeping routine.
3. Describe when and why 9's are moved to the master and transaction comparing areas.

PROJECTS

Project 1

Prepare a print chart and a flowchart for the following problem:

INPUT

MASTER RECORD

Positions	Description
1–15	Employee Name
16–24	Employee Number
25–28	Check Number
29–35	Check Amount
36–41	Check Date
42–44	Department Number

TRANSACTION RECORD

1–14	Check Number
5–11	Check Amount
12–17	Check Date
18–26	Employee Number

PROCESSING

Produce a bank reconciliation report for the Widget Wrecking Company. Matched records should cause the printing of the message "CHECK CLEARED" as well as all of the fields on the master record. Unmatched master records should be shown with the message "CHECK NOT YET RETURNED" as well as all of the master fields. You should print the message "NO SUCH EMPLOYEE" as well as the other fields on the transaction record for unmatched transactions. Employee name and department should be left blank for unmatched transactions. The files are in sequence by check number.

OUTPUT

1. Page and column headings should be provided.
2. Page heads should include report title, company name, current date and page number.
3. Columns should be provided for employee number, check amount, check date, check number and a status message.
4. Single space the detail lines on the output.
5. No more than 50 detail lines per page.

Project 2

Prepare a flowchart and a print chart for the following problem:

INPUT

MASTER RECORD

Positions	Description
1–6	Stock Number
7–10	Quantity on Hand
11–25	Description

TRANSACTION RECORD

1–7	Unit Price
8–13	Stock Number

PROCESSING

Produce a listing of the inventory for the Fly-By-Night Airline Co. Each of the items for which there are matched records should have the stock number, quantity on hand, description, unit price and extended value (unit price × quantity on hand) printed. Unmatched masters should have the stock number, quantity on hand and description printed in the appropriate columns as well as *'s in the unit price and extended value columns. Unmatched transactions should have the stock number printed in the appropriate column as well as a message "NO MATCHING MASTER" in a message column. The files are in sequence by stock number. There will be no more than one transaction record per master record.

OUTPUT

1. Page headings should be provided including company name, report title, current date and page number.
2. Column heads should be provided for stock-number, description, quantity on hand, unit price, extended price and message.
3. Single space the detail lines on the output.
4. No more than 50 detail lines per page.

12

THE UPDATE PROGRAM

OBJECTIVES

As a result of studying this chapter the student should be able to perform the following activities:

1. Describe the function of a file-update program.
2. Identify and describe the types of transaction records in an update program.
3. Flowchart the logic for additions to a master file.
4. Flowchart the logic for deletions from a master file.
5. Flowchart the logic for changes to a master file.
6. Describe why a sequential-file update needs to produce a new file for the updated version of the file.
7. Flowchart a file-updating procedure updating a master file where there is only one possible transaction record for any master record.
8. Describe what is needed when there are multiple transaction records needed to create or change a master record.

INTRODUCTION

A fairly common type of program that requires two sequential input files to be matched is an update program. An update program is used to bring the data in a file (usually a master file) up to date so that it reflects the current situation. When sequential files are updated it is necessary to create a new file. A simple analogy should clarify the need for a new file being created. If you have a cassette tape of music that you wish to add songs to and you wish to insert them in the middle of the tape, you have much the same problem. That is, you cannot insert the songs on the existing tape. You must create a new tape, copying to it those songs from the original tape that you still want and inserting the new songs at the places you want them to appear. Much the same process is followed in updating a standard sequential file. Since there is no room between existing records to add new records, a new file needs to be created and the new records added at the desired points. The transaction records which provide the updating data may be of three types: additions to the master file, deletions from the master file, and changes to items already in the master file.

Add records are those that are to be added to the master file. Adds are valid only if no record with the same control field contents already exists on the master file. Additions are found on the master-greater-than-transaction path when we are comparing the records from the two files.

Deletions are records that are to be removed from the master file. Deletions are valid only if there is a record on the master file with the same control field contents as the one that is to be deleted. Deletions are found on the equal path of the master/transaction comparison.

Change records are those that will modify the contents of the records already on the master file. Like deletions, change records are valid only if there is a record on the master file with the same control field contents as the change record. Changes also happen on the equal branch of the master/transaction comparison. Changes may occur to any part of the master record except the field on which the file has been sequenced (called the control field).

In order to know which type of transaction record is being processed at any given time, we need some sort of code in the transaction record, such as A (addition), C (change), or D (deletion), in addition to any data that is in the record. As these records are processed, a report should be produced showing any activity (updating) that takes place. The first few steps in the update program are the same as in the file-matching program. These steps are shown in Figure 12–1. There has been a slight addition to the logic from chapter 11—the setting of all the counters used in a file update equal to zero.

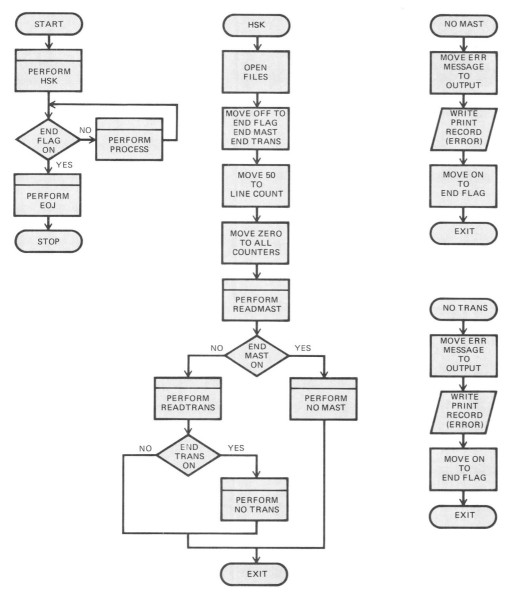

FIGURE 12–1

MASTER GREATER THAN TRANSACTION

The PROCESS routine is a little more complicated than the one in Chapter 11. The same basics still apply, but more steps are needed. One path of this process is shown in Figure 12–2.

Whenever the master is greater than the transaction, the record should be an addition to the file. It is, however, necessary to check to see if the transaction record has a valid add code. If it has no add code, it is in error and the BAD ADD routine is performed to handle the error.

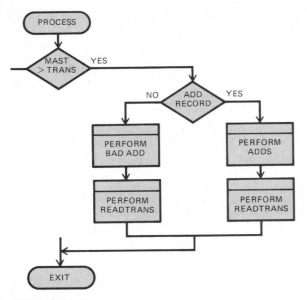

FIGURE 12–2

If it does have an add code, the ADDS routine is performed to add the record to the file. In either case, after processing the add or the error transaction record, the next transaction record needs to be read before returning to where the END-FLAG is checked in the mainline logic of the program. The logic for the BAD ADD and ADDS routine is shown in Figures 12–3 and 12–4, respectively.

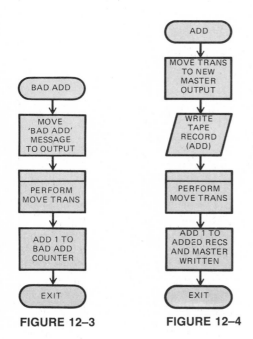

FIGURE 12–3   **FIGURE 12–4**

All that is being done for invalid add records in our example is to indicate what occurred, print the contents of the bad transaction (with an error message) and increment the BAD ADD counter. The BAD ADD counter is needed so that after all the records have been processed from both files it will be possible to tell how many invalid addition records were present in the transaction file.

The ADDS routine first moves all the data from the transaction record to the output area for the new master file and then writes the new master record. Besides adding the record to the new master, the contents of the new record were printed together with a message indicating that this addition has been made to the file. This serves as a visual indication of the processing taking place. A records added (ADDED RECS) counter was incremented so that at the end of the processing it will be possible to tell how many new records have been added to the master file. A MASTERS WRITTEN counter is also incremented.

MASTER LESS THAN TRANSACTION

Another path possible after the master and transaction records have been compared is that of the master being less than the transaction. In this situation the master record from the old master file is to be copied in its present form onto the new master file. This is shown in Figure 12–5 along with the COPY routine that actually moves the record from the old to the new file.

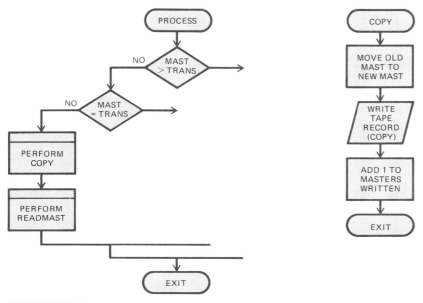

FIGURE 12–5

Notice once again that besides moving the data from the old master to the new master and writing the new master, the MASTERS WRITTEN counter was also incremented. This counter serves the same control purposes as in the previous example of additions.

MASTER EQUAL TO TRANSACTION (GENERAL)

The one remaining path left on the master/transaction comparison is that of the master and transactions records being equal. If the equal path is followed, then, to be valid, the transaction record must be either a change or a deletion. The logic for this is shown in Figure 12–6.

Once it has been determined that the comparing areas of the master and transaction records are equal, it is necessary to know if the transaction item represents a change or a delete. If it is a change, then the CHANGE routine needs to be performed to modify the existing master record's contents and the READMAST and READTRANS routines need to be performed to get the next master and transaction records. After reading the next record from both files it is time to exit the PROCESS routine.

If the transaction is not a change, it is necessary to check to see if it is a delete. If it is not a delete, it is in error, and the BAD EQUAL error routine needs to be performed to indicate the error and the READTRANS routine needs to be performed to get the next transaction record. If, on the other hand, it is a delete, then the DELETE routine needs to be performed to drop the record from the master file and the READMAST and READTRANS routines need to be performed before it is time to continue processing.

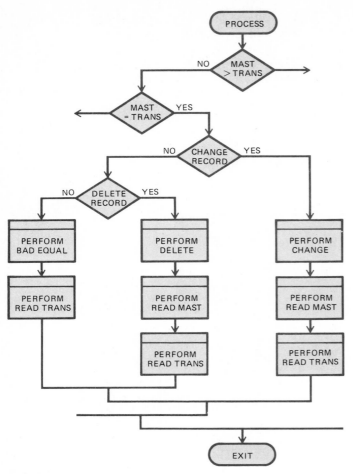

FIGURE 12–6

MASTER EQUAL TO TRANSACTION (BAD EQUAL)

The BAD EQUAL routine shown in Figure 12–7 prints the transaction record that is in error along with a message indicating a bad equal condition. Also, a counter is incremented so that at the end of the program there will be an indication of how many of this type of error occurred.

MASTER EQUAL TO TRANSACTION (DELETE)

The DELETE routine shown in Figure 12–8 prints the deleted master record with a message indicating that it has been deleted. Once again a counter is incremented so that at the end of the program there will be an indication of how many master records have been deleted.

MASTER EQUAL TO TRANSACTION (CHANGE)

The contents of a change record requires a little explanation before we discuss the logic. Change records contain all the same fields as the master record. If any fields in the change record are blank, then no change is being made to those particular fields. If any of the fields in the change record are not blank (except the control field), then the contents of the nonblank fields in the change record will replace the contents of the same fields in the master record. If the contents of the control field need changing they can be altered by deleting the record which is in error and adding a valid record.

Let's assume that the fields in our master and transaction record are NAME, date of birth

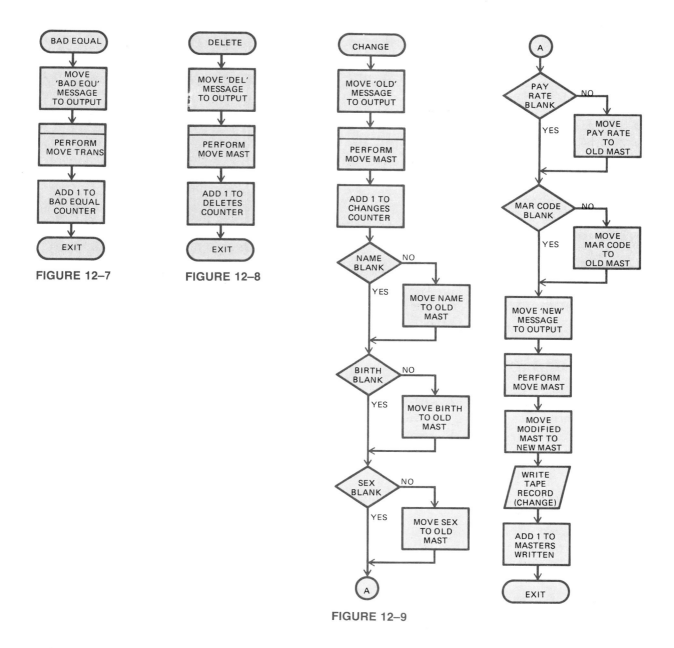

FIGURE 12–7

FIGURE 12–8

FIGURE 12–9

(BIRTH), SEX, PAY RATE, and marital status code (MCODE). In addition the transaction record contains the EMPLOYEE NUMBER and CHANGE CODE, and the master record contains the EMPLOYEE NUMBER. The logic for a change record is as shown in Figure 12–9.

The first step in the CHANGE routine is to print a record showing the original contents of the master record before any changes are made. Also, a counter is incremented so that it will be possible to indicate how many change records have been processed at the end of the program.

Next come a series of decisions which check each field on the change record to see if it is blank. If it is, nothing is done except to go on to the next decision. If it is not, then its contents are moved to the corresponding field in the old master record. Notice that the old master fields are the ones that are modified. Notice, too, that all the fields in the transaction record are individually checked, regardless of whether any of the fields are blank or have changes in them.

Once all the fields have been checked and changes have been made, the modified contents of the entire old master record are once again printed out to reflect its current status. After printing the modified contents the modified master record is moved to the new master and the new master is written. The MASTER WRITTEN counter is also incremented prior to exiting the CHANGE routine.

READMAST

Now for the READMAST routine. Its logic is shown in Figure 12–10. Notice that this routine is almost the same as the READMAST routine presented in Chapter 11. The only change is the addition of a comparison at the end of the routine to determine whether the MASTER READ counter should be updated. When attempting to read the master file, if no end-of-file is found, it is time to exit the READ MAST routine after incrementing the MASTERS READ counter. If an end-of-file is found, the TEST TRAN routine is performed. If in TEST TRAN it is found that the transaction file is not yet finished, 9's are moved to the master employee number area, the END MAST switch is turned on, and the logic proceeds to exit TEST TRAN and READMAST routines.

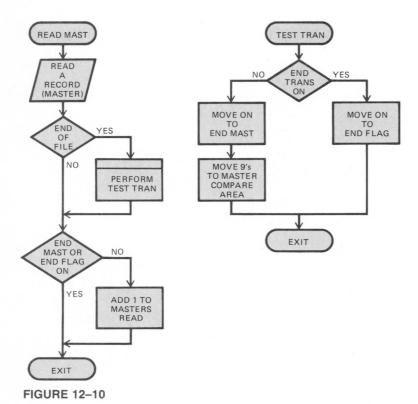

FIGURE 12–10

If an end-of-file is found and the transaction file is also ended, END-FLAG is turned on and it is time to exit the TEST TRAN and READMAST routines. Subsequently, it is also time to exit the PROCESS routine, perform the EOJ routine, and terminate processing.

If the transaction file is not already finished (END TRANS off) but the master file is finished (END MAST on), any further transactions that are adds will be added to the new master (via ADDS) and any further transactions that are not adds will be handled as errors (via BAD ADDS). When the end of the transaction file is finally reached, the END FLAG switch will be turned on in READTRANS and processing will be terminated.

READTRANS

The logic for reading the transaction file is shown in Figure 12–11. The logic in READTRANS has the same change at the end as compared to what was presented in Chapter 11 (adding to TRANS READ).

When the READTRANS routine is entered, an attempt will be made to read another transaction record. If another transaction is successfully read (that is, no end-of-file is found), it is

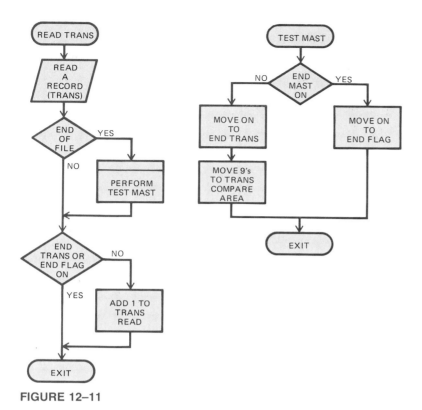

FIGURE 12–11

time to exit the READTRANS routine. If an end-of-file is found, the TEST MAST routine will be performed, where there are two possible paths. First, if the master file is also finished (END MAST is on), END-FLAG will be turned on and it will be time to exit TEST MAST and READTRANS routines. Second, if the master file is not yet finished (END MAST is off), 9's will be moved to the transaction employee number area, END TRANS will be turned on, and an exit of the TEST MAST and READTRANS routines will be accomplished.

Let's put all these parts together and see how it works. Figure 12–12 shows the entire update flowchart, including all the routines that are performed.

TEST DATA

A sample set of data is needed to see how this will actually work. The formats for the master and transaction records are shown in Figure 12–13. For simplicity the records have been kept small; in reality, many more fields would probably be present.

The sample data to be used is shown in Figure 12–14. For simplicity the high order (leftmost) zeros of the employee numbers have been deleted.

In performing the HSK routine the first record from both the master (employee number 1) and transaction (employee number 1) files is read into storage. Since the END FLAG switch is off, the PROCESS routine will then be performed.

When the master and transaction items are compared, they are found equal (1 = 1). The next step is to check whether the transaction item is a change record (C in position 80). Since it is not, the NO path is taken and a check is made to see if it is a delete record (D in column 80). It is, so the YES path in the logic is followed, where the DELETE routine is performed. Within the delete routine a copy of the record being deleted is printed together with a message indicating that it has been deleted. The DELETES counter is also incremented. After performing DELETE, the next step is to perform the READMAST routine.

If reading the master file no end-of-file condition is found, after reading the next master record (employee number 2), it is time to increment the MASTERS READ counter and exit the

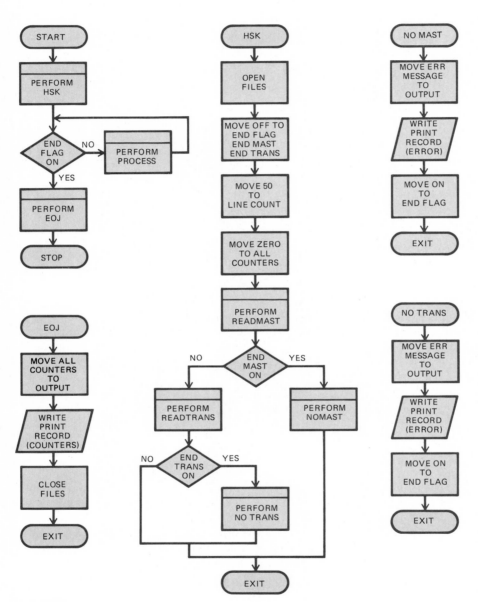

FIGURE 12–12

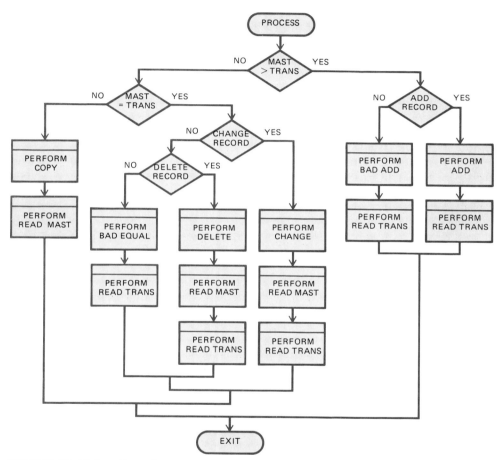

FIGURE 12–12 (continued)

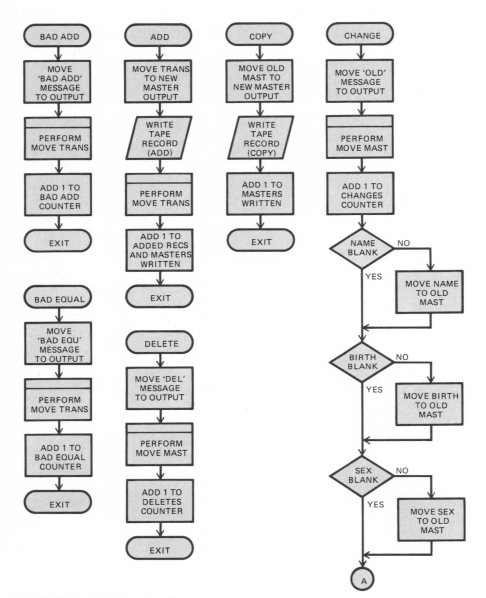

FIGURE 12–12 (continued)

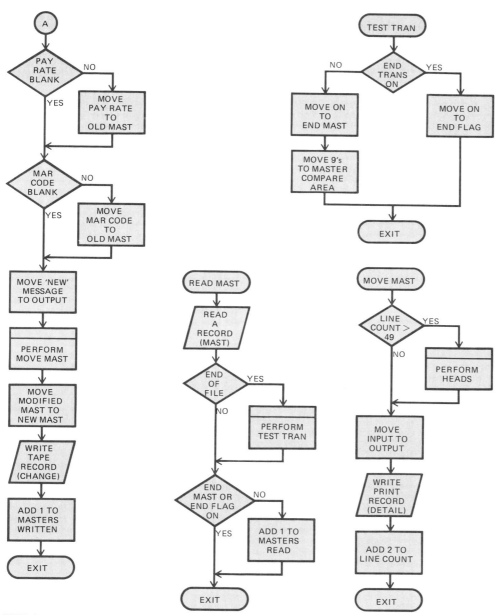

FIGURE 12–12 (continued)

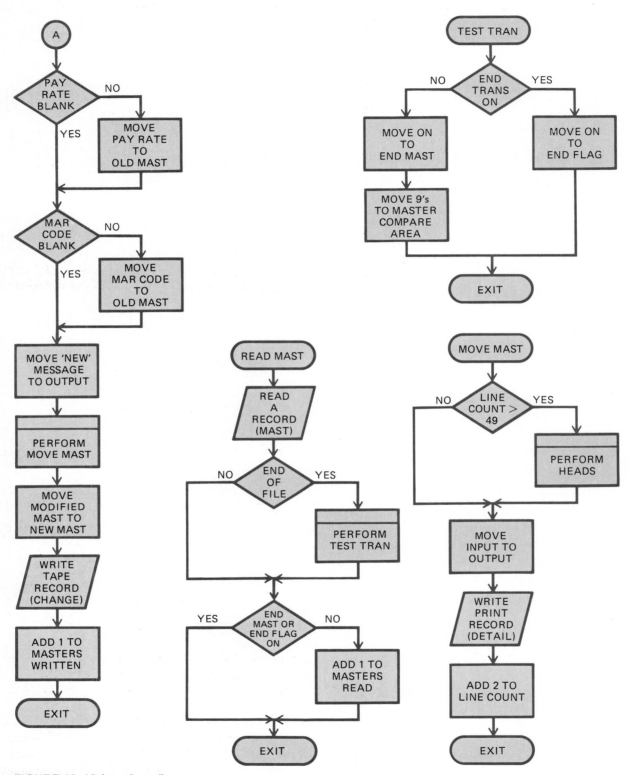

FIGURE 12–12 (continued)

MASTER RECORD FORMAT

DESCRIPTION	POSITION IN RECORD	
EMPLOYER NUMBER	1–9	
EMPLOYEE NAME	10–30	
BIRTH DATE	31–36	
SEX CODE	37–37	
PAY RATE	38–44	(7.2)
MARITAL STATUS CODE	45–45	
UNUSED	46–80	

TRANSACTION RECORD FORMAT

DESCRIPTION	POSITION IN RECORD	
EMPLOYEE NUMBER	1– 9	
EMPLOYEE NAME	10–30	
BIRTH DATE	31–36	
SEX CODE	37–37	
PAY RATE	38–44	(7.2)
MARITAL STATUS CODE	45–45	
UNUSED	46–79	
TRANSACTION CODE	80–80	

FIGURE 12–13

OLD MASTER DATA

EMP. NO.	EMP. NAME	BIRTH DATE	SEX	PAY RATE	MAR	UNUSED
1	TIMOTHY ABBOT	101240	M	2000000	S	
2	ROGER BENDER	033044	M	0180000	M	
4	DONALD CANTERBURY	092435	M	0090000	D	
6	BEN DONALDSON	122560	M	9500000	M	

TRANSACTION DATA

EMP. NO.	EMP. NAME	BIRTH DATE	SEX	PAY RATE	MAR	UNUSED	CODE
1							D
2	ROBER FENDER						C
3	SALLY BUTTONS	072540	F	0079000	S		A
4	DENISE DARNELL	091430	F	0098000	M		A
5	ROWLAND ROBERTS						C

FIGURE 12–14

READ MAST routine. Following this it is time to perform the READTRANS routine. In reading the transaction file, no end-of-file condition is found, so the next transaction record (employee number 2) is read, the TRANS READ counter is incremented, and the logic proceeds to exit the READTRANS routine. At this point it is also time to exit the PROCESS routine.

This brings us back to the point in the mainline logic of the program where a check is made to see if the END FLAG switch is on. It is not, so the PROCESS routine is once again performed. In comparing the master and transaction items, they are found to be equal (2 = 2). Taking the equal path, a check is made to see if the transaction is a change record. It is, (it has a C in position 80), so the CHANGE routine needs to be performed.

The CHANGE routine first prints a copy of the original master record and increments a counter for the number of change records processed. Then each field in the change record is individually checked to see if it is blank. The only nonblank field is the NAME field (ROGER FENDER), which is moved to the old master NAME field and replaces what was there (ROGER

BENDER). The modified version of the master record is then written on the printer. The last things done by CHANGE are to move the modified contents of the master record to the new master, write the new master, and increment the MASTERS WRITTEN counter.

After leaving the CHANGE routine, the READMAST routine is performed, which reads the next master record (employee number 4) into storage. Since no end-of-file condition was encountered in reading the master file, the MASTERS READ counter is incremented and it is time to exit the READMAST routine.

Next the READTRANS routine is performed, which reads the record for employee number 3 into storage. With no end-of-file condition occurring on the transaction file, the TRANS READ counter is incremented and an exit of the READTRANS routine is accomplished. It is also time to exit the PROCESS routine and return to check the END FLAG switch, which is still off. Since End FLAG is off the PROCESS routine will be performed.

While performing PROCESS this time the master and transaction items are compared and it is found that the master record is greater than the transaction record (4 > 3). The transaction is checked to see if it is an add record. It is, so the ADD routine is performed. The ADD routine moves the data (each of the individual fields) to the new master area and writes the new master record. The new master now has two records. The ADD routine also prints a message indicating that this record has been added and increments counters for the total records added (ADDED RECS) and master records written (MASTERS WRITTEN).

The next step is to perform the READTRANS routine. The next transaction record (employee number 4) is read into storage and, finding no end-of-file, the TRANS READ counter is incremented and it is time to exit the READTRANS routine. This in turn causes an exit from the PROCESS routine and a return to check the END FLAG switch. Since END FLAG is still not turned on, the PROCESS routine is performed.

When comparing master and transaction items, they are found to be equal (4 = 4). The next step is to check to see if a change record is present. It is not, so a check is made to see if it is a delete record. Since it is neither a change nor a delete, it is an error. At this point the BAD EQUAL routine is performed, which prints the error transaction record and an error message. It also increments a counter for the total number of this type of error (BAD EQUAL). Next it is time to perform the READTRANS routine. READTRANS brings the next transaction record (employee number 5) into storage. At this point the TRANS READ counter is incremented, an exit is taken from the PROCESS routine, and it is again time to check the END-FLAG switch.

Still finding END-FLAG off, when the master and transaction items are compared it is found that the master record is less than the transaction record (4 < 5). This in turn causes the old master to be moved and written on the new master. The MASTERS WRITTEN counter will be incremented and the next master (employee number 6) will be read into storage.

The next pass through the PROCESS routine finds the master high (6 > 5). Checking for an add record, it is found to be in error, since there is not an A in position 80. Because the transaction record is in error the BAD ADD routine is performed. BAD ADD prints a message indicating the error along with the contents of the transaction record and increments a counter for this type of error (bad add). After finishing BAD ADD it is time to perform the READTRANS routine.

This time when performing READTRANS an end-of-file condition is found. This causes the END TRANS switch to be turned on and 9's to be moved to the transaction area (in TEST MAST). Next it is time to exit the READTRANS and PROCESS routines and return to check END FLAG. Since both files have not yet ended END FLAG is still off. Therefore, the logic will again proceed to the PROCESS routine.

This pass through the PROCESS routine finds the master less than the transaction (6 < 9's). Remember that 9's were moved to the transaction area when an end-of-file was found on the transaction file. Since the master is low, the COPY routine is performed to move the old record to the new master and increment the MASTERS WRITTEN counter. Following COPY, the READMAST routine is performed. This time an end-of-file occurs on the master file. Since END TRANS is also on at this point, END-FLAG is turned on (in TEST TRAN) and it is time to exit the READMAST routine.

Finding END FLAG now turned on, it is time to perform the EOJ routine and terminate processing. EOJ moves and prints each of the individual totals (transactions read, masters read, masters written, adds, changes, deletes, bad adds, and bad equals) along with a message identifying each total. The files are also closed in the EOJ routine.

The new master file contents are shown in Figure 12–15, and the update report is shown in Figure 12–16.

NEW MASTER

EMP. NO.	EMP. NAME	BIRTH DATE	SEX	PAYRATE	MAR	UNUSED
	ROGER FENDER	033044	M	0180000	M	
	SALLY BUTTONS	072540	F	0079000	S	
	DONALD CANTERBURY	092435	M	0090000	D	
	BEN DONALDSON	122560	M	9500000	M	

FIGURE 12–15

EMPLOYEE FILE UPDATE REPORT

STATUS MESSAGE	EMP NO.	EMPLOYEE NAME	BIRTH DATE	SEX	PAY-RATE	MAR
DEL	1	TIMOTHY ABBOTT	10–12–40	M	02000.00	S
OLD	2	ROGER BENDER	03–30–44	M	01800.00	M
NEW	2	ROGER FENDER	03–30–44	M	01800.00	M
ADD	3	SALLY BUTTONS	07–25–40	F	00790.00	S
BAD EQU	4	DENISE DARNELL	09–14–30	F	00980.00	M
BAD ADD	5	ROWLAND ROBERTS				

CONTROL TOTALS

MASTERS READ	4
TRANSACTIONS READ	5
MASTERS WRITTEN	4
BAD ADDS	1
ADDED RECORDS	1
BAD EQUAL	1
DELETED RECORDS	1
CHANGED RECORDS	1
NEW MASTER	4

FIGURE 12–16

In looking at the report shown in Figure 12–16, notice the status message on the left side. This column is used to indicate the status of each record on the report. Notice also that the totals show how many times each type of activity occurred. These totals are for control purposes to indicate the processing that took place during the updating operation. One of these totals, however, was not created during the updating. The NEW MASTER total should match MASTERS WRITTEN and is generated at the time when the totals are printed out. It is computed as follows:

$$\text{NEW MASTER} = \text{MASTERS READ} + \text{ADDS} - \text{DELETES}$$
$$4 \quad = \quad 4 \quad + \quad 1 \quad - \quad 1$$

The process of updating a standard sequential file is one of the more complicated file-handling situations because of the logic needed in the PROCESS routine and in end-of-file situations. The COBOL and BASIC programs to do this update are shown in Figures 12–17 and 12–18.

MULTIPLE TRANSACTIONS PER SINGLE MASTER

When there are multiple transaction records per single master record then it is necessary to use a different set of steps to handle the files and process the data on the records. The "balance line algorithm" is logic that was dveleoped for this purpose. The flowchart for handling this type of situation is shown in Figure 12–19. The pseudocode is shown in Figure 12–20.

COBOL VERSION

PROCEDURE DIVISION.

MAINLINE-LOGIC.

```
        PERFORM HSK-ROUTINE.
        PERFORM PROCESS-ROUTINE UNTIL END-FLAG = 'ON'.
        PERFORM EOJ-ROUTINE.
        STOP RUN.
```

HSK-ROUTINE.

```
        OPEN INPUT C10MAST
                     C10TRAN
             OUTPUT  C10NEW
                       PRINT-FILE.
        MOVE 'OFF' TO END-FLAG.
        MOVE 'OFF' TO END-MAST.
        MOVE 'OFF' TO END-TRANS.
        MOVE 50      TO LINE-COUNT.
        MOVE ZERO TO PAGE-COUNT
                 MASTERS-READ-COUNT
                 TRANS-READ-COUNT
                 BAD-EQUAL-COUNT
                 BAD-ADD-COUNT
                 ADD-RECORD-COUNT
                 CHANGE-RECORD-COUNT
                 DELETE-RECORD-COUNT
                 NEW-MASTER-COUNT.
        PERFORM READ-MAST-ROUTINE.
        IF END-MAST = 'ON'
             PERFORM NO-MAST-ROUTINE
        ELSE
             PERFORM READ-TRANS-ROUTINE
                 IF END-TRANS = 'ON'
                 PERFORM NO-TRANS-ROUTINE.
```

PROCESS-ROUTINE.

```
        IF MAST-EMP-NO > MT TRANS-EMP-NO
             IF ADD-RECORD
                 PERFORM ADD-ROUTINE
                 PERFORM READ-TRANS-ROUTINE
             ELSE
                 PERFORM BAD-ADD-ROUTINE
                 PERFORM READ-TRANS-ROUTINE
        ELSE
             IF MAST-EMP-NO = TRANS-EMP-NO
                 IF CHANGE-RECORD
                     PERFORM CHANGE-ROUTINE
                     PERFORM READ-MAST-ROUTINE
                     PERFORM READ-TRANS-ROUTINE
                 ELSE
                     IF DELETE-RECORD
                         PERFORM DELETE-ROUTINE
                         PERFORM READ-MAST-ROUTINE
                         PERFORM READ-TRANS-ROUTINE
                     ELSE
                         PERFORM BAD-EQUAL-ROUTINE
                         PERFORM READ-TRANS-ROUTINE
             ELSE
                 PERFORM COPY-ROUTINE
                 PERFORM READ-MAST-ROUTINE.
```

FIGURE 12–17

```
EOJ-ROUTINE.

        WRITE PRINT-RECORD FROM FINAL-HEADING
            AFTER ADVANCING TOP-OF-PAGE.
        WRITE PRINT-RECORD FROM BLANK-LINE
            AFTER ADVANCING 1 LINES.
        MOVE 'MASTERS READ' TO SIDE-HEADING.
        MOVE MASTERS-READ-COUNT TO COUNT-OUT.
        WRITE PRINT-RECORD FROM FINAL-LINE
            AFTER ADVANCING 1 LINES.
        MOVE 'TRANSACTIONS READ' TO SIDE-HADING.
        MOVE TRANS-READ-COUNT TO COUNT OUT.
        WRITE PRINT-RECORD FROM FINAL-LINE
            AFTER ADVANCING 1 LINES.
        MOVE 'MASTERS WRITTEN' TO SIDE-HEADING
        MOVE NEW-MASTER-COUNT TO COUNT-OUT.
        WRITE PRINT-RECORD FROM FINAL-LINE
            AFTER ADVANCING 1 LINES.
        MOVE 'BAD ADDS' TO SIDE-HEADING.
        MOVE BAD-ADD-COUNT TO COUNT-OUT.
        WRITE PRINT-RECORD FROM FINAL-LINE
            AFTER ADVANCING 1 LINES.
        MOVE 'ADDED RECORDS' TO SIDE-HEADING.
        MOVE ADD-RECORD-COUNT TO COUNT-OUT.
        WRITE PRINT-RECORD FROM FINAL-LINE
            AFTER ADVANCING 1 LINES.
        MOVE 'BAD EQUAL' TO SIDE-HEADING.
        MOVE BAD-EQUAL-COUNT TO COUNT-OUT.
        WRITE PRINT-RECORD FROM FINAL-LINE
            AFTER ADVANCING 1 LINES.
        MOVE 'DELETED RECORDS' TO SIDE-HEADING.
        MOVE DELETE-RECORD-COUNT TO COUNT-OUT.
        WRITE PRINT-RECORD FROM FINAL-LINE
            AFTER ADVANCING 1 LINES.
        MOVE 'CHANGED RECORDS' TO SIDE-HEADING.
        MOVE CHANGE-RECORD-COUNT TO COUNT-OUT.
        WRITE PRINT-RECORD FROM FINAL-LINE
            AFTER ADVANCING 1 LINES.
        CLOSE C10MAST
            C10TRAN
            C10NEW
            PRINT-FILE.


ADD-ROUTINE.

        WRITE C10NEW-RECORD FROM C10TRAN-RECORD.
        MOVE 'ADD' TO MESSAGE.
        PERFORM MOVE-WRITE-TRANS-ROUTINE.
        ADD 1 TO ADD-RECORD-COUNT.
        ADD 1 TO NEW-MASTER COUNT.


COPY-ROUTINE.

        WRITE C10NEW-RECORD FROM C10MAST-RECORD.
        ADD 1 TO NEW-MASTER-COUNT.


CHANGE-ROUTINE.

        MOVE 'OLD' TO MESSAGE.
        PERFORM MOVE-WRITE-MAST-ROUTINE.
        ADD 1 TO CHANGE-RECORD-COUNT.
        IF TRAN-EMP-NAME = SPACES
            NEXT SENTENCE
        ELSE
            MOVE TRAN-EMP-NAME TO MAST-EMP-NAME.
```

FIGURE 12–17 (continued)

```
        IF TRAN-BIRTH-DATE = SPACES
            NEXT SENTENCE
        ELSE
            MOVE TRAN-BIRTH-DATE TO MAST-BIRTH-DATE.
        IF TRAN-SEX-CODE = SPACES
            NEXT SENTENCE
        ELSE
            MOVE TRAN-SEX-CODE TO MAST-SEX-CODE.
        IF TRAN-PAY-RATE = SPACES
            NEXT SENTENCE
        ELSE
            MOVE TRAN-PAY-RATE TO MAST-PAY-RATE.
        IF TRAN-MAR-STATUS = SPACES
            NEXT SENTENCE
        ELSE
            MOVE TRAN-MAR-STATUS TO MAST-MAR-STATUS.
        MOVE 'NEW' TO MESSAGE.
        PERFORM MOVE-WRITE-MAST-ROUTINE.
        WRITE C10NEW-RECORD FROM C10MAST.
        ADD 1 TO NEW-MASTER-COUNT.

    DELETE-ROUTINE.

        MOVE 'DEL' TO MESSAGE.
        PERFORM MOVE-WRITE-MAST-ROUTINE.
        ADD 1 TO DELETE-RECORD-COUNT.
        BAD-ADD-ROUTINE.
        MOVE 'BAD ADD' TO MESSAGE.
        PERFORM MOVE-WRITE-TRANS-ROUTINE.
        ADD 1 TO BAD-ADD-COUNT.

    BAD-EQUAL-ROUTINE.

        MOVE 'BAD EQU' TO MESSAGE.
        PERFORM MOVE-WRITE-TRANS-ROUTINE.
        ADD 1 TO BAD-EQUAL-COUNT.

    MOVE-WRITE-MAST-ROUTINE.

        IF LINE-COUNT > 49
            PERFORM HEADS-ROUTINE.
        MOVE MAST-EMP-NO TO EMP-NO-OUT.
        MOVE MAST-EMP-NAME TO EMP-NAME-OUT.
        MOVE MAST-BIRTH-DATE TO BIRTH-DATE-OUT.
        MOVE MAST-SEX-CODE TO SEX-CODE-OUT.
        MOVE MAST-PAY-RATE TO PAY-RATE-OUT.
        MOVE MAST-MAR-STATUS TO MAR-STATUS-OUT.
        WRITE PRINT-RECORD FROM DETAIL LINE
            AFTER ADVANCING 2 LINES.
        ADD 2 TO LINE-COUNT.

    MOVE-WRITE-TRANS-ROUTINE.

        IF LINE-COUNT > 49
            PERFORM HEADS-ROUTINE.
        MOVE TRAN-EMP-NO TO EMP-NO-OUT.
        MOVE TRAN-EMP-NAME TO EMP-NAME-OUT.
        MOVE TRAN-BIRTH-DATE TO BIRTH-DATE-OUT.
        MOVE TRAN-PAY-RATE TO PAY-RATE-OUT.
        MOVE TRAN-MAR-STATUS TO MAR-STATUS-OUT.
        WRITE PRINT-RECORD FROM DETAIL-LINE
            AFTER ADVANCING 2 LINES.
        ADD 2 TO LINE-COUNT.
```

FIGURE 12–17 (continued)

NO-MAST-ROUTINE.

    MOVE 'MASTER FILE NOT PRESENT' TO ERR-MESSAGE.
    WRITE PRINT-RECORD FROM ERROR-LINE
        AFTER ADVANCING 2 LINES.
    MOVE 'ON' TO END-FLAG.

NO-TRANS-ROUTINE

    MOVE 'TRANSACTION FILE NOT PRESENT' TO ERR-MESSAGE.
    WRITE PRINT-RECORD FROM ERROR-LINE
        AFTER ADVANCING 2 LINES.
    MOVE 'ON' TO END FLAG.

READ-MAST-ROUTINE.

    READ C10MAST
        AT END
            PERFORM TEST-TRANS-ROUTINE.
    IF END-MAST = 'ON' OR END-FLAG = 'ON'
        NEXT SENTENCE
    ELSE
        ADD 1 TO MASTERS-READ-COUNT.

TEST-TRANS-ROUTINE.

    IF END-TRANS = 'ON'
        MOVE 'ON' TO END-FLAG
    ELSE
        MOVE 'ON' TO END-MAST
        MOVE '999999999' TO MAST-EMP-NO.

READ-TRANS-ROUTINE.

    READ C10TRANS
        AT END
            PERFORM TEST-MAST-ROUTINE.
    IF END-TRANS = 'ON' OR END-FLAG = 'ON'
        NEXT SENTENCE
    ELSE
        ADD 1 TO TRANS-READ-COUNT.

TEST-MAST-ROUTINE.

    IF END-MAST = 'ON'
        MOVE 'ON' TO END-FLAG
    ELSE
        MOVE 'ON' TO END-TRANS
        MOVE '999999999' TO TRANS-EMP-NO.

HEADS-ROUTINE.

    WRITE PRINT-RECORD FROM HEADS1
        AFTER ADVANCING TOP-OF-PAGE.
    WRITE PRINT-RECORD FROM HEADS2
        AFTER ADVANCING 2 LINES.
    WRITE PRINT-RECORD FROM HEADS3
        AFTER ADVANCING 1 LINES.
    MOVE ZERO TO LINE-COUNT.

FIGURE 12–17 (continued)

```
'PROGRAMMERS: J AND J, INC.
'DATE: 10/11/89
'PROGRAM NAME: CASE 12
'*******************************************************************************
'*                         MAINLINE LOGIC                                      *
'*******************************************************************************
GOSUB HOUSEKEEPING.ROUTINE
WHILE END.FLAG$ = "OFF"
    GOSUB PROCESS.ROUTINE
WEND
GOSUB EOJ.ROUTINE
END
'*******************************************************************************
'*                      HOUSEKEEPING ROUTINE                                   *
'*******************************************************************************
HOUSEKEEPING.ROUTINE:
OPEN "A:C12MAST" FOR INPUT AS #1
OPEN "A:C12TRAN" FOR INPUT AS #2
OPEN "A:C12NEW"  FOR OUTPUT AS #3
INPUT "DO YOU WANT THE OUTPUT TO BE PRINTED - ENTER Y OR N",ANSWER$
IF ANSWER$ = "Y" OR ANSWER$ = "y" THEN
    DEVICE$ = "LPT1:"
ELSE
    DEVICE$ = "SCRN:"
END IF
OPEN DEVICE$ FOR OUTPUT AS #4
LET END.FLAG$ = "OFF"
LET END.MAST$ = "OFF"
LET END.TRANS$ = "OFF"
LET LINE.COUNT = 50
LET PAGE.COUNT = 0
LET FMT1$ = "\      \" + SPACE$(3) + "&" + SPACE$(5) + "\               \"
+   SPACE$(1) + "&-&-&" + SPACE$(2) + "&" + SPACE$(2) + "&.&" + SPACE$(4)
+ "&"
GOSUB READ.MASTER.ROUTINE
IF END.MAST$ = "ON" THEN
    GOSUB NO.MASTER.ROUTINE
ELSE
    GOSUB READ.TRANSACTION.ROUTINE
        IF END.TRANSK$ = "ON" THEN
            GOSUB NO.TRANSACTION.ROUTINE
        ELSE
        END IF
END IF
LET FMT2$ = "\      \" + SPACE$(3) + "&" + SPACE$(5) + "\               \"
RETURN
'*******************************************************************************
'*                        PROCESS ROUTINE                                      *
'*******************************************************************************
PROCESS.ROUTINE:
IF MASTER.EMPLOYEE.NUMBER$ < TRANS.EMPLOYEE.NUMBER$ THEN
    GOSUB COPY.MASTER.ROUTINE
    GOSUB READ.MASTER.ROUTINE
```

FIGURE 12-18

```
        ELSE
            IF MASTER.EMPLOYEE.NUMBER$ > TRANS.EMPLOYEE.NUMBER$ THEN
                IF TRANSACTION.CODE$ = "A" THEN
                    GOSUB ADD.TRANS.ROUTINE
                    GOSUB READ.TRANSACTION.ROUTINE
                ELSE
                    GOSUB BAD.ADD.ROUTINE
                    GOSUB READ.TRANSACTION.ROUTINE
                END IF
            ELSE
                IF TRANSACTION.CODE$ = "C" THEN
                    GOSUB CHANGE.ROUTINE
                    GOSUB READ.MASTER.ROUTINE
                    GOSUB READ.TRANSACTION.ROUTINE
                ELSE
                    IF TRANSACTION.CODE$ = "D" THEN
                        GOSUB DELETE.ROUTINE
                        GOSUB READ.MASTER.ROUTINE
                        GOSUB READ.TRANSACTION.ROUTINE
                    ELSE
                        GOSUB BAD.EQUAL.ROUTINE
                        GOSUB READ.TRANSACTION.ROUTINE
                    END IF
                END IF
            END IF
        END IF
END IF
RETURN

'***********************************************************************
'*                          EOJ ROUTINE                                *
'***********************************************************************
EOJ.ROUTINE:
PRINT #4,CHR$(12)
PRINT #4,"          CONTROL TOTALS"
PRINT #4,
LET MESSAGE$ = "MASTERS READ"
LET FMT3$ = "\                              \" + SPACE$(4) + "###"
PRINT #4,USING FMT3$;MESSAGE$,MASTERS.READ
LET MESSAGE$ = "TRANSACTIONS READ"
PRINT #4,USING FMT3$;MESSAGE$,TRANSACTIONS.READ
LET MESSAGE$ = "MASTERS WRITTEN"
PRINT #4,USING FMT3$;MESSAGE$,MASTERS.WRITTEN
LET MESSAGE$ = "BAD ADDS"
PRINT #4,USING FMT3$;MESSAGE$,BAD.ADD.COUNT
LET MESSAGE$ = "ADDED RECORDS"
PRINT #4,USING FMT3$;MESSAGE$,ADDED.COUNT
LET MESSAGE$ = "BAD EQUAL"
PRINT #4,USING FMT3$;MESSAGE$,BAD.EQUAL.COUNT
LET MESSAGE$ = "DELETED RECORDS"
PRINT #4,USING FMT3$;MESSAGE$,DELETED.COUNT
LET MESSAGE$ = "CHANGED RECORDS"
PRINT #4,USING FMT3$;MESSAGE$,CHANGED.RECORD.COUNT
LET NEW.TOTAL = MASTERS.READ + ADDED.COUNT - DELETED.COUNT
LET MESSAGE$ = "NEW MASTER"
PRINT #4,USING FMT3$;MESSAGE$,NEW.TOTAL
```

FIGURE 12–18 (continued)

```
CLOSE #1,#2,#3
RETURN
'***********************************************************************
'*                    NO MASTER ROUTINE                                *
'***********************************************************************
NO.MASTER.ROUTINE:
PRINT #4,"          MASTER FILE NOT PRESENT"
LET END.FLAG$ = "ON"
RETURN
'***********************************************************************
'*                    NO TRANSACTION ROUTINE                           *
'***********************************************************************
NO.TRANSACTION.ROUTINE:
PRINT #4,"          TRANSACTION FILE NOT PRESENT"
LET END.FLAG$ = "ON"
RETURN
'***********************************************************************
'*                    READ MASTER ROUTINE                              *
'***********************************************************************
READ.MASTER.ROUTINE:
IF NOT EOF(1) THEN
    LET MASTERS.READ = MASTERS.READ + 1
    INPUT #1  ,    MASTER.EMPLOYEE.NUMBER$   ,    MASTER.EMPLOYEE.NAME$
    MASTER.BIRTH.DATE$   ,    MASTER.SEX.CODE$   ,    MASTER.PAY.RATE$ ,
    MASTER.MARITAL$
ELSE
    GOSUB TEST.TRANSACTION.ROUTINE
END IF
RETURN
'***********************************************************************
'*                    TEST TRANSACTION ROUTINE                         *
'***********************************************************************
TEST.TRANSACTION.ROUTINE:
IF END.TRANS$ = "ON" THEN
    END.FLAG$ = "ON"
ELSE
    LET END.MAST$ = "ON"
    LET MASTER.EMPLOYEE.NUMBER$ = "9"
END IF
RETURN
'***********************************************************************
'*                    READ TRANSACTION ROUTINE                         *
'***********************************************************************
READ.TRANSACTION.ROUTINE:
IF NOT EOF(2) THEN
    LET TRANSACTIONS.READ = TRANSACTIONS.READ + 1
    INPUT#2,TRANS.EMPLOYEE.NUMBER$,TRANS.EMPLOYEE.NAME$,TRANS.BIRTH.DATE$,
    TRANS.SEX.CODE$,TRANS.PAY.RATE$,TRANS.MARITAL.STATUS$,TRANSACTION.CODE$
ELSE
    GOSUB TEST.MASTER.ROUTINE
END IF
RETURN
```

FIGURE 12–18 (continued)

```
'***************************************************************
'*                     BAD ADD ROUTINE                         *
'***************************************************************
BAD.ADD.ROUTINE:
LET MESSAGE$ = "BAD ADD"
PRINT #4,USING FMT2$;MESSAGE$,TRANS.EMPLOYEE.NUMBER$,TRANS.EMPLOYEE.NAME$
LET BAD.ADD.COUNT = BAD.ADD.COUNT + 1
RETURN


'***************************************************************
'*                      DELETE ROUTINE                         *
'***************************************************************
DELETE.ROUTINE:
LET MESSAGE$ = "DEL"
GOSUB PRINT.MASTER.FIELDS
LET DELETED.COUNT = DELETED.COUNT + 1
RETURN


'***************************************************************
'*                    BAD EQUAL ROUTINE                        *
'***************************************************************
BAD.EQUAL.ROUTINE:
LET MESSAGE$ = "BAD EQU"
GOSUB PRINT.TRANSACTION.FIELDS
LET BAD.EQUAL.COUNT = BAD.EQUAL.COUNT + 1
RETURN


'***************************************************************
'*                       COPY ROUTINE                          *
'***************************************************************
COPY.MASTER.ROUTINE:
WRITE#3,MASTER.EMPLOYEE.NUMBER$,MASTER.EMPLOYEE.NAME$,MASTER.BIRTH.DATE$,
    MASTER.SEX.CODE$,MASTER.PAY.RATE$,MASTER.MARITAL$
LET MASTERS.WRITTEN = MASTERS.WRITTEN + 1
RETURN


'***************************************************************
'*                      CHANGE ROUTINE                         *
'***************************************************************
CHANGE.ROUTINE:
LET MESSAGE$ = "OLD"
GOSUB PRINT.MASTER.FIELDS
LET CHANGED.RECORD.COUNT = CHANGED.RECORD.COUNT + 1
IF TRANS.EMPLOYEE.NAME$ = "" THEN
    GO TO CHECK.BIRTH
ELSE
    LET MASTER.EMPLOYEE.NAME$ = TRANS.EMPLOYEE.NAME$
END IF
CHECK.BIRTH:
IF TRANS.BIRTH.DATE$ = "" THEN
    GO TO CHECK.SEX
ELSE
    LET MASTER.BIRTH.CODE$ = TRANS.BIRTH.DATEE$
```

FIGURE 12–18 (continued)

```
END IF
CHECK.SEX:
IF TRANS.SEX.CODE$ = "" THEN
    GO TO CHECK.PAY.RATE
ELSE
    LET MASTER.SEX.CODE$ = TRANS.SEX.CODE$
END IF
CHECK.PAY.RATE:
IF PT$ = "" THEN
    GO TO CHECK.MARITAL
ELSE
    LET MASTER.PAY.RATE$ = TRANS.PAY.RATE$
END IF
CHECK.MARITAL:
IF MASTER.MARITAL$ = "" THEN
    GO TO WRITE.NEW
ELSE
    LET MASTER.MARITAL$ = TRANS.MARITAL.STATUS$
END IF
WRITE.NEW:
LET MESSAGE$ = "NEW"
GOSUB PRINT.MASTER.FIELDS
WRITE#3,MASTER.EMPLOYEE.NUMBER$,MASTER.EMPLOYEE.NAME$,MASTER.BIRTH.DATE$,
    MASTER.SEX.CODE$,MASTER.PAY.RATE$,MASTER.MARITAL$
LET MASTERS.WRITTEN = MASTERS.WRITTEN + 1
RETURN
'*******************************************************************************
'*                          HEADS ROUTINE                                     *
'*******************************************************************************
HEADS.ROUTINE:
PRINT #4,CHR$(12)
PRINT #4,SPC(16);"EMPLOYEE FILE UPDATE REPORT"
PRINT #4,
PRINT #4,"STATUS    EMP                        BIRTH"
PRINT #4,"MESSAGE   NO.     EMPLOYEE NAME       DATE   SEX PAY-RATE    MAR"
PRINT #4,
LET LINE.COUNT = 0
RETURN
'*******************************************************************************
'*                     PRINT MASTER FIELDS                                    *
'*******************************************************************************
PRINT.MASTER.FIELDS:
IF LINE.COUNT > 49 THEN
    GOSUB HEADS.ROUTINE
ELSE
END IF
PRINT #4,    USING FMT1$;    MESSAGE$    ,    MASTER.EMPLOYEE.NUMBER$    ,
    MASTER.EMPLOYEE.NAME$    ,    MID$(MASTER.BIRTH.DATE$,1,2)    ,
    MID$(MASTER.BIRTH.DATE$,3,2)    ,    MID$(MASTER.BIRTH.DATE$,5,2)    ,
```

FIGURE 12–18 (continued)

```
      MASTER.SEX.CODE$,MID$(MASTER.PAY.RATE$,1,5),MID$(MASTER.PAY.RATE$,6,2),
      MASTER.MARITAL$
PRINT #4,
LET LINE.COUNT = LINE.COUNT + 2
RETURN
'*************************************************************************
'*                        CHECK ADD ROUTINE                             *
'*************************************************************************
'IF RC$ = "A" THEN GOSUB 19000:GOSUB 8000:GOTO 18040
'RETURN
'*************************************************************************
'*                        ADD TRANS ROUTINE                             *
'*************************************************************************
ADD.TRANS.ROUTINE:
WRITE #3    ,    TRANS.EMPLOYEE.NUMBER$    ,    TRANS.EMPLOYEE.NAME$    ,
      TRANS.BIRTH.DATE$,TRANS.SEX.CODE$,TRANS.PAY.RATE$,TRANS.MARITAL.STATUS$
LET MESSAGE$ = "ADD"
GOSUB PRINT.TRANSACTION.FIELDS
LET ADDED.COUNT = ADDED.COUNT + 1
LET MASTERS.WRITTEN = MASTERS.WRITTEN + 1
RETURN
'WRITE #3,T,NT$,BT$,ST$,PT$,MT$
'*************************************************************************
'*                        TEST MASTER ROUTINE                           *
'*************************************************************************
TEST.MASTER.ROUTINE:
IF END.MAST$ = "ON" THEN
   LET END.FLAG$ = "ON"
ELSE
   LET END.TRANS$ = "ON"
   LET TRANS.EMPLOYEE.NUMBER$ = "9"
END IF
RETURN
'*************************************************************************
'*                      PRINT TRANSACTION FIELDS                        *
'*************************************************************************
PRINT.TRANSACTION.FIELDS:
IF LC > 49 THEN
   GOSUB HEADS.ROUTINE
ELSE
END IF
PRINT #4    ,    USING FMT1$;    MESSAGE$,TRANS.EMPLOYEE.NUMBER$    ,
      TRANS.EMPLOYEE.NAME$    ,    MID$(TRANS.BIRTH.DATE$,1,2)    ,
      MID$(TRANS.BIRTH.DATE$,3,2)    ,    MID$(TRANS.BIRTH.DATE$,5,2)    ,
      TRANS.SEX.CODE$    ,    MID$(TRANS.PAY.RATE$,1,5)    ,
      MID$(TRANS.PAY.RATE$,6,2)    ,    TRANS.MARITAL.STATUS$
PRINT #4,
RETURN
```

FIGURE 12–18 (continued)

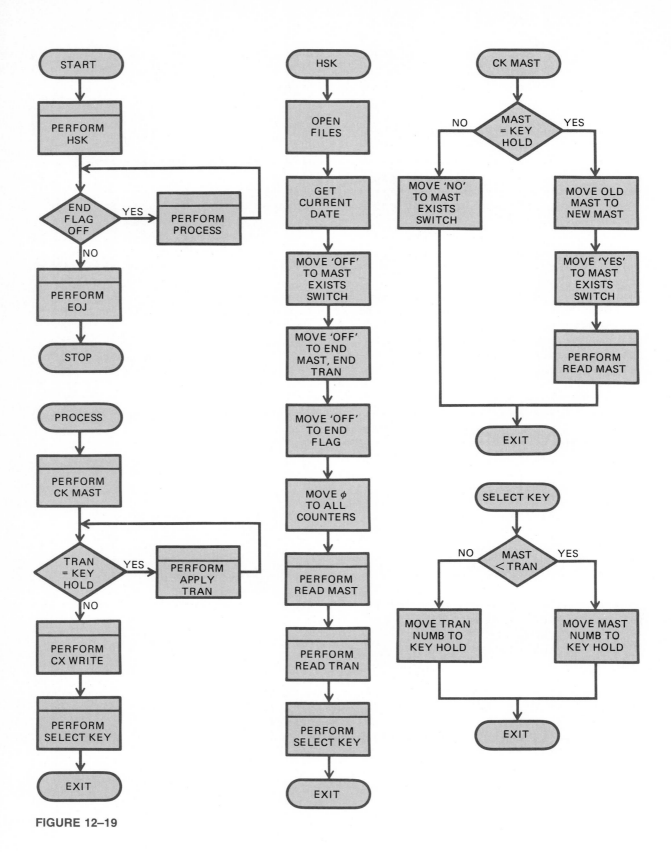

FIGURE 12–19

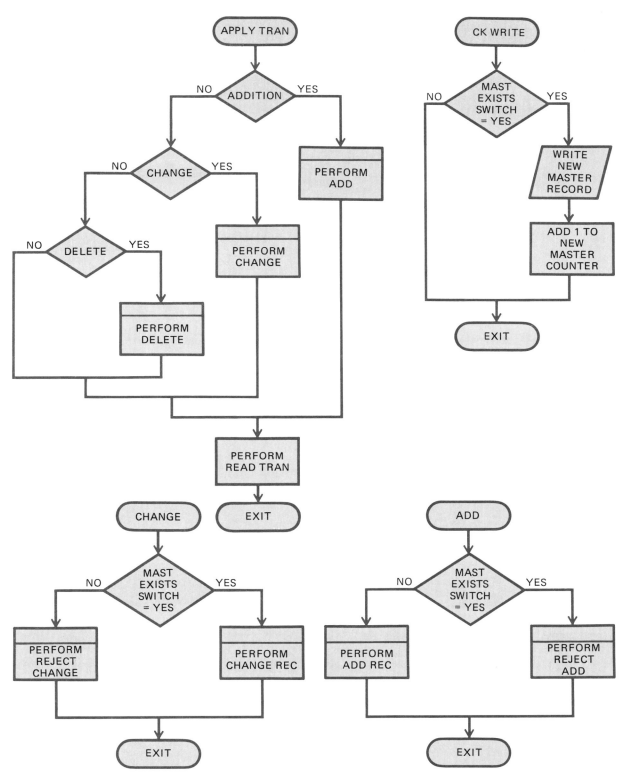

FIGURE 12–19 (continued)

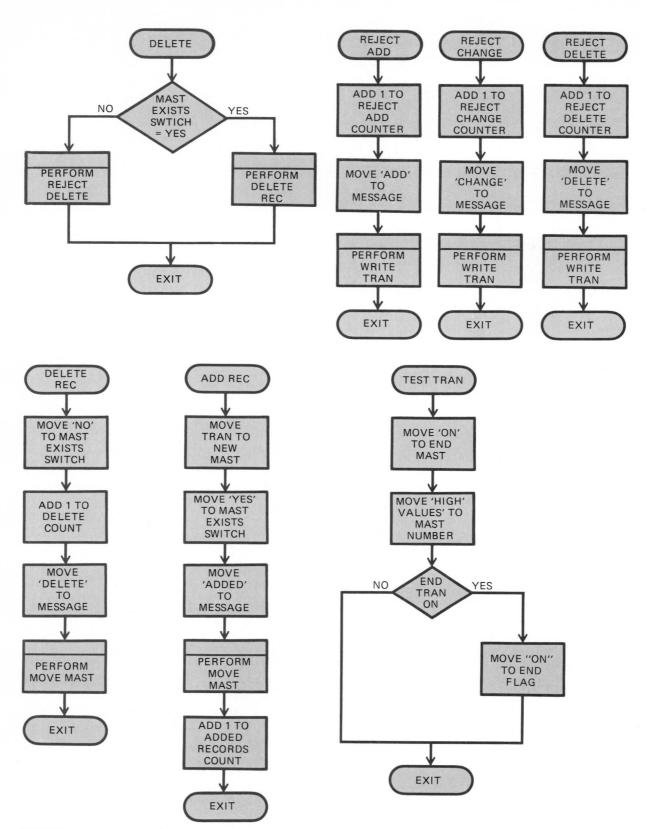

FIGURE 12–19 (continued)

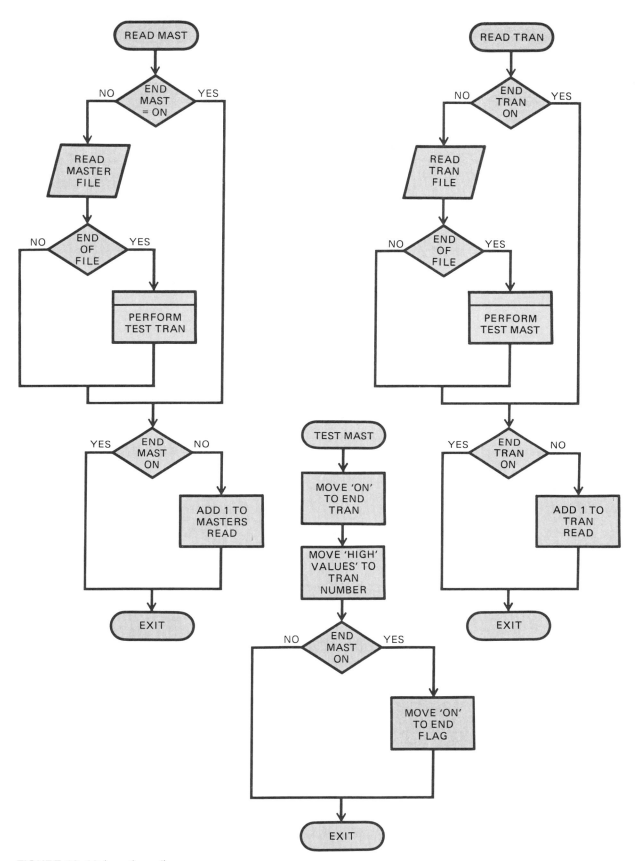

FIGURE 12–19 (continued)

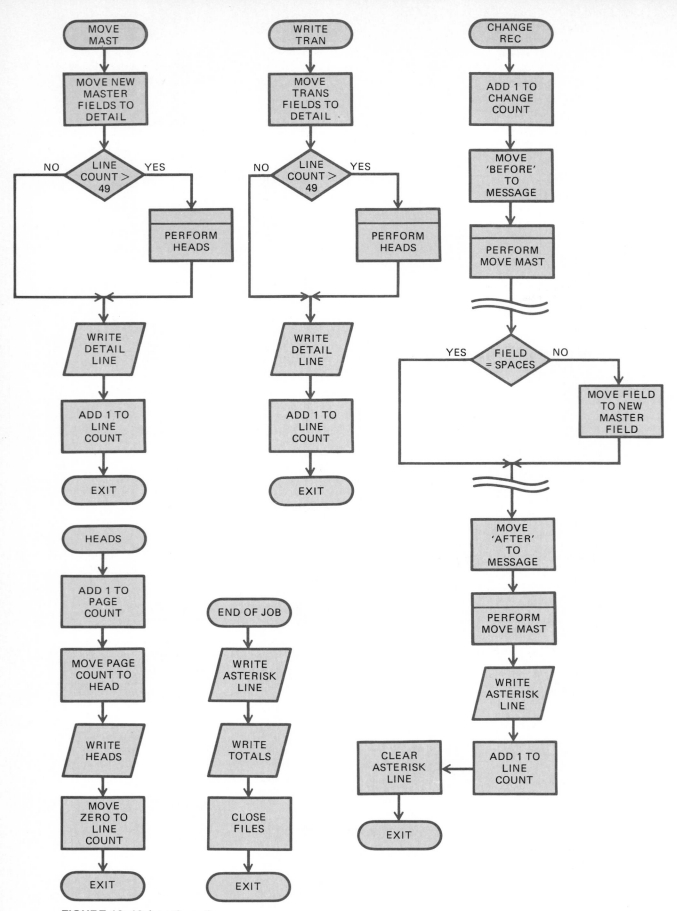

FIGURE 12–19 (continued)

MAINLINE LOGIC

PERFORM hsk routine
PERFORM process routine until end flag = on
PERFORM eoj

HSK routine

OPEN files
GET current date
MOVE "off" to mast exists switch
MOVE "off" to end-mast
MOVE "off" to end-tran
MOVE "off" to end-flag
MOVE zero to all counters
PERFORM read mast routine
PERFORM read tran routine
PERFORM select key routine

PROCESS routine

PERFORM ck mast routine
PERFORM apply tran routine until tran number = key hold
PERFORM ck write routine
PERFORM select key routine
CK MAST routine
IF mast number = key hold area
    MOVE old master to new master
    MOVE "yes" to mast exists switch
    PERFORM read mast routine
ELSE
    MOVE "no" to mast exists switch
ENDIF

SELECT KEY routine

IF master number < tran number
    MOVE mast number to key hold area
ELSE
    MOVE tran number to key hold area

APPLY TRAN routine

IF addition
    PERFORM add routine
ELSE
    IF change
        PERFORM change routine
    ELSE
        IF delete
            PERFORM delete routine
        ENDIF
    ENDIF
ENDIF
PERFORM read tran

CK WRITE routine

IF master exists switch = "yes"
    WRITE new master record
    ADD 1 to new master counter
ENDIF

FIGURE 12–20

CHANGE routine

    IF mast exists switch = "yes"
        PERFORM change rec routine
    ELSE
        PERFORM reject change
    ENDIF

ADD routine

    IF mast exists switch = "yes"
        PERFORM reject add routine
    ELSE
        PERFORM add rec routine
    END!F

DELETE routine

    IF mast exists switch = "yes"
        PERFORM delete rec routine
    ELSE
        PERFORM reject delete
    ENDIF

REJECT ADD routine

    ADD 1 to reject add counter
    MOVE "add" to message
    PERFORM write trans routine

REJECT CHANGE routine

    ADD 1 to reject change counter
    MOVE "change" to message
    PERFORM write tran routine

REJECT DELETE routine

    ADD 1 to reject delete counter
    MOVE "delete" to message
    PERFORM write tran routine

ADD REC routine

    MOVE tran record to new master record
    MOVE "yes" to mast exists switch
    MOVE "added" to message
    PERFORM move mast routine
    ADD 1 to added records count

DELETE REC routine

    MOVE "no" to mast exists switch
    ADD 1 to delete count
    MOVE "delete" to message
    PERFORM move mast routine

HEADS routine

    ADD 1 to page count
    MOVE page count to head
    WRITE heads
    MOVE zero to line count

FIGURE 12–20 (continued)

END OF JOB routine

    WRITE asterisk line
    WRITE totals
    CLOSE files

CHANGE REC routine

    ADD 1 to change count
    MOVE "before" to message
    PERFORM move mast routine
    IF field contents not = spaces
        MOVE field contents to new mast field

MOVE "after" to message

    PERFORM move mast routine
    WRITE asterisk line
    ADD 1 to line count
    MOVE spaces to asterisk line

MOVE MAST routine

    MOVE new master fields to detail line
    IF line count > 49
        PERFORM heads routine
    ENDIF
    WRITE detail line
    ADD 1 to line count

WRITE TRAN routine

    MOVE trans fields to detail line
    IF line count > 49
        PERFORM heads routine
    WRITE detail line
    ADD 1 to line count

READ MAST routine

    IF end mast = "on"
    ELSE
        READ master file
        AT end-of-file
            PERFORM test tran
    ENDIF
    IF end-mast = "on"
    ELSE
        ADD 1 to masters read
    ENDIF

TEST TRAN routine

    MOVE "on" to end-mast
    MOVE "high values" to mast number
    IF end-tran = "on"
        MOVE "on" to end flag
    ENDIF

READ TRAN routine

    IF end-train = "on"
    ELSE
        READ tran file

FIGURE 12–20 (continued)

```
        AT end-of-file
             PERFORM test mast
    ENDIF
    IF end-tran = "on"
    ELSE
         ADD 1 to tran read
    ENDIF

TEST MAST routine

    MOVE "on" to end-tran
    MOVE "high values" to tran number
    IF end-mast = "on"
    ELSE
         MOVE "on" to end-flag
    ENDIF
```

FIGURE 12–20 (continued)

In order to see how this works some sample data will be needed. To accomplish that the following master and transaction records will be used.

MASTER	TRANSACTION
1	1—change (C)
2	1—change (C)
3	2—delete (D)
5	4—add(A)
6	6—add(A)
9	7—delete(D)
	8—change(C)

In looking through the data it can be seen that item number 1 is being changed, number 2 is being deleted, 4 is being added, 6 is being added in error, 7 is being deleted in error, 8 is being changed in error, and numbers 3, 5, 6, and 9 are being left unchanged. To see how the logic for the problem works it will be helpful to walk through the flowchart and see what happens as each record is read and processed. After leaving the HSK routine the first record from both files (old master number 1 and transaction number 1—the first of two change records) have been read into storage via the READ MAST and READ TRAN routines. In CKMAST NO was moved to the MAST EXISTS switch. Since the transaction number does not equal KEYHOLD, the CKWRITE routine is performed where the MAST EXISTS switch is found to be off. In the SELECT KEY routine the old master number was not < the transaction number (1 is not < 1) so the transaction number was moved to the KEY HOLD area. The contents of the old master record area, transaction record area, KEY HOLD area, new master record area, and MAST EXISTS switch are shown below. Only the record numbers are shown for the master and transaction records—it is understood that the rest of the data in the record would also be present but has no affect on processing.

Old Master record area	1
Transaction record area	1 (code of C)
KEY HOLD area	1
New master record area	(nothing at this point)
MAST EXISTS switch	no
New file records	none at this point

It is once again time to perform the PROCESS routine. The first thing in the PROCESS routine is to perform CK MAST. Since the old master number is equal to the KEY HOLD area the old master record is moved to the new master record, YES is moved to the MAST EXISTS switch and the READ MAST routine is performed. Since END MAST is not on, an old master record is read (number 2) and 1 is added to the MAST READ counter. The current contents of the same areas are shown below.

Old master record area	2	
Transaction record area	1	(code of C)
KEY HOLD area	1	
New master record area	1	(unaltered)
MAST EXISTS switch	yes	
New file records	none at this point	

The next step in the PROCESS routine is to check to see if the transaction number is equal to the KEY HOLD area. In this case it is (1 = 1) so the APPLY TRAN routine is performed. When checking the code in the transaction record it is found to be a change record so the CHANGE routine is performed.

The MAST EXISTS switch = YES so the CHANGE REC routine is performed to effect the actual changes that are needed. The CHANGE REC routine adds 1 to the CHANGES counter, prints the contents of the master record prior to any changes being made, alters the contents of the fields needing change, prints the contents of the modified master record, and adds 1 to the line counter. The same process is used to determine which fields need to be changed that was used earlier in this chapter. That is, each of the fields in the transaction record (with the exception of the record number) are checked to see if they are blank. If they are not blank the contents of the transaction record field are moved to the corresponding new master record field. Blank fields in the transaction record will leave the contents of the corresponding new master record field unchanged. The changes are always made to the new master record since the old master record which is being changed has already been moved to the new master record area and another master record has been read into the input area for the master file. After the CHANGE routine has been performed the transaction file is read which brings transaction number 1 (the second of two change records for master number 1) into storage. The contents of the various areas are shown again for reference purposes.

Old master record area	2	
Transaction record area	1	(second change record)
KEY HOLD area	1	
New master record area	1	(changed by change 1)
MAST EXISTS switch	yes	
New file records	none at this point	

The next step in the logic is to check to see if the transaction number is equal to the KEY HOLD area. It is (1 = 1) so it is time to once again perform the APPLY TRAN routine. The transaction record is a change record so the CHANGE routine is performed once more and the next transaction record (number 2) is read. The current contents of the areas are shown below.

Old master record area	2	
Transaction record area	2	(code of D)
KEY HOLD area	1	
New master record area	1	(with changes from both change records)
MAST EXISTS switch	yes	
New file records	none at this point	

This time when the check is made to see if the transaction record is equal to the KEY HOLD area it is not, so the logic proceeds to performing the CK WRITE routine. Since the MAST EXISTS switch = yes the new master record is written and 1 is added to the NEW MASTER counter.

After finishing the CK WRITE routine the SELECT KEY routine is performed. The old master number is not < the transaction number (2 is not < 2) so the transaction number is moved to the KEY HOLD area. At this point it is time to return to checking to see if the END FLAG is on. Since it is not on, the PROCESS routine is performed. The current contents of the areas are shown below.

Old master record area	2	
Transaction record area	2	(code of D)
KEY HOLD area	2	
New master record area	1	
MAST EXISTS switch	yes	
New file records	1—changed	

In performing the CK MAST routine (the first step in the PROCESS routine) the old master number is found to be equal to the KEY HOLD area (2 = 2) so the master record is moved to the new master area, YES is moved to the MAST EXISTS switch, and the READ MAST routine is performed. This time the READ MAST routine reads old master record number 3 into storage. The current contents of the areas are shown below.

Old master record area	3	
Transaction record area	2	(code of D)
KEY HOLD area	2	
New master record area	2	
MAST EXISTS switch	yes	
New file records	1—changed	

When checking to see if the transaction record number is equal to the KEY HOLD area they are found to be equal (2 = 2). It is therefore time to perform the APPLY TRAN routine. This time the transaction record is found to be a delete record so the DELETE routine is performed. Within the DELETE routine the MAST EXISTS switch is found to be equal to YES so the DELETE REC routine is performed. Within the DELETE REC routine NO is moved to the MAST EXISTS switch, 1 is added to the DELETE counter, and a message is printed (via the MOVE MAST routine) to indicate that the record has been deleted. The record which is being deleted is the one that resides in the new master record area. After performing the DELETE routine the next transaction record (number 4) is read by the READTRANS routine.

Old master record area	3	
Transaction record area	4	(code of A)
KEY HOLD area	2	
New master record area	2	
MAST EXISTS switch	no	
New file records	1—changed	

Returning to check whether the transaction number is equal to the KEY HOLD area they are found to be not equal (4 is not = to 2). As a result the CK WRITE routine is performed. The MAST EXISTS switch is equal to no so no record is written to the new master file. The next step is to perform the SELECT KEY routine.

This time when the SELECT KEY routine is performed the old master number is found to be less than the transaction number (3 < 4) so the old master number is moved to the KEY HOLD area. END FLAG is not yet on so the PROCESS routine is again performed. The current contents of the areas are shown below.

Old master record area	3	
Transaction record area	4	(code of A)
KEY HOLD area	3	
New master area	2	
MAST EXISTS switch	no	
New file records	1—changed	

In performing the CK MAST routine within the PROCESS routine the old master record number is found to be equal to the KEY HOLD area (3 = 3) so the old master record is moved to the new master record area, YES is moved to the MAST EXISTS switch, and the READ MAST routine is performed. In performing the READ MAST routine, old master record number 5 is read into storage. The current contents of the areas are as follows.

Old master record area	5	
Transaction record area	4	(code of A)
KEY HOLD area	3	
New master record area	3	
MAST EXISTS switch	yes	
New file records	1—changed	

When comparing the transaction number and the KEY HOLD area they are found to be unequal (4 does not = 3) so the CK WRITE routine is performed. The MAST EXISTS switch is equal to YES so the new master record is written and 1 is added to the NEW MASTER counter. In performing the SELECT KEY routine the old master number is not less than the transaction number (5 is not < 4) so the transaction record number is moved to the KEY HOLD area. The current contents of the areas are as follows.

Old master record area	5	
Transaction record area	4	(code of A)
KEY HOLD area	4	
New master record area	3	
MAST EXISTS switch	yes	
New file records	1—changed	
	3—copied	

END FLAG is not on yet so the PROCESS routine is once again performed. This time when performing the CK MAST routine the old master number is not equal to the KEY HOLD area (5 is not = 4) so NO is moved to the MAST EXISTS switch. The current contents of the areas are shown below.

Old master record area	5	
Transaction record area	4	(code of A)
KEY HOLD area	4	
New master record area	3	
MAST EXISTS switch	no	
New file records	1—changed	
	3—copied	

The transaction number is equal to the KEY HOLD area (4 = 4) so the APPLY TRAN routine is performed. Since the transaction is an add record the ADD routine is performed. The MAST EXISTS switch is equal to NO so the ADD REC routine is performed. In ADD REC the transaction record is moved to the new record area, YES is moved to the MAST EXISTS switch, a message is printed to indicate the addition of a record to the file, and 1 is added to the ADDED RECS counter. Following this the next transaction record (number 6) is read via the READTRANS routine. The current contents of the areas are shown below.

Old master record area	5	
Transaction record area	6	(code of A)
KEY HOLD area	4	
New master record area	4	
MAST EXISTS switch	yes	
New file records	1—changed	
	3—copied	

In performing the CK WRITE routine the MAST EXISTS switch is found to be equal to YES so the new master record is written on the new file and 1 is added to the NEW MASTER counter. In performing the SELECT KEY routine the old master number is less than the transaction number (5 < 6) so the old master number is moved to the KEY HOLD area. The current contents of the areas are shown below.

Old master record area	5	
Transaction record area	6	(code of A)
KEY HOLD area	5	
New master record area	4	
MAST EXISTS switch	yes	
New file records	1—changed	
	3—copied	
	4—added	

At this point it is time to perform the PROCESS routine once more. This time when performing the CK MAST routine the old master number is equal to the KEY HOLD area (5 = 5) so the old master record is moved to the new master area, YES is moved to the MAST EXISTS switch, and the next old master record (number 6) is read into storage. The current contents of the areas are as follows.

Old master record area	6	
Transaction area	6	(code = A)
KEY HOLD area	5	
New master record area	5	

```
MAST EXISTS switch          yes
New file records            1—changed
                            3—copied
                            4—added
```

When comparing the transaction and KEY HOLD area values against each other they are not equal (6 is not = 5) so the CK WRITE routine is performed. The MAST EXISTS switch is equal to YES so the new master file record is written and 1 is added to the NEW MASTER counter. In performing the SELECT KEY routine the old mast number is not less than the transaction number (6 is not < 6) so the transaction number is moved to the KEY HOLD area. The current contents of the areas are as follows.

```
Old master record area      6
Transaction record area     6       (code = A)
KEY HOLD area               6
New master record area      5
MAST EXISTS switch          yes
New file records            1—changed
                            3—copied
                            4—added
                            5—copied
```

In performing the CK MAST routine the old master number and KEY HOLD area are found to be equal (6 = 6) so the old master record is moved to the new master record area, YES is moved to the MAST EXISTS switch, and the next old master record (number 9) is read. The current contents of the areas are shown below.

```
Old master record area      9
Transaction record area     6       (code = A)
KEY HOLD area               6
New master record area      6
MAST EXISTS switch          yes
New file records            1—changed
                            3—copied
                            4—added
                            5—copied
```

The transaction number is = to the KEY HOLD area (6 = 6) so the APPLY TRAN routine is performed. Since the code is for an addition, the ADD routine is performed. The MAST EXISTS switch is equal to YES so the REJECT ADD routine is performed. The REJECT ADD routine adds 1 to the REJECT ADD counter and prints a message indicating that an invalid add record has been processed. After printing the error message the next transaction record (number 7) is read via the READTRANS routine. The current contents of the areas are shown below.

```
Old master record area      9
Transaction record area     7       (code = D)
KEY HOLD area               6
New master record area      6
MAST EXISTS switch          yes
New file records            1—changed
                            3—copied
                            4—added
                            5—copied
```

When performing the CK WRITE routine the MAST EXISTS switch is found to be equal to YES so the new master record area is written to the new file and 1 is added to the NEW MASTER counter. In the SELECT KEY routine the old master number is not less than the transaction number (9 is not < 7) so the transaction number is moved to the KEY HOLD area. END FLAG is still off so the PROCESS routine is again performed. The old master number is not equal to the KEY HOLD area (9 is not = 6) so NO is moved to the MAST EXISTS switch. The current contents of the areas are shown below.

```
Old master record area      9
Transaction record area     7       (code = D)
KEY HOLD area               7
```

```
New master record area        6
MAST EXISTS switch            no
New file records              1—changed
                              3—copied
                              4—added
                              5—copied
                              6—copied
```

The transaction is equal to the KEY HOLD area so the APPLY TRAN routine is performed. The transaction record contains a code for a delete so the DELETE routine is performed. Since the MAST EXISTS switch is equal to NO the REJECT DEL routine is performed to handle the invalid deletion. The REJECT DEL routine adds 1 to a counter for invalid deletes and prints a message indicating that the invalid deletion transaction was present. The next transaction record (number 8) is then read into storage. When performing the CK WRITE routine the MAST EXISTS switch is found to be off so no record is written to the new master file at this point. The SELECT KEY routine finds the transaction record lower than the old master record and therefore moves the transaction number to the KEY HOLD area. The current contents of the areas are shown below.

```
Old master record area        9
Transaction record area       8        (code = C)
KEY HOLD area                 8
New master record area        6
MAST EXISTS switch            no
New file records              1—changed
                              3—copied
                              4—added
                              5—copied
                              6—copied
```

END FLAG still being off, it is again time to perform the PROCESS routine. In performing the CK MAST routine the old master number is not equal to the KEY HOLD area (9 is not = 8) so NO is moved to the MAST EXISTS switch. The transaction number does equal the KEY HOLD area (8 = 8) so the APPLY TRAN routine is performed. Since the transaction record contains a code of C the change routine is performed. The MAST EXISTS switch, however, is not equal to yes so the REJ CHANGE routine is performed to indicate that an invalid change record was present. When attempting to read the next transaction record an end-of-file condition is encountered on the transaction file. As a result ON is moved to the END TRAN switch and "high values" are moved to the transaction record number area. The current contents of the areas are shown below.

```
Old master record area        9
Transaction record area       999
KEY HOLD area                 8
New master record area        6
MAST EXISTS switch            no
New file records              1—changed
                              3—copied
                              4—added
                              5—copied
                              6—copied
```

The transaction number does not equal the KEY HOLD area (high values are > 8) so the CK WRITE routine is performed. The MAST EXISTS switch is equal to NO so nothing is written to the new master file at this time. In the SELECT KEY routine the old master number is found to be < the transaction number (9 < high values) so the transaction number (high values) is moved to the KEY HOLD area. END FLAG is still off so the PROCESS routine is performed again. The old master number is not equal to the KEY HOLD value so NO is moved to the MAST EXISTS switch. The transaction number is not equal to the value in the KEY HOLD area so the next step is to perform the CK WRITE routine. The MAST EXISTS switch is still off so the next step is to perform the SELECT KEY routine. The old master number is less than the transaction number so the master number is moved to the KEY HOLD area. At this point the CK MAST is performed and the master number is equal to the KEY HOLD area so the old master record will be moved to the new master record area, YES will be moved to the MAST EXISTS switch, and the next old master record will be read. The end-of-file condition on the master file causes ON to be moved to END-MAST and "high values" to be moved to the old master record number area. END-TRAN is on so ON is also moved to END FLAG. Since the transaction number is not equal to the KEY HOLD area value, the CK WRITE routine will be performed. The MAST EXISTS switch is on so the new record will be written to the new master file and 1 will be added to the NEW MASTER counter. The current contents of the areas are shown below.

Old master record area	999
Transaction record area	999
KEY HOLD area	9
New master record area	9
MAST EXISTS switch	yes
New file records	1—changed
	3—copied
	4—added
	5—copied
	6—copied
	9—copied

It should be noted that "high values" refers to a value greater than the maximum value within a field. In COBOL the term "high values" has a specific value.

CHAPTER VOCABULARY

Add	Changes	Key hold area
Adds	Copy	MAST EXISTS switch
Bad add	Delete	Record counts
Bad equal	Deletes	Updating
Change		

REVIEW QUESTIONS

All questions refer to sequential file matching with a single transaction per master unless otherwise specified.

MATCHING

A. Adds
B. Deletes
C. Master > transaction
D. END FLAG switch

E. Changes
F. EOJ routine
G. Master < transaction
H. 9's (or high values)

_____ **1.** Condition indicating that the record should be an add record.
_____ **2.** Transaction records used to modify the data in the file.
_____ **3.** Moved to the master or transaction compare areas on an end-of-file condition.
_____ **4.** Produces the final totals of the various record types encountered during processing.
_____ **5.** Transaction records to be included in the new master file which were not in the old master file.
_____ **6.** Turned on only after both files have ended.
_____ **7.** Condition that forces the old master to be moved and written as is on the new master file.
_____ **8.** Transaction records which cause old master records not to be included on the new master file.

TRUE/FALSE

T F **1.** The DELETE routine should be the result of a master = transaction comparison on the PROCESS routine.

T F **2.** Adds are permitted on a master = transaction comparison in the PROCESS routine.

T F **3.** The purpose of a file-updating program is to cause a file to reflect the current situation.

		4.	The only portion of a master-file record that should be changed is the contents of the field on which the file is sequenced.
T	**F**		
T	**F**	5.	The new master file can be created right over the old master file in order to save a second tape, disk, or other media.
T	**F**	6.	The only place that records are written on the new master is in the COPY routine.
T	**F**	7.	When the master compares lower than the transaction, the COPY routine will be performed.
T	**F**	8.	Deletes cause a null record to be created on the master indicating that a record has been deleted.
T	**F**	9.	Blank fields in change record cause the master-file fields to be changed to blanks.
T	**F**	10.	The READ MAST routine checks transaction records to see if they are additions to the file.
T	**F**	11.	Files are typically closed in the PROCESS routine.
T	**F**	12.	END FLAG is sometimes turned on when only one file has ended.

EXERCISES

1. Flowchart the PROCESS routine for a master-file update program (less subroutines).
2. Flowchart the READ MAST routine for a master-file update program.
3. Flowchart the READTRANS routine for a master-file update program.
4. Flowchart the entire update program for a master-file update program including all subroutines. The master file is sequenced on the employee-number field and has the following fields:
   EMPLOYEE NAME
   EMPLOYEE NUMBER
   DATE OF BIRTH
   SEX
   RATE OF PAY
   POSITION
   ADDRESS
   CITY
   STATE

DISCUSSION QUESTIONS

1. Discuss the use of control totals including when they are initialized, incremented, and printed. Of what use are they?
2. Describe the various types of transaction records in a master file update program and what they signify.
3. Describe why it is necessary to create a separate new master file when doing a sequential file update.
4. Discuss additional items which need to be considered when multiple transaction records are needed to add or change a master-file record.
5. Describe the function of a sequential file update program and what might be done if file updating in this manner were not possible.

PROJECTS

Project 1

Prepare a print chart and a flowchart for the following:

INPUT

MASTER PERSONNEL FILE

01–02	Personnel Record Code
03–03	Personnel Division Has a range of 1–5
04–05	Personnel Department Has a range of 1–5
	Personnel Employee ID
06–08	Personnel ID-1
09–10	Personnel ID-2
11–14	Personnel ID-3
15–34	Personnel Name
35–50	Personnel Street Address
51–52	Personnel State
53–57	Personnel Zip
	Personnel Date of Employment
58–59	Personnel Month
60–61	Personnel Day

62–63		Personnel Year
64–64		Personnel Experience Code
65–65		Personnel Responsibility Code
66–67		Personnel Skill Code
68–71		Personnel Vacation Days (4.1)
72–75		Personnel Sick Days (4.1)
76–80		Personnel Daily Rate (5.2)

TRANSACTION FILE

01–01	Transaction Record Code
02–02	Transaction Action Code (A=ADD, C=CHANGE, D=DELETE)
03–03	Transaction Division
04–05	Transaction Department
	Transaction Employee ID
06–08	Transaction ID-1
09–10	Transaction ID-2
11–14	Transaction ID-3
15–34	Transaction Name
35–50	Transaction Street Address
51–52	Transaction State
53–57	Transaction Zip
	Transaction Date of Employment
58–59	Transaction Month
60–61	Transaction Day
62–63	Transaction Year
64–64	Transaction Experience Code
65–65	Transaction Responsibility Code
66–67	Transaction Skill Code
68–71	Transaction Vacation Days (4.1)
72–75	Transaction Sick Days (4.1)
76–80	Transaction Daily Rate (5.2)

PROCESSING

Update the master file using the transaction file. Use column 2 of the transaction file to determine what updating action is to be taken. Fields requiring change will have data on the transaction file, other fields will be blank.

OUTPUT

Design a printed output which will identify the results of the update. This design is to include all adds, changes and deletes, but no copies.

At the end-of-file on the transaction file, print out a list of the new master file.

Project 2

Prepare a print chart and a flowchart for the following specifications:

INPUT

MASTER INVENTORY FILE

1– 2	Inventory Record Code	
	Inventory Stock Number	
3– 3	Inventory Type	Has a range of 1–5
4– 5	Inventory Class	Has a range of 01–10
6– 9	Inventory Part	
10–29	Inventory Description	
30–30	Inventory Location Code	
31–34	Inventory Quantity on Hand	
35–38	Inventory Quantity on Order	
39–42	Inventory Reorder Level	
43–43	Inventory Unit Size Code	
44–48	Inventory Unit Price (5.2)	
49–49	Inventory Discount Code	
50–55	Inventory Annual Usage (Units)	
56–58	Inventory Vendor Code	
	Inventory Transportation Code	

59–59	Inventory Category
60–60	Inventory Distance
61–80	Unused

TRANSACTION FILE

1– 1	Transaction Inventory Code	
2– 2	Transaction Inventory Action Code	A=ADD,C=CHANGE,D=DELETE
	Transaction Inventory Stock Number	
3– 3	Transaction Inventory Type	Has a range of 1–5
4– 5	Transaction Inventory Class	Has a range of 01–10
6– 9	Transaction Inventory Part	
10–29	Transaction Inventory Description	
30–30	Transaction Inventory Location Code	
31–34	Transaction Inventory Quantity on Hand	
35–38	Transaction Inventory Quantity on Order	
39–42	Transaction Inventory Reorder Level	
43–43	Transaction Inventory Unit Size Code	
44–48	Transaction Inventory Unit Price	(5.2)
49–49	Transaction Inventory Discount Code	
50–55	Transaction Inventory Annual Usage (Units)	
56–58	Transaction Inventory Vendor Code	
	Transaction Inventory Transportation Code	
59–59	Transaction Inventory Category	
60–60	Transaction Inventory Distance	
61–80	Unused	

PROCESSING

Update the master file using the transaction file. Use column 2 of the transaction file to determine what updating action is to be taken. Fields requiring change will have data on the transaction field, other fields will be blank.

OUTPUT

Design a printed output which will identify the results of the update. This design is to include all adds, changes and deletes, but not copies.

At end-of-file on the transaction file, print out a list of the new master file.

NONSEQUENTIAL FILES

13

OBJECTIVES

As a result of studying this chapter the student should be able to perform the following activities:

1. Describe the difference between a sequential and a nonsequential file.
2. Describe appropriate media for nonsequential files.
3. Describe the types of applications suitable for nonsequential files.
4. Describe types of nonsequential files.
5. Flowchart the logic for creation of an indexed file.

6. Flowchart the updating of an indexed file.
7. Describe methods of positioning records in a random file used on a microcomputer.
8. Flowchart the logic for the creation of an indexed file on a microcomputer.
9. Flowchart the logic for retrieving records from a random file on a microcomputer.

INTRODUCTION

Although the use of nonsequential files is common, we have left the flowcharting techniques for such files until the end of the coverage of program flowcharting. The reason for this is the ease with which we can flowchart some of the more difficult sequential file routines (matching, updating, and so on) when using a nonsequential file. In this chapter we will describe the difference between the types of files, the appropriate media for each, and the types of applications suitable for each. Examples of file creation and retrieval for both mainframes and microcomputers are given.

SEQUENTIAL VS. NONSEQUENTIAL

A sequential file is one whose records must be accessed starting at the beginning of the file and passing over (or reading) every record. We must read every record whether we are interested in it or not. To find a specific record, each record that is read is tested for the condition we are looking for. This process will continue from the beginning of the file through each record until the test is positive, indicating that the record we are looking for has been found.

A file with nonsequential access allows us to read any one record in the file just as easily as any other record. The program can locate any record without having to read all prior records. This makes a record in the middle of the file immediately available without having to read the first half of the file.

FILE MEDIA

Two types of media that are suitable only for sequential files are punched cards and magnetic tape. When punched cards are loaded into a card reader, they must be read one at a time from the beginning to the end of the deck. We are free to sort the cards into a particular sequence before loading them. After that the cards must be accessed (read) one card at a time until the reading of the deck is completed. The use of magnetic tape is similar. Once the records are on the tape in a sequence of our choosing, reading is generally started at the beginning of the tape and continued record by record until either the end of the file is reached, or all of the records we are interested in have been passed.

Nonsequential files are found most often on magnetic disks. On a large computer system a series of magnetic disk surfaces are usually assembled together in what is commonly referred to as a disk pack. The assembly includes read-write heads, which move over the disk surfaces either reading or writing data. The ability of these read-write heads to move across the disk surface to a predetermined location gives us nonsequential or random access. Figure 13–1 is an illustration of a disk pack.

On microcomputer systems the disk storage is often a single disk. These disks come in a variety of sizes from a large hard disk to the popular 5¼- and 3½-inch diskettes. Figure 13–2 is an illustration of a diskette for a microcomputer.

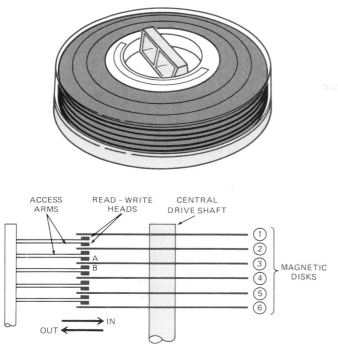

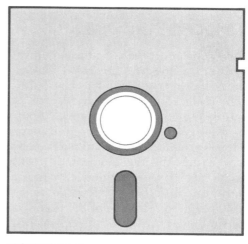

FIGURE 13–1

FIGURE 13–2

TYPES OF APPLICATIONS

A number of factors affect the decision to use sequential or nonsequential files. One is the speed with which we can complete a given job. Another is convenience. The decision on which method to use is based partly on the number of records from the file that need to be read. Sequential processing is the faster method per record read. This is because once we have read one record in a sequential file the file is in the correct position to read the next record, whereas with a nonsequential file each record must be located individually. If the project requires that a high percentage of the records in the file must be read, then sequential processing may be the choice. If, on the other hand, we need only a small percentage of the records from a file, we may choose nonsequential processing.

We have to balance the slower reading speed on a nonsequential file against the number of records we actually need to read from a file. Assume that it takes three times as long to access the average nonsequential record as the average sequential record in a file. This would mean that if we needed at least one-third of the records in a file, sequential processing would be just as fast. See Figure 13–3 for a comparison of the two methods. Notice that the amount of time required to read the sequential file does not change as the percentage of records needed changes. The time required to read the nonsequential file, however, changes in proportion to the number of records read.

PERCENT REQUIRED OF 1000 RECORDS	UNITS OF READING TIME, SEQUENTIAL FILE (1 UNIT OF TIME PER RECORD READ)	UNITS OF READING TIME, NONSEQUENTIAL FILE (3 UNITS OF TIME PER RECORD READ)
10	1000	300
50	1000	1500
90	1000	2700

FIGURE 13–3

Another factor is convenience. Many on-line real-time systems are built around the concept of random access. A student coming to register for classes wants to know if a seat is available in the class. A person buying an airline ticket wants to know if space is available on a particular flight. Neither of these people wants to wait until every class or every flight with a lower number has been checked out. Their need for a real-time reply to their request makes nonsequential processing the only practical method in such situations.

TYPES OF ACCESS

Two common types of nonsequential access are indexed sequential and direct access. **Indexed sequential** files are normally loaded or created originally in a sequential order based on a key field within a record. The key field of a record will contain a unique value that distinguishes that record from all other records in the file. Examples of key fields might be a social security number for personnel, payroll, school, or IRS records; a part number for manufacturing, inventory, or quality control records; and a customer number for marketing, shipping, or billing records. This key field is unique to each record and is used to sequence and identify the record.

When the file is created, an index is developed by the system representing the key for each record within the file. When additions are made to the file, records are rearranged to accommodate the new records, and the index is changed to keep track of the new location. The advantage to this type of file organization is that the records can be retrieved either sequentially or randomly. We can retrieve records from an indexed sequential file randomly by looking for the contents of a key field in a set of indices. The indices will pinpoint the physical location of the record we are looking for, allowing the read-write heads to access the record by going directly to that area.

As records are added to an indexed file, the file loses its original sequential order. Older methods of indexed access place new or displaced records in overflow areas. As this happens, the indices become more complicated and access is slowed. To remedy this, the file is reorganized periodically. In this process the records are sorted into the proper order and then written back to the original file and the indices are rebuilt.

The newer methods of indexed access allow for insertion of new records in the proper order by reserving free space in multiple locations within the file. When a record is added, there may be free space for the record within an existing group with the appropriate number range. If there is not, the records in that group are split to create two groups, each with free space. This planning for free space distributed within the file allows the file to remain in sequential order for a longer time and cuts down on the slowed access and need to reorganize.

These indices often have levels. When we start to locate a record based on its key, the system looks at the major index and finds that it is greater than the value we are looking for. This section of the index points to a minor index, where the same approach is used; locating the first area that is greater than the value we are looking for. This minor index points to a group of records one of which contains the record key. Using an index is much like looking a word up in a nice dictionary that has finger tabs for the alphabet. We can get to the proper letter by looking at the tabs. This is the major index. Next, we scan the page tops to find the correct range of letters or words. This is the minor index. Next we scan the page for the word we want. Assume we are looking for a record with a key of 135. Follow the shaded areas in Figure 13–4.

MAJOR INDEX

| 186 | 285 | 400 |

MINOR INDICES

| 101 | 140 | 186 | | 210 | 250 | 285 | | 300 | 340 | 400 |

80	120	145		190	217	261		287	306	365
86	129	180		193	250	278		293	325	400
90	135	186		201		283		300	331	
101	140			210		285			340	

FIGURE 13–4

In the case of direct file organization a relationship is developed that uses the key field of the record to assign a location for the record within the file. Usually a formula is applied to the contents of the key field, and the results of the calculation are used to assign a location within the file to the record. The record is then written in this location. When it is time to retrieve the record, the same formula is applied to the key field of the transaction record. The results point to the location in the nonsequential file where the matching record was stored.

CREATING AN INDEXED FILE

The flowchart to create an indexed file on a medium or large computer system is shown in Figure 13–5. This flowchart assumes an initial read in housekeeping. In the CREATE routine the key of each record is moved to an area where it is recognized by the computer to be the key used for indexing. Next, the record is written. The computer handles the creation of the index for the record. Figure 13–6 is the pseudocode.

When each record is written, a test is made for INVALID KEY. INVALID KEY is a condition which exists if, for any reason, the computer cannot use the key of the record the system just attempted to write (duplicate or no more space). If the key is invalid, an error message is moved to output and written. At that point END FLAG is turned on, because the loading of the file should not continue if an INVALID KEY is discovered. We are assuming here that the file can be loaded only if the sequence is proper. As long as an INVALID KEY condition is not encountered, the program continues to read records and write them on the file until there are no more records to be loaded.

In addition to the INVALID KEY test it is also possible to develop error-handling routines. The system will revert to the error handling routines whenever there is an input/output error. These routines are peculiar to the programming language and access method being used.

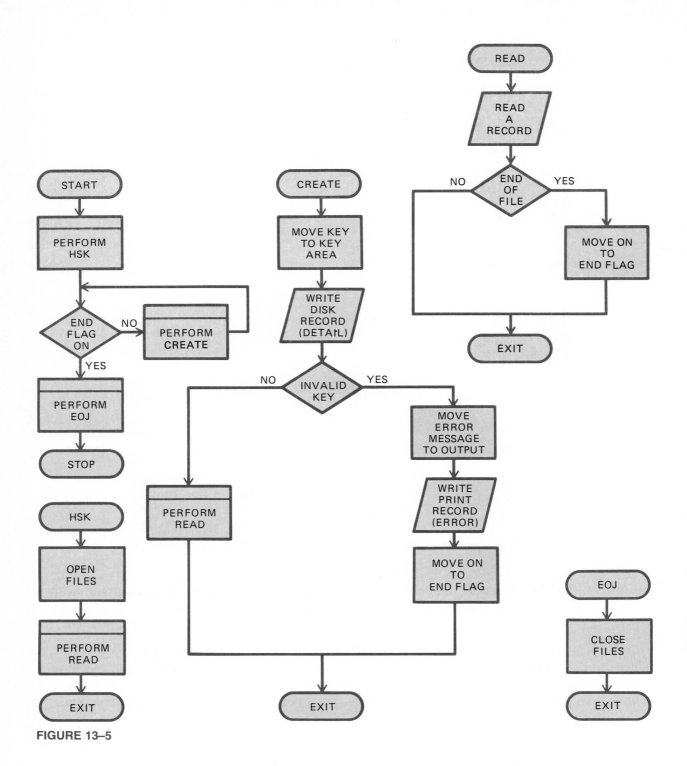

FIGURE 13–5

MAINLINE LOGIC

    PERFORM hsk routine
    PERFORM create routine until end flag = on
    PERFORM eoj routine
    STOP

HSK ROUTINE

    OPEN files
    PERFORM read routine

CREATE ROUTINE

    MOVE key to key area
    WRITE disk record (detail)
    IF invalid key condition
        MOVE error message to output
        WRITE print record (error message)
        MOVE on to end flag

    ELSE

        PERFORM read routine

    ENDIF

EOJ ROUTINE

    CLOSE files

READ ROUTINE

    READ a record
        AT END of file
            MOVE on to end flag

FIGURE 13–6

UPDATING AN INDEXED FILE

To update an indexed master file on a medium or large computer system we need a transaction file which contains all the additions, deletions, and changes. After reading the initial transaction record in housekeeping the UPDATE routine is entered and the transaction code is tested. If the transaction code is not an addition, deletion, or change, an error routine is performed. If the answer is yes to any of these codes, the appropriate ADD, DELETE, or CHANGE routine is performed. After the return from any of these routines another transaction record is read. If the END FLAG is not on, UPDATE is performed again. See Figure 13–7 for the flowchart and Figure 13–8 for the pseudocode.

The ADD routine requires that the key field from the transaction file be moved to the control field used by the computer to establish an index. Then the data is moved and the added record is written. Each time a record is written a test is made for INVALID KEY. If the answer is yes, it may mean the record we are trying to add is already in the file. A message is moved and written indicating a bad add and the routine is exited.

The DELETE and CHANGE routines are similar. In both cases we must establish the key by moving it from the transaction record to the key area for the indexed file and then use the key to locate and read the matching record in the master file. After an attempt at reading, if there is an INVALID KEY message it means the record we wanted to change or delete was not located. In this case an appropriate message is written. If the read was successful, either a delete code is moved to the record and it is rewritten or changes are moved to the record and it is rewritten. If as a result of the rewrite there is an INVALID KEY message, there is a serious

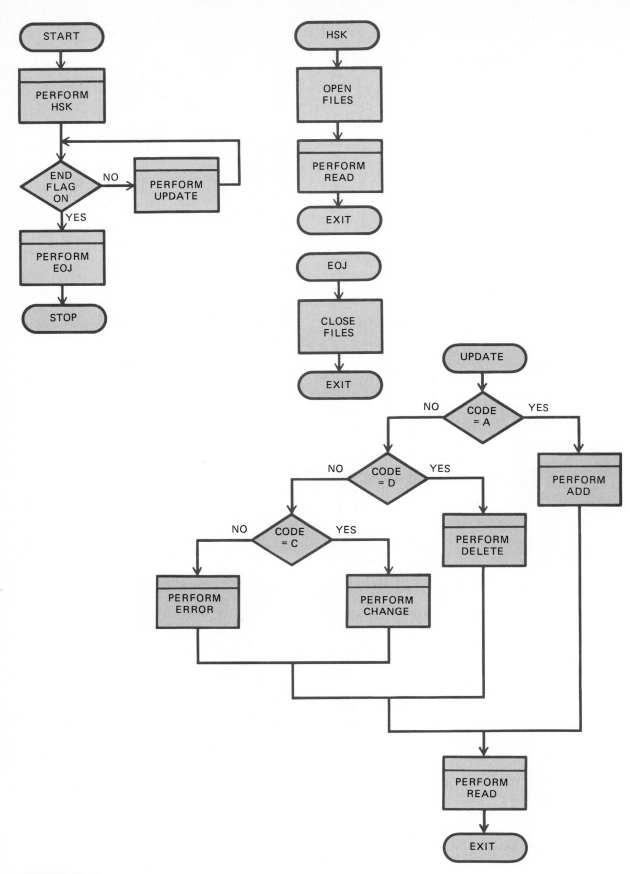

FIGURE 13–7

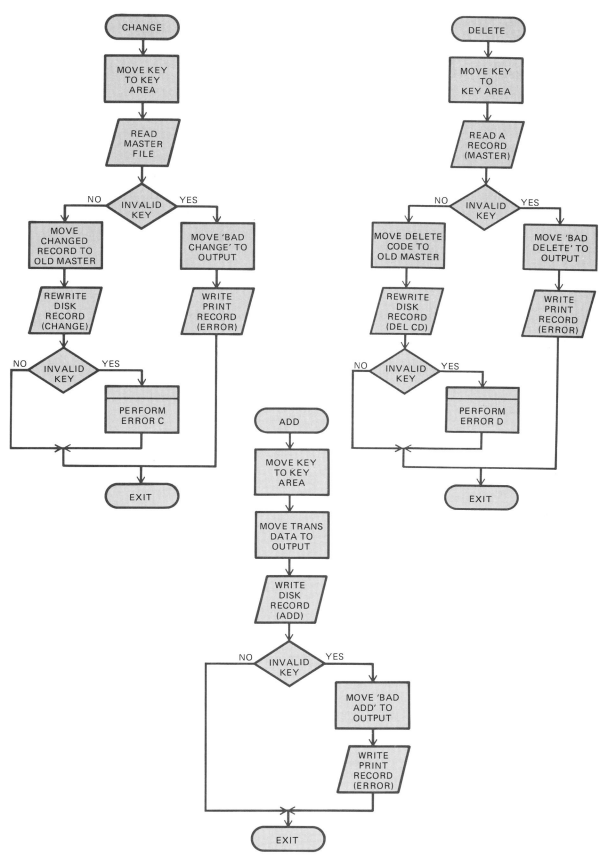

FIGURE 13-7 (continued)

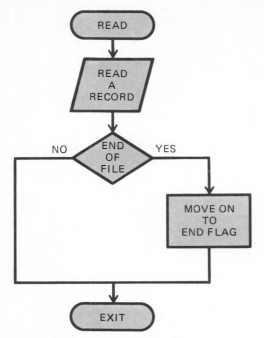

FIGURE 13–7 (continued)

MAINLINE LOGIC

      PERFORM hsk routine
      PERFORM update routine until end flag = on
      PERFORM eoj routine
      STOP

HSK ROUTINE

      OPEN files
      PERFORM read routine

UPDATE ROUTINE

      IF update code = A
          PERFORM add routine
      ELSE
          IF update code = D
             PERFORM delete routine
          ELSE
             IF update code = C
                PERFORM change routine
             ELSE
                PERFORM error routine
             ENDIF
          ENDIF
      ENDIF
      PERFORM read routine

EOJ ROUTINE

      CLOSE files

READ ROUTINE

      READ a record (transaction file)
          AT END of file
             MOVE on to end flag

FIGURE 13–8

ADD ROUTINE

```
MOVE key to key area
MOVE transaction data to output
WRITE disk record (add)
      IF invalid key
            MOVE bad add to output
            WRITE print record (error message)
      ENDIF
```

DELETE ROUTINE

```
MOVE key to key area
READ a record (master file)
      IF invalid key
            MOVE bad delete to output
            WRITE print record (error message)
      ELSE
            MOVE delete code to old master
            REWRITE disk record (delete code)
                  IF invalid key
                        PERFORM error routine (delete)
                  ENDIF
      ENDIF
```

CHANGE ROUTINE

```
MOVE key to key area
READ a record (master file)
      IF invalid key
            MOVE bad change to output
            WRITE print record (error message)
      ELSE
            MOVE changed record to old master
            REWRITE disk record (change)
                  IF invalid key
                        PERFORM error routine (change)
                  ENDIF
      ENDIF
```

FIGURE 13–8 (continued)

processing problem which doesn't allow the record to be rewritten and a suitable error routine is performed.

In this logic we have used techniques from the older style of indexed file in the DELETE routine. When we wish to delete a record, the record in the nonsequential is flagged for deletion but not physically deleted. Periodically, when the file is reorganized, the records which are flagged for deletion are actually deleted. This is accomplished by not copying the flagged records to the reorganized file. In new versions of indexed files the records we wish to delete can be physically deleted, using a delete command in the update program.

INDEXED FILES ON MICROS

Some versions of BASIC allow for the creation and retrieval of random files. In a popular version we can either use the key field in a direct manner to determine a record number (and position) for the record in the random file or we can place the records in the file in a sequential manner and then develop a method to determine which record number (position) is associated with a particular key field. If we use the direct method, where the record number and the key field have the same value, we must either have a compact range of numbers to use as the key field or create a file with a lot of wasted space. With a file of employees whose employee numbers ranged from 1 to 999 we could create a random file using the employee numbers as the record numbers for the file. We would need a file capable of holding 999 records to accommodate the records. It would not matter if we had 10 employees or 999 employees, we would still need

999 spaces if the numbers could range as high as 999. Notice all of the wasted space. See Figure 13–9.

Figure 13–10 shows the logic for creation of a random file where the key field is used directly as the record number. The important points in this logic include the description of an input/output area (DECLARE), the movement of data to that buffer area, and the writing of

RECORD 1   EMPNO 1
                   _____

RECORD 2
                   _____

RECORD 3
                   _____

RECORD 4   EMPNO 4
                   _____

RECORD 5
                   _____

RECORD 6
                   _____

RECORD 7
                   _____

RECORD 8   EMPNO 8
                   _____

RECORD 9
                   _____

RECORD 994
                   _____

RECORD 995   EMPNO 995
                   _____

RECORD 996
                   _____

RECORD 997
                   _____

RECORD 998
                   _____

RECORD 999   EMPNO 999
                   _____

FIGURE 13–9

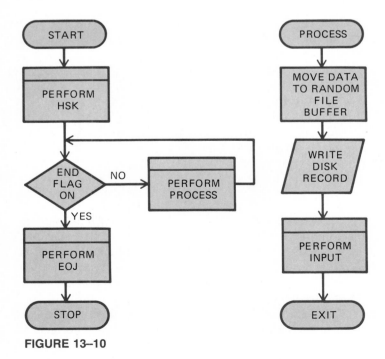

FIGURE 13–10

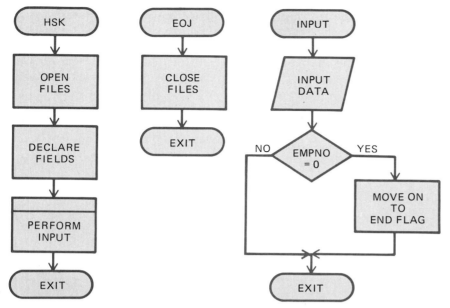

FIGURE 13–10 (continued)

the record in a location in the file based on the contents of the key field. Remember that versions of BASIC vary, and this logic is only representative of the approaches taken. Figure 13–11 is the pseudocode.

In order to access this file randomly we will use a transaction file which has EMPNO as one of the fields in the record. The EMPNO is then used directly as the record number to determine the record location. BASIC does this by calculating a location for the record based

MAINLINE LOGIC

    PERFORM hsk routine
    PERFORM process routine until end flag = on
    PERFORM eoj routine
    STOP

HSK ROUTINE

    OPEN files
    DECLARE fields
    PERFORM input routine

PROCESS ROUTINE

    MOVE data to random file buffer
    WRITE disk record, EMPNO (empno determines location)
    PERFORM input routine

EOJ ROUTINE

    CLOSE files

INPUT ROUTINE

    INPUT data (empno, etc)
    IF empno = 0
        MOVE on to end flag
    ENDIF

FIGURE 13–11

on the location of the file on the disk and the size of a record. Notice how EMPNO is used as a part of the read statement so it can supply the record number. Figure 13–12 is the flowchart for random access, and Figure 13–13 is the pseudocode.

The wasted space in the previous example of file creation and access occurs because we have a wide range of employee numbers and only a few records in the range. The space usage in this situation can be improved by reducing the range of numbers. We could do this by actually changing the employee numbers from an administrative viewpoint and assigning new numbers with a small range. When a change like this is impractical, we can create a sequential file to be used as an index for the random file when it is time to retrieve records from the random

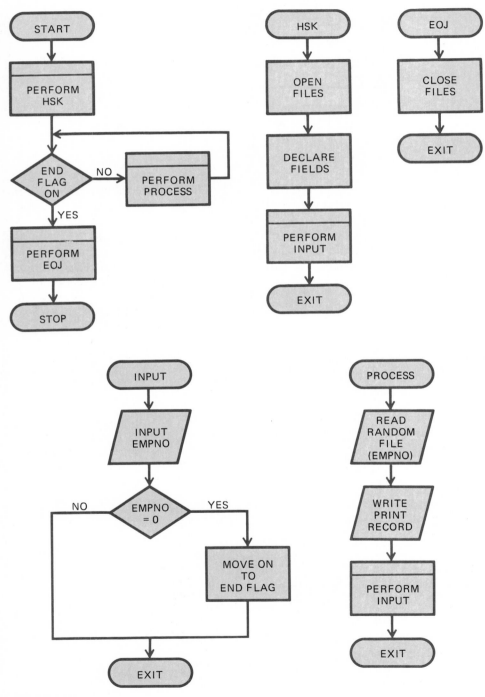

FIGURE 13–12

MAINLINE LOGIC

```
PERFORM hsk routine
PERFORM process routine until end flag = on
PERFORM eoj routine
STOP
```

HSK ROUTINE

```
OPEN files
DECLARE fields
PERFORM input routine
```

PROCESS ROUTINE

```
READ random file, EMPNO
WRITE print record
PERFORM read routine
```

EOJ ROUTINE

```
CLOSE files
```

INPUT ROUTINE

```
READ a record
      AT END of file
            MOVE on to end flag
ENDIF
```

FIGURE 13–13

file. The sequential file will contain only the contents of the key fields from each record of the random file. See Figure 13–14 for an example of the contents of the two files. Notice that the employee numbers are not in any order, the employees were added to the files as they were hired. There are no unused areas in the file even though there is a large range of employee numbers and few records in the file.

Now let's assume that we want to access the record for employee number 414540418 (normally printed as 414–54–0418). We can't go to record number 414540418, there aren't that many records; there are only 10 records in the small file. If we could not refer to the printed listing we would have no idea which position this record occupied in the file.

To determine which record contains the data for employee 414540418 we will use the sequential file that was created when the records were loaded into the random file. One of the first steps in the retrieval program is to load the sequential file into a table. This would normally be done in the housekeeping routine. Because the sequential file will be considerably smaller than the random file all of its contents can be stored in memory at one time.

```
Sequential            Random
File                  File
                          1    1    2    2    3    3    4    4    5
1...5....             ....5....0....5....0....5....0....5....0....5....0
502790936             502790936SIAVELIS      JOAN      01086405000000
601612754             601612754BABCOCK       RON       02106404850000
410533550             410533550LISSY         GEORGE    03126404500000
414540418             414540418FERGUSON      BETH      04146604300000
110932551             110932551HUMPHREYS     HELEN     01167004250000
418602856             418602856EVERETT       VALENE    05207504100000
110680083             110680083EBNER         KELLY     08258004050000
223355326             223355326WHITE         PETER     09308304500000
422184554             422184554CARROLL       JACI      11018504300000
416892323             416892323MURTHY        GEETHA    03238804200000
```

FIGURE 13–14

As each transaction record is processed the employee number from the transaction record is used as the search argument to search the table of employee numbers built from the sequential file. When searching the table, employee number 414540418 will be found on row four of the table. This row number will be stored in a hold area and used as the record number to retrieve the fourth (and matching) record from the random file. BASIC will use the file location on disk and record size to find the fourth record. Why didn't we just search the random file? In order to search for a specific value such as employee number (versus a position in a file) we would need the entire random file loaded into memory at one time. There is an assumption here that the random file will be too large to fit into memory all at one time.

Figure 13–15 shows the logic for the creation of a random file in which the range of the key field requires the creation of a sequential file to be used later as an index. Notice that the records are placed in the random file consecutively, rather than using their key field to select their position as in the previous example. This way there is no wasted space. Figure 13–16 is the pseudocode for this file creation.

Figure 13–17 shows the logic for retrieving records from the random file created in Figure 13–15. A loop is used in the HSK routine to read the sequential file containing the employee numbers. As the employee numbers are read they are loaded into a one-dimensional table. Since the table resides in memory the entire list of keys will be available at one time. The first transaction record is also read in the HSK routine. The transaction record contains an employee number and the number of hours worked. When a random file record is read with a matching employee number the pay rate from that record will be used with the hours worked from the transaction record to calculate gross pay.

In the PROCESS routine the employee number from the transaction record is used as the search argument and the table is searched for a matching employee number. If a matching number is found the subscript used in the search is saved and the search is ended. If no matching number is found an error message is printed. Since the subscript was saved at the point a match was found, it can now be used as the record number in the read statement for the random file. The read statement for a random file specifies which file is being read and which record number we want from that file. Once the random file record is read its contents are available to use in the gross pay calculation. Figure 13–18 is the pseudocode for the random file retrieval.

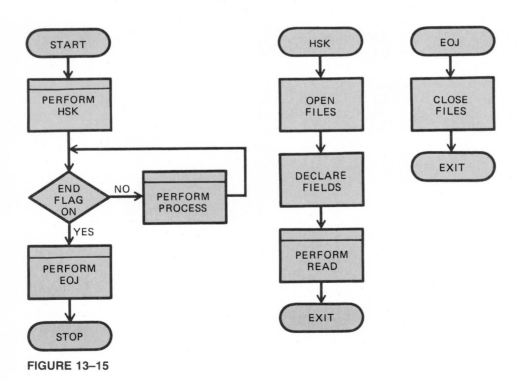

FIGURE 13–15

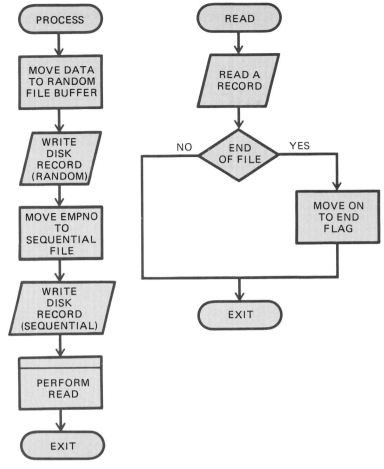

FIGURE 13–15 (continued)

MAINLINE LOGIC

    PERFORM hsk routine
    PERFORM process routine until end flag = on
    PERFORM eoj
    STOP

HSK ROUTINE

    OPEN files
    DECLARE fields
    PERFORM read routine

PROCESS ROUTINE

    MOVE sequential data to random file buffer
    WRITE disk record (random)
    MOVE empno to sequential file record
    WRITE disk record (sequential)
    PERFORM read routine

EOJ ROUTINE

    CLOSE files

READ ROUTINE

    READ a record (sequential)
        AT END of file
            MOVE on to end flag

FIGURE 13–16

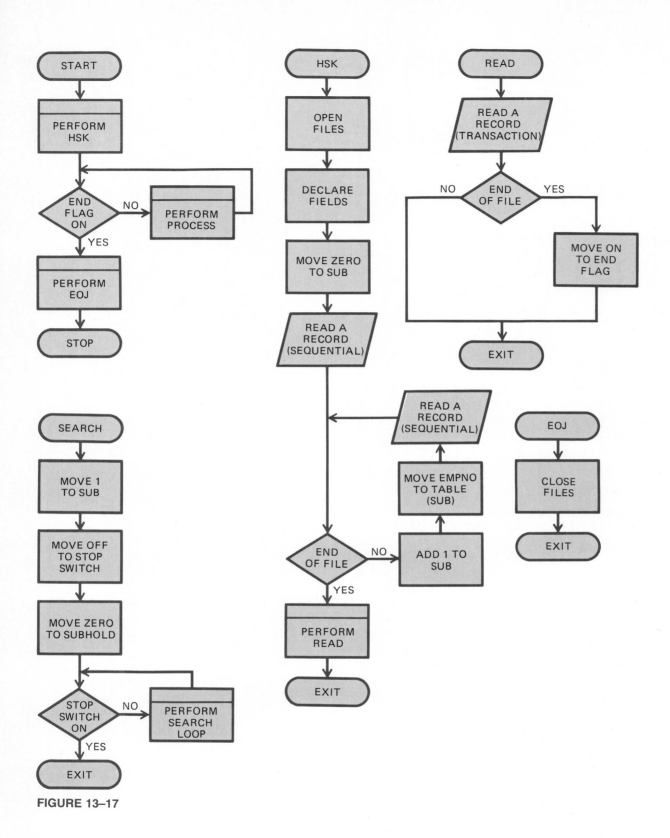

FIGURE 13–17

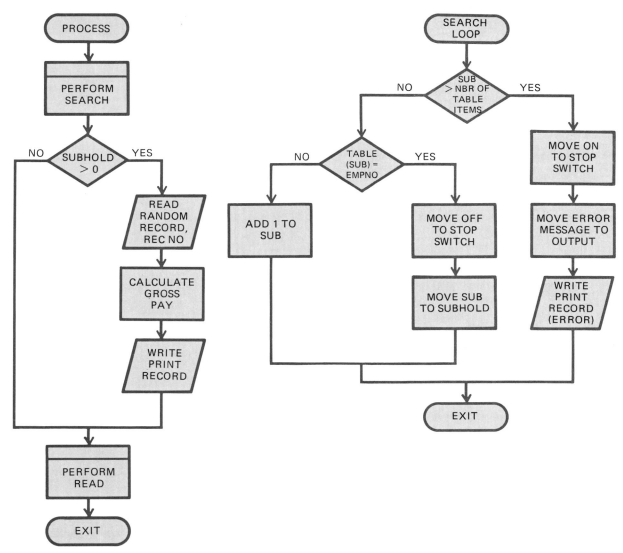

FIGURE 13–17 (continued)

MAINLINE LOGIC

    PERFORM hsk routine
    PERFORM process routine until end flag = on
    PERFORM eoj routine
    STOP

HSK ROUTINE

    OPEN files
    DECLARE fields
    MOVE zero to subscript
    READ a record (sequential file of employee numbers)
    DO WHILE not end of file
        ADD 1 to subscript
        MOVE employee number to table (subscript)
        READ a record (sequential file of employee numbers)
    ENDDO
    PERFORM read routine

FIGURE 13–18

PROCESS ROUTINE

```
PERFORM search routine
IF subhold > zero
        READ random file record
        CALCULATE gross pay
        WRITE print record
ENDIF
PERFORM read
```

EOJ ROUTINE

```
CLOSE files
```

SEARCH ROUTINE

```
MOVE 1 to subscript
MOVE off to stop switch
MOVE zero to subhold
DO WHILE stop switch = off
        PERFORM search loop routine
ENDDO
```

SEARCH LOOP ROUTINE

```
IF subscript > number of table items
        MOVE on to stop switch
        MOVE error message to output
        WRITE print record (error)
ELSE
        IF table (subscript) = employee number
                MOVE on to stop switch
                MOVE subscript to subhold
        ELSE
                ADD 1 to sub
        ENDIF
ENDIF
```

READ ROUTINE

```
READ a record (transaction)
        AT END of file
                MOVE on to end flag
```

FIGURE 13–18 (continued)

DATA BASES

Current data processing practices often consolidate what once would have been a group of files to form a data base. Software is available for a data-base system to 'manage' it. The routines to locate, extract, match, and update are a part of this data-base management system. This saves the programmer a number of the logic steps that would otherwise be necessary. Each data base management system has its own set of commands to allow adds, changes and deletes to the data base.

CHAPTER VOCABULARY

Access	Indexed file	Random access
File creation	Invalid key	Record number
File retrieval	Key field	Sequential
File updating	Nonsequential	

REVIEW QUESTIONS

MATCHING

A. magnetic disk
B. magnetic tape
C. key field

D. index
E. indexed file
F. sequential

_____ 1. A field in a record (unique to that record) used to access the record.
_____ 2. An access method whose records are available in a sequential or nonsequential manner.
_____ 3. A medium suitable only for sequential processing.
_____ 4. Used to locate records on an indexed file.
_____ 5. The most common medium for nonsequential processing.
_____ 6. The fastest access method per record read.

TRUE/FALSE

T F 1. The flowcharting for nonsequential files is more difficult than that for sequential processing.
T F 2. Sequential processing is practical only when 90 to 100 percent of the records in a file are needed.
T F 3. Sequential processing is the fastest method per record processed.
T F 4. Magnetic tape may be used only for sequential file.
T F 5. An indexed file is created by performing a randomizing routine on the key field.
T F 6. On-line real-time systems rely mainly on sequential files.
T F 7. An indexed file is normally created or loaded with the records in sequence by a key field.
T F 8. When an indexed file is updated, all transactions are read but only the master records needed are read.

EXERCISES

1. Flowchart a routine to check on the availability of an inventory item in a sales office.
2. Flowchart a routine to print transcripts for students who have requested them during the previous 24 hours.
3. Flowchart a routine to update a payroll master file.
4. Flowchart a routine to print a student's schedule. You will need more than one master file to do this. Identify the files you will need and the general type of data they will contain.
5. Flowchart a routine to answer customer inquiries about their account balances.

DISCUSSION QUESTIONS

1. What on-line real-time systems are you familiar with that must rely on a nonsequential access method?
2. Is there something in your job that could be made more efficient if it were handled with an on-line real-time system?
3. What are some ways to reduce the range of numbers when a smaller set of numbers is needed as the key field?

PROJECTS

Project 1

Flowchart a routine to register a student for a group of classes. Two master files exist for this purpose. The student master has 500 characters of general information for each student followed by 0–70 elements of a table. Each element of the table can represent a course enrolled for by the student. A counter is kept in the general information portion of the record to count the number of courses enrolled for so far.

The course master has 100 characters of general information about a course followed by 0–150 elements of a table. Each element of the table can contain the social security number of a student who enrolls for the course. A counter is kept in the general information portion of the record to count the number of students enrolled for the course so far.

Project 2

Flowchart the logic to update a random file which has been created using BASIC on a microcomputer. The key field is the employee number. The employee numbers range from 1 to 100 and there are currently 75 employees. Fields in the random file are:

ACTIVE FLAG
DIVISION
DEPARTMENT
EMPLOYEE NUMBER
NAME
ADDRESS
CITY
STATE
ZIP
NUMBER OF DEPENDENTS (STATE)
NUMBER OF DEPENDENTS (FEDERAL)
RATE OF PAY

Include in the logic any steps necessary to add, change, or delete a record based on data from a transaction file.

SYSTEMS FLOWCHARTING

14

OBJECTIVES

As a result of studying this chapter the student should be able to perform the following activities:

1. Identify the system flowcharting symbols and be able to use the proper one in a system flowchart.
2. Describe what file maintenance is in terms of the file updating process.
3. Describe the system flowcharting process and show where programs such as updates, edits, extracts, listings, and sorts fit into an overall system flowchart.
4. Draw system flowcharts for a file-updating process all the way from source documents to an updated file.

INTRODUCTION

As mentioned earlier, systems flowcharting is used to show the flow of data through a system. The logic of any given program within a system is not shown in a systems flowchart. Like program flowcharts, systems flowcharts have their own set of symbols.

SYSTEMS FLOWCHARTING SYMBOLS

Punched Card Symbol

This symbol represents an input/output function in which cards are used as the medium. It represents all types of cards (mark sense, stub, optical character recognition and so on). It also includes both card decks and card files. The data which is recorded in these cards may be recorded in the form of punched holes, magnetically encoded symbols, or characters which can be read by optical character recognition devices. Two variations on this symbol, which may be used to specifically represent card decks and card files, are shown below.

Punched Card Deck

This symbol represents a deck of cards. The cards are not necessarily related to each other. Additional cards may be depicted, each card representing a single card or group of cards (see Figure 14–1). The cards can be labeled to represent each component of the deck.

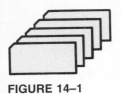

FIGURE 14–1

File of Cards

This symbol is used to depict a group of related cards. Since a file is a group of related records, this symbol is used to represent related card records comprising a file.

On-Line Storage Symbol

This is a general symbol for an input/output function using any type of on-line storage. It can represent magnetic tape, disk, or drum storage.

Magnetic Tape Symbol

This symbol is used when you wish to show that the input or output is on magnetic tape.

Punched Tape Symbol

This symbol shows that you are using punched tape as an input or output medium.

Magnetic Drum Symbol

This symbol indicates that the input or output medium being used is a magnetic drum.

Magnetic Disk Symbol

This symbol shows that the input or output medium is magnetic disk. If more than one file resides on a single disk, the names of the files being used are sometimes placed between the bands of the symbol (Figure 14–2).

FIGURE 14–2

Core Symbol

This symbol represents an input/output function in which the medium is magnetic core.

Document Symbol

This symbol represents either an input or an output function where the medium is a document. It is generally used to represent a source document or an output listing.

Manual Input Symbol

This symbol represents an input function in which the data is entered manually at the time of processing. An example would be input through a console typewriter.

Display Symbol

This symbol represents an output function in which the information is displayed for human use at the time of processing. Examples would be video devices, console printers, and plotters.

Communication Link Symbol

This symbol represents a situation where information is being transmitted by a telecommunication link, such as telephone, telegraph, or satellite microwave transmission.

Off-Line Storage Symbol

This symbol represents the function of storing information off line regardless of the medium on which the information is recorded. Off-line storage is not currently accessible by the computer. It could range from reports filed in a folder to cards on a shelf to a disk file in a safe.

Preparation Symbol

This symbol represents modifications of an instruction or a group of instructions which change the program itself.

Manual Operation Symbol

This symbol represents an off-line operation performed at the speed of a human being using no mechanical aid. This could include many things, such as physically sorting or altering parameter cards or making out a report for a program that just ended abnormally.

Auxiliary Operation Symbol

This symbol represents an off-line operation performed on equipment not under the control of the central processing unit. A typical example would be putting cards or optically read input on a tape or disk from a stand-alone device.

Merge Symbol

This symbol represents the combining of two or more sets of items into one set. Among other things it can be used to show the combining of a master and a transaction file or two transaction files.

Extract Symbol

This symbol represents the removal of one or more specific sets of data items from a single larger set of items. The extract is based on a set of criteria, which could be similar to those we used in Chapter 5.

Sort Symbol

This symbol represents the arranging of a set of items into a particular sequence. This operation is used to order a file on some field or series of fields in preparation for using it in a program.

Collate Symbol

This symbol represents merging with extracting. It is the formation of two or more sets of items from two or more other sets.

Process Symbol

Although this symbol was presented in Chapter 3 as a part of program flowcharting, it is also used in system flowcharting, where it represents an entire program, rather than a single instruction or group of instructions.

In addition to these symbols the flowlines used for program flowcharts (Chapter 3) are used in the same manner for system flowcharts.

A PAYROLL SYSTEM

In order to demonstrate the use of systems flowcharting symbols a payroll system will be developed. An employee master file is the major file used in a payroll system. This will be represented as an on-line file. The first flowchart shows the steps necessary to maintain or update the employee master file. The employee master file will then be used on a periodic basis to produce the output of a payroll system, paychecks, payroll register, voluntary deduction reports, state and federal tax reports, W2s, and so on. Two additional system flowcharts have been developed to show the production of these items, one for each payroll period and one for quarterly and yearly reporting. These three flowcharts will be presented for the payroll system along with a step-by-step explanation of the symbols used. The first step in the process is the update system flowchart shown in Figure 14–3.

PERSONNEL AND PAYROLL UPDATES

This symbol represents the source documents that contain the data we use to maintain the employee master file. These documents could originate in either the personnel or payroll department. They represent changes such as new hires, terminations, name changes, address changes, telephone number changes, voluntary deduction changes, and pay rate changes. These updates can also include hours worked, which would be entered prior to a payroll run.

These changes to the employee master file are entered through a terminal as input to the file-update program. The process box used in a system flowchart represents an entire program. The payroll-update program is designed to handle any necessary changes to the employee master file. Based on input received through the terminal, the appropriate employee record is read. If the record read is to be deleted, it is either flagged for deletion or physically deleted, depending

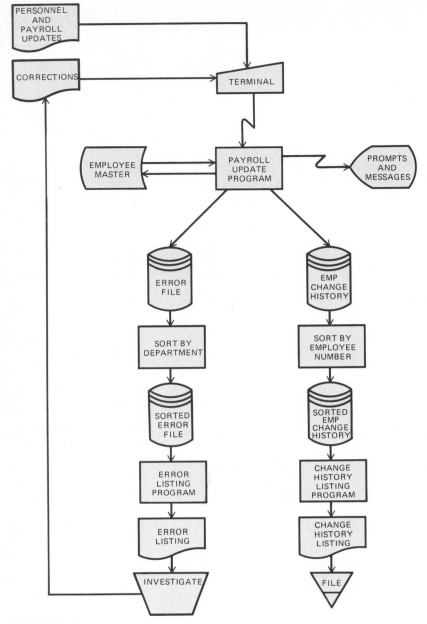

FIGURE 14–3

on the access method in use. If the input is for a new hire, an attempt may be made (again, depending on the file structure in use) to read the record first to insure that it is not already on file. If the record is not on file, it will be added to the file. If the terminal input is data needed to change an existing record, then the appropriate record is read, changed, and rewritten.

Notice that the employee master file is used as both input and output for the update program. Each time the update program is run, the employee master file is brought to current status. This updating process may be on a daily, weekly, or monthly basis. There is usually a cutoff day and time for each pay period, after which no more changes will be accepted by the departments doing the data entry. This same process may be used to enter data from time sheets that provide data on hours worked and account numbers to be charged for that work. The data entry process will be scheduled prior to each payroll run.

As the update program runs, aids for inputting changes are displayed on the screen. These aids point out choices (menus), provide input editing as the data is entered, and display error messages.

If, during the update process, any errors of a serious nature occur which cannot be corrected as a part of data entry, these errors are written to a separate file. If no errors exist, then no records will be placed in this output file.

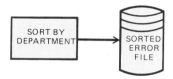

Assuming that errors requiring investigation and correction have been written to the error file, the error file is sorted by departments. This will allow a separation of errors by department.

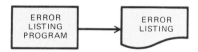

A control-break program is then used to produce an error report. After the report is printed, it is distributed to the appropriate departments.

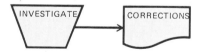

Each department is responsible for investigating the errors listed on its section of the report. The department is also responsible for submitting a source document to initiate the necessary correction. The source documents containing corrections are entered through the terminal and follow the same path as before. This process will be repeated until there are no errors to write to the error file or until the cutoff for the corrections has been reached.

At the same time the error file is being created (if errors exist), an employee history file is created. This file contains all alterations (adds, changes, and deletes) that are made to the employee master file. If a question were to arise as to when some alteration had been made to the employee master file, this alteration could be traced through the use of this history file.

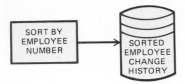

After all errors have been corrected and the current updated file is considered correct, the employee history file is sorted by employee number and used as input to a history listing program.

The listing program produces a printout which is the "hard copy" record of all alterations to the employee master file. Since the file was sorted on employee number, all alterations for one employee will be grouped together for the current pay period.

The historical listing document is placed in storage and remains there for a period which is determined by the records-retention policy of the company.

RUNNING THE PAYROLL

Figure 14–4 is the system flowchart for the periodic running of the payroll. Let us examine step-by-step the flow within the system.

The employee master file is the major file used in the payroll program. It is used as both input and output for the program. Records are read from the employee master, payroll calculations are made, and new data resulting from those calculations is written back to the master file. Updating of totals does not take place until the final run, after all the errors in the data have been corrected. The new data written back to the file includes current earnings as well as updated quarterly and yearly totals.

The payroll program also produces a number of other disk files for use in reporting and maintaining a payroll history. Since most of these files are produced with each payroll run, any that were created while the payroll data still had errors in it are recreated with the next running of the program.

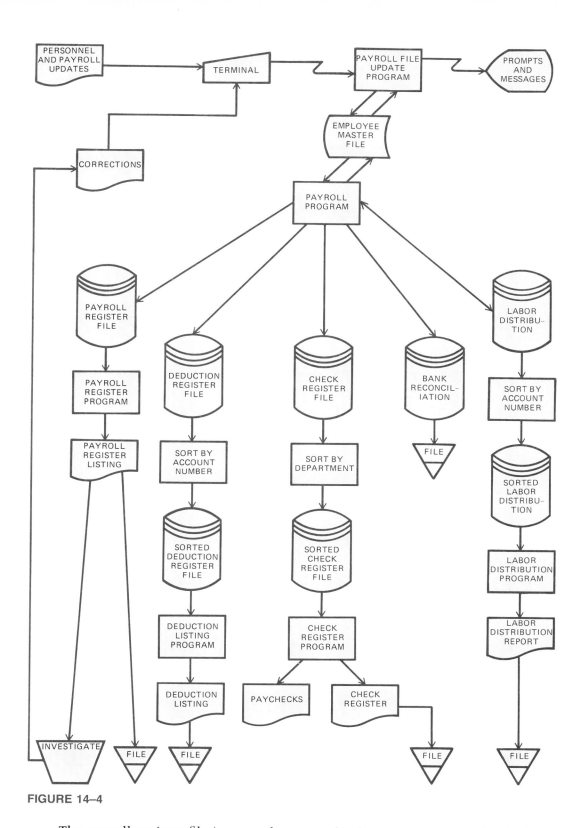

FIGURE 14–4

The payroll register file is created as a result of the current payroll calculations. The data from the payroll register file is used in a program which foots and crossfoots all fields and records to insure that no errors are present in the payroll.

```
PAYROLL
REGISTER
PROGRAM
```

This program produces a listing which contains all the detail involved in the current payroll. Any unusual conditions are flagged so that they can be reviewed.

The listing that is produced by this program is referred to as payroll register. It is reviewed before approval is given for the final payroll run.

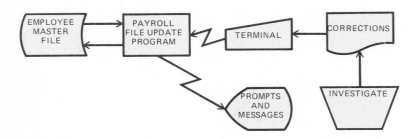

If there are any discrepancies on the payroll register, they must be corrected before the payroll run can continue. The update program can be used for this purpose. A document is prepared reflecting the corrections necessary. The contents of this document are entered through a terminal to the payroll-update program.

In addition to producing the payroll register, which leads into a possible error-correcting routine, the payroll program also produces a deduction-register file. All deductions are written on this file. They carry with them data necessary to identify whose pay they are a deduction from and to whom the deduction is to be forwarded.

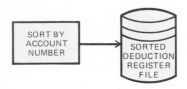

These deductions are sorted by employee number within the deduction account. This sort allows us to use the file as input to a control-break program which is capable of making separate lists for the various deductions. Examples would be credit union, employee purchase, health insurance, dental insurance, pension funds, and union dues.

After the file has been sorted, the report is produced. Since the report program has a control break on deduction type, each organization's portion of the report will start on a new page, with the page numbers starting at 1.

Each segment of this report is sent, along with a check to cover the amounts specified, to the proper recipient. Copies are also filed within the company preparing the report.

A check register file can be created to carry only the data pertinent to the paychecks. This file is not necessarily as complete as the payroll register file.

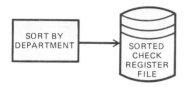

This check register file can be sorted in any order that will make distribution of paychecks easier. Alphabetical within department within division would be one possible method if the checks were to be disbursed within each department.

The check register program then utilizes the sorted check register file to produce two outputs, a check register and the paychecks. The check-register report is filed and the paychecks are disbursed. A carbon of the check may be retained in the files.

A fourth disk file can be created for purposes of bank reconciliation. This file would contain only check numbers, employee numbers, and amounts. This file would be used as checks were returned from the bank to reconcile the payroll bank account.

A fifth disk file is created on the final payroll run. Its purpose is to keep track of the hours allocated to various accounts. In a manufacturing environment this file may be used to keep track of the hours by project. This file is not created until the final run because it is used as both input and output to the payroll program. The hours for a particular account or project can be kept on both a current and to-date basis. If we are to add to hours for accounts or projects in the file, we want to do this only once, when we are sure the payroll is ready for the final run.

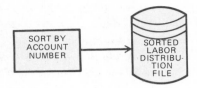

This labor distribution file is then sorted by account or project number. After being sorted it becomes input to the labor distribution program.

The labor distribution program produces a report by account number of the labor used by the company. The account numbers may represent departments, specific products, research projects, and the like.

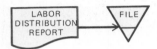

The labor distribution report is distributed based on the account numbers and filed by the appropriate departments.

QUARTERLY AND YEARLY REPORTING

The third system flowchart covers the periodic reporting required primarily by governmental agencies. This flowchart is shown in Figure 14–5.

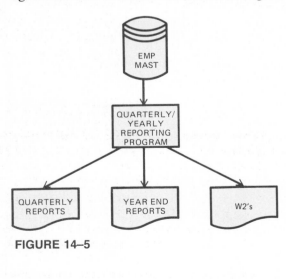

FIGURE 14–5

EMPLOYEE
MASTER
FILE

The employee master file is used as input to produce the periodic reporting required for tax purposes. Notice in this system flowchart that the employee master file is used as input only.

PERIODIC
REPORTING
PROGRAM

The same program is used for quarterly and yearly reporting. A parameter record can be incorporated in the programming to indicate which period the reports are for or the type of report or both.

 QUARTERLY TAX REPORTS

 YEARLY TAX REPORTS

W2's

Three separate reports can be produced by the quarterly/yearly reporting program: quarterly tax reports, year-end tax reports, and W2s.

CHAPTER VOCABULARY

Auxiliary operation
Collate symbol
Communications link
Core
Display
Document
Extract symbol
Magnetic disk

Magnetic drum
Magnetic tape
Manual input
Manual operation
Merge symbol
Menu
Off-line storage
On-line storage

Preparation
Process symbol
Punched card
Punched card deck
Punched card file
Punched tape
Sort symbol
Systems flowchart symbols

REVIEW QUESTIONS

MATCHING

_____ 1. Sort symbol.
_____ 2. Card file symbol.
_____ 3. Communication link symbol.
_____ 4. Magnetic disk symbol.
_____ 5. Merge symbol.
_____ 6. Document symbol.
_____ 7. Punched card deck symbol.
_____ 8. Manual input symbol.
_____ 9. Collate symbol.
_____ 10. Punched tape symbol.
_____ 11. Display symbol.
_____ 12. Manual operation symbol.
_____ 13. Punched card symbol.
_____ 14. Auxiliary operation symbol.
_____ 15. Extract symbol.
_____ 16. On-line storage symbol.
_____ 17. Magnetic drum symbol.
_____ 18. Off-line storage symbol.
_____ 19. Magnetic tape symbol.

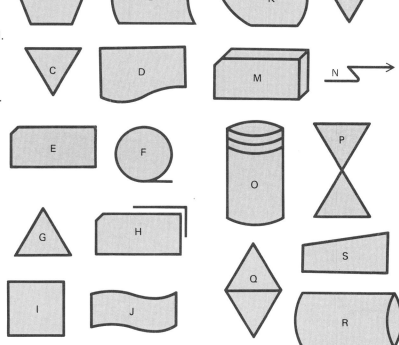

TRUE/FALSE

T F **1.** System flowcharts depict the logic of the programs in a system.

T F **2.** The punched card symbol can be used to represent mark sense cards.

T F **3.** Multiple files may be shown on the disk symbol.

T F **4.** Off-line storage could be used for any media.

T F **5.** Flowlines are not needed in system flowcharting.

T F **6.** Sequential file updating requires that the transaction items be the same sequence as the master file.

EXERCISES

1. Draw a system flowchart of a program that has a card file and magnetic tape file as inputs and a disk file and a printed report as outputs.

2. Draw a system flowchart for the following activities: Keypunch and verify the data from personnel information sheets. Sort the cards produced on employee number.

3. Draw a generalized flowchart for updating a master file. Include the handling of both master and transaction files.

DISCUSSION QUESTIONS

1. Discuss the uses and values of system flowcharting.

2. Could the principles of system flowcharting be applied to nonprogramming tasks?

3. Discuss the need for master file updating and how often it needs to be done.

4. What types of errors might be found in the input-edit and file-updating programs that would appear on the error reports?

ALTERNATIVE CHARTING METHODS

15

OBJECTIVES

As a result of studying this chapter the student should be able to perform the following activities:

1. Name the parts of a decision table.
2. Describe the advantages of decision tables.
3. Describe the disadvantages of decision tables.
4. Differentiate between limited-entry, extended-entry, and mixed-entry tables.
5. Construct a decision table for a situation with which the student is familiar.
6. Describe the use of Nassi-Schneiderman and hierarchy charts.
7. Describe the advantages of Nassi-Schneiderman charts.
8. Describe the disadvantages of Nassi-Schneiderman charts.
9. Construct a Nassi-Schneiderman chart for a situation with which the student is familiar.
10. Describe the advantages of hierarchy charts.
11. Describe the disadvantages of hierarchy charts.
12. Construct a hierarchy chart for a situation with which the student is familiar.

INTRODUCTION

Up to this point the text has concentrated on flowcharts and pseudocode. There are, however, other methods of depicting the logic steps in the solution to a problem. These methods include such items as decision tables, Nassi-Schneiderman charts, and hierarchy charts. These methods will be explored individually and then applied to a single problem.

DECISION TABLES

Decision tables are planning tools used in ways similar to flowcharts. They provide a concise format for examining a situation with many decision steps. Their compact nature makes them an excellent planning and documentation tool but also limits them. Each individual decision table usually deals with the logical decisions and actions present in a situation; however, it does not show the overall flow of the logic that a flowchart shows.

LIMITED-ENTRY TABLES

In order to build a decision table we first need a problem to solve. Given a college setting, an ongoing problem seems to be registration. In particular, people are often disappointed by the lack of openings in classes they wish to take. The circumstances we will describe cover the registration process as it is currently handled at a typical college. It reflects the timing of the registration process. For our first example we will use what is known as a limited entry table—a table in which each condition has only two possibilities, Yes or No (True or False).

First, let's examine the structure of a decision table. Decision tables are divided into four segments (see Figure 15–1). The two items on the left are referred to as stubs and the two items on the right as entries.

CONDITION STUBS | | CONDITION ENTRIES

ACTION STUBS | | ACTION ENTRIES

FIGURE 15–1

The condition stubs list all the important, usual conditions. It would be nice to say "all the **possible** conditions," but that would be like asking you to describe the universe in 10 words or less and give three examples. Each condition that we can identify is listed on a separate line. We have chosen the conditions shown in Figure 15–2. The fourth condition may seem out of place, but if you watch where the X's fall, you will find that it may well be an overriding factor in the registration process.

TIMING OF REGISTRATION

APPLICATION COMPLETE

FULL–TIME STUDENT

RETURNING STUDENT

PROCRASTINATOR

FIGURE 15–2

The lower or action-stubs section lists all the usual actions that may be taken as a result of the various condition stubs. The actions in our example reflect the time that a student registers for each of the possible combinations of conditions (see Figure 15–3).

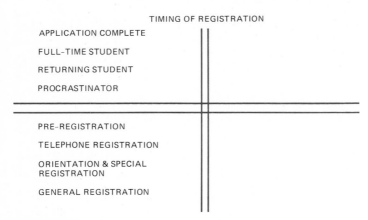

TIMING OF REGISTRATION

APPLICATION COMPLETE

FULL-TIME STUDENT

RETURNING STUDENT

PROCRASTINATOR

PRE-REGISTRATION

TELEPHONE REGISTRATION

ORIENTATION & SPECIAL REGISTRATION

GENERAL REGISTRATION

FIGURE 15–3

Once you have formulated the conditions and the actions possible based on those conditions, it is time to start systematically examining the results of the possible combinations of conditions.

We do this in our limited-entry table starting in the first column or our condition entry with all Ys and Ns (**Y means yes and N means no**).

In many tables one specified condition may make other listed conditions not feasible. In this case the square is left blank, or a hyphen is inserted. In our example, as long as an application has been completed we are able to fill out all the other squares (see Figure 15–4). Notice in particular the systematic way the Ys and Ns are grouped. This is not always possible, but proceeding in this manner will assure that you have not overlooked any possibilities.

TIMING OF REGISTRATION

APPLICATION COMPLETE	Y	Y	Y	Y	Y	Y	Y	Y	N
FULL-TIME STUDENT	Y	Y	Y	Y	N	N	N	N	
RETURNING STUDENT	Y	Y	N	N	Y	Y	N	N	
PROCRASTINATOR	Y	N	Y	N	Y	N	Y	N	
PRE-REGISTRATION									
TELEPHONE REGISTRATION									
ORIENTATION & SPECIAL REGISTRATION									
GENERAL REGISTRATION									

FIGURE 15–4

The remainder of the decision table is shown in Figure 15–5. Our table, as constructed, can deal effectively only with people who have made application. Actions needed for the item with the N and no other entry in the condition entry segment will be covered shortly. The way that the table in Figure 15–5 is constructed it is referred to as a closed entry table. That is, all possible activity is shown within the single table.

TIMING REGISTRATION

APPLICATION COMPLETE	Y	Y	Y	Y	Y	Y	Y	Y	N
FULL-TIME STUDENT	Y	Y	Y	Y	N	N	N	N	
RETURNING STUDENT	Y	Y	N	N	Y	Y	N	N	
PROCRASTINATOR	Y	N	Y	N	Y	N	Y	N	
PRE-REGISTRATION		X				X			
TELEPHONE REGISTRATION								X	
ORIENTATION & SPECIAL REGISTRATION				X					
GENERAL REGISTRATION	X		X		X			X	

FIGURE 15–5

OPEN-END TABLES

Although the table in Figure 15–5 is valid, by being a closed table it has left those persons who have not completed an application out in the cold. There is nothing being done for these individuals. Two things are possible. Either the table could be expanded to allow for this possibility or a separate table can be constructed to handle the situation. For purpose of example, we will refer to a separate table (although the individual steps for handling the situation will not be included). Figure 15–6 is similar to Figure 15–5 except that a reference to TABLE 2 has been added in the action entry segment of the table. This addition points to a separate table where the actions needed for persons who have not filled out an application will be covered.

TIMING OF REGISTRATION

APPLICATION COMPLETE	Y	Y	Y	Y	Y	Y	Y	Y	N
FULL-TIME STUDENT	Y	Y	Y	Y	N	N	N	N	
RETURNING STUDENT	Y	Y	N	N	Y	Y	N	N	
PROCRASTINATOR	Y	N	Y	N	Y	N	Y	N	
PREREGISTRATION		X				X			
TELEPHONE REGISTRATION								X	T A B L E 2
ORIENTATION & SPECIAL REGISTRATION				X					
GENERAL REGISTRATION	X		X		X		X		

FIGURE 15–6

This addition to the table (the reference to TABLE 2) makes the table in Figure 15–6 an open-end table rather than a closed table. Open-end tables have one or more sub-tables which are used to complete all of the necessary steps in the solution to a problem. TABLE 2 referred to in Figure 15–6 would be described elsewhere.

EXTENDED-ENTRY TABLES

It is also possible to have a table which allows entries in the condition-entry area, such as $<$, $>$, $<$ or $>$, with each of these related to a quantity. Such a table is referred to as an extended-entry table. Limited and extended entries are not allowed on the same horizontal line of a table, but they are allowed in the same table on a separate line in the condition-entry portion of the table. If both types of entries appear in one table, it is called a mixed-entry table. Figure 15–7 is an example of an extended-entry table. It represents the grading scale in a course.

GRADING SCALE

POINTS EARNED	> 378	> 336	> 294	> 252	< 252
A	X				
B		X			
C			X		
D				X	
F					X

FIGURE 15–7

In any of these types of decision tables a condition entry together with the related action entry is called a **rule.** For example, the decision table in Figure 15–7 has five rules. One rule is that if the points earned are > 378, the person's grade will be an A. Each rule in a decision table represents one path in a flowchart depicting the same problem.

NASSI-SCHNEIDERMAN CHARTS

Another method used to show the steps in the solution to a problem is a Nassi-Schneiderman chart. These charts utilize rectangles and diagonal lines to represent the various actions which need to be accomplished. The parts of these charts are shown in Figures 15–8 through 15–11.

Sequence

Figure 15–8 shows the equivalent of sequence structure. Each horizontal bar is used to describe a single activity. Sequence activities may involve either a single bar or a series of successive bars. A PERFORM statement refers to a separate chart, where the steps in the process being performed are described.

COMPUTE GROSS = RATE * hours
COMPUTE OVERTIME = OVERTIME HOURS * 1.5
COMPUTE TOTAL PAY = REG PAY + OT PAY
PERFORM TAXES
COMPUTE NET = GROSS − TAXES

CLOSE FILES

FIGURE 15–8

Decision (Two-Way)

The segment of a Nassi-Schneiderman chart shown in Figure 15–9 indicates how the process routine of a typical program would be started. It represents an IF/THEN-ELSE situation similar to a decision structure. There is to be a control break on a change in department, and no more than 50 detail lines are to be printed on a single page. Each decision is represented by diagonals drawn from top corners of the bar to a point at the bottom of the bar or segment of a bar. The condition being tested goes above the diagonals, and the possible outcomes of the decision are written under each diagonal line.

In this example there are two successive decisions. However, it is possible to have only one decision or several decisions, depending on the needs of the problem. When no action takes place on one of the paths, this is indicated by a dash or the word NULL. This situation is illustrated in Figure 15–9, when DEPT = DEPT HOLD and LINE COUNT is not > 49.

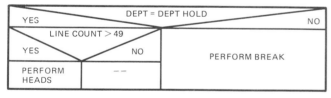

FIGURE 15–9

Multiple-Path Decisions

When decisions have three or more exit paths, the decision is still written above the diagonals. The diagonals meet the bar line offset quite a bit from center to allow for the several outcomes of the decision(s) being made. When the horizontal lines are drawn from the diagonals to the outer edges and vertical lines are drawn downward from the diagonals, you have a series of three (or more) columns produced with a triangle at the top of each column. Each of these triangles at the top of a column represents one of the possible resulting conditions. In Figure 15–10 we are testing a code to see if it is CHANGE, DELETE, or OTHER. The actions to be taken for each resulting condition are then written under that condition. Figure 15–10 is a segment of a chart for a sequential file-updating program. The flowchart was presented in Chapter 12.

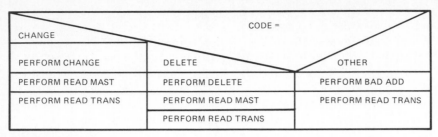

FIGURE 15–10

DO WHILE

The DO WHILE segment in Figure 15–11 represents the process routine for reading and writing the contents of a file. In order to keep this chart simple, no provision was made for any forms overflow. The first record was read in the housekeeping section prior to entering the DO WHILE. Each of the steps written in a bar between the one with **DO WHILE** and the one with **END DO** will continue to be performed as long as the condition specified on the DO WHILE line is true.

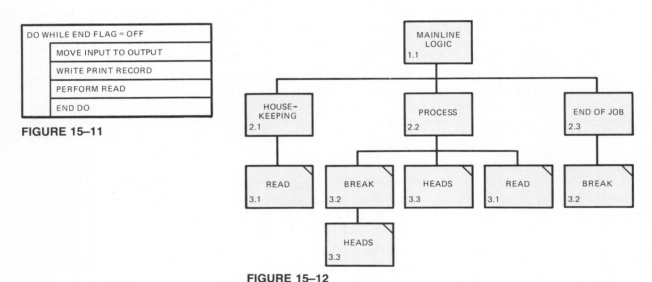

FIGURE 15–11

FIGURE 15–12

HIERARCHY CHARTS

The last method of showing the logic for a problem that will be presented is hierarchy charts. Such a chart is shown in Figure 15–12. These charts somewhat resemble the typical organizational chart for a company. All the steps are shown in rectangles, with subordinate relationships going down the chart. Although the general concepts of hierarchy charts are relatively consistent, there are almost as many variations as there are companies that utilize them. Figure 15–12 is a general example for a program with one level of control break with totals and final totals.

Each level of the chart, starting with the mainline logic at the top, shows which processing steps are performed within it. That is, the MAINLINE performs the HOUSEKEEPING, PROCESS, and END OF JOB routines while PROCESS performs the BREAK, HEADS, and READ routines. END OF JOB performs only the BREAK routine.

The boxes may or may not be numbered. If they are numbered, then there is a scheme to the numbering process. Our scheme utilizes numbers within the format **n.n.** The **n** to the left of the decimal identifies the level from the top where the routine is first used. Therefore the MAINLINE logic is numbered 1. HOUSEKEEPING, PROCESS, and END OF JOB are 2, and so on down the chart.

The **n** to the right of the decimal indicates whether it is the first, second, third, . . . item on a given level. Thus HOUSEKEEPING is 2.1, PROCESS is 2.2, and END OF JOB is 2.3. This scheme carries on down to the items under HOUSEKEEPING, PROCESS, and END OF JOB. There are exceptions to this in that when a routine is to be used in more than one level on the chart then it carries a number large enough that it is not part of the regular numbering scheme for the chart. Once this number has been assigned it carries that number with it whenever the same routine is used again in the chart. Notice that READ is numbered 3.1 under both HOUSE-KEEPING and PROCESS, BREAK is numbered 3.2 under both PROCESS and END OF JOB, and HEADS is numbered 3.3 under both PROCESS and BREAK.

All of the routines are shown in boxes, however all of the individual steps that are part of each of the routines are not included. This is one of the drawbacks of a hierarchy chart. It is supplemental to some other charting method, such as a flowchart or pseudocode, since it does not give the detailed description of the activities performed within a routine. A hierarchy chart is a good summary of the routines being performed and where they are performed, but it has its limitations due to the lack of detail.

ALTERNATE CHARTING METHODS—EXAMPLE 1

Now let's draw a decision table, a Nassi-Schneiderman chart, and a hierarchy chart for two programming problems. The first program will produce a departmentalized listing of the female personnel in a company. Totals will be produced for the number of dependents for each department and for the entire company. No more than 50 detail lines will be printed on a single page with provision being made for forms overflow. The pages are to be sequentially numbered. The decision table for this program is shown in Figure 15–13.

DECISION TABLE

HSK ROUTINE	Y	—	—	—	—	—
PROCESS ROUTINE	—	Y	Y	Y	Y	—
EOJ ROUTINE	—	—	—	—	—	Y
FEMALE	—	Y	Y	Y	N	—
LINE COUNT > 49	—	—	Y	N	—	—
NEW DEPT	—	Y	N	N	—	—
OPEN FILES	X					
ZERO LINE COUNT	X	X	X			
ZERO PAGE COUNT	X					
ZERO DEPT HOLD	X					
READ	X	X	X	X	X	
ADD DEPS TO DEPT TOTAL		X	X	X		
WRITE DETAIL LINE		X	X	X		
ADD TO LINE COUNT		X	X	X		
PRINT DEPT TOTALS		X				X
ROLL DEPT TO FINAL TOTAL		X				X
ZERO DEPT TOTAL		X				X
UPDATE HOLD		X				X
ADD TO PAGE COUNT		X	X			
PRINT HEADS		X	X			
PRINT FINAL TOTALS						X
CLOSE FILES						X

FIGURE 15–13

When many actions are being performed, it may be beneficial to replace the Xs in the action entry segment of the table with numbers. When this is done, the action entries in each column are numbered in the sequence in which they are to be performed. Remember that the condition entries together with the action entries in each column are called a rule.

Figure 15–14 is the Nassi-Schneiderman chart for the same problem. Each step in Figure 15–14 has been written in the sequence in which it was needed. The chart can be condensed by showing a perform for those items such as break and heads and producing a separate chart for the performed routines. The method used is a matter of personal preference or company policy.

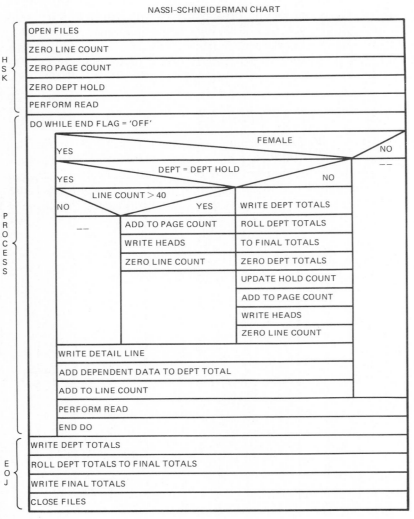

NASSI-SCHNEIDERMAN CHART

FIGURE 15–14

HIERARCHY CHART

As you can see in Figure 15–15, there is less detail in the hierarchy chart than in the decision table or the Nassi-Schneiderman chart. The hierarchy chart does, however, give an overall picture of which routines are performed and where they are performed.

ALTERNATE CHARTING METHODS—EXAMPLE 2

The second problem to be illustrated is the one that was presented in Chapter 12. It is the logic needed for a sequential file-update program for a situation where there is only one transaction record for any given master record. The decision chart for the problem is shown in Figure 15–

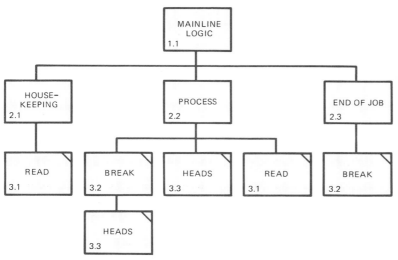

FIGURE 15–15

DECISION TABLE

	1	2	3	4	5	6	7	8	9	10
HSK ROUTINE	Y	Y	Y							
PROCESS ROUTINE				Y	Y	Y	Y	Y	Y	
EOJ ROUTINE										Y
MAST > TRANS				Y	Y					
MAST = TRANS						Y	Y	Y		
MAST < TRANS									Y	
CHANGE RECORD						Y		N		
DELETE RECORD							Y	N		
ADD RECORD				Y	N					
END MAST ON	Y	N	N							
END TRANS ON		Y	N							
OPEN FILES	X	X	X							
MOVE OFF TO END FLAG	X	X	X							
MOVE OFF TO END MAST	X	X	X							
MOVE OFF TO END TRANS	X	X	X							
MOVE ZERO TO ALL COUNTERS	X	X	X							
PERFORM READ MAST	X	X	X			X	X		X	
PERFORM READ TRANS		X	X	X	X	X	X	X		
PERFORM CHANGE						X				
PERFORM DELETE							X			
PERFORM ADD				X						
PERFORM BAD EQUAL								X		
PERFORM BAD ADD					X					
PERFORM COPY									X	
PERFORM NO MAST	X									
PERFORM NO TRANS		X								
MOVE COUNTERS TO PRINT										X
PRINT TOTALS										X
CLOSE FILES										X

FIGURE 15–16

16. The Nassi-Schneiderman chart is found in Figure 15–17 and the hierarchy chart is found in Figure 15–18.

The logic for each of the individual routines has not been included in order to reduce the size of the chart. The individual steps in the performed routines could either be included as individual lines in the action stub section of the chart or shown separately as a set of action stubs and entries for the given set of conditions.

One of the drawbacks of the Nassi-Schneiderman charts is that if there are complex decision structures to be accomplished the jumping from chart to chart to find the needed logic can be

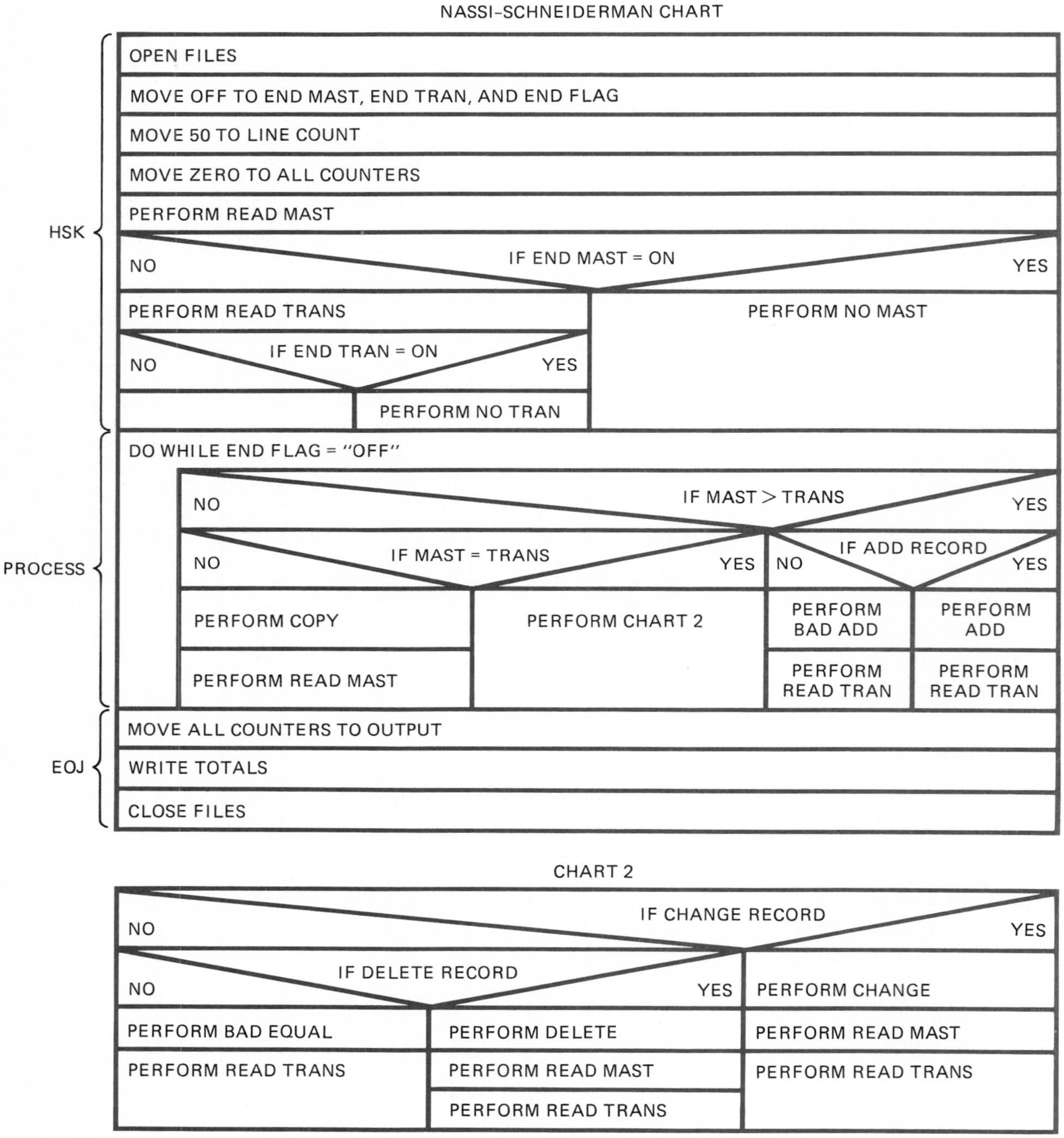

NASSI-SCHNEIDERMAN CHART

CHART 2

FIGURE 15–17

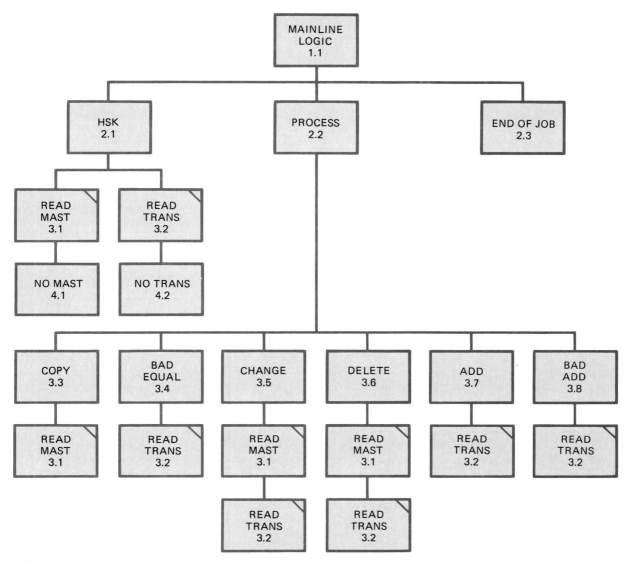

FIGURE 15–18

cumbersome. In the above chart it was necessary to go to the second chart to see what was needed if the master was equal in value to the transaction.

The charting methods in this chapter may be used independently (except hierarchy charts) or in combination with flowcharts and pseudocode. Your selection of method(s) is based on a decision of how much detail you need to show and how you want to describe the flow of the logic. A variety of methods have been presented to give you an opportunity to choose the one most suited to your needs.

CHAPTER VOCABULARY

Action entries
Action stubs
Closed table
Condition entries
Condition stubs

Decision table
Extended-entry table
Hierarchy chart
Limited-entry table
Mixed-entry table

Nassi-Schneiderman chart
Open-end table
Rule

REVIEW QUESTIONS

MATCHING

A. Condition stub
B. Hierarchy chart
C. Action stub
D. Condition entry

E. Action entry
F. Nassi-Schneiderman chart
G. Limited entry
H. Extended entry

_____ **1.** The area where the specific status for each condition is specified.
_____ **2.** A list of the conditions which need to be considered.
_____ **3.** A table in which only yes or no, true or false, is allowed in the condition entries.
_____ **4.** A charting form which utilizes rectangles and connecting lines that show subordinate relationships.
_____ **5.** A list of actions that may be taken.
_____ **6.** A table in which $<$ or $>$ may be used.
_____ **7.** The area where an action is identified for each combination of conditions.
_____ **8.** A charting form which utilizes bars and diagonals.

TRUE/FALSE

T F **1.** Each decision table is divided into four sections.
T F **2.** The left side of the decision table contains all the conditions and the right side contains all the actions.
T F **3.** Limited-entry tables use yes or no condition entries, while extended-entry tables use true and false.
T F **4.** If a condition makes other conditions infeasible, a blank or hyphen may be used to indicate this situation.
T F **5.** An open-end table allows us to refer to another table for additional areas of decisions.
T F **6.** Yes, no, $<$, and $>$ are all permissible on a single horizontal line of a decision table.
T F **7.** Hierarchy charts have different methods for showing each of the structures from flowcharting.
T F **8.** Nassi-Schneiderman charts cannot be used to represent DO WHILE structures.
T F **9.** Nassi-Schneiderman charts are limited to decisions with either two or three outcomes.
T F **10.** A hierarchy chart shows much more detail than a decision table.

EXERCISES

1. Draw a decision table to determine if you should attend a movie. Consider homework, money, and the appeal of the movie.
2. Draw a decision table to aid in the granting of credit by a retail establishment. Set your own conditions.
3. Draw a decision table to aid you in buying a house. Set your own conditions.
4. Draw a Nassi-Schneiderman chart and a decision table for a complete sequential file-update program.
5. Draw a hierarchy chart for a sequential file-update program.

DISCUSSION QUESTIONS

1. What are the advantages of decision tables, Nassi-Schneiderman charts, hierarchy charts, and flowcharting?
2. What are the disadvantages of decision tables, Nassi-Schneiderman charts, hierarchy charts, and flowcharting?
3. What are some uses for decision tables, Nassi-Schneiderman charts, and hierarchy charts outside the area of computer programming?

PROJECTS

Project 1

Given the following information prepare a decision table, Nassi-Schneiderman chart and a hierarchy chart for the following problem:

INPUT

STUDENT MASTER FILE

01–09	Student Identification Number
10–29	Student Name

30–50	Student Address
51–65	Student City
66–67	Student State
68–68	Student Residency Code
69–69	Student Sex Code
70–75	Student Date of Birth
76–78	Student Major Area Of Study Code
79–79	Student Enrollment Status Code
80–89	Student Work Phone Number
90–99	Student Home Phone Number

PROCESSING

The student file is in sequence by major area of study code. Produce a list by area of study of the students with majors of engineering (122) or chemistry (224) who are currently enrolled (2) and live within the district (1). Control breaks should be taken on major area of study.

OUTPUT

A printed listing of the students meeting the above criteria should include provisions for the following items:

1. Use 132 print positions per line.
2. Double-space the output.
3. Appropriate page and column headings should be provided.
4. Each new area of study should start on a new page.
5. Page numbers should be reset for each new area of study.
6. All input fields should be included on the output.
7. Use a line count of 50 lines per page.

Project 2

Given the following information prepare a decision table, Nassi-Schneiderman chart, and hierarchy chart for the following problem:

INPUT

MASTER INVENTORY FILE

01–02	Inventory Record Code
	Inventory Stock Number
03–03	Inventory Type
04–05	Inventory Class
06–09	Inventory Part
10–29	Inventory Description
30–30	Inventory Location Code
31–34	Inventory Quantity on Hand
35–38	Inventory Quantity on Order
39–42	Inventory Reorder Level
43–43	Inventory Unit Size Code
44–48	Inventory Unit Price (5.2)
49–49	Inventory Discount Code
50–55	Inventory Annual Usage (Units)
56–58	Inventory Vendor Code
	Inventory Transportation Code
59–59	Inventory Catagory
60–60	Inventory Distance

PROCESSING

List the contents of the inventory file and compute the following items. Compute the value of the quantity on order, quantity on hand and necessary reorder quantity (if reordering is necessary). Reordering is necessary if the quantity on order plus the quantity on hand is less than the reorder level. If reordering is necessary order one half of the reorder level. If there is no reorder for an item, zero should appear in the column for the value of the reorder quantity and reorder amount.

OUTPUT

Produce a listing of the inventory file by inventory type. Control breaks should appear on type. The listing should provide for the following items:

1. Use 132 print positions per line.
2. Single space the detail lines on the output.
3. Each new type should start on a new page.
4. Appropriate page and column heads should be provided.
5. All of the input fields should appear in the output (type should only be in the heads) in addition to the value of the quantity on hand, quantity on order, reorder amount, and value of the reorder, if there is a reorder.
6. The pages are to be numbered consecutively. They are not to be restarted on a new type.

GLOSSARY

ACCESS Retrieval of a previously stored item. This may be getting an item from a table or reading a record from a file.

ACTION ENTRIES The items which appear in the lower-right-hand quarter of a decision table. They show which of the possible actions are performed for each possible combination of conditions.

ACTION STUBS The items which appear in the lower-left-hand quarter of a decision table. They are a listing of the various options that will be taken by the program.

ADD RECORDS Transaction records that are to be added to the master file in a file-update program.

ADDS Subroutine designed to add new records to a master file in a file-update program.

AND LOGIC Checking of two or more separate conditions, where both or all of them must be true for some activity to take place.

ANNOTATION SYMBOL A symbol used to add more comments to a flowcharting symbol when there is not room to put them inside the symbol.

ARROWHEADS Directional indicators drawn on flowlines at the point where the flowline connects with a symbol.

ASCENDING ORDER Items which have been placed in an order by some key field(s) such that the key fields range from smallest to largest.

AUXILIARY OPERATION SYMBOL A symbol representing an off-line operation on equipment not under the control of the central processing unit. This includes such activities as putting cards or optically read input on magnetic tape.

AUXILIARY (EXTERNAL) STORAGE The storage of data outside of a computer on a medium such as a magnetic disk or a printed report.

BAD ADD In a sequential file-update program, a subroutine designed to process records on the master-greater-than-transaction path which should be additions to the master file but have the wrong code present in the transaction record.

BAD EQUAL In a sequential file-update program, a subroutine designed to process records on the master-equal-to-transaction path which should be changes to or deletions of an existing record but have the wrong code present in the transaction record.

BINARY SEARCH An efficient method of searching a sequential table, where each successive comparison eliminates half of the remaining items in the table.

BRANCHING An alteration in the normal sequential execution of program instructions such that execution continues at some point other than the next physical instruction in the program.

BUBBLE SORT A sort where adjacent items are compared and exchanged if necessary until the desired order (ascending or descending) has been achieved.

CHANGE A subroutine designed to alter the contents of an existing master-file record in a file-update program.

CHANGE RECORD In a file-update program, a transaction record that contains the new or corrected data for an existing master-file record.

CHARACTER A single symbol used in representing data. This may be a letter, number, or special symbol such as $.

CLASS A category of data such as numeric or alphanumeric.

CLOSED TABLE A decision table which is complete by itself and does not refer to any succeeding table for other components to be considered.

CODE To write instructions for a computer in a particular, programming language such as BASIC or COBOL.

COLLATE SYMBOL A symbol that represents merging with extracting. This is the formation of two or more sets of data items from two or more other sets.

COLLATING SEQUENCE The order in which letters, numbers, or symbols will be placed based on the internal data representation scheme used to form the characters.

COMMUNICATIONS LINK SYMBOL A symbol representing a situation where information is being transmitted by a telecommunications link. This includes such items as telegraph, telephone, and microwave.

COMPILE-TIME TABLE A table in which the actual values are coded directly into the program when the program is written and compiled and become a part of the object code.

CONDITION ENTRIES The items which appear in the upper-right-hand corner of a decision table. They show each of the various combinations of conditions relevant to the problem solution.

CONDITION STUBS The items which appear in the upper-left-hand quarter of a decision table. They are a listing of the various conditions which must be considered in the solution of the problem.

CONDITIONAL BRANCHING The following of one of two or more paths in the logic based on whether some condition is true (or false).

CONNECTOR SYMBOL A symbol used to show an

exit from, or an entrance into, some point in the logic of a flowchart.

CONSISTENCY   A comparison of two or more fields to determine if the data in them is in agreement.

CONSTANT   A value used by the program which is coded directly into the program when the program is written. The value of a constant does not change during the execution of the program.

CONTROL-BREAK HEADINGS   Page and column headings which are produced when a control break occurs. These usually require some updating of the heading information and are normally produced at the top of a new page.

CONTROL-BREAK TOTALS   Totals which are shown when a control break occurs such as a state total or a department total. If higher level or final totals exist then it is on the control break when these totals are rolled, or added, to the next higher level or final total. After any necessary rolling the control-break totals are reset to zero to accommodate the next control group.

CONTROL BREAKS   A method of breaking the contents of a report down into more meaningful units, such as starting each new department on a new page so the report is easier to distribute. Breaks are recognized when the contents of a field (control field) change during sequential reading of the records in a file.

COPY   A subroutine designed to transfer a record from the current version of a file to the new version being created in a sequential file-update program.

CORE SYMBOL   A symbol that represents an input/output function in which the medium is magnetic core. Magnetic core storage is located within the computer itself.

COUNTER (LOOP CONTROL)   A storage area whose contents are being increased or decreased. The value in the counter is used to determine whether the steps in a loop are to be continued or the loop should be terminated.

DATA   Raw facts which will be processed in some manner so as to provide information.

DATA EXCEPTION   An error condition that may occur when a program is run. It is caused by such things as nonnumeric data in a numeric field or numeric data in a format other than the one specified.

DATA PROCESSING   The transformation of raw facts (Data) into information.

DATE RECORD   A special-purpose record read in the housekeeping routine. It is used when the date is not available on the computer system being used, or when a date other than the current date is needed for processing.

DECISION SEQUENCE   The order in which we check a series of decisions. Depending on the decision being made, the most efficient sequence can be either most to least likely or least to most likely.

DECISION STRUCTURE   A structure that depicts a decision being made and the alternate logic paths to be followed (with actions performed) as a result of that decision.

DECISION SYMBOL   A single symbol depicting a decision being made with a program and the possible outcomes (e.g., yes, no,.>,<, or =) of that decision. The actions performed as a result of the decision are not a part of the decision symbol.

DECISION TABLE   A planning tool used to show the steps in the solution to a problem. It provides a concise format for examining a situation with several decision steps.

DELETE   A subroutine designed to eliminate, or flag as obsolete, records from a master file in an update program.

DELETE RECORD   In a file-update program, a record that will cause an existing master-file record to be flagged as obsolete or not included on the new master file.

DESCENDING ORDER   Where items have been placed in an order so that the key field ranges from largest to smallest.

DESK CHECKING   The testing of a flowchart by working through it with the various types of good input data that can be expected as well as bad input data to determine whether the desired results will be produced.

DESTRUCTIVE READIN   Replacing the contents of the input area in storage with the contents of the next input record read into storage.

DIMENSION   A method of subdividing the data in a table. Each separate level of subdivision is said to be a dimension.

DIRECT ACCESS (TABLES)   Retrieving or using an item in a specific location in a table based on its location as opposed to searching for a particular value.

DISPLAY SYMBOL   A symbol which represents an output function in which information is displayed for human use during processing. This display may be on a typewriter, video terminal, or other such device.

DO-UNTIL STRUCTURE   Performing the steps in a loop until some condition becomes true (or false). With do-until structures these actions will be performed at least once, regardless of whether the initial condition is true or false.

DO-WHILE STRUCTURE   Performing the steps in a loop while some condition is true (or false). With do-while structures these actions may or may not be performed, since the test is made before the action is performed the first time.

DOCUMENT SYMBOL   A symbol that represents either an input or an output function in a system flowchart where the medium is a document. It is generally used to represent a source document or an output listing.

DOCUMENTATION   In reference to a program, the written backup for the program. This includes such items as record (card, tape, disk, and so on) layouts, print charts, source program listings, record descriptions, program narratives, run sheets, flowcharts, sample output, and job control language (JCL).

EDIT   To check the validity of the data contained in each of the records in a file and indicate what errors exist so they may be corrected.

END FLAG   A switch in a program that is used to control whether the process routine or the end-of-job routine will be the next to be executed. This switch will remain off until all files being used have reached an end, or the file is missing.

END-MAST SWITCH   A switch specifically set up to indicate whether the master file has ended when two or more files are present in a program. If the end-mast switch is on when the end of the transaction file is encountered, then the end-flag switch will be turned on.

END-OF-FILE LOGIC   In file-matching operations, the standard actions performed when an end-of-file condition is encountered. When one of the two files ends, a check is made to see if the other file has also ended. If it has, then the end-flag switch is turned on; otherwise the end switch for the file that just ended is turned on and a maximum value is moved to the control field for the file that ended.

END-OF-JOB TOTALS   Totals which are shown after all of the data has been processed. These may be single items such as total sales or total records read. They may also be something such as a series of control-break totals which have been saved (usually in a table) during processing and are listed at the end of the processing.

END-TRANS SWITCH   A switch specifically set up to indicate whether the transaction file has ended when two or more files are present in a program. If the end-trans switch is on when the end of the master file is encountered, then the end-flag switch will be turned on.

ENTRY   A point of entrance into the logic of a flowchart other than the normal sequential execution of the steps. Entries are made into flowlines, not symbols.

ERROR COUNTER   A counter set up to accumulate the total number of error records found or, if multiple types of records are present in a program, the number of each type of error record.

ERROR SWITCH   A switch used in an input edit program to determine if any errors were found in a record after each of the fields in the record has been checked for validity.

EXECUTION-TIME TABLE   A table for which storage is reserved but no data is provided at the beginning of the program. The table is filled with data as a result of processing the program.

EXISTENCE   The use of a table or another file to determine if a piece of data exists in that file or table, as in a list of part numbers or employee numbers.

EXIT   A point in the flowchart where the logic is being continued elsewhere than at the next physical symbol.

EXTENDED-ENTRY TABLE   A decision table where the condition entries depict more than a yes/no result. This includes such items as $>$, $<$, or $<>$, with each of these related to some quantity.

EXTERNAL SUBROUTINE   A predefined process which is not part of the program in which it is being used.

EXTRACT PROGRAM   A computer program which utilizes only a portion of the records in a file to produce a report. Which records in the file are used depends on the criteria established for selection.

EXTRACT ROUTINE   A routine that contains the criteria for selecting certain records from a file.

EXTRACT SYMBOL   A symbol representing the removal of one or more specific sets of data items from a single larger set of data items. Which records are extracted is based on some set of criteria.

FIELD   One or more consecutive characters of related data such as name, age, or rate of pay.

FILE   A collection of one or more related records organized for a particular purpose, such as an employee master file or a membership file.

FILE CREATION   The initial writing of the records on a file which previously did not exist.

FILE MATCHING   Comparing the records in two files to determine where there are unmatched records on both files. What the unmatched conditions represent depends on the type of program utilizing the file-matching process.

FILE RETRIEVAL   Transferring data from a file into memory.

FILE UPDATING   Altering the contents of a file through additions, deletions, or changes so that the file reflects the current situation. File updating is a process usually performed on master files.

FINAL TOTALS   Totals that are accumulated during processing and printed at the end of the report, sometimes referred to as grand totals. They serve as control totals and are part of the audit trail created for files.

FIRST-RECORD PROCESSING   There are two separate areas in which we deal with first-record processing. The first is at the end of the housekeeping routine to insure that the first record has been read from each file present prior to entering the process routine. If no record is found when attempting to read the first record, the end flag is turned on to terminate processing. The second area is found within the major break routine if control-break totals are present. This means checking a first-record switch to prevent totals from being produced prior to the first group on the report.

FIRST-RECORD SWITCH   A switch used to prevent totals printing for a group prior to the first group, when a control break is encountered while processing the first record of a file.

FLOWCHART   A set of symbols with predetermined meanings used to show the flow of logic (program flowchart) or the flow of data (system flowchart).

FLOWLINES   Used to connect the various symbols in a flowchart and indicate the directional flow of the logic. Without arrowheads the flow is assumed to be to the right and down.

FORMS OVERFLOW   The point at which the allotted maximum number of lines has been written on a page and it is time to move the paper to a new page.

GAP   A term used with a Shell sort which determines which records will be compared.

HARDWARE   Input or output devices used for processing media such as a disk drive, a magnetic tape drive, or the computer itself.

HEADINGS   Descriptive information printed at the top of the pages in a report.

HIERARCHY CHARTS (HIERARCHICAL DIAGRAMS) Charts used to show which routines are present in a program. They utilize rectangles to show the routines and resemble a corporate organizational chart. Subordinate relationships are shown by the lines connecting the rectangles.

HOLD AREA An area in storage set aside by the programmer to allow checking for control breaks. It contains the value of the last group processed and is updated when a new group is encountered. It is initialized in housekeeping to a value less than the value of the first group.

HOUSEKEEPING ROUTINE A preparation step which is found at the beginning of the program and executed only once during the execution of the program. It does such tasks as opening files, fetching the date, setting switches, and reading the first record on the input file(s).

INDEXED FILE When the file is created, an index (directory) is produced which points to the location of each record in the file. The records in the file are located based on the value of a "key" field found within each record. The contents of this key field will determine where the record will be placed when the file is created and where it may be found when the record is accessed in subsequent processing. This includes such file structures as VSAM and ISAM.

INFORMATION The meaningful results produced by manipulating or transforming raw data in some predefined manner.

INITIALIZE To assign a beginning value to a storage area being used for some specific purpose, such as a page counter or control-break hold area.

INPUT The raw data needed to produce the desired information or output. It will be read into the computer and processed by a program.

INPUT-EDIT PROGRAM A computer program which validates the data in each record of a file so that errors in the data may be corrected. Errors that are found may be displayed on a terminal or printed on a report.

INPUT/OUTPUT SYMBOL Used in a program flowchart to show the reading or writing of an individual record.

INSTRUCTIONS Statements or commands in some programming language which cause an action to take place or identify a particular data item being used in, or by, the program.

INTERMEDIATE BREAK/TOTAL When there are three or more levels of breaks present in a program, the one(s) that occur between the major- and minor-level breaks are called intermediate-level breaks. There may be one or more levels of intermediate-level breaks. Intermediate-level totals are printed when the corresponding intermediate-level break occurs and are rolled to the next higher intermediate-level totals, or to the major-level totals if there is only one intermediate-level break.

INTERNAL SUBROUTINE A predefined process located within the program where it is being used.

INVALID KEY An error condition that may occur when processing an indexed file. It means various things, such as attempting to write a duplicate record, no such record exists on the file, a changed record is being rewritten at a location different than where it was read, and so on.

JOB CONTROL A set of instructions to the computer indicating the actions to be performed in the execution of a program. This includes such items as identifying the job, assigning files to devices, and initiating execution of the program.

KEY FIELD A field in a record that is used to access or compare data located either in a file or in a table.

LEAST TO MOST (LIKELY) The preferable sequence in which to check multiple fields when each field must have an acceptable value or values for the record to be selected.

LIMITED ENTRY TABLES A decision table in which each condition present has only two possible outcomes (yes/no or true/false).

LINE COUNT A counter to keep track of how many lines have been printed on a page so that we can determine when an end-of-page condition is encountered.

LINEAR SEARCH Searching of a table in a sequential manner. The search is terminated when a matching table element is found or we reach the end of the table.

LISTING PROGRAM Printing of a report with provision made for ejecting to a new page on either forms-overflow or control-break situations.

LOADING Placing the desired values in a table that will be used by the program. This can be done by coding the table into the actual program (compile-time table), reading the values in from an external source in the housekeeping routine (preprocess table), or filling in the values as they are developed during the execution of the program (execution-time table).

LOGICAL OPERATORS Operators such as AND and OR used to combine conditions. AND between two conditions means that both conditions must be true in order for the whole expression to be true. OR between conditions means that one or the other or both conditions may be true in order for the expression to be true.

LOOPING Executing a series of instructions in a program over and over as many times as needed.

MAGNETIC DISK SYMBOL A symbol used to show that the input or output medium is magnetic disk. File names may be written on the bands in the symbol.

MAGNETIC DRUM SYMBOL A symbol used to show that the input or output medium is magnetic drum.

MAGNETIC TAPE SYMBOL A symbol used to show that the input or output medium is magnetic tape.

MAINLINE LOGIC The overall logic of the program which performs the three (or sometimes more) major routines (Housekeeping, Process, and End of Job) within the program. The mainline logic is sometimes referred to as the "driver."

MAJOR BREAK/TOTAL The highest level of break possible if control breaks are present in a program. If only one level of control break is present, it is a major-level break. If there are multiple-level breaks, the major break is the one that occurs least frequently. Totals printed on a major break are major break totals. They will be rolled to final totals if final totals are present.

MAJOR KEY   The most important of the key fields in a record.

MANUAL INPUT SYMBOL   A symbol representing an input function in which the data is entered manually during processing on a device such as console typewriter.

MANUAL OPERATION SYMBOL   Represents an off-line operation performed at human speed using no mechanical aid, such as physically sorting cards or preparing a report for a program which terminated abnormally.

MAST-EXISTS SWITCH   A switch which is used to indicate whether or not a record has been moved to the new mast record area in a sequential file-updating process using the method for multiple transactions per master record.

MEDIUM (MEDIA)   An item on which data is stored, such as a magnetic disk, printed report, punched tape, or time sheet.

MENU   Single-line or full-page messages which are displayed for the operator. These may be informational, but it is likely they will seek a response of some sort from the operator.

MERGE SYMBOL   A symbol that represents the combining of two or more sets of data items into one set.

MINOR BREAK/TOTAL   The lowest level of break possible, if two or more levels of control breaks are present in a program. If there are various levels of control breaks, minor-level breaks are the ones that occur most frequently. Minor-level break totals are printed when a minor break occurs and are rolled to the next-higher-level total (intermediate or major).

MINOR KEY   The least important of the key fields.

MIXED-ENTRY TABLE   A decision table which contains both limited and extended entries. Both types of entries may not be on the same horizontal line of the table.

MODIFY   To change the contents of an area in storage, as in altering the contents of a loop control counter or the end-flag switch.

MOST TO LEAST (LIKELY)   The preferable sequence in which to check for one of multiple values in a single field.

MULTIPLE-LEVEL TOTALS   Totals that are being accumulated and printed on more than one level of break. That is, there are at least major- and minor-level (and possibly intermediate) totals being accumulated.

MULTIPLE RECORD TYPES   Two or more types of records (record formats) present in a single file.

NASSI-SCHNEIDERMAN CHART   A method of showing the steps in the solution to a problem. They utilize a series of vertical bars to list the steps. The vertical bars are subdivided by diagonal lines when decisions are being shown.

NESTED LOOP   A loop that is performed within another loop in a program or flowchart.

NO-MAST ROUTINE   A routine performed if no master file is present when an attempt is made to read the first record in the housekeeping routine. This routine turns on the end flag to force termination of the program and prints a message indicating what went wrong.

NO-TRANS ROUTINE   A routine performed if no transaction file is present when an attempt is made to read the first record in the housekeeping routine. This routine turns on the end flag to force termination of the program and prints a message indicating what went wrong.

NONSEQUENTIAL FILES   A type of file in which the records may be retrieved either sequentially or randomly.

OBJECT PROGRAM   A program which has been converted from code written by the programmer into a form usable by the computer.

OCCURS   A reserved word used in COBOL to indicate the number of times an area of memory is being subdivided to form a table.

OFFLINE STORAGE SYMBOL   A symbol representing the function of storing information offline on any medium. Offline storage is not currently accessible by the computer. It could range from a file on a shelf to a disk in a safe.

OFFPAGE CONNECTOR SYMBOL   An IBM-only symbol used to indicate that a path in the logic of a flowchart is continued on a separate page of the flowchart.

ONLINE-STORAGE SYMBOL   A generated symbol for an input/output function using any type of online-storage medium. It could be magnetic tape, disk, or drum storage.

OPEN-END TABLE   A decision table which refers to another decision table for a continuation of the steps in the solution of the problem.

OPERANDS   The portions of an instruction that indicate which items are to be processed. In the following instruction A, B, and C are operands: 40 LET A=B*C.

OPERATION CODE   The portion of an instruction that indicates what action is to be performed, such as ADD or MOVE.

OR LOGIC   Checking of two or more conditions, when at least one of them must be true for some activity to take place.

OUTPUT   The results of having processed data. It may be a written report, a disk file, a display on a terminal, or other similar items.

PARAMETER RECORD   An input record usually read at the beginning of the program in the housekeeping routine. The data on this record is used to define processing limits or establish the value of a data item within the program.

PREDEFINED PROCESS SYMBOL   A subroutine which has had its steps defined at a point other than where it is being used. It may be either an internal or an external subroutine.

PREPARATION SYMBOL   A symbol which represents the modification of an instruction or group of instructions which alter the program itself.

PRE-PROCESS TABLE A table whose data is loaded in the housekeeping routine and then used to process the records from the major files in a program.

PRESENCE An edit test to determine if any data is present in a field of a record.

PRIMARY (INTERNAL) STORAGE Storage inside the computer, such as core, semiconductor, or bubble memory.

PRINT CHART (PRINTER LAYOUT) A form containing a gridwork of boxes utilized to plan the format of a printed report.

PROCESS The transformation or manipulation of data to produce some form of useful or meaningful output.

PROCESS SYMBOL A symbol in a program flowchart to depict a single step in the solution to a problem other than reading, writing, or making a decision. It is also used in a system flowchart to depict a program.

PROGRAM FLOWCHART One method of showing the steps in the solution to a problem, including the sequence in which these steps are to be performed. The symbols used are those accepted by the American National Standards Institute. In a structured flowchart these symbols are combined into structures and the structures are combined to produce the solution.

PROGRAM INTERRUPT An error which occurs during the execution of a program that causes execution of the program to be terminated. There are many possible reasons for this event.

PROGRAM SPECIFICATION A written overview of the purpose of a program. It identifies such things as files being used as input, the source of input files, actions being performed by the program, files being created as output, and the disposition of output files.

PROGRESSIVE TOTALS Totals which are incremented but are never reset to zero, such as record counts and final totals.

PSEUDOCODE A list of English-like statements that identify the steps in the solution to a problem.

PUNCHED CARD DECK SYMBOL A symbol that represents a deck of punched cards which may or may not be related to each other.

PUNCHED CARD FILE SYMBOL A symbol that represents a group of related punched cards that comprise a file.

PUNCHED CARD SYMBOL A symbol that represents an input or output function in which cards are being used as the medium.

PUNCHED TAPE SYMBOL A symbol that represents an input or output function in which punched tape (paper or mylar) is being used as the medium.

RANDOM ACCESS (RETRIEVAL) The ability to read any record in a file as easily as any other record without reading all the preceding records to find the one you need.

RANGE The beginning and ending values which are acceptable. This may refer to the contents of a field or to the records on a file that are to be processed.

READMAST A routine that reads the records from the master file in a program with two or more sequential-input files.

READTRANS A routine that reads the records from the transaction file in a program with two or more sequential-input files.

RECORD A group of one or more related fields that refer to one person, place, or thing.

RECORD COUNT An area for accumulating the number of records processed that belong to a given category, such as records read, error records, records changed, records deleted, and so on.

RECORD DESCRIPTION A written description of the attributes of each field in a record. This includes the name of each field, location of each field within the record, type of data (alphabetic, numeric, etc.) contained in each field, recording format of the data in the fields, size of the fields, and brief explanation of the contents of each field.

RECORD LAYOUT A form showing the fields present in a record in the order that they actually occur, including any blank or unused areas in the record.

RECORD NUMBER Used to identify a record in a nonsequential file written for a micro. It determines the position of the record in the file.

RECORD TYPE When multiple kinds of records are present in a file, each record type is one that contains a specific portion of the data relative to a given item, such as an employee or an asset owned by the company. In a personnel situation, for instance, a file might contain name-and-address records, work-history records, special-skill records, and so on.

REPORT Output of the data-processing cycle in printed form. This might include payroll checks or a listing of the inventory.

REPORT PROGRAM Program which utilizes the data from one or more input files to produce a report containing the information requested.

RESETTING TOTALS Moving zero to a total when needed. This could be to restart the page number so that each group of a report would start at page one or to move zero to lower-level control-break totals after rolling them to the totals on the next higher level.

ROLLING TOTALS Adding totals for one level of control break to totals for the next higher level of control break when a control break occurs on the lower-level item.

RULE A column in the entry section (right half) of a decision table. This represents one combination of the conditions present and the resulting actions to be taken. It would correspond to a single path in a flowchart or subroutine.

RUN SHEET A written document informing the operations department of what items and actions are necessary to run the program. It also informs operations of what to do if errors occur when the program is run.

SEARCH A process where elements of a table are compared to a field in a record called a search argument. The objective is to find a match in the table, to find a range into which the search argument fits, or to determine that there is no match in the table.

SECONDARY STORAGE Storage outside of the computer memory as on tape or disk.

SELECTED RECORD COUNT A type of record count

that indicates how many records were selected in an extract program.

SELECTED RECORDS Records chosen in an extract program because they contain certain criteria.

SEQUENCE STRUCTURE A series of one or more successive symbols including the process, input/output, or predefined process symbols.

SEQUENTIAL FILE A file arranged in some predetermined order on a particular field, such as part number or employee number.

SEQUENTIAL RETRIEVAL Reading of the records on a file one after the other in the order in which they were written on the file.

SHELL SORT A sort in which the key fields in the records are compared across successively smaller gap to determine if exchanges are necessary.

SINGLE-LEVEL TOTALS Totals which are initialized to zero at the onset of execution and are accumulated during the entire running of the program without being reset to zero. These would include such items as record counts and page numbers (assuming that page numbers are not being reset on control breaks.)

SOFTWARE Computer programs, written or recorded.

SORT To arrange the records in a file in sequence (ascending, descending, or both) according to the contents of a field or fields in each record. This field must be in the same location in each record.

SORT SYMBOL A symbol that depicts the arrangement of a set of data items into a particular sequence (ascending, descending, or both).

SOURCE PROGRAM A program written by a programmer using the instructions of a particular language, such as COBOL or BASIC.

STRUCTURED FLOWCHARTING A flowcharting technique using the four structures (sequence, decision, do until, and do while.) These structures are designed to provide ease in coding and maintaining programs. There is always one entrance into and one exit from a structure, thus providing a modular or "pluggable" format for adding, deleting, or changing routines in the program.

STRUCTURES Standardized groupings of flowcharting symbols. The four structures are the sequence, decision, do-until, and do-while structures.

SUBROUTINE A group of instructions that performs one identifiable part of the overall program, such as computing federal tax or determining the age of an asset.

SUBSCRIPT A number used to refer to a specific item or a dimension of a table. If there are two dimensions in a table, then two subscripts will be needed, one for the row and one for the column within the row. Three-dimensional tables require three subscripts. The following shows how subscripts relate to dimensions:

ITEM (A, B, C)
Third dimension reference
Second dimension reference
First dimension reference

SWAP A term used for exchanging rows in a table when sorting.

SWITCH An area in storage defined by the programmer and used to control which path in the logic is taken. The value in this area and the testing of that value are the responsibility of the programmer.

SYSTEM DATE The date kept by the computer system either through an internal clock or set by the operator.

SYSTEM FLOWCHART A graphic representation of a computer-based system which shows the flow of data (files) through the system.

SYSTEM FLOWCHART SYMBOLS A set of symbols used to show various media, such as tape or disk, and various actions, such as sorting or merging, on a system flowchart.

TABLE A collection of related data items which are subdivided on one or more dimensions. Subscript notation is needed to refer to an item in a table in higher-level languages.

TABLE ACCESS The retrieving of an item from or the placing of an item into a table. Retrieval may be done either by searching or by direct access.

TABLE SEARCH The retrieving of an item from a table when we know the value we are looking for but not its location in the table. The searching may be done with either a linear or a binary search.

TERMINAL SYMBOL A symbol used to indicate the beginning or ending point in a flowchart. The beginning point is given the label START in the mainline logic and the name of the routine in a subroutine. The ending point is labeled STOP in the mainline logic and EXIT or RETURN at the end of a subroutine.

TEST A check of the contents of an area to determine which path in the logic to follow.

UNCONDITIONAL BRANCH An alteration of the normal sequential execution of a program's instructions, regardless of whether a condition is true or false.

UPDATE PROGRAM A program used to bring the contents of a file, usually a master file, up to date.

UPDATING The process of bringing the data in a file (usually a master file) up-to-date so it reflects the current situation. This includes additions to the file, changes to existing records in the file, and deletions of records from the file that are no longer needed.

UTILITY PROGRAM A program provided by the manufacturer or written by the user to perform standardized functions, such as sorting, merging, listing, and copying of files.

VARIABLES Data items used in a program that do not have a constant value. Their value changes during the execution of the program. A change of values requires that the data item have a name.

INDEX

A

accessing table data, 165
add records, 264
alphanumeric data, 56
analysis, 4
AND/OR, 88
annotation symbol, 18
APPLY TRAN routine, 299
ASCII, 88
assembling, 10
assumed decimal, 56
auxiliary operation symbol, 332

B

balance line algorithm, 279
binary search, 168, 174
bit, 88
bubble sort, 203
byte, 88

C

CHANGE REC routine, 299
change records, 264
character, 2
CK MAST routine, 298
CK WRITE routine, 299
class, 210
closed table, 345
coding, 4
collate symbol, 333
collating sequences, 88
column, 158
column headings, 61
communication link symbol, 331
compile-time table, 167
compiling, 10
conditional branching, 41
connector symbol, 16
consistency, 214
constant, 72
control breaks, 108
control fields, 110
control-break headings, 113

S

SELECT KEY routine, 298
selected record counts, 100
sentinel record, 29
sequence structure, 12, 20
sequential files, 308
shell sort, 205
simple listing, 71
software, 3
sort symbol, 332
sorting, 202
source program, 7
structured flowcharting, 11
structures, 11, 12, 19
subroutine, 73
subscript, 159
subscript range, 166.
switch, 72
symbols, 13
syntax errors, 4
system flowchart, 5, 54
systems flowcharting symbols, 329

T

table, 157
table access methods, 172

U

unconditional branching, 40
update program, 8, 264
utility program, 8

V

variable, 72
variable name, 72

W

writing out a table, 177
writing output data, 26

terminal symbol, 13
test data, 5
TEST MAST, 252
testing, 4
three-dimensional table, 164
trans file ending first, 252
two-dimensional table, 161